LOREN REID, 1905 –
University of Missouri

First
Principles
of
Public
Speaking

**SECOND
EDITION**

ARTCRAFT PRESS
Columbia, Missouri

LIBRARY OF CONGRESS CATALOG CARD NO. 62-15056

Printed in the United States of America

Contents

Appendix

A List of Speaking Assignments

A List of Illustrations

Line Drawings

Preface

In preparing this revision I have adopted many suggestions from students and teachers who used the original text, principally to strengthen the sections on outlining, expand the chapters on persuasion, and add a chapter on discussion.

I have also further reviewed the illustrative material, substituting and adding freely in order to make the book reflect current times. I have dipped a little more deeply still into long-established principles of communication, and especially into helpful findings of experimentalists in speech, social psychology, and psychology.

My purpose continues to be to state principles as cogently as possible, illustrating them with a variety of examples, so that the student may see for himself how various speakers, some from his own day, have applied the principles.

Note to the Student

As nearly every older student would like to say to every younger student: The better your study habits, the more you will learn from any text, and, accordingly, the more you will value it.

When you are assigned a chapter in this book, instead of beginning with its first page, reading line 1, line 2, and so to the end, try this better way:

1. Read the *title* of the chapter.
2. Read the *italic sentences* at the head of the chapter.
3. Turn the pages, glancing at center headings and side headings and do other casual reading that will give you an impression of the material as a whole.

This procedure will help you understand better the purpose of the chapter. It will supply you with main headings with which you can associate detailed ideas and examples. Finally:

4. *Read the chapter carefully, idea by idea.*

Experienced students also advise that one should be *mentally active* while studying. Work at a desk, therefore, so you can jot notes about your reading in the margins of the text itself. *Think and reflect* about what you read. *Mental attitude* is all important.

No textbook writer can be sure to get his chapters in the order that will best meet the needs of every class. What seems to him to be a desirable arrangement may not be entirely pleasing in every circumstance. The instructor may rearrange chapters, omit chapters, or assign supplementary materials, to make the text more suitable to the students on his own campus. You can aid him in his desire to help you. Read ahead of any given assignment; in this way you can even better adapt the book to your needs.

Note to the Instructor

A purpose in planning this text has been to make it fairly *self-teachable* by utilizing a method and a style that will encourage each student to master the principles himself. The book is written with the beginning public speaker in mind.

To help achieve this goal, I secured from about a hundred institutions copies of outlines used in the first course in speech on their campuses.[1] A study of this foot-high stack of documents showed that most beginning courses include a personal experience or narrative speech; short speeches to introduce the problem of organization; expository speeches stressing clarity of presentation, one utilizing a visual aid; persuasive speeches emphasizing evidence, reasoning, and the motivating processes; shorter talks such as introducing a speaker, presenting, accepting, welcoming. The syllabi also reflect an interest in parliamentary discussion. Furthermore, they place a strong emphasis on teaching speech structure, utilizing factual and other authoritative materials, employing valid reasoning, analyzing audience and occasion, using effectively language, voice, and body.

Chapters of the text have been arranged with the foregoing assignments and standards in minds. The instructor should be able to say to his class, for example, "Read Chapter 8 on 'Organizing: The Short Speech'; study for yourselves how to plan and rehearse such a talk." He may give supplementary material for amplification and motivation, but the chapter itself should provide the information the student needs to get him started. Headings are numbered and lettered; since subtle changes in typography do not always say with immediate clarity what is *principal* and what is *subordinate,* "I" and "II" identify one level of headings, "A" and "B" a lower level. This old textbook device I think well worth reviving. All in all the instructor should be able to give more class time to individual help with student problems and additional material from his own study and reflection.

At the end of most chapters will be found *speaking assignments.* Not all of these will be used in any one course, but many can be adapted to most courses. *Questions for discussion* are designed not so

[1] A partial list of the institutions surveyed, and a descriptive report of the study, appears in *Teaching Speech,* 3rd ed. (Columbia, Artcraft Press, 1960), Chapter 4, "The College First Course."

much for review as to allow students and instructor to talk about additional problems almost sure to arise. *Speech-related projects* call for individual investigation. *References* provide supplementary material or a different point of view.

Acknowledgments

Much that is in this book comes from the, by now, well-established body of theory and principle developed over the centuries by those interested in public speaking. Obviously I have drawn generously from classical rhetoric as expounded by Aristotle, Cicero, and Quintilian, from older textbooks like those of A. E. Phillips, Charles H. Woolbert, and James A. Winans, and from contemporary textbooks such as those listed as references at the end of the various chapters. I have a heavy obligation to the professional discussions, research papers, and table talk heard and overheard at state, regional, and national conventions. Much I owe to former professors like John P. Ryan of Grinnell, and A. Craig Baird and H. Clay Harshbarger of the University of Iowa, all of whom aroused my concern about methods of teaching public speaking. I have profited by a long connection with regular and visiting members of the staff at the University of Missouri, and at other campuses where I have taught for shorter intervals.

My colleagues at the University of Missouri have given this enterprise much encouragement. Frances L. McCurdy and Robert P. Friedman have read one or more chapters, and Christopher Reid has supplied useful material. Charles R. Row has provided suggestions for strengthening and clarifying the text. Jay E. Adams, E. Gene Ritter, and Randall M. Fisher have helped with specific problems of organization and outline. Helen Brookshire Adams, State Normal and Industrial College, Ellendale, North Dakota; James C. Ching, Tulane University; Stanley D. Travis, University of Buffalo; Joseph O'Rourke, Wabash College; have made suggestions. I am deeply appreciative of their interest, and equally desirous to hold them blameless for any faults and shortcomings that yet remain.

To check and recheck classroom theory against the practice of business and professional men and women engaged today in speech making, I undertook to correspond with many well-known people about the nature of their training and the number and kind of speeches they make. Although most of these busy individuals would disclaim the title of *professional* speaker, necessity and opportunity have combined to call upon them for frequent public appearances. They have supplied copies of speeches and many of them also have added their reflections about the speaker's responsibilities and problems. My quotations from these speeches have in many instances been all too brief; a reader needs to see the entire speech in order to get the full force of the speaker's reasoning, but I have had space only to print short passages to illustrate highly specific principles of effective speaking. In addition to the acknowledgments that appear in the body of the text, I should like to extend here also my thanks to the following:

Paul C. Ackerman, vice president in charge of engineering, Chrysler Corporation; Florence E. Allen, chief judge, United States Court of Appeals, sixth circuit; George V. Allen, former director, United State Information Agency; Bruce Barton, chairman of the board, Batten, Barton, Durstine & Osborn, Inc.; L. K. Bishop, vice president, National Conference of Christians and Jews; Roger M. Blough, chairman of the board, United States Steel Corporation; Ernest R. Breech, chairman of the board, Ford Motor Company; Charles H. Brower, president, Batten, Barton, Durstine & Osborn, Inc.

Monk Bryan, pastor, Missouri Methodist Church, Columbia, Missouri; Harlan Cleveland, assistant secretary of state; F. G. Crawford, former trustee, Power Authority of the State of New York; George Cochran Doub, law offices, Weinberg and Green; Paul H. Douglas, United States Senate; Henry B. du Pont, vice president, E. I. du Pont de Nemours & Company; Lt. Gen. Ira C. Eaker (USAF Ret.), Douglas Aircraft Company, Inc.; Elmer Ellis, president emeritus, University of Missouri.

Richard S. Emrich, bishop of Michigan, Protestant Episcopal Church; J. W. Fulbright, United States Senate; Harold Evans, secretary to Harold Macmillan; Louis Hadley Evans, Board of National Missions of the United Presbyterian Church; Benjamin F. Fairless, late adviser to the board, United States Steel Corporation; Ernest S. Fields, Cincinnati Gas & Electric Company.

G. Keith Funston, former president, New York Stock Exchange; Barry Goldwater, Phoenix, Ariz.; W. Dennis Grubb, Peace Corps, Westport, Conn., now Zipacón, Cundinamarca, Colombia; E. J. Hanley, president, Allegheny Ludlum Steel Corporation; Bryce N. Harlow, director of governmental relations, Procter and Gamble; Henry T. Heald, president, The Ford Foundation; Ben W. Heineman, chairman of the board, Chicago and North Western Railway Company.

Paul G. Hoffman, managing director, United Nations Special Fund; Kenneth B. Keating, Rochester, N. Y.; Gerald Kennedy, bishop of the Methodist Church, Los Angeles; John F. Kennedy, press secretary Pierre Salinger, associate press secretary Andrew T. Hatcher; Willy Ley, scientist and author; Francis McCarthy, for Henry Cabot Lodge, New York.

Harold R. Medina, circuit judge, United States Court of Appeals, second circuit; Lionel B. Moses, *Parade Magazine;* Richard M. Nixon, Los Angeles; Charles Nutter, managing director, International House, New Orleans; T. S. Petersen, Standard Oil Company of California; H. G. Rickover, vice admiral, United States Navy.

Jack Rosenthal, assistant director of public information in the Department of Justice, for Robert F. Kennedy; Governor George Romney, Lansing; Carl Sandburg, Connemara Farm, Flat Rock, North Carolina; John M. Seabrook, Woodstown, N. J.; Tom E. Shearer, president, The College of Idaho; H. Richard Steding, executive engineer, Chrysler Corporation; C. Langdon White, professor of geography, Stanford University; P. B. Wishart, president, Minneapolis-Honeywell Regulator Company.

Gerald Pease, John Red, and Louis Rittmaster, students in public speaking courses, have given me permission to reprint excerpts from speeches made in class.

For permission to quote from periodicals and books I am indebted to:

Appleton-Century-Crofts, Inc., for material from Henry Lee Ewbank and J. Jeffery Auer, *Discussion and Debate*. (Copyright, 1951.)

The Free Press of Glencoe, Inc., for excerpts from Elihu Katz and Paul F. Lazarsfeld, *Personal Influence: The Part Played by People in the Flow of Mass Communications* (Copyright, 1955) and Joseph T. Klapper, *The Effects of Mass Communications*. (Copyright, 1960.)

Harcourt, Brace and World, Inc., for an excerpt from *Abraham Lincoln: The Prairie Years* by Carl Sandburg. (Copyright, 1926.)

Harvey Harmon, executive director, The National Football Foundation and Hall of Fame, and Paul Basco, administrative aide to General Douglas MacArthur, for excerpts from General MacArthur's speech in *Footballetter*.

Harper and Brothers, for an excerpt from *Mark Twain's Speeches*. (Copyright, 1923.)

Holt, Rinehart and Winston, Inc., for an excerpt from Halbert E. Gulley, *Discussion, Conference, and Group Process*. (Copyright, 1960.)

Houghton Mifflin Company, for excerpts from *The Second World War* by Winston Churchill (Copyright, 1949), and from *The Dynamics of Discussion* by Dean C. Barnlund and Franklyn S. Haiman. (Copyright, 1960.)

John Jamieson, editor of general publications, The H. W. Wilson Company, for excerpts from *Representative American Speeches*, edited by A. Craig Baird, and more recently by Lester Thonssen, and for helpful information about speech texts and copyrights.

Robert C. Jeffrey, executive secretary, Speech Association of America, for excerpts from *Speech Monographs, The Speech Teacher*, and *The Quarterly Journal of Speech*.

King Features Syndicate, for an excerpt from a syndicated column by George E. Sokolsky.

The Macmillan Company, for excerpts from the *Elements of Style* by William Strunk, Jr. and E. B. White. (Copyright, 1959.)

McGraw-Hill Book Company, Inc., for an excerpt from *Oral Communication in Business* by David C. Phillips (Copyright, 1955); for a reference to *Are You Listening?* by Ralph G. Nichols and Leonard A. Stevens (Copyright, 1957); for excerpts from W. Norwood Brigance, ed. *History and Criticism of American Public Address* (Copyright, 1943); for illustrations from *Phonetics*, by James Carrell and William R. Tiffany. (Copyright, 1960.)

Charles W. McLane, director of admissions and registrar, University of Missouri, for an excerpt from *Improving Transition from High School to University* (Columbia, University of Missouri, 1961).

Robert L. Morris, director, University of Missouri Press, for excerpts from Loren Reid, ed. *American Public Address: Studies in Honor of Albert Craig Baird*. (Copyright, 1961.)

Oxford University Press, for excerpts from *The Rhetoric of Aristotle*, trans. W. Rhys Roberts. (Copyright, 1924.)

Princeton University Press, for a reference to *Logic and Rhetoric in England* by Wilbur S. Howell (Copyright, 1956), and excerpts from Carl I. Hovland, Arthur A. Lumsdaine, and Fred D. Sheffield, *Experiments in Mass Communication* (Copyright, 1949).

Rutgers University Press, for excerpts from *The Collected Works of Abraham Lincoln*. (Copyright, 1953.)

The Viking Press, for an excerpt from *Benjamin Franklin*, by Carl Van Doren. (Copyright, 1938.)

Yale University Press, for excerpts from *Communication and Persuasion* and *The Order of Presentation* by Carl I. Hovland and others (Copyright, 1957, 1959), and for a reference to Theodore Clarke Smith, *The Life and Letters of James Abram Garfield* (Copyright, 1925).

I am also indebted to *The Colorado Quarterly, Forbes, Fortune, Journal of Abnormal and Social Psychology, Journal of Communication, Journal of Marketing, Journal of Social Issues, Journal of Social Psychology, Life, The Listener, Nation's Business, Newsweek, New York Times, Public Opinion Quarterly, Public Relations Journal, Reader's Digest, Saturday Evening Post, Science, Time, Vital Speeches of the Day,* and *Wall Street Journal,* for permission to quote excerpts from these publications; more specific acknowledgment is gratefully made in the appropriate place in the body of the text.

Elsewhere I have noted my appreciation of the counsel of Nelson Heath Meriwether, of Artcraft Press, but I want to express here my further thanks for his continued help with all sorts of editorial and typographical details.

Other acknowledgments are also made at appropriate places in the text.

To students I should particularly like to say: In these days when much emphasis is placed on the *practical,* I hope you will enjoy discussing *ideas* in your public speaking class. You will grow in competence and self-assurance, in respect for evidence and reasoning, in ability to use the spoken word with accuracy, vividness, and force. Most of all I hope your classroom experiences in speech making will help you put whatever you may achieve in the way of information, wisdom, good sense, and good judgment at the service of your profession, your community, and your fellow man.

LOREN REID

University of Missouri
Columbia

First
Principles
of
Public
Speaking

CHAPTER 1

Speech Making in the Sixties

Scope of speech making in this decade: in government, in business, in the professions. ■ *Nature of classroom instruction in speech making, and its importance in training the student for his life's work.* ■ *Public speaking as a form of communication, comprising five practical arts.*

THE FIFTIES HAVE LONG HENCE DEPARTED, and the sixties have ushered in what may prove to be an age of impressive speech making. John F. Kennedy's speech of January 20, 1961, on assuming the presidency, has been ranked with Lincoln's second inaugural ("With malice towards none, with charity for all . . . let us strive on to finish the work we are in, to bind up the nation's wounds") and Franklin D. Roosevelt's first ("This great nation will endure as it has endured . . . the only thing we have to fear is fear itself"). As on those other occasions, young and old citizens alike are once more facing critical problems, reflected in such moving language as:

> Let every nation know, whether it wishes us well or ill, that we shall pay any price, bear any burden, meet any hardship, support any friend, oppose any foe to assure the survival and the success of liberty.
>
> . . . civility is not a sign of weakness, and sincerity is always subject to proof. Let us never negotiate out of fear. But let us never fear to negotiate.[1]

---

[1] From a copy of the official text furnished this book by Pierre Salinger. Quoted by permission. The complete address appears in the Appendix.

The importance of speech making to the national interest is strongly urged in the paragraph below:

"Why is the United Nations of value to the United States? The answer is that we need a forum where our representatives can speak directly to the world. John F. Kennedy's speech before the United Nations did more to clear the atmosphere

I. The Scope of Speech Making

Others in public life are discussing with conviction the many far-reaching issues that come before us. The Vice President travels to Berlin to assure the German people that "we pledge our lives, our fortunes, and our sacred honor" to their cause and ours, these historic words reminding the twentieth century of the eighteenth.[2] The Attorney General makes a plea to a southern audience for a better understanding of the grave problems growing out of civil rights.[3] No one is especially surprised to read that these or other national officials have made important speeches of policy in Europe, in Asia, in India, in Latin America; wherever they can best serve the cause of world peace. On scores and hundreds of occasions, on campuses and elsewhere, speakers remind citizenry that the review of national policy is the proper concern of a free people.[4] Vital issues produce thoughtful and serious speech making; it has always been so, and especially seems so today.

Turning from the political to the business world, we can see that issues growing out of steadily-intensifying competition again lead to significant speech making. The European common market, much the most effective economic development so far this decade, has already eminently proved to be a way of stimulating production by reducing tariffs on goods moving between member nations. As other countries come into the market, a splendid vision will appear: through learning to discuss together their economic problems, national leaders of Europe will accustom themselves to discuss their political concerns, and may, one day, lead themselves to a United States of Europe, with a common currency, a common parliament. The emergence of a third powerful economic group, with a potential membership of 300 million people, should prove a strong influence for peace. Meanwhile, however, American business is to face stronger competition than ever, as overseas production becomes more efficient and as tariff

---

than miles of propaganda releases could do. He defeated Soviet Russia in Africa with one speech. This will not happen every time. We face a very tough period in our history . . . but our chances will be better if the instruments available are beneficial to us." This excerpt from a column by George F. Sokolsky was distributed to several hundred newspapers in 1962. It appears here through the courtesy of King Features Syndicate, Inc.

[2] Lyndon B. Johnson, Aug. 19, 1961.

[3] Robert F. Kennedy, on Law Day, May 7, 1961, campus of the University of Georgia, Athens.

[4] Former president Harry S. Truman, former president Dwight D. Eisenhower, former vice president Richard M. Nixon, Hubert Humphrey, Robert S. McNamara, McGeorge Bundy, J. W. Fulbright, Paul Douglas, countless others.

barriers are lowered; so again, in economic as well as in political areas, weighty issues set the stage for influential speech making. Quite appropriately this text includes excerpts from speeches of American business and professional men as well as from American statesmen.

All of this increased speech-making activity has not gone unnoticed by the press. "Americans suddenly seem to be all ears," say the editors of *Life,* surveying the interest of American listeners in hearing speeches packed with *information.* Scientists like Harold Urey, Linus Pauling and Ralph E. Lapp, observers of current affairs like Vincent Sheean, William Laurence, and James J. Wadsworth, reporters on women's interests like Amy Vanderbilt and Marguerite Higgins, artists like choreographer Anne Wilson, command the attention of audiences from coast to coast.[5] Says W. Colston Leigh, for 37 years a manager of lecturers: "Lecturing is more popular than ever." He continues:

> There will probably be 100,000 lectures given in this country this year. . . . Every luncheon group, every lodge, every church social group and temple brotherhood, and women's club and educational group wants lecturers. There are 20,000 or 30,000 customers, each buying for some organization.[6]

Overseas, *The Times Literary Supplement* editorializes that "we live in an age of dialog and of the spoken word."[7]

Little need to tell students today that the speech making that goes on in the outside world is only a continuation of the discussion of issues that they grapple with in their own speeches. Many who hardly thought of themselves as speakers all at once find themselves elected, or promoted, or hand-picked, for an office or position in which speech making is necessary. Take for example the officers of the groups to which you belong; or the hundreds of members of the Peace Corps who find themselves in such remote regions as East Pakistan, Ghana, Tanganyika, Colombia, the Philippines; young men like Dennis Grubb, of Westport, Connecticut, who addressed a South American audience:

> We're here to work with our hands with your hands. We don't have any gifts for you. We don't have any money for you. We're

---

[5] *Life,* LI (November 10, 1961), 18.
Wrote the editors of *Time:* "One of the biggest booms in the nation comes from all those businessmen who are getting up to speak" (February 8, 1960).
[6] *Newsweek,* LVIII (December 25, 1961), 68.
[7] Quoted in *The Listener,* LXV (January 26, 1961), 198.

trying to show you through democracy that we can make your
lives better.[8]

The public speaker of today may be thought of as a lawyer, physician, minister, engineer, salesman, housewife, public relations person,
teacher, office holder, agricultural expert, military officer, editor,
nurse, accountant, or executive—any of scores of different businesses,
professions, callings—talking to small or medium-sized groups, or
occasionally to large groups, on topics growing out of business, professional, religious, social, civic, educational, or economic problems
and issues. Modern classes in public speaking stress a clear, practical,
interesting, effective type of presentation; they do not offer instruction
in the more formal type of eloquence popular generations ago. Yet
old beliefs and old prejudices about the scope and purpose of public
speaking classes die hard. This spot is therefore as good a place as
any to state that with your public speaking instructor, the *content*
of your speech comes first: your reasoning, your evidence and proof,
your ideas, the clarity and force of your language. Your *delivery*
(voice, action) comes second: a close second, to be sure, as you want
to free yourself from awkwardness and mannerisms and acquire a
serviceable, practical, functional type of presentation that helps make
content convincing. Concern with *flowery language, excessive emo-
tionalism,* and *artificial gesture* is, however, *not for us.*

The May, 1952, *Fortune* article states well the need for training in
speaking and writing:

> As soon as you move one step up from the bottom, your effective-
> ness depends on your ability to reach others through the spoken or
> the written word. . . .
>
> The larger the organization of which you are an employee, the
> more important it will be that you know how to convey your
> thoughts in writing or speaking. . . .
>
> The foundations for skill in expression have to be laid early; . . .
> if you do not lay these foundations during your school years, you
> may never have an opportunity again.[9]

[8] Reported in *Life,* LII (January 5, 1962), 20.
Before enrolling in the Peace Corps, Dennis Grubb was a high school debater
and a student in the basic speech course at Pennsylvania State University. In
his South American project he found it necessary to talk daily "with the people
of the region, either formally or informally"; to "organize community action
groups" and "present proposals for their most pressing problems." (Letter of
March 23, 1962.)
[9] Peter F. Drucker, "Some Truths that Every Young College Graduate Should
Know," in "How to be an Employee," *Fortune,* XLV (May, 1952), 127.
Forbes describes Dr. Drucker as "probably the most sought-after consultant to

Nation's Business asked the question, "What does business want most in business school graduates?" Replied the 73 business men who responded: (1) "ability to think clearly and communicate with facility," (2) "beginnings of maturity and judgment," (3) "understanding human behavior."[10] Point One is obviously a principal concern of the public speaking course; Point Two emerges insofar as your class helps you develop "maturity and judgment" in weighing and appraising ideas; and Point Three is developed and strengthened every time you consider a speech in relation to the understandings and feelings of the human beings who are to listen to you. *Newsweek* in a feature story mentions 11 prominent businessmen who frequently speak in behalf of their firms. "Few company presidents can get by without making four or five speeches a year . . . the nation's 4,500 Rotary clubs alone consume almost a quarter million speeches each year. . . . Speech making is a unique and valuable channel of communication."[11]

As to the importance of speaking to technical men, the Executive Engineer of the Engineering Division of Chrysler Corporation had this to say:

> . . . For every hour of good creative work, of . . . work to improve existing products or create new ones, there are many more hours of talking, writing, arguing, persuading, cajoling, soothing, praising, and selling required in order to bring that creative effort to the point of favorable acceptance by the people who must use it. . . .

> If engineers can be made 10 per cent more effective . . . in their ability to communicate more effectively—the potential rewards to

---

big business in the U. S. today. "More than 50 top U. S. firms currently engage Drucker to stimulate the thought processes of their high-paid brass. . . . His book, *The Practice of Management,* is a classic and is required reading at the Harvard Business School" (issue of February 15, 1962, pp. 34-35).

The author wrote Dr. Drucker inviting him to comment further, for the benefit of readers of this text. He wrote (letter of March 5, 1962): "Let me say that the more I see—and in my daily work I see a great many promising young executives in government, in academic life and in business—the more distressed I am by the tremendous waste of ability, effort and talent that results from the lack of skill in presenting one's ideas in speaking or in writing.

"I see far too many people with real ability who get nowhere because they can not say what they have to say, either on paper or through the spoken word. And the man who can do so, even though he may have much less ability and much less to contribute, gets the big job, gets effectiveness, gets attention every time."

10 XLVI (March, 1958), 101.

11 LIV (November 23, 1959), 94-98. "Yet the average business speaker should be run out of town," comments the president of one firm. "He doesn't give himself adequate time to prepare. He deals in generalities. He is not well organized, and his talk is usually too long." (Page 94.)

be realized are far greater than are those waiting to be tapped through a like increase in technical creativity. This is why I like to refer to this part of the engineer's job as creative communication.

He praises the technically-trained man for using statements that are well-organized, accurate, and clear—to himself and others of his background—"but too frequently he stops there":

He concludes that he has done his job and it is now up to the listener to [act]. He often fails to realize that maybe the listener isn't sufficiently interested to expend the effort necessary to do this. Someone has said that effective communication is the art of telling people who don't want to listen something they don't want to hear and doing it in such a way that they will do something they didn't want to and, at the same time, leave them pleased with both themselves and you. . . .

When you can get him to appreciate that his total job includes . . . communication . . . that he hasn't really accomplished anything until he has gained acceptance for the products of his technical efforts, then he will pursue the subject as scientifically and as enthusiastically as he will the solution of any problem in the physical sciences.[12]

Considering the necessity of public speaking in civic affairs, a judge of the United States Court of Appeals has written:

The importance of public speaking to our community life cannot be overestimated. . . . Without the opportunity to speak in public, how would the high-minded public servant have a chance to meet with his constituents, to express his views to the persons

---

[12] H. Richard Steding, at the annual meeting, American Society for Engineering Education, Michigan State University campus, April 22, 1961. Text of this speech supplied through the courtesy of Mr. Steding.

Mr. Steding, executive engineer for the Chrysler Corporation, wrote the author as follows: "I seem to find myself involved in some kind of speech making assignment on the order of two or three times a year. . . . Public speaking on the part of our engineers and excutives is important both from the standpoint of fulfilling our obligations as good citizens where we can make a useful contribution, and also because in so doing we help to project a good image of our company and its products.

"I did indeed have considerable experience in speaking before various kinds of groups during my college years and I believe strongly that such experience is vital to the development of anyone's full potential. However, as I am sure you would agree, public speaking is not an end in itself; the primary objective of having something important to say before getting up seems too often overlooked." (Letter of February 22, 1962.)

Information forms completed by 778 graduates of the College of Engineering, University of Missouri, revealed that physics, mathematics, English composition, and public speaking were the non-engineering courses considered "to be of most value to them in the profession." They also felt a need for additional

whose support is so vital to his program, and finally to win authorization for worthy projects?[13]

In similar vein the Athenian statesman, Pericles, is said to have observed that "one who forms a judgment on any point but can not explain himself clearly to the people, might as well have never thought at all on the subject."[14] This statement would certainly be true of a citizen who not only wanted to vote wisely himself, but who also desired to be able to inform, encourage, and persuade others.

II. What is Public Speaking?

Public speaking is, as has been suggested, a form of communication. As with all communication, its function is to seek to get others to react as the communicator wishes them to react. The speaker may wish to explain an idea, or share a mood. If he explains, he wants his listeners to understand him; if he persuades, he wants them to believe him.

The *means of communication employed* is oral language, thus including the shades of meaning that vocal inflection gives words. The speaker also communicates through gesture, facial expression, action, personal bearing. He may use charts, graphs, other objects.

Attempts suggests that the speaker does not always succeed. Circumstances may be beyond his control. Some other speaker, perhaps one with greater knowledge and experience, might have done better.

To get others to react as one wishes them to react suggests that the speaker has a *purpose:* to share *information;* or *entertain;* or change a *belief* or *urge* action; or *stimulate, impress, inspire.* The purpose should be one that is worthy of a man of integrity; in the long run, a speaker of doubtful character will be discovered, and his influence destroyed. The word *others* suggests that people are listening. This group may be large or small.

The situation in which public speaking takes place is one in which the *speaker* is usually, in one or more ways, set apart from the *listeners.* He may have a special place from which to talk; he may be intro-

training in public speaking and English. From an unpublished doctoral dissertation, University of Missouri, by Jay L. Logue. Quoted in Donald D. Shook, "Improving Transition from High School to University" (Columbia, University of Missouri, 1961). p. 17.

13 Letter to the author, January 24, 1962, from Judge Florence E. Allen, sixth circuit, Cleveland, Ohio. Judge Allen's distinguished services to the bar and bench and to the nation is recognized in part by the fact that she has been awarded an honorary LL.D. by more than 20 institutions of higher learning.

14 Quoted in Richard Whately, *Elements of Rhetoric* (Louisville, John P. Morton & Co., n.d), p. 21.

duced or identified as the speaker. Others present will sense that, for a time, they should *listen;* this relationship between speaker and listener is another useful clue to help describe public speaking.[15]

III. Public Speaking Comprises Five Arts

The study of public speaking helps the student to improve himself in five practical arts.[16] The basic idea was first expressed by Cicero and has been developed in various ways throughout the ages.

Art number 1 is the art of creating or discovering good and sensible ideas. The speaker accumulates evidence, argument, example and illustration, testimony from authority. From this storehouse he evolves comparisons, relationships, solutions. Obviously, finding arguments, establishing relationships, and reasoning to conclusions, is an important aspect of speaking.

Art number 2 is the art of selecting and organizing. Mastery of this art guides the student as to what to leave out of his speech and what to put in; and in what order to arrange what is selected.

Art number 3 is the art of using language. Certain words are more forceful, vivid, persuasive, and accurate than others. "Four score and seven years ago" has a different impact from "87 years ago." "Iron curtain" was retained in the mind of nearly every listener, whereas "great wall" would likely have passed unnoticed. Relevant, pertinent facts call for clear, incisive language.

Art number 4 is the art of memory. A student needs to have ideas at the tip of his tongue, so he can draw upon them *when* he needs them. He may also be called upon to answer questions, to develop his ideas at greater length, to defend his evidence or reasoning.

Art number 5 is delivery. This art of using voice and body helps the student immeasurably in making words effective.

The point of view of this text is that you should improve yourself in *each of these five aspects.* Don't be like a person who tries to go around a golf course with one club, a putter.

Imagine a speaker *weak in ideas.* His information would be inaccurate, his judgment unfounded, his counsel superficial. Although

---

[15] The student may wish to compare and contrast public speaking with *conversation* or *interviewing.* He may wish to modify this definition and discussion to fit *public speaking* by *radio.* He may also reflect upon how *small* the group may be to which one may give a *public* speech.

[16] For a good exposition of this concept, see Wilbur Samuel Howell, *Logic and Rhetoric in England, 1500-1700* (Princeton University Press, 1956), Chapter 3, pp. 66-116. He cites the phrase, "an art made up of five great arts." Donald Lemen Clark, in *Rhetoric in Greco-Roman Education* (New York, Columbia University Press, 1957), speaks of "the five resources of the speaker" (pp. 71 ff.).

he might be impressive in other ways, his influence could not be lasting among thoughtful people.

Imagine a speaker *weak in selecting and organizing.* His speeches would be formless blobs, difficult for him to present, difficult for listeners to remember.

Imagine a speaker *weak in the use of words.* His ideas would seem vague and colorless; his utterance would consist of trite sayings. Some people mistakenly think that public speaking is principally concerned with the use of fancy language; they believe the speaker is one who continually whips up a froth of words of little sense or meaning. The two great arts of having ideas and of clothing them in well-chosen words are almost inseparable. As soon as you take any crude, raw idea and begin to shape and form it, even just to make it clear and understandable, you are calling upon the principles of using language.

Imagine a speaker of *weak memory.* He would have to write his speeches and read them. He would hardly dare take his eyes off the page. He would be helpless in a question and answer period. Yet we are not interested in memorizing speeches word by word. In rehearsal a speaker should encourage himself to use different wordings each time. Many of his wordings he may like—and these he will want to hold on to—but other wordings will be improved, and important improvements may be created at the actual moment of giving the speech to the audience.

Imagine a speaker of *poor delivery.* He might be so inaudible that you could hear him only with great difficulty. He might mumble so much that you would miss the meaning. He might lull you into inattention by a chant or singsong presentation.

Master each of these five aspects of good speaking. Unplanned speeches are likely to be long-winded, rambling, wearying. A test missile has built-in devices so that the experimenter can explode it in midair if it gets off its course. How relieved an audience would be if, in similar fashion, an unplanned, experimental, tentative speech could be halted in midair once the speaker got off his course. Improve in *all five ways* your abilities to speak.

Questions for Classroom Discussion

1. In his first important address of 1962, John F. Kennedy declared: "The United States did not rise to greatness by waiting for others to lead. This nation is the world's foremost manufacturer, farmer, banker, consumer and exporter. The Communist economic offensive is underway. The opportunity is ours—the initiative is up to us."

Comment on how those who make up these foremost manufacturing, farming, banking, consuming and exporting groups can exert leadership—inside each individual group, and outside of it.

2. Consult a file of local community or student newspapers for the last month, and report on the different kinds of speeches that have made the news. To this list add other examples from your own observation.

Speech-Related Project

Select a field of interest in which you plan to do study and research in preparation for later speeches. This field should be a current social, political, literary, artistic, religious, industrial, or economic problem. Perhaps you would like to explain, interpret, or defend modern art, modern music, exploration of outer space, trends in religious thinking, labor unions, investing in the stock market, our relations with a foreign country, medical practices or innovations, national defense. This subject should be a significant one—preferably one in which you now have an above-average interest and would like to extend your study.

Speaking Assignment 1
A Speech Introducing Yourself

Make an informal talk in which you introduce yourself. Tell us unknown, little-known, or notorious facts about you that will help us get acquainted with you. Draw upon such items as: home town, hobbies or interests, vocational goal, politics, special talents, likes, or dislikes. Not all of these will come into any one talk. Time limit (to be suggested by your instructor) .... minutes.

Note: This text contains 25 speaking assignments, numbered for the convenience of the student and the instructor. Presumably some of them will be omitted and others modified; your instructor may also substitute other assignments. He will advise about time limits, outlines, other requirements.

CHAPTER 2

Preparing for
Speech Making

Aspects of the intellectual basis of speaking. ■ *The usefulness of habits of observing, recording, thinking about the
audience, thinking about the subject.* ■ *Methods of presentation: memorized, manuscript, impromptu, extemporaneous.*

LOOK BACK OVER your high school career, and recall the contributions of this earlier education *that now matter.* One of them will
likely be the *habits of thinking* that you developed. Perhaps you
learned to think as a physical or social scientist thinks, as a mathematician thinks, or as an artist thinks. What you learned about
thinking—those ways in which you toughened your mind—came after
the mastery of facts, principles, data of one kind or another. You had
to learn to work rigidly and accurately with formulas, conjugations,
concepts of behavior of men or matter, the arranging of ideas into a
speech or theme. Many of these little bits and pieces tend to dis-
appear (although we believe not permanently) but habits of thinking
remain. Your teacher had to show you the way and help you with
the first steps, but if he taught well and you learned well, before long
you were able to proceed onward by yourself.

Speech making is also an intellectual discipline; a speaker should
draw upon a wide range of information and experience, of reflection
and judgment; he should have the faculty of putting these thoughts
into words, in the presence of small or large audiences. Cicero, who
was soldier, lawyer, writer, and speaker, who held the highest political
office in the gift of the people of Rome, who had a wide acquaintance in these many fields, thought that the art of public speaking was
the most difficult of all; to help prove his point, he would point to
the scarcity of good speakers. Yet he was a great believer that one
could improve his ability to speak and was himself a continual stu-

dent of speech making. We can very well therefore give attention to the intellectual side of speech making.

I. The Intellectual Basis of Speaking

Just as in order to become a better scientist one should develop and practice the methods of thinking like a scientist, to become a better speaker one should develop the habits of thinking that good speaking requires. In general a speaker is forever on the search for materials that he can use in his speeches; he records these so that he will have them at hand in the moments of speech preparation, and he selects and interprets and reasons from them in such a way as to make them clear or persuasive or memorable to listeners.

A. OBSERVE LIKE A SPEAKER

Speeches are composed of reasons, examples, facts, and other materials, put together in various kinds of arrangements. Most of these materials come from what you hear and what you see. You must be on the watch for new ideas, new points of view, new details.

Many will see the sign in front of the municipal building, "Give Blood Today," but the *speaker* may observe that as a possible speech subject. If he gives blood, he will note details of procedure, so that he can give a more vivid and interesting talk. Many will drive aimlessly along the new interstate highway, but the *speaker* may ask himself whether he should make a timely speech about problems of superhighway driving. If a speaker likes to make talks about rocketry, he will especially be aware of new developments in that field. If he likes to make talks about sports cars, the population problem, the art of selling, new procedures in agriculture, engineering, medicine, or home-making, he will be observant in those areas.

B. RECORD LIKE A SPEAKER

Early in his career the good speaker, like the good student, realizes that *unless he writes an item down, he may forget it.*

Observing and recording go together. If you run across something interesting, *write it down.* Some speakers carry 3x5 cards or slips in their pockets. Whenever they see a useful item, they write it on the card and later file it. Others use a loose-leaf notebook.

Everyone who has kept such a file has had this experience: in sorting his cards or his loose-leaf sheets, he finds he has *recorded* ideas which he has since *forgotten.* Seeing the written record, however, refreshes the memory. Perhaps you have heard a humorous story, and suddenly, part way through the recounting, have realized you had heard this story yourself weeks or months ago, and had forgotten it. Next time, write it down; then you can be the narrator.

Idaho's great senator, William E. Borah, used large envelopes or folders, labelled with appropriate titles, in which he filed letters, pamphlets, petitions, newspaper clippings, articles from magazines, and notes taken on his reading.[1] The speaker must observe, read, reflect, and, to keep from losing the fruits of his study, record.

If you are going to make eight or ten speeches in your public speaking class, you can not be content simply to give the audience eight or ten installments from your biography. Select a current social, economic, or political problem, preferably, to be sure, one with which you already have concern, and read further about it. Review your resources by reading the lists on pages 45-49 and 347-348; choose topics close to your heart, and as you discover material, *note and file*.

C. REFLECT UPON THE SUBJECT LIKE A SPEAKER

Not only must the speaker observe, read, and record, but he must look at his materials with a speaker's eye—he must reflect upon his subject as a good speaker does. Good thinking is the basis of good speaking; and this good thinking may be described in several ways.

1. *Thinking that creates*

Although a classroom speaker's ideas may not be new in every particular, they can at least show originality and creativity in adaptation or application. The speaker's personal experiences may be new and original, and when he applies these to an explanation or a problem he may be thinking creatively. He may study a speech or essay and talk about it; mere paraphrase or summary is not creative, but a reaction, critique, or appraisal could be. In the public speaking class speakers sometimes evolve original (but sensible) solutions, proposals, procedures, applications, as well as original methods of organizing, adapting, and phrasing. Speakers operate at different levels of inventiveness: the ideas may be new, or new at a particular time, or in a particular context; or the ideas may be old, but the presentation or adaptation of them may be new and fresh.

---

1 Waldo W. Braden, "The Political Speaking of William E. Borah," in *American Public Address: Studies in Honor of Albert Craig Baird* (Columbia, University of Missouri Press, 1961), 196.

2. *Thinking that makes an idea clear*

While reflecting upon his subject, the speaker may say to himself, "A special problem with a speech on this subject is to make it *clear*." The material may be clear to the speaker and to those of like background, but if it is to be presented to a non-specialized audience, it must somehow be made more communicable. One with a speaker's training will therefore begin to think about vocabulary, examples, illustrations; ways of organizing and arranging; possibilities of preview, transition, summary. One without a speaker's training might overlook these vital points, and not succeed in making the subject clear at all.

Every speaker is called upon to address two great kinds of audiences: those in his field and those out of it. When physicians talk among themselves, their technical vocabulary is in the highest degree accurate and communicative. These same terms, however, are usually meaningless to the patient. A football coach should be able to discuss the fine points of the game to the student body as well as to the squad. An engineer should be able to speak understandably to the mayor and city council as well as to other engineers in the same professional society. Moreover, in a given firm or factory, the expert from research and development should be able to talk to the expert from accounting or sales. Next time you hear a speaker broadcasting on the wrong wave length, remind yourself that when next you take the platform you will broadcast on a frequency suitable for your listeners.

Keep ever in mind what Dale has appropriately labelled the "clear only if known" fallacy. Some speeches are clear only to those who already know the information.[2]

3. *Thinking that makes an idea persuasive*

During his reflections the speaker may decide that basically his subject is clear and simple, but he must do some special thinking about ways of making it persuasive. He wants his listeners to accept his belief or to undertake the positive action he has in mind: to sign, vote, buy, do. So he gives thought to his selection of examples, statistics, reasoning, testimony; he wonders whether he will encounter prejudice, bias, tradition, habit; he considers appeals to duty, affection, patriotism, perhaps fear or anger.

When a speaker undertakes to persuade listeners, he must reason about the probable course of future events. Since no one can read

[2] Edgar Dale, "Clear Only if Known," *The News Letter*, Bureau of Educational Research, Ohio State University, XXVII, 6 (1957). Originally appeared in the issue of January, 1952, and cited here by permission of Dr. Dale. Quoted in David K. Berlo, *The Process of Communication* (New York, Holt, Rinehart and Winston, 1960), 193.

the future accurately, the speaker must weigh and appraise assumptions, probabilities, likelihoods—*after* studying and analyzing all the available facts that can be brought to bear. Thus we can say that a certain speaker (Churchill, for example) displayed good judgment and statesmanship because, secure in his knowledge of what had happened and of what was going on at the moment, he could advise listeners about what was likely to happen. This kind of reasoning is highly involved in the making of decisions. When in a classroom speech a student persuades his listeners to vote for Spangler instead of Ashlock, he is combining what he knows about Spangler or Ashlock with what he expects they would do in office. No one can be positive how either Spangler or Ashlock will operate once in office, but if one of them has shown more initiative and responsibility in the past, the likelihood is that he will show more in the future. When a classroom speaker urges that his state adopt a point-system for automobile drivers, he is combining what he knows about the experience of this plan in another state with what he hopes will be the effect of legislation in his own state. His case is helped if traffic conditions seem to be similar in the two states; to determine the extent of the similarity certainly calls for preliminary study that will help listeners to make up their minds as they try to weigh how the proposal would be received in their own state. Making speeches on topics that demand a forward-looking view will help train the student for this important kind of thinking about the future that is necessary for all citizens.

In a widely-quoted address, Sir Charles Percy Snow illustrated this kind of reasoning about the probable course of future events when he addressed the members of the American Association for the Advancement of Science:

We are faced with an either-or, and we haven't much time. The *either* is acceptance of a restriction of nuclear armaments. This is going to begin, just as a token, with an agreement on the stopping of nuclear tests. The United States is not going to get the 99.9 per cent "security" that it has been asking for. It is unobtainable, though there are other bargains that the United States could probably secure. I am not going to conceal from you that this course involves certain risks. They are quite obvious, and no honest man is going to blink them. That is the *either*. The *or* is not a risk but a certainty. It is this. There is no agreement on tests. The nuclear arms race between the U.S.A. and the U.S.S.R. not only continues, but accelerates. Other countries join in. Within, at the most, six years, China and several other states will have a stock of nuclear bombs. Within, at the most, ten years, some of those bombs are going off. I am saying this as responsibly as I can. *That* is the certainty.

On the one side, therefore, we have a finite risk. On the other side we have a certainty of disaster. Between a risk and a certainty, a sane man does not hesitate.[3]

4. *Thinking that makes an idea memorable*

As the classroom speaker ponders his subject he may ask himself, "How can I make my speech one that will be remembered longer?" This question leads him to reflect upon the techniques of repetition (often incorporated into transitions and summaries) or of language (*big stick, forgotten man, new frontier*). Or a speech may become memorable by the force of the idea or of the personality behind it.

D. OTHER ASPECTS

One may indeed hope that when he stands before an audience he may achieve 80 or 90 or 100 per cent of his intellectual potential, not merely 40 per cent or zero. Training in speaking should add to one's fluency and command of language. It should lead him into a study of important topics, so that his range of information will be increased. It should encourage him to take a stand on urgent issues. Three types of students can be identified: those who lead, those who follow, and those who do not know what is going on. Training in speech making should lift the student out of the last category into one of the other two.

Society can not train one set of men to do the work, another to make the speeches. The president, chairman, sales manager, or chief engineer, *must make his own speeches.* Ghost writing is bad enough, but ghost speaking is worse. If *you* climbed the mountain, saved the child, flew in the space ship, won the contest, attained the office, solved the problem, swung the deal, audiences want to hear *you* and not some one sent by you. If you send your message by some one else, part of it is likely to get lost. When you arrive on the scene, the listeners are gratified to see you, the person they have heard about and have come to listen to. Let them, then, hear from you in your words, so they can enjoy your own recital of the situation, your own grasp of the problem, your own proposal for the future.

II. Methods of Presentation

Speakers are likely to use one of four methods of presentation, to be described below. The kind of intellectual activity that you will

[3] Reprinted by permission of the author and The American Association for the Advancement of Science; first published in *Science* Magazine; Copyright © by The American Association for the Advancement of Science.

be called upon to use depends in part upon the method of presentation called for by the occasion.

A. THE MEMORIZED SPEECH

The method of writing the entire speech and memorizing it, used by many speakers a century or more ago, is little used today. Listeners today are inclined to show lessened interest in speeches that sound memorized; and the art of presenting an entire speech in a way that conceals the memorizing is difficult indeed. Many speakers, however, practically memorize parts of their speech: opening sentences, concluding sentences, key phrases here and there, statistics or quotations, the order of presenting key arguments. And if you find yourself in a situation where you give the same speech more than once, you will eventually have large sections of it committed to memory.

Ordinarily, however, your instructor does not recommend that beginners memorize speeches. He wants to develop a style that is more direct and spontaneous. Perhaps in an earlier speech course you leaned too heavily on rote memorization. Or perhaps because of excessive stage fright you feel insecure unless you have memorized every word. Discuss this problem with your instructor. You are quite right to rehearse your speeches, but perhaps you can adopt the plan of changing your wording from one rehearsal to the next in order to evolve more fluency in picking and choosing your words as you speak.

B. THE SPEECH READ FROM A MANUSCRIPT

Teachers of public speaking are of differing opinions about the advisability of reading speeches in a public speaking class. Unquestionably they agree that it is not desirable for a beginning speaker. As everybody knows, a speech that is read is likely to be dull in its presentation. The speaker is inclined to use a monotonous tone that makes it difficult for listeners to sustain attention. In general, therefore, do not write out and read speeches except for those assignments when the instructor specifically asks you to do so. Before making those assignments he will no doubt give the class special suggestions so that speakers can avoid the worst faults of using a manuscript.

C. THE IMPROMPTU SPEECH

Occasions arise when the speaker has literally no time for specific preparation. He must call upon his reserves as well as he can on the spur of the moment. A speaker should train himself to speak impromptu as effectively as he can. Even a carefully planned speech may have an impromptu moment, as when the speaker inserts a comment inspired by a question, a reaction from the audience, or a remark of a previous speaker. If you are at a banquet or other function where you think you may be introduced to the guests and called upon for a few remarks, ask yourself in advance what you will say if you are suddenly invited to speak. Foresight of this sort will save you a little embarrassment.[4]

D. THE EXTEMPORANEOUS SPEECH

Impromptu means *immediately, at once, right now. Extemporaneous,* however, as used by speech teachers, describes a speech for which the speaker may have prepared hours or days, but at the moment of delivery he speaks from a mental or written outline. In preparing a speech by this method the speaker pores over his material and arranges it in the most effective order, adding here and deleting there so as to secure proper balance and emphasis. He may rehearse his talk many times, so that he will know what idea to take up first, what second, and so on. He is not concerned about the precise language he will employ, leaving that to the occasion itself, except for special places in the speech where he has exact wording well in mind. The conclusion, for example, may be well planned and carefully worded.

Using this method, the speaker is most likely to use a delivery that is conversational and direct. Even if he stumbles momentarily, that hesitation seems to reassure the listeners that the speaker is communicating directly with them. What is lost in fluency is gained in spontaneity. Such a speaker may glance at his notes now and then, but for the most part he will be looking at his hearers and will be communicating to them about his topic.

E. CONSULT YOUR INSTRUCTOR

Consult your instructor about the method of presentation to be used in your class. Generally the extemporaneous, conversational method will prevail, though special assignments from time to time may exploit other methods. Most men and women active in business or professional life today find that they need to be trained in different methods of presentation in order to meet the requirements of different kinds of situations.

A famous flute teacher, Timotheus, who had a fixed fee for beginners, followed the practice of doubling it if the young musician had had previous instruction under some other master. Timotheus

4 See Chapter 19, "Reading a Speech; Impromptu Speaking."

reasoned it would be twice as difficult to correct bad habits instilled by another teacher as it would to begin with one who frankly appeared in a state of ignorance; his extra tuition is often called "the double fee of Timotheus."

Let us hope that the combined efforts of this text and your instructor will help you improve your speaking from the outset. Remember, of course, that any misconceptions you may have about speaking, or preconceived notions, or reluctance to learn new ideas, or fear of trying different methods, are as costly in their way as was the double fee assessed by Timotheus. Begin this intellectual enterprise as you would any other worthwhile one: as a learner, in the spirit of inquiry.

Questions for Classroom Discussion

1. What personal qualities—intellectual, social, emotional—are valuable assets to a speaker?

2. In which businesses and professions is the ability to speak effectively an asset? Note ways in which this ability makes an individual a better citizen.

3. To what extent are women called upon to speak?

4. Comment on the following statement by John F. Kennedy:

An open society grows or withers according to the power of its ideas and the vitality of its interior dialogue.

If ever the United States should reach a point where the clash of ideas comes to an end, where debate disappears, where everybody agrees with everybody else on everything, then we are finished as a nation—and the ideal of freedom, to which our nation has been dedicated since the times of Washington and Adams, Jefferson and Hamilton, perishes.

Speech-Related Projects

1. Start a file (note cards, loose-leaf sheets) of anecdotes, quotations, examples, illustrations that may fit into a later speech. Hand in five typical cards or sheets.

2. Make a list of possible topics on which you think you might speak.

3. Select a field of interest in which you plan to do study and re-

search in preparation for later speeches. This field should be a current social, political, literary, artistic, religious, industrial, or economic problem. Perhaps you would like to explain, interpret, or defend modern art, modern music, exploration of outer space, trends in religious thinking, labor unions, investing in the stock market, our relations with a foreign country, medical practices or innovations, national defense. This subject should be a significant one—preferably one in which you now have an above-average interest and would like to extend your study.

Speaking Assignment 2

A Personal Background Speech

Continue Assignment 1 further by telling in more detail about one important aspect of your life: vocational, social, educational, athletic, artistic, political, or the like. Time limit (to be suggested by your instructor) .... minutes.

CHAPTER 3

Stage Fright

What surveys and experimental studies show about stage fright in student speakers. ■ *Nine ways of managing stage fright.* ■ *Customs of speech making to know in order to feel more at home in front of an audience.*

~~~~~~

MOST OF US EXPERIENCE a kind of anxiety, apprehension, or worry between the time we agree to make a speech and the time we deliver it. After receiving an invitation or an assignment to speak, we begin a mental countdown, each count a nervous and awesome one, beginning with "Ten: I've got to make a speech," on through the perplexing steps of locating and arranging material, and so on down to "One: The chairman is calling my name," and "Zero: Here I am, on my feet." And there we stand, like a missile on its launching pad, hoping to rise into the heavens, but not knowing exactly how successful this firing will be.

I. The Problem of Stage Fright

The more that we learn about the principles and practice of public speaking, the more confident we can be about the probable outcome of our speaking.

Speech flights usually end like missile flights; you may not reach the back side of the moon but you do not completely fail, either. If a missile plunges into the sea, scientists report that they made valuable observations and collected priceless data, all to be put to splendid use next time. Such reports can be made only about missiles that are guided and *speeches that are planned;* no one is interested in chance, random, purposeless efforts. The very fact of planning introduces a wonder and a concern about the outcome; and this concern, by heightening our eagerness to do well, brings us face to face with the phenomenon known as stage fright. This anxiety is a part of the *emotional basis of speaking.*

A. STAGE FRIGHT: PRELIMINARY STUDY

Two questions may usefully be asked about stage fright.

1. *How frequently does it occur?*

Public speaking teachers have made informal surveys of frequency of stage fright to show students how often it occurs. As a broad estimate, from 60 to 75 per cent of college students have reported that they worry about their nervousness in speaking. More than thirty per cent of them consider it their most serious problem.[1] Specifically, 384 students at the State University of Iowa described their stage fright as follows: 6 per cent as severe, 45 per cent as moderate, and 33 per cent as mild; 16 per cent stated that they had no stage fright.[2] When still another investigator surveyed two groups of University of Minnesota students, 56 per cent of one and 61 per cent of the other listed a form of nervousness as an important speech problem.[3] Other Minnesota students checked statements like those below, the figures representing the percentage of the total group:

I am in a state of nervous tension before getting up to speak (70 per cent).

It is difficult for me to search my mind calmly for the right word to express my thoughts (57 per cent).

My voice sounds strange to me when I address a group (37 per cent).

Only 6 per cent of the group reported that speaking in public was a pleasurable experience unaccompanied by any doubts or fears.[4] In a University of Southern California study, two researchers secured pulse and blood pressure readings of 50 men and 50 women college students in a beginning course immediately before and immediately after two classroom speeches. More than 90 per cent of all the readings showed fluctuations from normal.[5]

What happens to these students who say, at the outset of a course,

[1] A. Craig Baird and Franklin H. Knower, *General Speech: An Introduction,* 2nd ed. (New York, McGraw-Hill Book Company, 1957), p. 114.
[2] Floyd I. Greenleaf, "An Exploratory Study of Stage Fright," *Quarterly Journal of Speech,* XXXVIII (October, 1952), 327.
[3] Franklin H. Knower, "A Study of Speech Attitudes and Adjustments," *Speech Monographs,* V (1938), 131.
[4] Howard Gilkinson, "Social Fears as Reported by Students in College Speech Classes," *Speech Monographs,* IX (1942), 144-145.
[5] Milton Dickens and William R. Parker, "Physiological, Introspective, and Rating Scale Techniques for the Measurement of Stage Fright," *Speech Monographs,* XVIII (November, 1951), 259.

that they are in a state of nervous tension before getting up to speak, that it is difficult for them to search their minds calmly for the right word to express their thoughts, that their voices sound strange when they address a group? After the course, do they report that they are in a state of collapse, mental processes completely paralyzed and voices entirely gone? No; classes in public speaking would not have enjoyed a steady and continual increase in enrollment if this had been the situation. A University of Minnesota investigator, studying a group of 56 students, reported that both men and women showed significant increases in confidence.[6] An analysis of a number of experimental investigations concluded: "Almost without exception studies which have tested specific methods for the development of confidence have shown that repeated performances will increase confidence."[7] A small class participating in an experiment at Northern Illinois University reported extreme nervousness during the first speaking performance and practically no stage fright in the final speech.[8]

From the history of American public speaking comes this story of one who as a boy first suffered, then outgrew, the agonies of stage fright. He describes his experiences in his *Autobiography:* "One thing I could not do . . . I could not speak before the school. . . . Many a piece did I commit to memory, and recite and rehearse in my own room over and over again, yet when the day came, . . . and I saw all eyes turned to my seat, I could not raise myself from it. Sometimes the instructors frowned, sometimes they smiled. . . . When the occasion was over, I went home, and wept bitter tears of mortification." That was Daniel Webster, then a student at Phillips Exeter academy. Later, at Dartmouth, Webster became one of the fine speakers of the campus.[9]

2. *What are the symptoms of stage fright?*

From public speaking textbooks and experimental studies, Clevenger and King, aided by a group of other experienced teachers, have compiled a list of phrases describing *visible* symptoms of stagefright. They group them as follows:

Fidgetiness: shuffles feet, sways, swings arms, arms stiff, lacks eye contact, paces back and forth.

[6] Stanley F. Paulson, "Changes in Confidence During a Period of Speech Training," *Speech Monographs*, XVIII (November, 1951), 260-265.
[7] Edward R. Robinson, "What Can the Speech Teacher Do About Students' Stage Fright," *Speech Teacher*, VIII (January, 1959), 10-11.
[8] Louis Lerea, "The Verbal Behavior of Speech Fright," *Speech Monographs*, XXIII (August, 1956), 233.
[9] George Ticknor Curtis, *Life of Daniel Webster*, I (New York, D. Appleton & Co., 1870), 20.

Inhibition: deadpan, knees tremble, hands in pocket, face pale, returns to seat while speaking, hands tremble.

Autonomia (indicating excess of activity of the autonomic nervous system): moistens lips, blushes, breathes heavily, swallows repeatedly.[10]

In addition the speaker may have such *mental* symptoms as dread of speaking, fear of forgetting, or feeling that listeners are not approving.

Three general categories of stage fright have been suggested:

Audience tension: A speaker may be troubled with nervousness, excitement, anxiety, and even increase of pulse rate, constriction in throat or chest, and trembling of hands or legs. After he has begun his speech, however—in fact, almost immediately after he has started —his symptoms lessen and he feels more at ease. Most beginning speakers fall into this category. Experienced speakers, especially when about to make an unusually important speech, may feel some of these symptoms, but *their past experiences reassure them* that the uncomfortable feelings will vanish.

Audience fear: A speaker may have such severe symptoms that the speech making process itself is affected. His flow of ideas may falter, his words may sound muffled, his voice may become weak. He may stumble over sentences or mispronounce words. The ordeal of speaking is prolonged throughout the speech or throughout most of it.

Do not be in too much of a hurry to promote yourself into the *audience fear* category when you have only a relatively mild disturbance. A little stumbling or hesitation is entirely normal; much inner fear and anxiety is *never suspected by listeners, even trained listeners.*[11]

Audience panic: This category represents those with the greatest disturbance; these are the people who are too frightened to attempt to speak, or if they do, they have to stop after a few sentences. This category is rare: most classes of 20 or so would not have a single person who could be described as having audience panic.[12]

10 Thomas Clevenger, Jr. and Thomas R. King, ". . . Visible Symptoms of Stage Fright," *Speech Monographs*, XXVIII (November, 1961), 296-298. See also Greenleaf, 329.

11 A University of Southern California experimenter asked 61 speech teachers and graduate students to check observable degrees of stage fright in beginning public speakers. When he compared the reports of these listeners with reports that the students themselves made about their stage fright, he found that listeners *underestimated* student fears more frequently than they *overestimated* them. In other words, speakers appeared *more at ease* than they themselves realized.—Robinson, 9-10.

12 For further description of these three categories of stage fright, see Loren Reid, *Teaching Speech*, 3d ed. (Columbia, Artcraft Press, 1960), Chapter 5, "The Alleviation of Stage Fright."

B. STAGE FRIGHT: WAYS OF MANAGING

What we have discussed so far is the negative part of the emotional basis of speaking; the problems wrapped up in anxiety, tension, and worry. Your speech teacher will help you manage these problems, although, actually, his interest in you goes further; for even if you and he working together eliminated them, you would still be simply at a neutral position. What you need to do is to get over to the positive side: the side of self-confidence, self-assurance, self-reliance, poise.

The important suggestion is: Get actual speaking experience before an audience. Although the advice below is written for those who suffer stage fright, it will help any one improve his speech making:

1. *Prepare thoroughly*

Your first speeches especially should be on topics where you feel intellectually at home, where you have the advantage of advance study or experience. In this way you can draw upon your storehouse of ideas and information. Later, as you become familiar with the requirements of speaking, you can and should go further afield.

Solid preparation will give you a feeling of assurance as nothing else can. "What I lack as a speaker is more than made up by the subject."

Though you should be serious about your subject, you can avoid some tension by refusing to take yourself too solemnly. Advice like this needs to be dispensed cautiously as one should do his sober best in every situation. And it is a real fault for a student to do less than his best. The simple fact remains, however, that the world will not cave in if you stumble over a word or two. Set a modest standard for yourself at first, not an unattainable one. Do your best. Don't try to do somebody else's best. As you improve, raise your goal. Constant worriers should recall the advice of Frank Lloyd Wright: "You can't pull yourself up by the roots to see if you are growing."

2. *Study the theory of speech making*

Ignore the student who says, "I don't want to read about speech making; I want to get in there and make speeches." That would be like a dentist who said, "I don't want to know the principles of dentistry—I just want to get in there and yank teeth." Although the making of speeches is not an exact science, it *is* an art; to call it an art is another way of saying that it is solidly rooted in theory and principle. In the event you think speaking was invented by Sir Winston Churchill over there and Patrick Henry or Daniel Webster over here, be reminded that twenty-five centuries of speech making have transpired in the Greco-Roman-Anglican tradition alone. Twenty-five centuries have taught speakers how to begin a speech; how to state, partition, and develop ideas; how to adapt to audiences; how to use example, illustration, and other forms of argument and appeal; how to use voice and gesture; how to employ words and phrases; how to conclude. A lawyer ignorant of law is only a little worse off than a speaker who relies upon hunches, guesses, instinct, or inspiration instead of upon a solid grasp of principle. Almost any situation you will ever face has already been faced thousands of times. The theory of speech making has evolved from those thousands of experiences.

Note, however, that although the *principles* of good speaking remain fairly steadfast, speakers of different generations evolve different ways of applying those principles, so that it is entirely correct to say that yesterday's approach may be labelled old-fashioned today. Style, manner, language, change. Moreover, different individuals devise their own variations of the principles and themes. So you will find Samuel Gompers, John L. Lewis, and Walter Reuther, representing different generations of labor leaders, utilizing different speaking styles. And somewhere on a campus is a labor leader of tomorrow, and though he will face the same old problems (how to get higher wages, how to lessen unemployment, how to improve working conditions) he will likely use the style, manner, and language of his own generation, adapted to his own character and personality.

This is why new textbooks in speaking (and in writing) continually appear: the principles change but little, but the applications change greatly. Each textbook includes a little of what Emerson called "the conventional, the local, the perishable," the examples, the incidents, the personalities that must be continually changed in order to make the book meaningful to the current generation of readers.

3. *Don't offer unnecessary explanations*

Act as confidently as you can; don't indulge in negative thinking—not even to yourself, and certainly not in public. If you cough, stutter, stumble, forget, or repeat, don't bother with "excuse me," or "pardon me," or "I don't claim to be an expert on this subject," or "I left my notes at home," or "I haven't prepared this as carefully as I should have."

4. *Organize*

It is as hard to carry ideas in your mind without a plan as it is to carry an armful of groceries without a basket. Even an experienced speaker would get rattled if he tried to proceed without organization. Let us say that, early in the year, you want to tell us that the school team is certain to have a good season. Instead of merely rambling along, prepare a little outline. Talk first about the team's *offense,* offering examples; talk second about the team's *defense,* with other examples. Such a plan has a wonderfully steadying effect.

5. *Use visual aids*

Visual aids are not appropriate for every talk, but can sometimes be used, and help lend assurance to the speaker. Use charts, on which your principal ideas are displayed; or the actual object itself, which you can explain part by part; or a map, to which you can relate the ideas of your talk. Write a difficult word or a key phrase on the blackboard. By giving you work for your hands, these visual helps assist in dissipating your stage fright. Since they give a listener something to look at, they may help you feel less conspicuous. This topic is developed in full in Chapter 11, "Using Visual Aids."

6. *Rehearse*

Judge Harold R. Medina, circuit judge of the United States Court of Appeals, wrote the following on the importance of training, practice, rehearsal:

> I think such capacity as I developed for public speaking is wholly the result of experience.
>
> I got a prize in prep school in a public speaking contest at commencement the year before I graduated but never had any formal training at all . . . but practically from the time I got out of law school I was speaking constantly.
>
> I would practice . . . arguments in appellate courts for hours on end in my office or in my apartment or in my library building down at Westhampton so that I could proceed without notes and with considerable flexibility.[13]

Say your talk aloud several times. Become accustomed to hearing yourself. While rehearsing, time yourself; you may have too much material. If so, chop some of it out, and that will make your task simpler. Don't be shy about discussing your talk with a friend. As you rehearse, don't try to memorize; follow your planned train of thought, but feel free to change the wording.

7. *Develop other personal qualities*

Among them are: enthusiasm, sincerity, fairness, conviction, interest in others. These help you abandon the negative side, lead you through

[13] Letter of December 10, 1959.

the neutral zone, and place you squarely on the positive side. As you develop a little more self-assurance, that in itself will generate a certain amount of momentum.

8. *Deep breathing, and such*

A deep breath, just before speaking, may quiet some of the fluttering. Yawning, or stretching, may relax part of the nervousness. Professional actors and actresses have reported that these and similar procedures are useful because they help counteract the physical strain and tension.

9. *Take a speech course*

This step you have taken, or may take, to enroll in a public speaking course, is *the best way possible* to learn to manage stage fright. In *no other situation* will you be exposed so frequently to the two factors the beginner most needs: (1) actual speaking experience and (2) perceptive and sympathetic suggestions for improvement. Recall the young painter who shut himself in his studio and laboriously worked out his own methods. One day he came forth jubilant, and imparted his discovery to his teacher. "My dear boy," answered the master, "I could have shown you that in five minutes, and saved you two years of time."[14]

Teachers do not seem to need to employ spectacular methods to help beginning speakers with their anxieties. In most instances regular classroom instruction, plus now and then individual conferences, is sufficient. As a student acquires mastery of the helpful principles of selection and organization of material, and as he realizes that he and his classmates are slowly improving, he gradually learns to manage his nervousness.

II. Customs of Speaking

You will feel easier in your mind about your first speeches if you discuss with your instructor the things that are expected of speakers. You may ask him to show you how to stand, or how to manage lecterns, or what to do about notes. The following suggestions will bring to mind other questions to discuss.

[14] This story, a century old, comes from the teachings of the French philosopher and teacher, Francois Delsarte. See Genevieve Stebbins, *Delsarte System of Expression* (New York, Edgar S. Werner, 1902), 77.

See these articles in the January, 1959, *Speech Teacher*: Theodore Clevenger, Jr. and Gregg Phifer, "What Do Beginning College Speech Texts Say About Stage Fright?" (VIII, 1-7); Edward R. Robinson, "What Can the Speech Teacher Do About Students' Stage Fright?" (VIII, 8-14).

A. MAKING A DATE TO SPEAK

When you are invited to make a speech, be sure about the exact day, the exact place, and the precise time limits. Once you have agreed to talk, show up as agreed. If, because of illness, you are unable to speak, have in mind suggestions for substitutes, so that if your program chairman does not have an alternate speaker in mind, you can help him locate one. Adopt the same responsibility toward your classroom schedule.

A speaker often needs to ask the program chairman about the length of the speech. If he says, vaguely, "Speak as long as you like," pin him down to a specific answer. Ask, for example, how long previous speakers on his program have spoken. If the figure turns out to be 20 minutes, or 30, hold yourself to that time. If the program runs behind time, be prepared to shorten your remarks.

Arrive at the place where you are to speak ahead of time. Seek out the program chairman so he will know that his speaker is available. Get the feel of the place so you will know how loud to talk. Visit with the early arrivals; you may pick up information you can work into your talk. You may find yourself becoming more at ease. This advice is also good for the classroom. If you are so rushed that you have to make a hurried, late entrance, you will miss the chance to sense the mood and atmosphere of the class and to think through once again the opening sentences of your talk.

B. BEING INTRODUCED

The presiding officer, the chairman, or the instructor, will introduce you. Sometimes he talks about your qualifications, on occasion employing humor. The chairman's remarks traditionally end either with the name of the speaker or with the topic of his talk—neither being mentioned previously—thus: "Marion Anders will now talk to us on the topic, 'Can We Thaw Out the Cold War?' " or, "I am glad to present the next speaker, who is to discuss 'Can We Thaw Out the Cold War,' Marion Anders."

When your name is called, stand, walk to the lectern or to the center of the room, turn, and acknowledge the chairman with a smile and a slight nod. Don't be in a hurry to start talking—give the group a good, friendly looking over. Don't be afraid someone will think you have forgotten your talk—the listeners will see that you are simply pausing for them to give you full attention. Only a beginner lets himself get so eager that he starts talking before he reaches the center of the room. Experienced speakers are deliberate. You can quickly learn to emulate this trait of the skilled speaker.

You may then say, "Mr. Chairman," or call him by name: if the presiding officer is your teacher, you may say "Dr. Thornton," or "Professor Axton," or "Miss Hesler," using whatever title is customary in your class. Then you should address the listeners. "Ladies and gentlemen" is formal and dignified, appropriate for most adult audiences. "Fellow classmates" or "Friends" may be suitable for the informal atmosphere of the classroom. But say *something* appropriate by way of greeting: this procedure is conventional, it is courteous, and it helps you to command a respectful hearing.

You will need to acknowledge the introduction of your chairman, especially if gracious compliments have been paid you. "Thank you, Mr. Chairman; ladies and gentlemen" may do if the introduction has been brief; but if it has been complimentary or in some way original, you may say "Mr. Chairman, ladies and gentlemen," and then begin with a few comments of your own about the introduction. "I certainly want to thank Dr. Thornton for his gracious remarks," etc., etc. Your own language, however, adapted to the situation, is better than any formula.

An experienced speaker usually says a few words also about a speech that has just preceded his, or an event that has just taken place in the classroom or auditorium; this practice shows adaptability to the situation. "Just before class started I heard Dr. Thornton say . . ." or "I was really startled to hear Miss Jasmine say in her talk that . . ." The "Miss Hesler's story reminded me . . ." type of opening may also be used to good effect.

You may wonder where to *look* during your talk. The oldest advice is the best: Look at your listeners. Look at each one of them, if possible. Look them directly in the eyes. If a listener makes you too self-conscious, you can give him rather less of your concern. Say to yourself, "I want to talk to these people—" and look at them while you talk to them. Good *eye contact* is a primary requisite.

You may wonder how to *stand*. Stand in a comfortable position, your weight about equally distributed. Avoid having your feet either too close together or too far apart. You may have one slightly ahead of the other. Take a good, easy stance. You may walk about, if you do not overdo it. A good place to change your position is *between main points*: the shift of position serves as a visual announcement that you are moving to a new thought in your discourse. Don't make the shift too mechanical, however, or too pronounced. Stand straight, and tall; not in the military posture of attention, but comfortably erect. Don't lean on the furniture, or at least not more than you can help;

as you gain experience in speaking, you should gradually free yourself of these visible props. Males should keep hands out of their
pockets, although it is true that in informal situations a speaker may
slip a hand in a side or coat pocket. The sooner, however, you get
your hands out of your pockets, the better the listeners will like it.
Females should adjust their skirts and sweaters or blouses before
reaching the front of the room. Males should give their ties a final
tug well ahead of time; everybody should make sure attire is correct
before beginning, then forget about it.

The foregoing are the *usual* customs, the *usual* formulas. They are
stated here to acquaint you with what is conventional and traditional.
They are not inflexible rules. As you read them you will likely agree
that they make good sense for most situations; you will probably
also be able to visualize unusual situations where you would want to
act differently.

If you stand erect, look at your listeners, and use a natural, conversational voice, you are on the right track. On these points your instructor's suggestions will help make sure that the general principles
here discussed are executed by you to the best advantage. Ask him
about individual variations and adaptations that may fit your own
style and personality.

C. WHEN CLOSING

Occasionally a speaker will say "Thank you" at the conclusion of
his speech. President Eisenhower often said, "Thank you very much."
President Truman has said, especially when talking to audiences of
young people, "Thank you; you couldn't have been nicer to me."
Probably most speakers quite properly do not thank the audience at
all; they finish their speeches, give their audiences a smile and a slight
nod, and take their seats. This procedure is recommended for most
situations, including most classroom speeches. If, however, you feel
the audience has been unusually courteous and attentive, say so, in a
short sentence of your own phrasing, rather than through a set formula like "Thank you."

III. Concluding Note

If you have stage fright, surveys show, you are in a handsome majority. The experience of thousands of teachers is that stage fright
lessens materially as one gives more and more speeches.

The suggestions given in this chapter about studying the principles
of effective speaking, about organizing and rehearsing and generally

doing the things that help generate confidence, will help you get under way. Read ahead in this text for further guidance.

Moreover, instead of giving too much concern to fears and worries, cultivate positive emotional attitudes of a good speaker: enthusiasm, sincerity, conviction.

Questions for Classroom Discussion

1. Is stage fright found only on stages? Do you see any resemblance between the worry of a speaker before a speech and the nervousness of a musician before a concert, or of an athlete before a game?

2. Can you recall situations of various kinds in which experience increases *confidence* and decreases *fear*?

REFERENCES ON STAGE FRIGHT

If you would like to make a speech about stage fright, or report additional information to the class, read the references to the *Quarterly Journal of Speech, Speech Monographs,* or the *Speech Teacher,* cited in the opening dozen footnotes of this chapter. One or more of these journals will be found in most college and university libraries. If stage fright is one of your own serious problems, you will find that some of these articles will clarify your perspective.

Consult also these textbook references:

A. Craig Baird and Franklin H. Knower, Chapter 8, "Developing Confidence," in *An Introduction to General Speech,* 2nd ed. (New York, McGraw-Hill Book Company, Inc., 1957).

W. Norwood Brigance, Chapter 2, "The Mental Attitude," in *Speech Communication,* 2nd ed. (New York, Appleton-Century-Crofts, 1955).

Milton Dickens, Chapter 3, "Gaining Confidence and Poise," in *Speech: Dynamic Communication* (New York, Harcourt, Brace and Company, 1954).

John E. Dietrich and Keith Brooks, Chapter 3, "Alert Your Mental Attitude," in *Practical Speaking for the Technical Man* (Englewood Cliffs, N. J., Prentice-Hall, Inc., 1958).

Lester Thonssen and Howard Gilkinson, Chapter 4, "Social Adjustment," and Chapter 5, "Personality," in *Basic Training in Speech,* 2nd ed. (Chicago, D. C. Heath, 1953).

Choosing Subject and Purpose

As the problem of choosing a subject is persistent, come back to this chapter frequently. ■ *Consult first your own storehouse: jobs, hobbies and other experiences, travel, opinions, everyday life. Consult also books, newspapers and magazines, the calendar, classmates, periodical indexes.* ■ *To test subjects: Ask the three questions suggested in this chapter. To limit and sharpen your subject: Inquire into your purpose.*

CHOOSING A SUBJECT IS A DIFFICULT ASPECT of speaking. One naturally seeks a subject that grows out of his own background and challenges his own intellect; that stimulates his listeners at the time they hear his speech, and perhaps even commands their respect as they think about it later on. "If I could think of a good subject," students say, "the rest would be easier."

In your situation you can:

1. *Wait for an inspiration.* Not dependable. Creativity often follows vigorous reflecting. Sir Winston Churchill stated it in these words: *"Effort generates creative force."*

2. *Worry, fret.* Not productive. This procedure leads you away from good ideas instead of towards them.

3. *Review your resources.* Good; time-tried and speaker-tested. Get paper and start thinking with a pencil in your hand. Write down ideas. Some will be good, some indifferent, some bad; never mind. A good idea often comes by way of a poor one. To uncover a new idea, start a search or exploration. The pages that follow will help you begin that search.

The suggestions given in this chapter are designed for a wide variety of speakers and speaking situations. The topics range in difficulty from narratives drawn from an individual's experience to topics of international significance that even a well-read speaker might properly hesitate to discuss without additional study. Many students find it wise to begin with a modest, unpretentious subject, one on which they are well-informed, until they feel more comfortable in front of an audience; later they should move into topics that are more significant and challenging.

I. Your Own Storehouse

Subjects for speeches are close at hand. In fact *if they are not close at hand they probably are not anywhere.* As Charles Dickens wrote, "The world is full of subjects. All you have to do is reach out and put a little salt on their tails."

Mark Twain won fame as a writer because of *The Adventures of Huckleberry Finn,* in which he drew upon his boyhood in Missouri, and the first half of *Life on the Mississippi,* in which he narrated his experiences as a riverboat pilot. He is not well known for his *Joan of Arc,* largely because he really knew little about Joan. Though he read and travelled widely, the details of this last-named book are not so striking as are those in the other two.

The pamphlet, *Common Sense,* a rousing call to independence, was written by Thomas Paine, who had had many experiences in England as a tax-collector and corset-maker. His life was so miserable that he came to the colonies to start a new life. Arriving on this side of the Atlantic, he became involved in the struggle for independence. He saw, more clearly than most colonists, the nature of the struggle in which they were engaged. He understood the faults of the British monarchy because he had been a victim of the hardships it created. Out of his personal experiences and reflections he drew ideas for stirring pamphlets.

A. VOCATIONS, EMPLOYMENT

Many college men and women have had their education interrupted by work in business or industry. If you have never labored for a living, skip this paragraph; otherwise: Have you worked in an ice cream plant, launderette, grocery store, restaurant, postoffice, newspaper, dairy farm, chinchilla ranch? Have you delivered papers, sat on babies, washed dishes, flung hash, mowed yards, given golf lessons, worked on playgrounds or at summer camps, tended store, hopped cars, worked on a chain saw gang? This list is only a beginning; make your own. Your listeners will not have had quite your experience.

Moreover, as Justice Oliver Wendell Holmes wisely observed, "every calling is great when greatly pursued."

Some who read this book will be already established in a business or profession. They will naturally turn to aspects of their life careers that are suitable to present to an audience.

B. AVOCATIONS, HOBBIES

Do you like to fish? tie flies? Do you work with wood or metal tools? Do you collect stamps? Are you an expert barbecuer? a wizard at steak fries? a master with shish kabobs? Do you know about stereo? hi fi? low fi? Shakespeare? baseball? Zen? Do you fly a plane? or drive a hot rod? or water ski? Do you judge horses, sheep, cattle, poultry, carrier pigeons? Are you interested in judo or jiu jitsu? Do you sew, knit, crochet, or hook rugs? Are you an expert beauty parlor operator or home permanent giver? or makeup artist? or trading stamp hoarder?

A student who was compelled to spend six months convalescing in a hospital spent much of that time reading the novels of Thomas Wolfe. Ordinarily he discussed technical subjects like "The Future of the B-70" or political subjects like "England's New Pacifist Movement." On one occasion, however, he delighted his listeners with information from what had become an avocation; he revealed his deep interest in and sensitivity to the style of Wolfe, supported by his quoting of brief passages from this favorite novelist.

Sometimes a good topic is so close to a speaker that he overlooks it altogether. Remember, however, that you will not be able to tell all you know in a single speech, so limit your subject according to what appears to be the probable interest of the audience.

C. OTHER EXPERIENCES

Have you had a tour of duty in the armed forces? Have you gone to summer training camps? Is summer school different from year-round school? Is Sunday School and church a part of your background? Have you attended a corporation training school or an officers' training school? Have you known the great or near great? Have you mingled with the mighty, or with plain and ordinary, though uncommonly fine, people? Have you administered first aid to broken legs and sprained ankles at ski resorts? provided refreshments to donors at a blood bank? handled dice at a casino? managed children when the parents were away? helped fight a forest fire? hustled sandbags to control a flood? Have you, a girl, done something that boys usually do? or have you, a man, worked at a job that girls are usually hired for?

Have you visited Florida, California, Lake Louise, Quebec, or the Gaspé peninsula? Have you driven to Key West, hiked into Lower California, flown to the Bahamas, or bicycled to Alaska? Have you had a week in Washington, New York, San Francisco, New Orleans, Philadelphia, Denver, or Salt Lake City? Have you spent time in Hawaii, Okinawa, Manila, Japan? Do you have opinions about the English? the French? the Germans? the Italians? the Spaniards? the Brazilians? the Puerto Ricans? the Arabs? the Moslems? Or maybe you have had a different kind of travel experience, like the student who bought maps of his own township and hiked over every part of it. Maybe you have seen every cathedral in England or Germany, every mission in California. Says British philosopher Alfred North Whitehead: "First-hand knowledge is the ultimate basis of intellectual life."

D. OPINIONS, JUDGMENTS

What goes on in the discussion sessions in your home, residence hall, shop, company, or office? Any opinions about rules and regulations? the world series? jet planes? reenlistment? careers? standards of morals and living? small towns or small college vs. large? Are you concerned about fallout? conduct of teen-agers? upward spiral of inflation? overseas competition to our manufacturers? deterioration in quality of prepared foods? educating the masses? Personal judgments, backed by evidence, have been used as subjects for countless speeches.

E. PLAIN, EVERYDAY LIFE

Maybe you are just you. So far you haven't made anybody's All-American or honor roll. You haven't won any medals or ribbons recently; promotion has been slow. You haven't met unusual characters, held unusual jobs. Trying to do your daily work may be your most challenging venture.

If you have imagination and a sense of detail, however, you may discover here a thoughtful topic. Perhaps you can tell about problems that come to one who lives in a small town or a large city. Or about the pleasures and burdens that accompany working one's way through school. Or what it's like to be shy; or to be an only child, or to be the youngest, the oldest, or the in-between; or to be adopted; or to be one in a family of twelve; or to have poorer schooling than one's associates; or to come from a different region or country; or what it's like to have too few dates, or too many with the wrong persons; or to combine marriage with education, or to compete in business or in a profession under unfair competition. Reflecting upon these *ex-*

periences may lead you into a discussion of the vaster social or economic issues of which they are a part.

F. FOR WOMEN ONLY

Most of the foregoing topics are as suitable for women as for men. An English major explained "What Communism Is"; a nurse denounced the flagrant use of broad-spectrum antibiotics. But to get a better feeling for the kind of subject that women might use either in co-ed classes or in mixed classes, flip the pages of women's magazines. Let your imagination range. "Problems that women have with husbands" suggests "problems that women have with courses," or, "problems that women have with careers." In business and industry, women have repeatedly declared that they are unfairly treated in matters of salary and promotion.

Perhaps you see an article on the growth of nursing as a profession. This article about nurses may suggest other professions that can be interestingly discussed: the aircraft hostess, the policewoman, the receptionist, the executive's secretary, the long list of women who hold important jobs usually reserved for men: federal judge, senator, state legislator, executive, the treasurer of the United States, the chief of the passport section in the Deparment of State.

All this having been read, the woman student may reassure herself that although she may speak purely and simply from the viewpoint of her sex, she may also, like the men, speak for her generation and as a prospective or voting citizen, on any of the massive social, economic, and political problems that confront the world today.

II. Additional Sources of Subjects

When you need to go beyond subjects based on personal experiences, you may consult other sources.

A. BOOKS

Many try to read the outstanding books not only in their own field, but in related fields, and in fields of general interest. "I read all the time, and read omnivorously," says Harry Emerson Fosdick, eminent pastor and counselor.[1] Get the reading habit early, and

---

[1] Roy C. McCall, "Harry Emerson Fosdick: A Study in Sources of Effectiveness," in *American Public Address: Studies in Honor of A. Craig Baird* (Columbia, University of Missouri Press, 1961), p. 63. See also Bishop Richard S. Emrich's comment, this book, p. 233.

you will be in the best tradition of speaking well. You will open up a wider field of subjects for yourself; you will gain in effectiveness because of the significant content of your speech.

B. CURRENT NEWSPAPERS AND MAGAZINES

An article may suggest a subject to you. Reading about the pollution of our streams and waterways may start you on an investigation of purifying industrial wastes. Reading about a strike may start you thinking about improving relations between management and workers.

Seek out magazines covering fields for which you already have background. The forty-one year old *Current History* follows the events of the day with articles on problems growing out of Latin America, the New Frontier, national defense, and the like; at times an issue focusses on a single topic like the government's role in education, or rising nationalism in Africa. The sixteen-year old *Changing Times* presents the viewpoint of the consumer-taxpayer. *Fluoridation* is a hot issue in some communities; *capital gains* arouses interest towards the end of the tax year; *snow tires and chains* may one day be a required accessory like safety glass or direction signals. These magazines are two of hundreds.

The news columns and editorial features of your school or community newspaper, or of the daily or Sunday paper that serves your region, may start you thinking about a subject. In all cases give full credit to your source; be fair to yourself and honest with your audiences by stating what you have borrowed; do not content yourself with a mere summary of what you read, but bring your own thinking and reflecting into the speech.

Please note: if you have an interest in some current problem and *read widely about it,* you may develop more than one speech on the subject.

C. THE CALENDAR

Some calendars give not only the usual holidays, but other anniversaries: on September 29 Balboa discovered the Pacific, on March 3 the inventor of the telephone was born, on April 2 the United States Mint was established, on April 26 Confederate memorial day is observed, on May 8 V-E day is commemorated, on June 14 Flag day is noted, on July 28 World War I began. Your library has a reference book listing important events for each day of the year. Every day of the year commemorates *something.* You may consult Mary E. Hazeltine's *Anniversaries and Holidays* with its 196 pages of information about dates,[2] or George William Douglas's *The American Book of Days*, which contains a select list of events for each date, with a helpful paragraph to assist a speaker in his research about each date.[3] This source of suggestions for speeches does not invariably yield a speech topic, but on occasion may remind you of an anniversary that, because of a strong interest, you will want to research further.

Like scores of other suggestions briefly listed in this chapter, this one needs to be reflected upon with imagination. John P. Ryan of Grinnell College was one of the great professors of public speaking in the years 1903-1951. The anniversary of an eminent man or woman would see his students exposed to a little birthday biography—of Patrick Henry, Florence Nightingale, Robert G. Ingersoll, Robert E. Lee. Centennial anniversaries also offer inspiring subjects—for example, the centennial of a thousand events of Civil War and Reconstruction days. Carl Sandburg opened an address on the occasion of the one hundredth anniversary of the inaugural of Abraham Lincoln, delivered on the East Front of the United States Capitol on March 4, 1961—with these impressive words:

> Here one hundred years ago to the day were 10,000 people who hung on the words of the speaker of the day. Beyond this immediate audience were 30 million people in 34 States who wanted to know what he was saying. Over in the countries of Europe were more millions of people wondering whether the American Union of States would hold together or be shattered into fragments.[4]

And so this speaker continued, gathering strength from the fact that he spoke "one hundred years to the day" after Lincoln's speech, recreating hopes and events that made up the other March 4, in 1851.

D. YOUR CLASSMATES

Study your prospective listeners. Has something happened in the class that will serve as a springboard for an additional speech? Do you want to say more about an idea that provoked a lively debate? If the class had a discussion about income tax reform, or the feasibility of putting a man on the moon, and you, too, have ideas on this subject, develop them further. Perhaps your classmates have shown an interest in art, music, standards of morality, building a vocabulary, or an essay or speech that was assigned. Maybe some one said he did

[2] Chicago, American Library Association, 1944.
[3] New York, The H. W. Wilson Company, 1948.
[4] Text supplied this book by Carl Sandburg, and quoted with his permission.

not appreciate poetry, or did not approve of federal aid to schools, whereas you hold another point of view, and want to explore your beliefs at greater length.

E. PERIODICAL INDEXES

The Readers' Guide to Periodical Literature, The Education Index, and other indexes to magazines and journals, and *The New York Times Index,* and other indexes to newspapers, contain lists of articles classified by authors and subjects. Looking over these subjects may give you a suggestion and may reveal a title that you want to read. *Don't base your speech, however, on a single article.* Read different articles and in addition bring in your own considered reactions and reflections. Other reference sources are described in Chapter 5.

If you wanted to consider the possibilities of a speech about General Douglas MacArthur, and reflected upon the year 1942 as a high point in his career, you might consult the *New York Times Index* for that year; here you would locate headlines of 15 or 20 news stories that you could read for interesting detail. For in 1942, under orders from his commander-in-chief, he left the Philippines, eluded the Japanese ships, and arrived in Australia, to begin the task of planning the military campaign in the Far East ("I shall return"). You would find a wide variety of headlines: "US Cong members urge Cong Medal of Honor award," "Honored by Sons of the Amer Revolution," "New sweet-pea named in wife's honor," "Awarded highest Polish mil decoration," "Awarded Wis Univ honorary degree; sends message to graduation exercises," and many others attesting to the general public esteem. In another vein you could consult a 1966 or later volume for late developments in *elections, motion picture censorship, premiums and trading stamps, airline and railroad mergers, the situation in Red China* or any other country in the news, *UN debates, labor and management problems, legislation curtailing gambling,* and others.

F. SPEECHES AND SPEECH MAKING

Since you and your classmates share a common interest in speaking, you may on occasion consider a topic dealing with a speech of historic significance. For example, you could recreate the circumstances under which Patrick Henry delivered his "liberty or death" speech; Lincoln's first or second inaugural addresses, or the Gettysburg address; Wilson's declaration of war against Germany; the Bryan-Darrow courtroom debate at the Scopes' trial; one of Roosevelt's fireside chats or inaugural addresses. For material, search out the larger, more comprehensive biographies, and where feasible, consult bound volumes or microfilms of newspaper files; ask your instructor for advice. Or you might find it stimulating to read widely about some important aspect of speech making; investigate what speech texts and scholarly journals say about organization, audience adaptation, stage fright, listening, speech making in business. Again, consult your instructor, and read the references listed in this text.

III. Tests of a Subject

Not every new book or cinema is a good subject for *your* speech. After selecting a likely subject, you should predict its probable success, just as, if you were going to build a drive-in, you would want to know how much traffic was in that locality. Test your proposed subject by asking questions like these:

A. IS THIS THE BEST SUBJECT I CAN THINK OF?

That is not an easy question to answer, but you can say "Yes" more wisely if you have considered a number of subjects. As a rule your chosen subject will be better if it comes after a survey of many possibilities.

A kind of straw-clutching effect characterizes the search for a suitable topic. A speaker may become discouraged as he rejects one possibility after another—he reads a long list of suggestions, saying to himself, "These are not for me"; then, hope almost dead, an idea comes that possesses a faint possibility of success, and he clutches grimly at this wisp, this filament, this *straw,* and tries to build it into something substantial. So the advice is worth repeating: keep searching until you uncover a topic of, for you, genuine merit.

B. IS THIS SUBJECT CLOSE TO MY HEART?

Has a part of your thinking and feeling gone into it? If your community had been shocked by the disaster that followed a flood, if you personally saw the suffering that resulted, if you had been moved by the way the Red Cross transported supplies of clothing and drugs, if you were on your feet forty-eight hours helping avert disease, you might do something eloquent with phases of this experience. If your big sister arrived home from college with her diploma, if she were in your thoughts as she arranged one interview after another, if you recall the day she came home after landing a teaching position, if you helped her get her wardrobe together and sometimes late at night brought her coffee as she sat up writing lesson plans, if you caught a little of her wondering and apprehension as she boarded the bus enroute to her new position, if you read her letters that first week, you might arouse enthusiasm for "The First Day of School—Teacher's Kid Sister's View." You might also do well with "A City Manager Plan for Roseburg" or "A New Cure for Mental Illness" if you read so much on the subject, and talked to so many authorities, that, despite your lack of first-hand experience, that subject, too, grew close to your heart.

C. WILL MY LISTENERS BECOME INTERESTED?

Will it strike them because it is timely, vital, curious, of human interest? If you decide that your subject is too technical, perhaps you can say to yourself, "If I use clear language, and simplify my presentation wherever practicable, I can hold the interest of my audience even with this specialized subject." Or you may decide, "People may have the opinion that this subject is not a vital one—so I will begin with an example that shows its importance." Or you may have to say, "It is not interesting, and I can't think of any way to make it come to life, so I will seek another subject."

You may ask other questions to test your topic. The time, the occasion, the season, the opportunities for preparation, the time allotment for the speech, the other subjects to be discussed on the same program, may each be relevant. If your subject seems worthy after this analysis, you may proceed with greater confidence.

IV. Your Purpose

A speaker will be more successful in his search for a topic if he asks, "What do I want to achieve in this speech? Do I want to amuse the listener, inform him, remove a prejudice he may have, or get him to take action?"

The notion that a speech should have a distinct purpose goes back, in one form or another, to Greece and Rome. It is, accordingly, one of the great lessons handed down from the past.

The general purposes of speech making may be classified under these headings:

A. THE SPEECH TO ENTERTAIN

The speaker's purpose is to amuse, to divert, to arouse delight and enjoyment. His speech may or may not be humorous; suspense, novelty, human interest, evoke delight and enjoyment just as wit and humor do. Examples: "Tips for Surviving Military Service," "How to Survive Campus Fallout," "Advice to New Employees."

B. THE SPEECH TO INFORM

The speaker's purpose is to explain, to make clear, to simplify. He has important, significant information to present to his listeners. Examples: "Recent Improvements in Highway Construction," "How the New Labor Law Affects Unions," "The Story Behind the Berlin Wall," "How the Gas Turbine Works," "What Is an Autopsy?"

C. THE SPEECH TO PERSUADE

The speaker's purpose may be either to change belief or to influence action. Examples of speeches intended to change belief: "Should the College Course Be Shortened to 3 Years?" "Should the Sales Tax Be Extended to Include Services As Well As Goods?" These are subjects about which listeners can be expected to have beliefs, but deal with problems somewhat beyond their power to act upon. Examples of speeches intended to influence action: "Vote for the Reform Ticket," "Increase Your Silent Reading Rate," "Build a Community Recreation Center," "Read *Crime and Punishment.*"

D. THE SPEECH TO STIMULATE OR IMPRESS

The speaker's purpose is not to *change* a belief but to *heighten* the listener's appreciation. Examples: "The Priceless Gift of Education," "Our Debt to the Police," "What July 4 Really Means."

E. COMBINATION OF PURPOSES

In the same talk the speaker may have moments of entertainment followed by moments of impressiveness or persuasion. At times the best way to persuade may be to offer a clear explanation. Such a speech would be classified according to its predominant purpose. In a public speaking course the instructor usually invites the student to make one or more speeches of each of the four sorts, in order to give the student experience in handling methods of interesting, methods of informing, methods of persuading, and methods of stimulating.

Often listeners get more out of a speech than the speaker intended. He may intend merely to inform, but later a listener will take action or change belief because of the information. He may intend to persuade, yet nothing seems to happen; months or years later, however, someone recalling the speech may find himself believing or doing what the speaker advocated. Even so, when attempting to classify a speech, the student should search out what appears to be the predominant purpose of the speaker.

Sometimes a speaker seems to have as his purpose something entirely different from the above: to confuse, to obscure, to frighten, to conceal, to draw attention away from. These purposes, usually associated with propaganda, are here mentioned to call attention to a kind of speaking that seems unduly prominent in this century.

F. SPECIFIC VS. GENERAL PURPOSE

If you decide that your basic purpose, for example, is to explain, then your next step is to make your purpose even more specific: *inform about what? How* a teaching machine works? *How* to improve study habits? *How* to tell a communist from a socialist? *How* to survive when lost in the woods? *How* to build a hot rod?

Note that your basic purpose to be *expository* would govern your development of each of the foregoing topics; otherwise you might slide over into a persuasive, entertaining, or even inspirational category. As you become more and more specific about purpose, you gain a better concept of your subject.

If you decide that your basic purpose is *entertaining,* or narrative, in nature, you need to make that purpose still more specific. Exactly what incident do you wish to narrate—what do you wish to be entertaining about? Your trials during registration? The time you were lost in the Kaibab Forest? An incident that happened at boot camp or at the State Fair, during the Easter holidays, on Inauguration Day? An occasion when you were embarrassed, frightened, injured? Again, determining your basic purpose helps you develop your specific theme. You can tell about being lost in a forest simply to be entertaining, or you can use that incident as a reason to persuade young men and women to learn survival techniques. Your embarrassing incident might be a prelude to a thoughtful discussion that as one goes from high school to adult age he becomes less self-conscious and learns to handle himself with poise even in awkward situations.

So the concept of *purpose* helps you mold and shape ideas for speeches. If your basic purpose is to *persuade,* then ask yourself exactly what it is you want to persuade about. Should some regulation be changed or relaxed? Do we need better morale? Should this group sign up for square-dancing lessons? If your purpose is to *stimulate,* then your motive will likely be one of praise, and you need to answer the further question, praise what or whom? An individual? An institution? A tradition? A place? An ideal? The list is limitless.

Perhaps your mind will work something like this, as you move from the broad concept of purpose to a more specific topic:

"I want to inform. As I am a physical education major, I want to inform about health or hygiene. I believe I will talk about posture, since that topic is fresh in my mind and since it is significant. I could talk about the psychological value of good posture. I could give my listeners reasons why people should improve their posture—but that is persuasive, and I want this talk to be expository. I believe I will demonstrate simple exercises that help to improve posture. We learned twenty, but that many would be burdensome—I'll pick just three, and explain and demonstrate them."

Or this: "We're supposed to talk about some one who has influenced us. Could talk about Abraham Lincoln—I've read about him—visited his home in Springfield—and at New Salem—Lincoln's birthday is coming soon. Let's see if I can limit it—can't tell everything I know about Lincoln—might tell about ten or a dozen of his experiences—of course that's too many, though—why not illustrate his sense of humor—or his courage." Now the purpose is getting specific.

Or this: "I want my listeners to vote for my candidate in the election tomorrow. I want to give them two reasons for doing so, and I want to make these two reasons so strong that when my listeners find themselves in the polling places they will cast their votes as I suggest."

With a clear statement of purpose in mind, you will have made your topic more specific; you will better be able to know what materials to use and what to leave out. Those decisions help you plan how to begin the talk, how to develop it, how to close it.

V. A List of Suggested Topics

The following subjects are included in order to illustrate the wide variety of topics that other students have used. Many of them will suggest still other possibilities: "How to Buy a Second-Hand Car" calls up "How to Buy a Man's Suit," "How to Buy a House," "How to Buy Your First Insurance Policy."

A. EXPOSITORY TOPICS

How the FBI Catches Kidnapers.
What the European Common Market Is.
The Art of Survival.
Advantages of a Small College.

How to Get the Most out of Military Service.
Analyzing the Outcome of the Election.
How to Hedge Against Inflation.
Why Color TV Is Here to Stay.
New Kinds of Fertilizers.
Rackets and Pools.
Our Investment in Panama (or Cuba, or Venezuela).
Safety Engineering in the Automotive Industry.
When Disaster Strikes.
Diversification in Stock Buying.
Catastrophe Insurance.
New Methods of Weather Forecasting.
New Ideas on Prison Reform.
Courtesy on the Superhighway.
American Music Overseas.
Winning an Argument Without Too Much Arguing.
Isometric muscle exercises.
Sources of Our Fears.
Good Teachers I Have Known.
How Benzedrine (or some other drug) Acts.
How a Satellite is Launched (or operates).
Some Aspect of Modern Art (or Music) (or Poetry).
How something works (electronic brain, offset printing, transistors, radar, photoelectric cell; investigation of credit insurance applications or automobile accidents).
The Chemical Revolution on the Farm.
New Trends in (Church) (Hospital) (Home) (Office Building) Architecture.
Danger of High Altitude Explosions.
Peace Time Uses of the Atom.
New Discoveries About the Diet.
Fighting Forest Fires.
Proper Gear for Mountain Climbing.
Increasing Traffic on the Lakes.
New Developments in Instrument Flying.
Mach 3 or other advanced aircraft.
Keeping Up With the New Books.
Financing State Government (sales tax, income tax).
What the Egyptians (or Russians) (or Moslems) Want.
Fraudulent Advertising.
New Nations of Africa (or some one of the new nations).
DNA: What We Have Learned About Heredity.
Atlas, Titan, Minuteman, Polaris, or some other missile.

How to Buy a Share of Common Stock in the Stock Market.

The Importance of Ghana in African Politics.

The Greatest Blunder of (Civil War, World War I, Korean War, etc.).

How to Succeed in Business.

Air (or water) Pollution.

A recent discovery or invention (DDD) (transistorized ignition) (lasers).

B. PERSUASIVE TOPICS

Is TV educational?

Should capital punishment be abolished?

Should science education be improved?

Are the humanities sufficiently emphasized?

Should the sales tax be extended to include services?

Should students buy insurance while they are in college?

Should athletics be deemphasized?

Should we amend the state liquor laws?

Should the college course be shortened to 3 or 3½ years?

Should the GI bill of rights be extended?

Should you invest in common stocks?

Should public speaking be required?

Should we have more superhighways?

Should social security be extended?

Should Puerto Rico be admitted as the 51st state?

Should the rating system (industrial, military) be modified?

Should students grade their professors?

Should we change the state divorce laws?

Should universal fingerprinting be required?

Should industry hire the handicapped?

Should the streams be purified?

Should pleasure-boat drivers be licensed?

Should you join the Rod and Gun Club (or Toastmasters' Club) (or Le Cercle Français)?

Will communism expand in Latin America (or Africa)?

Should you read the works of (Thomas Wolfe, or your favorite author), (or become familiar with the architecture of Saarinen, or your favorite architect) (or with the music of Chopin, Copland, or your favorite composer)?

Should all instructors be required to take a course in public speaking?

Should less weight be placed on final examinations?

Should the wage scale for student employees be increased?

Is functionalism commendable in architecture?
Should swimming be a graduation requirement?
Does Congress have the right to investigate individuals?
Should high schools prepare for college entrance examinations?
Is the criticism of modern art justified?
Should we approve of Europeanism?

C. ENTERTAINING TOPICS

How to Drive in Rome.
The Hand is Quicker than the IQ.
Prospecting for Future Wives.
How to Meet and Marry a Millionaire (or a Doctor).
Tips on Surviving Military Service.
Lost on a Used-Car Lot.
A New Code for Pedestrians.
How to Fail in Business.
Short-Cuts to Success in Society.
I Was an Investigator for the IPA.
An Egghead on Diamond Head.
First Day Out of the Army.
How I Got into the Oil Business.
A Strange Experience at Camp.
Learning to Sell the Hard Way.
Working in a Factory in Illinois.
How a New Lake Changed Our Town.
My German Wife in America.
An Experience in a Concentration Camp.
Some Experiences with Mules.
The Championship Finals.
An Adventure in Reno.
Advantages of Being a Minister's Son.
Passing the Finals at ORC.
The Strange Case of the Lost Passport.
Experiences in Selling Bibles.
Five Sisters Are Too Many.
A Trip to Rockefeller Center.
I Am Not Superstitious, But—
The Fable of the Wise Fox.
Prisoner of War for a Day.
Why I Collect Autographs.
The Incident That Sent Me Back to School.
How to Stop Drinking.

New Rules for Rushing.
If I Were President (or the Boss) (or Commandant).
My Favorite Comic and How I Met Him.
Some of the Splendors of Love.
My Tastes, Alas, Are Expensive.
How to Cash a Check in a Strange Place.
Kid Brothers Should Be Leashed.

D. OTHER LISTS OF TOPICS

See this text: pages 68, 245, 347-348.

Questions for Classroom Discussion

1. Compile on the blackboard a list of suitable topics for speeches. Each member of the group should contribute topics from his own experience that he thinks will interest the others.

2. After each topic, write the word *entertain, explain, persuade,* or *stimulate,* to suggest the probable purpose of the speaker in talking about this topic. After most topics you may be able to write more than one term.

3. Take a vote on the list, each person selecting the best five. Tabulate the results. Can you explain the vote by descriptive terms like *importance, novelty, originality, timeliness?* Consider a topic not favored in the balloting. Does it have possibilities not immediately obvious?

Speech-Related Projects

1. Read your favorite daily newspaper for a week and construct a list of subjects for speeches. Include on your list only subjects that might have interest for the members of your class.

2. Explain the difference between a subject explanatory or informative in nature, and one that is persuasive. List five informative subjects (you may use or adapt subjects in the foregoing list) and show how you would revise them to make them persuasive.

3. Select five subjects from the list of persuasive subjects, and rewrite them into *titles* of themes or speeches. (Thus: "Should We Have a Compulsory Chapel" might be entirely acceptable as the title

of a speech. "Should High Schools Prepare Students for College Entrance Examinations" may be too long; rewrite it.)

4. Consult a dozen recent issues of the periodical, *Vital Speeches*. List the ten topics that seem most vital. What people are making these significant speeches, and what positions do they hold? Develop your study by reading a recent volume of *Representative American Speeches,* edited by A. Craig Baird to 1959-1960, by Lester Thonssen thereafter, published by the H. W. Wilson Company. For speeches on literary, social, and historical topics, consult the British Broadcasting Corporation's publication, *The Listener*. Occasionally also speeches on provocative topics appear in *Saturday Review* and *U. S. News and World Report*.

REFERENCES ON CHOOSING A SUBJECT

Donald C. Bryant and Karl R. Wallace, Chapter 5, "Selecting the Subject," in *Fundamentals of Public Speaking,* 3d ed. (New York, Appleton-Century-Crofts, Inc. 1960). Has a good list of suggestions for topics at the end of the chapter.

James H. McBurney and Ernest J. Wrage, Chapter 5, "Subjects for Speaking," in *The Art of Good Speech* (New York, Prentice-Hall, Inc., 1953). Suggestions for finding topics, plus a list, may help you review your capabilities.

Raymond G. Smith, Chapter 4, "Selecting the Speech Purpose, Topic, and Title," in *Principles of Speaking* (New York, The Ronald Press Company, 1958). Note the list of audience responses, and the topic list at the end of the chapter.

Paul L. Soper, Chapter 3, "Selecting the Speech Subject and Aims," in *Basic Public Speaking,* 2nd. ed. (New York, The Oxford University Press, 1956). Thoughts about wording the title, and a substantial, classified list of subjects.

Eugene E. White and Clair R. Henderlider, Chapter 2, "Selecting the Speech Subject," in *Practical Public Speaking* (New York, The Macmillan Company, 1954). Discusses speech purpose, with illustrative situations. See also pages 106-109 for lists of subjects.

CHAPTER 5

Gathering and Recording Material

Although a speech may be based entirely on one's own knowledge, many subjects call for additional materials to be secured through observing, interviewing, books and periodicals. ■ *The latter are located through guides, indexes, card catalogs. Familiarize yourself also with other reference works used by speakers.* ■ *Suggestions for taking notes and for quoting authorities.*

ONCE THE SPEAKER HAS CHOSEN his subject and is clear about his purpose, his next step is to gather material, writing down in usable form ideas he thinks will be of value.

I. Review Your Own Knowledge

Reviewing your own knowledge is the starting point for speeches on most subjects. Personal experience and previous reading and reflection get you started on sure, solid ground.

If you narrate your visit to Pearl Harbor, your trip on the Alaska highway, your first view of the Normandy beaches, the fact that you have seen these famous places with your own eyes helps your speech to carry interest and conviction. If you wish to take a more vital topic, one growing out of the events of the day, you should undoubtedly choose a topic on which you have previous knowledge. For if you start on a Monday to prepare a speech for Friday on a topic about which you have done no previous thinking whatever, you may find yourself relying so heavily on a single borrowed source or two that your listeners will sense that only a scant few hours of hurried reading separates you from them. But if you have been interested for some time in the problem of strengthening the U.N., or in new kinds of automotive propulsion like the rotary engine or the gas turbine, or in the spread of right-wing groups in the country, or the complex issues growing out of trying to write federal legislation for aid to education, you have a background of knowledge to fall back on. No doubt you will be able to use phrases like "I have been following this situation for some time," or "I am now convinced that," or "During the last several weeks I have come to the position" that show your previous thought and your long-sustained interest.

II. Locate Additional Material

Once you have made a sharp focus on your subject, you may need additional information to add clarity and detail to your previous knowledge. You may have in the past read something about the gas turbine, but now you must bolster your recollections with precise data. You may feel that an interesting talk may be made on "Critical Moments in the History of ———," but must first interview some one who has had a long connection with the college or company concerned. Let us review various sources of speech materials.

A. OBSERVATION

Observation is an excellent way of locating material. If you want to speak upon prison reform, do as one student did: visit a prison. Look around and see what goes on. If you are inquiring into the question of whether student drivers are better than town drivers, observe both types in action. Stand on a busy corner, as one young woman did, and report what you see. If, as one man did, you wonder whether the campus is intellectually stimulating, find the answer by observing talk sessions, checking attendance at recitals and lectures, and looking over the shoulders of readers in the periodical room. If you feel that the efficiency of the American laboring man is underrated, visit a shop, factory, or construction job, and note layouts, handling of materials, use of power tools and other modern methods.

B. INTERVIEWING

One student wanted to talk about cancer. As a relative had died after a long illness, the student had this experience in her memory. She visited the cancer hospital nearby and arranged an interview with the chief surgeon. As she told him she was planning a talk on the prevention of cancer, he took an interest in her project. He conducted her through the wards to talk to patients, and showed her before-and-after pictures of operations. He gave her a chart to display to her classmates. After her interview she felt so full of ideas that she could have talked an hour, but she combined in a ten-minute speech the highlights of her visit and her previous experiences. She spoke with the conviction of an expert; in a small way she had made herself one.

Another kind of interview is the opinion poll. Suppose you think your organization should have a magazine. To test the practicality of your idea you ask twenty-five of your colleagues the question, "Should we publish a magazine?" Some replies may be flippant, but others will be provocative; and when you have finished your poll you can be assured that you have felt the pulse of a part of the organization. Or perhaps you believe your school should have more low-rent apartments for married students, or a different student government. A young man who believed that students should not be allowed to have automobiles at school discovered, after conducting a poll, so many difficulties that he needed to revise his original proposals. "What struck me at first as a simple problem," he said, "proved to be highly complex."

The strong appeal of the findings of polls lies in the way interviewees phrase their answers. Newspapers, magazines, and radio and TV stations use the interview technique not only because they want to announce that 54 per cent favored the question and 46 per cent were opposed to it, but also because the answers reveal varieties of opinion. Undoubtedly you will find yourself quoting the responses of a few of your interviewees because of striking wordings of their answers to your question.

Whether you plan to interview classmates or experts, you should decide in advance what kind of information you want. If you enter the office of Professor Bloom, the distinguished sociologist, and tell him that you want information about marriage, he will likely respond in vague language. But if you say, "Professor Bloom, I have written down three questions I would like to ask you," he will likely be more impressed by your procedure. Your questions will get the interview off to a better beginning.

C. BOOKS AND PERIODICALS

Every person who desires to speak should acquaint himself with the vast range of information to be found in books.

Poets, dramatists, and novelists often get factual details from books and develop them imaginatively and creatively. "The Rhyme of the Ancient Mariner" by Coleridge, with its ghost-like ship, its strange crew, its wandering mariner, and its general flavor of the occult and the supernatural, seems to be entirely a work of the imagination; but Harvard scholar John Livingston Lowes brilliantly demonstrated that

Coleridge got many of his details from books, and that the imaginative part consisted largely in the working of these details into an artistic whole. In writing *Cimarron,* a novel about the pioneer West, novelist Edna Ferber consulted books, records, newspaper files, and documents, located in the Oklahoma state historical library collection and other places, and located actual incidents to work into her narrative. "Only the more fantastic and improbable events contained in this book are true," she writes in the preface.

It would therefore appear, if you want to give your speeches a vivid, striking, and even dramatic quality, you should stick to truth; and you can augment your facts by adding to them the wealth of incidents found in printed sources. Novelist Kenneth Roberts got ideas for the exciting yarns found in *Northwest Passage* and other sturdy sellers not from Indian chiefs and frontier scouts, not from Whig patriots and Tory loyalists, all of whom were long since dead; but from the archives of the New York State library, the New York Historical Society, the Portsmouth, N. H., public library, and books like *Travels Through the Interior Parts of America* by Anburly. The greatest writer that ever lived, whose tragedies, comedies and historical plays are studied in every high school and college in the English-speaking world, drew plots from old books and chronicles.

So it is literally true that there is nothing new under the sun; the old ideas, someone has said, are in the new books, and the new ideas are in the old books. Speakers read widely, picking up a thought here, relevant evidence there, illustrations and examples somewhere else; their genius consists in building these ideas and their own, into a significant plan, clothing them in words or phrases that are striking, and dedicating them to a moral or a purpose that has a special meaning. Rules and conventions, of course, govern what can be borrowed, and what credits and acknowledgments must be made. Remember that what the speaker borrows should be woven in and around his own experiences. Edna Ferber could not only read books, but she could travel the breadth and length of present-day Oklahoma; Kenneth Roberts could browse in libraries, but he could also familiarize himself first-hand with the New York and New England scenes of his books; Shakespeare could read Plutarch's *Lives* and Holinshed's *Chronicles* but he also knew at first hand a thousand facets of Elizabethan England. Thus we read *books* but we try to keep from being *bookish.*

A speaker, therefore, needs to form a partnership with librarians and to spend hours in libraries. Hercules once fought a battle with a giant, Antaeus, whose strength increased tenfold every time the giant touched the ground; Hercules could win the final victory only when he lifted Antaeus off the ground and crushed him in midair. To give the figure a novel application, a speaker becomes stronger if he keeps in touch with libraries; keep him away from books and periodicals, and his strength wanes.

Despite the best efforts of librarians, a library is not always an easy place in which to work. Even when a student compiles a list of books he may find that some of them are out on loan, and still others in a remote part of the building. This fact could be true even of the colossal Library of Congress in Washington, so it is likely true of the modest collection of your own school. Collections are rearranged; just when one learns that the *Dictionary of National Biography* sits next to the *Encyclopedia Britannica,* it is transported to a safe refuge behind the reference librarian's counter. At times the aims of the librarian seem to run counter to those of the scholar; the scholar likes to cart the books away and keep his borrowings out of circulation for a year or two; the librarian sometimes appears to like them tidily arranged on the shelves, the 808.91's nestling the 808.92's. But it is amazing how patient and helpful librarians invariably are to those who show enough interest to ask questions.

D. THE CARD CATALOG

Your first stop is usually at the card catalog, the alphabetical guide to the books and periodicals of the library. Each item is represented by one or more cards; author, subject, and title. For example, *Abraham Lincoln: The Prairie Years and the War Years* by Carl Sandburg is listed under an author card (Sandburg, Carl), a title card (*Abraham Lincoln: The Prairie Years and the War Years*), and subject cards ("Abraham Lincoln: President of the United States"). All these listings are in one alphabetical file. If you know the exact title and author of a book, you can turn to the author card or the title card. If you are unsure of either an author's name or the title, look under a subject heading that might reasonably be expected to contain it. If you come to the library with no particular book in mind and you want something about *Mozart,* look for that entry under the M's.

Once you locate the item you want, you may be required to fill out a call slip if you want to take the book out of the library, but as procedure differs from library to library this chapter will not attempt any generalizations. Eventually you will get either the book or some interesting information as to why it is not available.

One or two tricks of the trade in using the card catalog need to be called to your attention. Suppose you find a dozen different cards about *air conditioning*—which ones should you try first? From the *title* you can make a shrewd guess as to whether the treatment will be simple or technical. From the *number of pages* you can judge the comprehensiveness of the treatment. From the *copyright date* you tell the age of the book. A notation like "Third Edition" followed by a recent date suggests that the book is in demand.

Although this section has candidly pointed out difficulties of finding exactly the book you need at the instant you need it, the author also wants to say that many a student has gone to the library with only a vague notion of what he wanted to talk about, and after a session of study has discovered rewarding materials. Few things in this world are more exciting than intellectual adventure, and if you make a beginning along his line while you are still in school, you may, to quote the brilliant psychologist, William James, wake up some morning to find yourself one of the world's anointed.

E. READERS' GUIDE TO PERIODICAL LITERATURE

The preceding chapter mentioned the *Readers' Guide to Periodical Literature* as a publication to locate when in search of a subject. It is also useful to consult when you are in search of additional ideas. This publication is about as old as your grandmother; it was started in 1900, about midway between the end of the Spanish-American War and the first airplane flight at Kitty Hawk by the Wright Brothers. It is discovered anew every year by (author's rough estimate) 4,200,000 high school and college students.

The *Readers' Guide* is an index to magazine articles. If you wanted to read what the magazines had to say about new developments in synthetic penicillin, consult Volume 22 for 1959-61 or a later volume. If you wanted to get the latest reports on missiles, you would look up that subject in the most recent issues. Many subjects get into magazines that never reach books; for example, each year sees articles forecasting the season's athletic championships, and if you want to read these, you can locate them through the *Readers' Guide*. Or perhaps you are thinking about the subject of exercise and recall seeing a good article on a new method of calisthenics. You can not recall the name of the magazine, or the exact date—you think it was the *Saturday Evening Post,* and it was sometime during 1960 or 1961. Your procedure is to look under the heading "exercise" for the years in question, hoping that when you see the title of the article you will recognize it (turns out it was "Get Strong Without Moving: Isometric Contraction," in *Sports Illustrated,* October 30, 1961, pages 18-21).

Your library will also likely have the following indexes: *Education Index, Industrial Arts Index, Agricultural Index, Public Affairs In-*

formation Service, Art Index, Song Index. Still other indexes are available to serve special fields. *The New York Times Index* is a guide to news stories and features appearing in that publication; as the *Times* is one of the distinguished newspapers of the country, its *Index* is a good research tool.

F. FACTBOOKS

The World Almanac, The Statesman's Yearbook, The Statistical Abstract of the United States, and similar compilations are valuable to bolster a discussion with a statistic or other evidence: elections, populations, geographical data about cities and countries, memorable dates, world's records of various sorts, track and field marks, and scores of others. Annual compilations like *The World Almanac* are priced so reasonably that a student who does more than average amount of speaking should have a copy on his own desk. On the reference shelves of your library you will find other titles which are cumulations of facts of one sort or another.

G. DICTIONARIES, ENCYCLOPEDIAS

Well-known abridged dictionaries are: *The Concise Oxford Dictionary, Funk and Wagnall's Standard Dictionary, Webster's New Collegiate Dictionary, Winston's Simplified Dictionary, The American College Dictionary.* A publishing event of 1961 was the appearance of the unabridged *Webster's Third New International Dictionary.*

Still another valuable reference work is the encyclopedia. Often it is badly used, as when the investigator gets huge chunks of material from the encyclopedia and incorporates them into his speech without proper assimilation. *The Encyclopedia Britannica, The New International Encyclopedia, The Encyclopedia Americana,* and the one-volume *Columbia Encyclopedia* are well known. The supplementary yearbooks of the first three named are of great help to speakers. If you want to learn important events of a given year in football, TV, art, music, politics, or a thousand other subjects, you would find them capably summarized in the yearbooks.

H. OTHER REFERENCE BOOKS

Your library probably has a copy of Constance M. Winchell's *Guide to Reference Books,* seventh edition, published in Chicago in 1951 by the American Library Association. This useful work describes some 5500 entries. It is based on the former editions of this work edited by Isadore Mudge. Supplements issued in 1954, 1956, and 1960 supply additional titles. Your library may contain, besides the card catalog of its own books, volumes listing the holdings of certain of the great libraries of the world. One of these, for example, is the *Library of Congress Catalog of Printed Cards,* with various supplements dealing with authors and subjects. *The British Museum Catalog of Printed Books* and its supplements list the principal holdings of that great London library.

Sometimes a speaker wishes to know what books have been written on a particular subject, or whether any books at all have been written on it. A useful and comparatively new work is *Subject Guide to Books in Print,* which indexes books in English that are still in print; the volume is compiled from the various publishers' catalogs.

You may also profit by reading books explaining how libraries may be used efficiently. Typical volumes of this sort are by Robert L. Callison, *Library Assistance to Readers,* 2nd ed. (New York, J. de Graff, 1956); Lucyle Hook and M. V. Gaver, *The Research Paper,* 2nd ed. (New York, Prentice-Hall, Inc. 1952); Harold G. Russell, *The Use of Books and Libraries,* 8th ed. (Minneapolis, University of Minnesota, 1955); Robert W. Murphey, *How and Where to Look It Up: A Guide to Standard Sources of Information* (New York, Mc-Graw-Hill Book Co., Inc., 1958). Your own library may issue pamphlets or booklets describing its facilities.

Additional volumes are coming out steadily. A walk around your library reference room will help you locate recent publications. Colleges and universities do not require so much memory work as they did decades ago, but they do like students to know where facts can be found. All of us owe a debt to the considerable army of scholars and compilers, who, largely for the love of knowledge, have patiently and accurately assembled so many different kinds of facts.

III. Note Taking

You may recall that as you went through high school you seemed to need to do more and more note taking in class. Perhaps you experimented with various styles of loose-leaf and spiral-bound notebooks before you evolved a system you liked. You may also remember that some classmates took down each assignment systematically and also had readable notes when review time rolled around. Others copied assignments and other notes on backs of envelopes or sheets of note paper borrowed from their fellows—and at times these assorted scraps disappeared when they were needed.

Haphazard note taking is not good enough for serious speech making. Once you begin intensive reading for a speech, you need to take notes systematically. You could jot them on assorted scraps of paper, just as you can go fishing with a carpet pole, a string, and a bent pin; but good ideas are slippery as fish and the biggest ones may get away.

The system described on the following few pages is one that has had the endorsement of researchers in many different fields. It has been taught for decades on campuses all over the country. Law firms, newspaper offices, engineering laboratories, business analysts, and others who need to keep files of data use this plan or a modification of it. The general principles of the system follow.

A. KEEP NOTES ON CARDS OF UNIFORM SIZE

Speech materials are examples, statistics, striking quotations, statements of reasons, points of view, processes. Secure a supply of ordinary 4x6 file cards, and record your data on these. You may also buy boxes or cabinets, with alphabetical or plain dividers, for filing your cards. If your notes are likely to be brief, use the 3x5 size. If your data are complicated and extensive, you may need 8½x11 sheets of paper and manila filing envelopes. If you use a typewriter, you may want stiff paper instead of cards. Basically, however, this system is one you can follow all of your researching days.

B. PUT SOURCE AT TOP OF CARD

This notation need be only complete enough to identify the source. Suppose you are working with a book by Ernest Watson Burgess and Paul Wallin, *Engagement and Marriage*, published by Lippincott in 1953. All of this information, along with one or two other items, will be recorded on a *bibliography card* to be described later. For the time being, "Burgess and Wallin, *Engagement and Marriage*," followed by the page number, will identify the source. Further abbreviation of the title could be used, if you are planning to work over your materials immediately; if, however, your note cards are to go into any kind of permanent or semi-permanent file, too much abbreviating will serve simply to confuse you after your notes get cold. (And why shouldn't you plan to keep your note cards? If your subject is a significant one, you might use it for various occasions after you leave the class. You might continue to read about it, and to gather material upon it, and thus have a fund of basic data for many speeches or articles. Take the long view toward work done in this and other college courses.)

Your card may contain, besides the source, only a brief statistic; or it may be full on both sides; or you may have a note long enough that requires you to clip two or three cards together. Avoid, however, the temptation to put *two* ideas on the same card—you may need them for different parts of the speech.

C. WORK WITH AN OUTLINE IN MIND

Leave space at the top of each card so that later you may pencil in an appropriate heading. After you have done a part of your research you may modify your outline somewhat, and thus you will be more certain what the major divisions and subdivisions of your speech are to be. When your research is completed you can sort your cards and insert the headings you have devised, thus simplifying your organizing.

As you read, keep in mind purpose and central idea; look principally for facts or arguments, but also for illustrations that will be useful in the introduction or conclusion.

D. TYPICAL NOTE CARDS

Here are sample cards illustrating the foregoing principles:

SIZE

G. W. James, *The Grand Canyon of Arizona,* p. 23.

The canyon system of the Colorado River is vast in its extent. . . . For it consists of such a maze of canyons— the main canyons through which the river itself runs; the canyons through which the tributaries run; the numberless canyons tributary to the tributary canyons; the canyons within canyons. . . . If these canyons were placed end for end in a straight line they would reach over twenty thousand miles!

Note that although the words of the author are kept intact, the quotation is shortened by the use of dots (. . .). The phrasing itself is intriguing, and the picture is impressive. The figure of 20,000 miles, while not pretending to be accurate, sounds like a good guess. You can make it more striking by adapting the idea: "Imagine a big ditch, in some places eighteen miles wide and in others a mile deep, running across the country from New York to San Francisco—you would agree that would be a very imposing ditch. But imagine that it turned back upon itself, forming another gorge parallel all the way back from San Francisco to New York, turning and again making a complete round trip, so that you would have a geological structure four canyons wide!"

SALARIES IN HOME ECONOMICS

Changing Times, XVI (January, 1962), 34.

As a demonstrator on TV for a network or a large advertiser, your salary could go into five figures, depending on your arrangement with the sponsor. Other typical salaries . . . for those in extension work—$6,000 to $7,500; dieticians—$4,500 up to $12,000 and more.

This note card seemed important to the researcher because it contained specific figures. It is also reprinted because it illustrates a citation from a periodical.

NUMBER OF SETS

Britannica Book of the Year, 1961, p. 586.

About 331,000,000 radio sets were in operation throughout the world in 1960. There were also 76,000,000 TV sets, of which 52,500,000 were in the U.S.

This note is a condensation of a somewhat longer entry in the *Britannica Book of the Year* for 1961. Here the essential item is the statistical information, put in a few words. In using these facts, however, the speaker may place all sorts of interpretations upon them; an obvious one is that the United States had approximately 69 per cent of the world's television sets in 1960.

Consider the following paragraph:

Metropolitan Life Insurance statisticians say . . . nearly 17 per cent of all girls at ages 15 to 19 are married now or have been married, as compared with only 12 per cent in 1940. . . . Almost half the men at ages 20 to 24 are or have been married, as compared with only 28 per cent in 1940.

—*Science Digest*, XXXIV (October, 1953), 33-34.

These statistics seem too complicated to put into the average talk; they need simplifying. If you do a part of the necessary rewording and rephrasing before you copy them into your notes, you may save time later on. Your note could read as follows:

EARLIER MARRIAGE

Science Digest, XXXIV (October, 1953), 33-34,

Girls are marrying earlier now than they did in 1940. Metropolitan Life Insurance statisticians studied a group of girls aged 15 to 19 and found that, fifteen years ago, only 12 per cent of them got married; now the figure is 17 per cent. . . . Today almost half the men aged 20 to 24 have undertaken marriage, as compared with only 28 per cent in 1940.

The researcher's paraphrase is not so detailed as the original, but it is easier to follow; and if he wishes, he can simplify it still further; here a chart or graph would help.

This note contains an interesting bill of particulars:

QUALIFICATIONS FOR DATES

Whitbread and Cadden, "Dating and Marriage," *Mademoiselle*, XXXVIII (August, 1954), 330.

At the University of Michigan last year Prof. Robert Blood of the sociology department . . . asked girls and men to rate the qualifications they considered important in a date. . . . Being prominent in activities, belonging to a fraternity, having access to a car, having plenty of money, were at the bottom of the list. Instead, Michigan girls sought a date who was considerate, pleasant and cheerful, neat in appearance, humorous, a good sport,

Whitbread and Cadden, card 2.

willing to join in a group, and intelligent. The Michigan man's prescription for a good date, in order of importance, was that she be pleasant and cheerful, neat in appearance, considerate, dependable, attractive, and appropriately dressed.

This set of cards illustrates the poll technique; it also suggests a topic of perennial interest if the speaker gathers timely material.

The researcher may also search books of quotations. A note like the following has a variety of applications:

QUOTATION

Always do right. This will gratify some people and astonish the rest.

MARK TWAIN

Or maybe you like these better: "He is either dead or teaching school," by Zenobius, quoted as a proverb by Erasmus; "Despise not a rustic orator," a Greek proverb; or "Every one is eloquent in behalf of his own cause," from Ovid.

IV. Citing Sources

Although the foregoing pages have stressed the form of note taking, their real purpose is to suggest that speaking is more convincing when statements and assertions are backed up by *evidence*.

A speaker may say, "A lot of GI's stationed in England marry English girls," or "The number of deaths each month caused by automobile accidents is staggering." Listeners and readers are more convinced, however, if the communicator makes his statements more specific: "Each month 300 GI's marry English girls," or "More than 3,500 people were killed last month in automobile accidents."[1]

Ask yourself, furthermore, "What is the source of this fact—and how can I indicate that source in my speech?" In almost the same breath in which we urge you to read and study, we must warn you of careless or deliberate practice that makes you guilty of plagiarism.

Plagiarism is a form of dishonesty in which the speaker (or writer) offers the ideas of someone else as his own. Suppose you hear a lecture on "The Mission of the Air Force." You are stimulated by the discussion, and you prepare a speech on that topic, using some of the same reasons or examples, *without giving credit to your source.* Suppose you read an editorial proposing a solution to the traffic snarl. You make a speech proposing a similar solution, again *without giving credit to your source.* In both these examples you are dishonestly borrowing the ideas of another person, presenting them as if you had analyzed the problem and had devised the solution. Give credit where credit is due.

Sometimes plagiarism occurs because the speaker hesitates to confess that he has borrowed from *one single source.* The solution is to do a more conscientious job of researching. You may very well be sufficiently intrigued by a lecture or an editorial and want to speak on that subject. Do not, however, be content simply to summarize or paraphrase it; do further investigating so that you can bring in another source ("I was so fired-up by this editorial in the *Tribune* that I went down to talk to the chief of police about it"), and do not fail to let us see that you are also *thinking about* and *reacting* to the topic.

These procedures will not only assure your intellectual honesty but should also result in a better speech. Audiences like to feel that the speaker is *thoroughly prepared,* and if listeners can see the sources of the speaker's evidence, they will have an increased interest in the conclusions he reaches.

As the personal integrity of the speaker is one of his most persuasive assets, he should establish and maintain a reputation for intellectual honesty. He can hardly appropriate the idea of someone else without running the risk that his cheating will be detected. Audiences hear

[1] The importance of accuracy is discussed further in Chapter 16, "Improving In Use of Words."

lectures and read editorials, and so do professors of public speaking. If the audience is large, or if the speech is reported in the newspapers, the plagiarism may be noted by many. The solution, again, is to let your speech represent your own interest, your own experience, your own point of view; support your ideas with materials from other sources, but *identify those sources.* One wants to give credit where credit is properly due in order to avoid any suggestion of pilfering; moreover, one may effectively add *to his own personal authority* the *weight of his source,* by announcing and identifying it.

Speakers employ various phrases in acknowledging sources of their information. John Bright, a famed English speaker of the last century who used a modern style of speaking, wove in his citations as naturally as breathing. The listener must have felt as if he were in Bright's living room, hearing Bright talk about something he had just read. For example:

> I was reading the other day a very interesting pamphlet by Mr. R. Elliott, who has been a planter in India, and is well acquainted with many parts of the county. . . . Mr. Elliott said that . . . nearly 3,000,000 persons had been proved to have died from famine. . . . Now, the question is, How long is this to go on? . . .

> I quote from an interesting article in the *Fortnightly Review* by Colonel Chesney, who will be admitted to be a great authority. . . . He goes on to say that the Indian Government is like a father who spends a great deal on the doctor, if his child is ill and ready to die, but in ordinary times does not take care of him whatever. . . .

In like manner, you might say in a talk of yours:

> While I was planning this talk I picked up a copy of *Current History* for January, 1962, and read an article by Arthur P. Whitaker on "Yankeephobia: The United States and Latin America." Professor Whitaker, who is professor of Latin American history in the University of Pennsylvania, and who has studied in Peru and Colombia, makes the point that we should not take unilateral military action against Cuba. He goes on to say, and here I will read his own words, "Armed intervention by the United States in Cuba would wreck the Organization of American States, poison our relations with the rest of Latin America for decades to come, and destroy the credibility of our chosen role in world affairs as a champion of law, order, and the sanctity of treaties."

> I brought the magazine to class in the event that any of you wishes to read the article.

This informal approach is preferable to the mechanical, stereotyped rendering that follows:

Allow me to support my contention by quoting an article by Arthur P. Whitaker, which is in the January, 1962, issue of *Current History*. I quote: "Armed intervention by the United States in Cuba would wreck the Organization of American States . . . etc., etc." Unquote.

Probably much of the casual documenting we hear from speakers, like calling lawyer Silas Jones simply "a well-known attorney," fails to stir us at all. A speaker will be more effective if he can document his authority more accurately, at the same time avoiding mechanical means of doing so. Especially when the audience is well informed about the speaker's topic, or when the speaker is preceded or followed by others talking about the same topic, as in a panel or debate, does it become necessary to use accurate citations.

V. Preparing a Bibliography

When you locate a reference source from which you plan to take notes, prepare a bibliography card for that source. Bibliography cards are usually 3x5 in size. Having certain information on the bibliography card means that you will not need to repeat all of that information on each note card.

Enough information about the source should be given so that any listener can be directed to the material you have used. If the source is a book, give the author, title, number of edition, place and date of publication, and publisher.

Cousins, Norman, *Dr. Schweitzer of Lambaréné* (New York, Harper and Brothers, 1960).

If the source is a magazine article, the form differs:

London, P. H. "The Coming Revolution in Automobiles," *Popular Digest*, LXV (December, 1960), 25-28.

Newspaper stories frequently are published without the name of the author.

"Fall-out Will Double Strontium 90 Level on Ground," *New York Times*, November 1, 1961, p. 17, col. 1.

If you are required to hand in a bibliography, all you need to do is to arrange your cards in alphabetical order and copy them. A sample bibliography follows:

Bibliography for

WEDDING BELLS ON THE CAMPUS

Bowman, Henry A., *Marriage for Moderns,"* 3d ed. (New York, McGraw-Hill Book Company, Inc., 1954).

"Brides and Grooms Are Now Closer to Same Age," *Science News Letter*, LXVI (July 17, 1954).

Burgess, Ernest Watson and Paul Wallin, *Engagement and Marriage* (Philadelphia, J. B. Lippincott Co., 1953).

"Dr. H. V. Dicks Links Unhappy Marriage to Partners' Family Background," *New York Times*, August 19, 1954, p. 21.

Duvall, Evelyn Ruth, *Saving Your Marriage* (New York, Public Affairs Committee, 1954).

Kane, John Joseph, *Marriage and the Family: A Catholic Approach* (New York, The Dryden Press, 1952).

Mead, Margaret, "Student Marriage: Good or Bad?" *Reader's Digest*, LXXVII (September, 1960).

Pope, E., "Why Do They Marry?" *Good Housekeeping*, CXLVIII (May, 1959).

Popenoe, Paul, *Marriage Is What You Make It* (New York, The Macmillan Company, 1950).

"She's Working His Way Through College," *McCall's*, LXXX (March, 1953).

Shultz, G.D., "How Young Is Too Young To Marry?" *Ladies Home Journal*, LXXI (January, 1954).

Questions for Classroom Discussion

1. What special difficulties does a speaker create for himself when he undertakes to talk about a subject wherein he has no first-hand knowledge or experience?

2. Assume, however, that a speaker wants to go beyond his own knowledge and experience and bring in the results of his reading and other research. How can he do this without becoming dull or bookish?

Speech-Related Projects

1. Visit the reference room of your library and become acquainted with important works that every researcher should know. Inspect indexes to periodicals, dictionaries, encyclopedias, books of quotations, wordbooks, and special references. Look at: *Readers' Guide to Periodical Literature, Education Index, Industrial Arts Index, Poole's Index, Funk and Wagnall's New Standard Dictionary, Webster's New International Dictionary, New English Dictionary, Encyclopedia Britannica, Encyclopedia Americana, World Almanac, Who's Who in America, Statistical Abstract.* Broaden your acquaintance with each work.

2. Select a volume of the *Readers' Guide to Periodical Literature* (volume 22 for the period March, 1959, to February, 1961, or a more recent bound volume). Locate ten different subjects in this volume, and record a specific article about each subject, giving the author, publication, date, volume, and page. Look for subjects for which you have some previous experience or about which you have a strong curiosity. Following are suggested subjects: as you turn the pages, however, your eye may light upon subjects of even greater interest:

1. Americans in foreign countries	17. juvenile delinquency
2. Australia	18. Mars
3. ballet	19. marriage
4. buffet meals	20. Negroes in the United States
5. cameras	21. noise
6. cold (disease)	22. parakeets
7. cookery	23. political parties
8. dentistry	24. prize fighting
9. ecumenical	25. refugees
10. Egypt	26. roads; superhighways
11. employees	27. sailing
12. festivals	28. secret service: Russia
13. flower arrangements	29. strikes
14. frying	30. television: color
15. girls	31. war: psychological aspects
16. Honolulu	32. wire tapping

3. Encyclopedia yearbooks are often of significant help to the speaker or writer. In a late volume find answers to these questions (these are based on the *Americana* yearbook for 1961): a. What are

the principal products of the Federation of Nigeria? b. What are the chief drugs in illicit traffic (see *Narcotics*). c. What are the principal musical comedies of Oscar Hammerstein? d. What has been the progress of desegregation (see *Education*). e. How many students were enrolled in your college (or the state university of your state) (see *Colleges and Universities*).

4. Familiarize yourself with a standard dictionary by looking up the answers to the following:

Define bibliography, camouflage, knave, laissez-faire, orthography.
What and where is the Colosseum?
What does "A.B." stand for?
Who was Samuel Langhorne Clemens and when did he die?
What is a lute? Study the picture and compare with a violin.
What are compounds formed with *hollow*? (i.e. *hollow*-chested).
Name five members of the Hall of Fame.
When will Halley's great comet be seen again on this planet?

5. What reference works index each of the following publications: *Scribner's Magazine, Journal of the American Concrete Institute, Canadian Historical Review*.

Speaking Assignment 3

A Speech About a Speech

In a collection of speeches such as the annual *Representative American Speeches* (found in the reference room of most libraries), the periodical *Vital Speeches* (found in the periodical room of most libraries), or other collection, select a speech that seems both interesting and significant.

Make a short speech of .... minutes (your instructor will suggest the time length) on a principle of effective speaking illustrated by the speech you selected. You may discuss, for example, your speaker's wide fund of knowledge, his methods of gathering material, the way in which he blends personal experience or reflection with materials from books or other sources.

You may need to look at several speeches before you find one that will satisfy you as being helpful to you and to the class.

Do not try to cover too much ground; limit yourself to one or two features of your speech, with examples from the speech. What is wanted is not so much a summary of the speech as your reaction to it ("this speech is effective because"). Rehearse your talk aloud several times: partly to help adjust the length to fit the assigned time limit, partly to accustom yourself to hearing yourself speak, partly to improve your fluency. Feel free to change the wording from one rehearsal to the next; do not try to memorize a set and fixed wording.

REFERENCES ON GATHERING AND RECORDING MATERIAL

Donald C. Bryant and Karl R. Wallace, Chapter 4, "Sources of Materials," in *Oral Communication,* 3rd ed. (New York, Appleton-Century-Crofts, Inc., 1962). Note also the discussion of "Originality" on pages 60-63.

Wilbur E. Gilman, Bower Aly, and Loren Reid, Chapter 3, "Discovering Material," in *The Fundamentals of Speaking* (New York, The Macmillan Company, 1951). Systematic treatment of gathering and recording.

CHAPTER 6

Adapting to the Audience

Since the speaker wishes a desired response from his listeners, he needs information about them while he is still preparing his speech. ■ *He should know about one or more of the following: age, sex, marital status, occupations, nationalities, races, religious faiths, affiliations.* ■ *He also needs information about the occasion: time, place, nature of the program. He should study relationships between him and his listeners, the probable attitude of listeners toward his subject.*

AS YOU READ THE PRECEDING CHAPTERS you probably noted that the principles explained considered not only speaker and subject, but also the listener. Ways of analyzing the audience and adapting to it will be further discussed in this chapter. A speaker needs to develop a sensitivity to listeners that will guide him as he makes various decisions about selecting and arranging speech materials. This sensitivity is of great importance. Some evidence exists to show that it is a requirement not only of good speakers, but of all who win places of leadership: that like a good speaker, a good leader shares and understands the attitudes and standards of the group.[1]

I. What Audience Adaptation Is

When a speaker plans to *adapt to the audience,* he does not propose to sacrifice principles or beliefs. Speakers do *not* proclaim, "I hope everybody in this wonderful audience will be completely and totally delighted with everything I have to say." What the speaker does

[1] See Elihu Katz and Paul F. Lazarsfeld, *Personal Influence: The Part Played by People in the Flow of Mass Communications* (Glencoe, Ill., The Free Press, 1955), 101-102.

attempt is to be *clear,* so that listeners can understand him; to sustain *interest,* so that listeners will give their attention; and to reflect qualities of personality like competence, fairness, sincerity, and judgment, so that listeners will find him believable and convincing.

Sometimes an audience is composed of such widely-differing people that the problem of adaptation becomes intensely difficult. If you returned to the school from which you were graduated, and were invited to address an assembly of junior high students, senior high students, and faculty, you would see that a serious problem would be to choose a topic that could be made interesting to this wide age-group. You would also probably incorporate into your speech various illustrations and examples, since this kind of material has wide interest and appeal. Most audiences do not present this range of ages, but even a classroom audience has individuals with a challenging variety of backgrounds in education, vocation, religion, activities, and the like. All of these factors you attempt to weigh and appraise as you choose a subject, gather materials, and in other ways plan your speech.

II. Studying the Audience

You will need to answer questions like this:

1. What range of ages is represented?
2. Are both sexes represented?
3. What is the marital status of listeners?
4. What trades, businesses, or professions are represented?
5. What nationalities are represented?
6. What races are represented?
7. What religious faiths are represented?
8. What organizations are represented?
9. To what political parties do the listeners belong?
10. What is the educational background of listeners?
11. Is the group essentially liberal or conservative?
12. What interests, needs, hopes, attitudes are represented?
13. What is the economic level of the group?

Not all of these questions provide meaningful information for *every speech.* Religious beliefs may have no bearing on the subject you propose to talk about; for certain subjects, however, a knowledge of the religious faiths represented in your audience would be of the *utmost* importance. A knowledge of the age, sex, marital status, and educational background of your listeners, however, would be useful in many instances.

If you know the audience well, you can make a good guess about its interests and backgrounds. Or you may add to your information with a short questionnaire: "In connection with my speech on January 20, I should like to have each member of this group answer the following questions."

If you do not know the audience, ask questions of the person who invites you to speak to it. "Is this a men's organization? Will women be present? Are most of the members single or married?" or whatever information seems pertinent. Another good way to ponder the probable reception of the group to your speech is to inquire: "What other speakers have talked to your organization? What subjects have been discussed? Do you have a program theme for the year?"

You may, furthermore, find it possible to visit in advance the audience you are to address. If you are a speaker at a two-day convention of law enforcement officers, and your talk is scheduled for the second day, you may profitably attend earlier sessions in order to judge the responsiveness of listeners. If you are to talk to the Lions, the P.E.O.'s, the City Council, or the Junior High, you may perhaps visit an earlier meeting to see what the audience is like.

Sometimes a principal factor about your audience is that it is all grocers, or all insurance brokers, or all nurses, whereas you know little or nothing about these vocations. By reading trade publications, house organs, and professional journals, you can saturate yourself with the problems of your future listeners. You will find these specialized periodicals in a college library, although a still better source may be a city public library. A student invited to talk to a convention of specialty salesmen, on the topic of applying principles of public speaking to selling, prepared in part by reading dozens of issues of periodicals dealing with salesmanship.

Find out how large the audience is to be. You will prepare quite differently for an audience of 500 than you will for an audience of 15. If you are to hand out materials, demonstrate objects, or show slides or pictures, you need to know how many will be present.

Some speakers like to arrive a few minutes early at the room in which they are to appear, in order to get a better feeling for the temperament and mood of the audience. A speaker may think of two possible ways of opening a speech, and leave until the last minute the decision of which one to use, hoping that after seeing the audience and observing its response to other speakers he can make a wiser decision. Even after he begins his speech he continues his study of the audience; the responses of listeners to his ideas as shown by facial expression, attitude, laughter or applause, or intent silence, serve as feedback to help him judge how to proceed. If they are friendly and cordial, he will proceed with more confidence; if they are indifferent, he may decide to use more earnestness; if they are unfavorable, he may be more disarming. This feedback may lead him to bring in different examples, or to omit parts of his planned outline and thus shorten his speech. Your study of the audience therefore starts as soon as you begin your preparation and continues until you have finished your speech; even after the speech is over, you may indulge in self-questioning to determine how wise your decisions were.

III. Studying the Occasion

Chapter 3 has already suggested that you should inform yourself about the occasion at which you are to speak.

Seek answers to questions like the following:

When is the speech to be given? Is there anything special about this particular date?

Where is the speech to be given? How small or how large is the room? Are the acoustics favorable? Is a microphone provided? Are conditions suitable for the use of visual aids? Is there a speaker's table? a lectern? a reading light?

Are there special features about the occasion? Is it Founders' Day? ladies night? is it a dinner occasion? will well-known guests be present? is special dress required?

How is your speech to fit into the occasion? Are you the principal speaker? are you one of several speakers? Do you follow a 7-course dinner? or a long program of musical or other events? How much time is allotted you for your speech? Does the meeting have to adjourn at a fixed hour? You will be able to judge from this information something about the mood of the listeners, and whether you may have to cut out part of your speech at the last minute to compensate for another part of the program that ran too long.

An important way in which a speaker must adapt himself to the occasion (and to the audience as well) is to respect the *time limit* set for the speech. An occasion may be such that by custom or arrangement the speeches are expected to be of a certain length. If sermon-time is customarily 20 minutes, a half-hour sermon may seem long and forty minutes uncommonly so. If a business men's club has traditionally scheduled 30-minute addresses, members may become restless if the speech grows longer (and would perhaps be surprised and disappointed if the speech were only 10).

The length of speeches on such occasions is fixed in part because of a previously-scheduled time for adjournment; a church service must end on time in order to make way for the next, a businessmen's club adjourns at 1:15 because members must go back to work. Other occasions, however, are open ended; that is, they have no set time of adjournment. Suppose the local chamber of commerce is having an evening banquet followed by speeches. Although a century ago such a function might have run into the early morning hours, this generation prefers to stop at 10 p.m. or so—earlier if listeners have to drive long distances home that same evening. Your program chairman should give each speaker a time allotment for his speech; even so, each speaker should, that evening, reassure himself that events planned for the occasion are moving on schedule. For if the dinner service is delayed and the master of ceremonies long-winded, the speaker may sense that although earlier in the evening the audience might have listened happily to each moment of his 30-minute speech, realistically he must now conclude that he will be more effective with a compact 20-minute version of it.

IV. The Audience and You

A good question to ask yourself is: *What do I know that will be useful to this audience?* Are there topics of interest to listeners about which I may be better informed than they are? People like baseball, but you have been an umpire. People are interested in safe driving, but you have administered drivers' tests. People know about the Salvation Army or the Red Cross, but you have worked with them. People enjoy popular music, but you are a life-long fan.

A related question is: Do I have a reputation that will lead audiences to expect me to talk on certain topics? You would probably rather hear a great sports writer talk about his experiences in that field than discuss a topic like "The Future of the Panama Canal" that he understood only at second hand. You would be pleased to hear a prominent and successful automobile executive talk about "Success in Life," but you would anticipate with special pleasure his including first-hand experiences with the manufacture of automobiles. Your own reputation may be a more modest one, yet you may be able to capitalize upon it. Or maybe your reputation needs some bolstering. You come from a rival firm; you have received bad publicity recently; your former speeches have been soundly criticized for their faulty information; in the past you have been humorous, but today you want to be serious; you are a defeated candidate, or an erring prophet. In these situations get yourself on firm ground, not by apologizing, but by showing your tact and friendliness, or by poking fun at yourself, or by candidly confessing your faults (not to be confused with apologizing for them). Perhaps the *title* of your speech can help with the problem of adaptation.

Still another important question to ask is, How can I make this subject useful to this audience? To remind your listeners that your information will have practical value later on, when they are married, when they have children, when they are established in their careers, is of course helpful. Still better is to remind them that your information has value in the immediate future, or *right now*. Audiences tend to remember better the facts that they will personally put to use.

Soldiers about to participate in an operation known as Desert Rock, involving atomic warfare, were carefully indoctrinated before the maneuvers began. They were instructed about the purpose of the maneuvers, the military nature of the atomic weapons, and ways of treating personal injuries. Naturally they improved in their attitude and increased their fund of knowledge, but their learning was selective: the information about personal injuries was remembered better than the other groups of facts presented.[2] This last category of facts was more *immediate*.

In another experiment of interest to students of public speaking, two sets of arguments were composed about teachers' salaries. One set of arguments *favored* increasing salaries and the other set *opposed*. Two imaginary audiences were invented: "The National Council of Teachers" was described as favoring increases, and the other, "The American Taxpayers Economy League," was described as seeking to reduce the heavy burdens on the taxpayer.

A group of journalism students was selected and told that each member of the group was to plan a talk of from three to five minutes to "The National Council of Teachers" on the subject of increasing salaries. So far as the students knew, the audience actually existed as it was described. In preparation for this talk, the group was read, twice, a series of 25 statements in favor of increasing salaries. When tested immediately after hearing the statements, they scored, on the average, 17.7 statements out of the 25. A week later they were called back and retested, and they still recalled 13.7 statements. In other words, since they had been given information that they would put to immediate use, they tended to hold it in mind.

Another group of journalism students was also told that each member was to give a talk to "The National Council of Teachers." They heard read, twice, a series of 25 statements *opposed* to increasing

---

[2] Shepard Schwartz and Bertron Winograd, "Preparation of Soldiers for Atomic Maneuvers," *Journal of Social Issues*, X, 3 (1954), 52.

salaries. When tested immediately afterwards they remembered, on the average, 17.6 statements of the 25; but a week later, on the second test, they could recall only 6.1 statements. In other words, they must have felt that the arguments they heard, being opposed to salary increases, would not be of especial help in their talks to a group of members of "The National Council of Teachers" who would naturally favor salary increases. Accordingly, they tended to forget about twice as much as the other group.[3]

The "Desert Rock" experiment and the "National Council of Teachers" experiment remind the speaker that when possible he should tell his listeners in what ways his information is useful, important, and significant to them at this moment.

V. The Audience and Your Subject

You need also to anticipate the possible attitude of your audience toward your subject.

Will it be friendly? If your topic is not controversial, your audience will give you a hearing provided you select materials with care and judgment. Perhaps you can use humor, suspense, novelty in a way that will make attention-gaining and attention-holding relatively simple. If your topic is persuasive, and provides listeners with a quick, easy decision, you should get a favorable response.

Will it be indifferent or neutral? Although your topic is important, is it one that your listeners have perhaps neglected? Is it more significant than at the outset they will realize? Have they heard so many speeches on the same topic that they may ignore another? If your answer to these questions is yes, you will see that you need to use material that will seek to get the listener off his dead-center position.

Will it be hostile, antagonistic, prejudiced? Is your position unpopular? Will you be in the minority? Will you run into deep-seated prejudices? If your answer is *yes,* you will need to use a disarming approach in order to get a fair hearing. Good evidence, calmly presented, would be especially helpful here.

Actually, the hostile audience may be more rare than one supposes. One is more inclined to attend meetings that favor his own interests and attitudes than he is to attend meetings that are opposed to his views. This principle has been surveyed in connection with such widely-varying topics as political campaign issues, bond purchas-

---

[3] Claire Zimmerman and Raymond A. Bauer, "The Effect of an Audience on What Is Remembered," *Public Opinion Quarterly,* XX (Spring, 1956), 238-248. Other groups were coached in preparation for talks to "The American Taxpayers Economy League." The complete article should be read for other details.

ing, donating blood, the relationship between smoking and cancer, the U.N. Behavioral scientists argue that persuasion is more likely to reinforce or modify a listener's position than it is to convert him to the other side; they therefore speak of *selective exposure,* or the tendency to choose communications that one favors, and *selective retention,* or the tendency to remember ideas in harmony with one's own. For example, a well-advertised documentary film stressing such highly-important civic activities as donating blood and buying bonds was attended mainly by individuals *already prominent* in community affairs. Another investigator reported that articles dealing with the possible relationship between smoking and cancer was read by 60 per cent of male non-smokers, 32 per cent of male smokers. Still another reported that twice as many Republicans as Democrats viewed a Republican-sponsored TV program. The speaker to a public speaking class, a Rotary or Kiwanis club, a junior chamber of commerce, a congregation, will, however, pretty much have to deal with his audience as he finds it.[4]

Tannenbaum stresses the importance of understanding the *initial attitude* of those who are to receive a communication. The more strongly a reader or listener holds a belief or conviction, the less likely he is to change it. When no change in attitude follows communication, it may be that the reader or listener had "intense attitudes to begin with." Even being neutral, he emphasizes, does not necessarily imply passiveness—it is possible to be "intensely neutral."[5]

During World War II, psychologists and sociologists had unparalleled opportunity to study the impact of various kinds of information upon large numbers of troops. A film, "The Battle of Britain," was shown to companies of infantry, who, five days after the showing, were quizzed on what they remembered. Other troops that saw the film were questioned nine weeks later. Still others, used as control groups, were not shown the film but were given the quiz.

As can be expected, those who took the quiz at the nine-week interval remembered much less—about 50 per cent less—than those who took it five days after viewing the film. Again, as can be expected, some items were remembered better than others. A minor fact such as "after the fall of France the British could equip only one modern division" tended to be rapidly forgotten. A vivid statement like "Never

4 See Joseph T. Klapper, *The Effects of Mass Communication* (Glencoe, Illinois, The Free Press, 1960), 19-22. The studies reported deal with various forms of mass communication, but the conclusions are worthy of consideration in connection with speech making.

5 Percy H. Tannenbaum, "Initial Attitude Towards Source and Concept as Factors in Attitude Change Through Communication," *Public Opinion Quarterly,* XX (Summer, 1956), 420, 425.

in the field of human conflict was so much owed by so many to so few" seemed to be remembered as well by the nine-week group as by the five-day group. Surprisingly, some items seemed to be remembered better by the nine-week group than by the five-day group. These furnished evidence of a *delayed influence,* referred to as a *sleeper effect.* Often these items involved not *details* but *judgments,* such as "the British are doing their fair share of the fighting," or "If England had been conquered the U.S. would have been attacked next." As these judgments did not persist so firmly among troops in the control group that had not seen the film, the investigators felt that a part of the content of the film was making a steadily-increasing impression even after the nine weeks lapse.

The sleeper effect has also been observed in experiments in which written information was presented by (a) a source believed trustworthy and (b) a source believed to be untrustworthy. The trustworthy source proved more effective in changing opinion immediately, but this change of opinion began to decrease with the passing of time. The untrustworthy source was not so effective in bringing about an immediate change of opinion, but with the passing of time some individuals found themselves more in agreement with the source. A reason was that although the individual at first resisted getting information from an untrustworthy source, the *content* of the communication later proved influential.

Returning to "The Battle of Britain" film, the reader may be interested to know that sometimes information *boomerangs*—i.e., has an effect other than the one intended. One of the quiz questions revealed that after seeing the film the number of individuals decreased who felt that "the Russians will probably help us fight the Japanese." This was a boomerang because those who planned the film wanted to portray the English war effort but did *not* wish to detract from the effort of the other allies.[6]

Although these experiments were based on motion pictures and reading material, not speeches, the theoretical implications are worth noting. For what kinds of speech material is a delayed impact or sleeper effect possible? Though lesser facts may fade away, the major judgment that they support may become increasingly a part of the lis-

---

[6] For the "Battle of Britain" study, read Carl I. Hovland, Arthur A. Lumsdaine, and Fred D. Sheffield, Chap. 2, "The Orientation Film" and Chap. 7, "Short-Time and Long-Time Effects of an Orientation Film" in *Experiments in Mass Communication,* III (Princeton, Princeton University Press, 1949), 182-200. See also Hovland and Walter Weiss, "The Influence of Source Credibility on Communication Effectiveness," *Public Opinion Quarterly,* XV (1952), 635-650; Herbert C. Kelman and Hovland, " 'Reinstatement' of the Communicator in Delayed Measurement of Opinion Change," *Journal of Abnormal and Social Psychology,* XLVIII (July, 1953), 327-335.

tener's beliefs. The importance of solid content, well organized and carefully tied in to the major point it supports, is thus reaffirmed. So although a listener, like a film viewer, may forget the lesser fact that "after the fall of France the British could equip only one modern division," he may nevertheless gradually strengthen his conviction that "the British are doing their share of the fighting." Nor can a speaker interested in long-range influence rely exclusively on his charm or reputation; he must come with evidence and judgment that will persist after the effect of the charm has worn off. Vivid, striking language, like "owed by so many to so few" also has the power to lodge these flashes of wisdom and judgment in the listener's memory.

To speculate a bit, using the terminology of this magical space age, one may envisage a speech as containing material that may be described as *booster* and also material that may be called *capsule*. The booster represents the facts, the evidence, the details—put in well-organized form that gives the presentation order and structure. The capsule is the gist of the message—the point of view, recommendation, interpretation, conclusion. The booster serves its purpose, then falls harmlessly behind; the capsule goes into orbit of indefinite length. In contemplating the behavior of listeners, think of the possibility that they may make not only immediate responses to your communication, but also that part of what you say may linger in their memories for long periods of time.

The speaker may also take notice that spoken arguments, like film presentations, can boomerang. Many teachers trying to lecture students to persuade them to put forth a greater effort have probably, instead, discouraged them. And no doubt a few coaches could be located who, trying to make the pointed remarks that would instill confidence in their teams, overplayed their psychology and instead stimulated a disastrous overconfidence.

To speculate further, assume that a speaker is urging his listeners to install seat belts. His statistics and testimony lead sensibly to the conclusion, *You should install seat belts.* Some listeners will accept this judgment readily; others react in neutral fashion, but as time goes on, even though they forget the statistics, they may still remember that a good case can be made for seat belts, and thus eventually adopt this judgment as their own. But another individual with a strong initial prejudice may use these same facts to convince himself more determinedly than ever that seat belts are not the answer. With him the speech has boomeranged. That people react differently, regardless of the form of the communication, has been observed by many. Understanding these basic principles, the speaker should strive for the most favorable immediate reception possible, hoping also that his evidence is good enough so that with the passing of time some of the more sluggish reasoners may come to his point of view, and leaving those he can neither inform nor persuade to some later speaker.

The speaker must ever be aware of the interests, the information, and the attitudes of each specific audience that he is to address. In many passages in his *Rhetoric*, Aristotle reflects the awareness of the Greeks in the possible response of listeners to a speaker's message. "For of the three elements in speech making—speaker, subject, and person addressed—it is the last one, the hearer, that determines the speech's end and object." And again: "Argument based on knowledge implies instruction, and there are people whom one cannot instruct." He further observed that the speaker is not always successful in persuading; he can only come "as near such success as the circumstances of each particular case allow."[7]

The problem of audience adaptation is vital to the welfare and the prosperity of the speech. In following chapters you will learn to adapt more specifically to listeners. Your selection of ways of beginning and ending a speech for example is guided in large part by your understanding of your audience. Your choice of words, of illustrations, of reasons, of visual devices, again is governed by your analysis of the interests and capacities of your listeners.

Questions for Classroom Discussion

1. Discuss the concept of audience adaptation. To what extent can a speaker maintain his views in the face of strong opposition?

2. After a speaker analyzes his audience, how can he use the information? Give examples showing:

a. How it might lead him to change his subject.

b. How it would affect his choice of examples.

c. How it would determine the amount of preliminary or background information to include in his speech.

d. How it would affect his use of technical terms.

e. How it would determine whether the approach should be conciliatory, or forceful.

f. How it would affect his decision to use more transitions or fewer transitions; whether to make use of repetition, restatement, and summary.

[7] *Rhetoric*, trans. by W. Rhys Roberts. Quoted through the courtesy of Oxford University Press.

g. How it would guide him in the use of visual aids.

h. How it would affect his choice of a method of presentation. impromptu, extempore, manuscript, memorized.

3. Suggest topics from your own experience where knowledge about the *age* of the audience would be especially relevant. Consider also: sex, marital status, vocation, nationality, race, religious faith, educational background, membership in a specific organization.

4. From your knowledge of some other member of the class, suggest a topic that a local audience would like and expect to hear him discuss.

5. Report an experience you have had in studying a particular group to which you were to speak.

Speech-Related Project

1. Prepare a questionnaire to distribute to members of this class designed to yield specific information to help you prepare a speech on a specific topic. (Suggestion: One planning a speech on the subject, "Compulsory Chapel," could formulate questions designed to describe the church preferences or religious interests of each person who filled out the form.)

REFERENCES ON AUDIENCE ANALYSIS

David C. Berlo, Chapter 6, "Social Systems," in *The Process of Communication* (New York: Holt, Rinehart, and Winston, Inc., 1960). See the sections on communication and social systems, communication breakdowns.

W. Norwood Brigance, Chapter 6, "The People To Whom You Talk," in *Speech: Its Techniques and Disciplines in a Free Society,* 2nd. ed. (New York, Appleton-Century-Crofts, Inc., 1960).

Lionel Crocker, Chapter 21, "Analysis of the Audience," in *Public Speaking for College Students,* 3rd ed. (New York, American Book Company, 1956).

Milton Dickens, Chapter 11, "Audience Analysis," in *Speech: Dynamic Communication* (New York, Harcourt, Brace and Company, Inc., 1954).

Giles W. Gray and Waldo Braden, Chapter 5, "Audience and Occasion," in *Public Speaking: Principles and Practice* (New York, Harper and Brothers, 1951).

Carl I. Hovland, Arthur A. Lumsdaine, Fred D. Sheffield, *Experiments on Mass Communication,* III (Princeton, Princeton University Press, 1949). Discusses the "Battle of Britain" and other experiments with World War II troops as subjects.

Elihu Katz and Paul F. Lazarsfeld, *Personal Influence: The Part Played in the Flow of Mass Communications* (Glencoe, Ill., The Free Press, 1955). Much of the material presented is helpful in understanding the behavior of listeners.

Joseph T. Klapper, *The Effects of Mass Communication* (Glencoe, Ill., The Free Press, 1960). Analysis of research in the effectiveness and limitations of mass media in influencing the opinions, values, and behavior of their audiences. From an investigation of more than 1000 studies, the author selects more than 270 for discussion.

Ralph A. Micken, Chapter 4, "Analysis and Management of the Audience," in *Speaking for Results* (Boston, Houghton Mifflin Company, 1958).

Alan H. Monroe, Chapter 9, "Analyzing the Occasion and the Audience," in *Principles and Types of Speech*, 4th ed. (Chicago, Scott, Foresman and Company, 1955).

Lee Norvelle, Raymond G. Smith, and Orvin Larson, Chapter 4, "Audience Analysis," in *Speaking Effectively* (New York, The Dryden Press, Inc., 1957).

Raymond G. Smith, Chapter 3, "Planning for the Audience and Occasion," in *Principles of Public Speaking* (New York, The Ronald Press Company, 1958).

Eugene E. White, Chapter 9, "The Audience and the Occasion," in *Practical Speech Fundamentals* (New York, The Macmillan Company, 1960).

CHAPTER 7

Being a Better Listener

Since more of our day is spent in listening than in any other activity involving words, we should study attitudes and skills that make up good listening. ■ Understanding traits of good and poor listeners helps one to listen better (and to speak better). ■ Develop your ability to listen wisely by learning to appraise (1) generalizations, (2) predictions, (3) polls and surveys, (4) expert opinion, (5) majority opinion, (6) propagandistic devices.

EPICTETUS ONCE WROTE, "There is an art of hearing as well as of speaking. . . . To make a statue needs skill; to view a statue aright needs skill also. . . . One who proposes to hear philosophers speak needs a considerable training in hearing. Is that not so? Then tell me, on what subject are you able to hear me?"

Throughout this book references have repeatedly been made to the *listener*. Speakers ponder over topics covering the range of their own experience but the final choice of subject and selection of materials is directed towards the *listener*. Ideas are organized partly to add to the speaker's comfort and assurance but primarily to aid the comprehension of the *listener*. The examples we select and the words with which we clothe ideas are aimed at the *listener*. All in all, public speaking requires us to be thoughtful about the ultimate consumer of speeches—*the listener*.

How much of our day is spent in listening? From 40 to 50 per cent, say the experts; each one can adjust this figure to his own situation. Do we listen well? Most people do not, say the experts; in a few weeks' time 75 per cent or more of a given lecture has slipped away. Does the ability to listen vary? Yes, widely, say the experts; some retain much more than others. Some students have a listening efficiency of only 10 per cent; others range as high as 70 per cent.

I. Differences Between Good and Poor Listeners

A large group of freshmen on the University of Minnesota campus listened to lectures given on a variety of subjects. After each lecture, the students took an objective test over the material.[1] The 100 best listeners and the 100 poorest listeners were selected and were given various tests, followed by a personal interview. Investigators then formulated a number of differences between good and poor listeners; a few of these differences follow:

1. *Poor listeners usually decided, after hearing a few sentences, that the material would be dull.* Good listeners were more patient and more willing to assume that the material would have a future, if not a present, usefulness; they therefore listened more attentively.

2. *Poor listeners often found immediate fault* with the speaker's personality or delivery. A poor listener easily forgets that speakers come in all sizes, shapes, lengths, breadths, and talents. They have a variety of voices and postures, and they gesture in different ways. Some are more fluent than others—some have mannerisms that distract. The poor listener was inclined to assume that if the personality or delivery of the speaker was displeasing, the ideas would not be worth while. The good listener refrained from making snap judgments until he had listened to the *ideas.*

3. *The poor listener listened best when the speaker's message was carefully outlined.* Often he was lost if the speech were not clearly organized. The good listener had several systems of taking notes; if the lecture did not follow a methodical plan, he caught its gist with another system of outlining.

4. *The poor listener listened mainly for facts.* His long exposure to objective tests had probably made him sensitive to dates, names, formulas, and other specific items. The good listener not only caught the facts, but was also more likely to seize upon *interpretations, generalizations, implications, applications, trends.*

---

[1] See Ralph G. Nichols and Leonard A. Stevens, "Listening to People," in *Harvard Business Review,* XXXV (September-October, 1957), 85-92. And see also, by the same authors, Chapter 9, "Six Bad Habits," and Chapter 10, "Pencil and Paper Listening," in *Are You Listening?* (New York, McGraw-Hill Book Company, Inc., 1957). Used by permission. The material in this section is based largely on the research of these authors.

5. *The poor listener had had less experience in difficult listening than had the good listener.* The poor listener preferred television and radio programs that were easy to follow, like westerns, instead of more difficult programs like interviews with thoughtful persons. The good listener could draw upon a wider background of listening experience, and therefore, when the speaker's exposition became more complex or his reasoning more profound, the good listener gave even closer attention to the discussion and tried to follow it.

II. Implications for Listening and Speaking

As you read this selected list of differences between good and poor listeners, you may catalog your own skills and preferences. How well did you listen in your high school days? How earnestly do you try to comprehend the information presented in your college classrooms? When you find yourself in later years in a position of responsibility, will you be able to listen with understanding and comprehension to superiors, colleagues, and subordinates? Experience shows that the ability to listen can be cultivated; you may want to exert yourself to listen better.

1. *The interestingness of material.* Even though material seems dull, try to wrest from the speech everything you can. *Interest grows with knowledge.* The more you learn about something, the more you become interested in it.

Implication for speakers: Since the poor listeners in your audience are likely to make a quick judgment about the interestingness of your speech, *give especial care to the opening sentences.* Advice is given in Chapter 12 to open with a striking statement, an example or illustration, a quotation.

2. *The personality and delivery of the speaker.* Let your own experiences as a speaker teach you to be tolerant of the shortcomings of others. Although a share of the speaker's effectiveness depends upon his personality and delivery, a larger share depends upon the quality and worth of his ideas. Lincoln was called a *baboon;* but those who called him that were deaf to some of the greatest eloquence ever uttered in America.

Implication for speakers: Since listeners can not be changed overnight, give thought to your appearance. You can be neat and well-groomed. You can have a pleasant smile for your listeners. You can be sincere. Good posture or mental and physical alertness will help win over critical listeners who mistakenly think that delivery and appearance are everything. An audience can be made to forget physical handicaps. Roosevelt was a hopeless cripple from the waist down, had to be escorted to the platform, and had to steady himself by holding to the lectern; but his voice and bearing radiated such assurance that listeners scarcely realized he had been a victim of paralytic polio.

3. *The speaker's organization.* If the speech is organized, fine; take it down point by point as the speaker develops it. If it is not, listen to it for its other virtues.

Implication for speakers: If you organize your speech, you should hold the attention of a greater percentage of your listeners, *good or poor.*

Evidence is accumulating that individuals generally listen better if they are told what the speaker's message is to be about. Thus the listener's anticipating a message, and his comparing what he hears with what he expected, may cause him to listen more carefully to see whether or not his anticipations are fulfilled. A specifically-stated central idea ("I want to discuss two advantages that the Latin-American common market will have for that region") should help the listener get ready to listen, to interpret and infer.[2] A speech that follows a readily-perceived plan of organization—time order, space order, or the more imaginative designs described in Chapter 21—should stimulate the listener's anticipation of what is to follow. I. A. Richards has suggested the term *feedforward* to describe a procedure in which the communicator reveals part of the structure in such a way that the whole plan is likely to be anticipated; he thus "paves the way for what is to follow."[3]

4. *The speaker's facts.* Listen not only for the details, but for the inferences and generalizations.

Implication for speakers: Use examples, illustrations, and statistics, but *drive the story home. Clinch the idea. Make the point.* Use a question: "Now what does this mean?" or "In what direction do these facts point?" Use an assertion: "If you forget everything else, remember this," or "Here is the key to the problem."

5. *The listener's experience or inexperience in listening.* You may

<hr>

[2] See Charles T. Brown, "Studies in Listening Comprehension," *Speech Monographs,* XXVI (November, 1959), 288-294. "Listener anticipation of the purpose of a message is an important factor in his comprehension. . . . Students at all levels of listening ability were equally aided by the statements of purpose" (p. 291).
[3] See Paul W. Keller, "Major Findings in Listening in the Past Ten Years," *Journal of Communication,* X (March, 1960), 29-38, and Isabella H. Toussaint, "A Classified Summary of Listening—1950-59," *Journal of Communication,* X (September, 1960), 125-134.

need to school yourself to listen with greater concentration. Don't abandon your listening when the going becomes rough.

Implication for speaking: Erect no unnecessary barriers between you and your listener. Though some listeners may have soft, tender minds, they are still potential consumers of your idea. But note that one who finds it difficult to follow a discussion of modern poetry may have a tough, competent thinking apparatus for social science or mathematics. Clarifying technical terms, using summaries and transitions, interpolating a little humor for mental relief, employing examples to stimulate the imagination, providing visual aids—all of these should help the listener. In the presence of good speaking the listener finds it easier to listen than not listen. He pays attention more and lets his mind wander less. David Lloyd George, Britain's World War I prime minister and himself one of the eminent speakers that twentieth century England has produced, liked to tell the story of the shipbuilder who said that when he listened to an ordinary sermon he could design a new ship from keel to topmast but complained that when he listened to the great preacher, Whitefield, he could not think of a single plank.

III. Critical Listening

A special kind of listening that we need to give speeches helps you develop your ability not only to appraise the speaker's delivery but also the quality of his ideas.

1. *Delivery.* As you listen to a speech, consider what the speaker adds to or subtracts from the speech by his delivery. Does his voice, for example, suggest interest, enthusiasm, conviction? Does his facial expression reflect his seriousness, his sincerity, his strength, his gentleness—in short, does it help to make the words he is uttering more communicative? Does his gesture help to emphasize his ideas?

You would not be wise to imitate some one else exactly, but you may very well ask yourself this question: Would my delivery be better if I could show a little more of my enthusiasm, sincerity, conviction, and earnestness? Good student speakers can stimulate one another; a good model encourages good examples; one reward of your discriminating listening may be to encourage you to work on delivery more during your next rehearsal period.

2. *Selection, organization.* Note how the speaker leads into his central idea, how he states it, how he develops it. How wide a variety of materials does he use: only statistics, only examples, only quota-

tions from experts? And if he does seem to be resting his case on a single type of material, does this procedure seem justifiable, or would he be even more effective had he used different kinds? Do you hear transitions, internal summaries, recapitulations, enumeration of main points, or other evidences of good speech structure? When he has finished, can you say with some confidence what his point of view is? Like this: "Madison said that the liberal arts college has a fault that few would suspect: the tendency to graduate students whose training has been overspecialized. He showed that this tendency is the result of two powerful pressures. One is the desire of students to take repeated courses in a field they like rather than to open up a new field of study. The other is the likelihood of professors to encourage a student to strengthen his major continually rather than to advise him to broaden and diversify." To be able to make a concise summary like this shows good speaking on the part of the speaker—good listening on your part.

Moreover, since a speaker presumably has more materials than he can use, he therefore selects certain facts and omits others. You may therefore reflect, "This speaker is making the best possible case that he can. If he had a better reason or a more convincing fact he would use it. Is his case *good enough?*" You may also reflect: "Are his examples typical? Is he aware of exceptions? Has he weighed, appraised, sorted the good from the shoddy, or must I do this for him?"

Whenever another speaker, in class or out, demonstrates some aspect of good selection and organization, let his talent encourage you to give additional thought to the planning of your own speeches.

3. *Reasoning.* Since speakers often deal with complex issues, they should not only be well grounded in facts and evidence, but they should display a high quality of reasoning about the facts. To say that ten years ago 90 million Americans attended movies at least once a week, whereas today attendance has shrunk to 30 million a week, is no doubt an entirely credible fact, supported by attendance and tax records. To offer reasons for this decline, however, or to make statements about ways of reversing the trend, puts the speaker on controversial ground. So far as the statistic is concerned, the listener might ask: "Where did these figures of 90 million and 30 million come from?" So far as the reasoning is concerned, he might inquire: "Why do you think so? Are you sure? Who else thinks so?"

Listen attentively to speakers whose viewpoint differs from your own. Impressions, attitudes, beliefs, opinions formed in your grade school days need not necessarily dominate your thinking for the rest of your life. This text has already commented (pp. 77-78) on *selective exposure* (seeking communications that favor rather than oppose your point of view) and *selective retention* (tending to remember the facts with which you agree, to forget those with which you disagree). Educated people should be more open-minded and judicial than the non-educated. Good habits of listening can contribute to the development of your own good sense and judgment. Note the following:

a. SWEEPING GENERALIZATIONS. Assure yourself that the conclusions follow from the evidence offered. Assertions without proof can mislead. In 1848 Daniel Webster stoutly declared that California and New Mexico "are not worth a dollar." But before the year was out, the great gold rush had begun.

b. PREDICTIONS. When the speaker foretells the future, whether it concerns the stock market, the election, or the possibility of war, remind yourself that a prediction is only a prediction, and that prophets can be mistaken. You can certainly apply the usual tests of causal reasoning to help determine whether, in your own judgment, it is probable that what he thinks will happen will actually happen.

Even when the prediction is based on facts, remember again to keep in mind the strong possibility that another speaker might have interpreted the same facts differently. Economists, for example, have access to the principal facts about unemployment, income, capital expenditures, carloadings, the various indexes; but at a given moment one economist may feel that the country is headed for further recession, a second that it has hit the bottom of the recession, a third that it is beginning to head upward out of the recession.

c. POLLS, SURVEYS. Polls are sometimes right, sometimes wrong. Surveys are sometimes helpful, sometimes misleading. Once there was an automobile named the Edsel. The decision to build it was reached after an intensive analysis of the market. Meanwhile, people changed their minds and decided they could live without an Edsel. In 1948 the polls elected Dewey, but the voters picked Truman. Polls and surveys are useful, and this book recommends them, but they are not conclusive evidence, and the listener must still use his best judgment.

d. EXPERT OPINION. Nearly always good, but sometimes experts get set in their ways, and others have to come along with a fresh outlook. Especially be wary of the testimony of experts when they testify outside the field of their speciality.

e. EVERYBODY'S DOING IT. At times speakers want us to do what everybody's doing. But the majority is sometimes right, sometimes wrong. Anatole France wrote: "If 50 million people say a foolish thing, it is still a foolish thing."

Social psychologists have long established that individuals have a strong desire to conform to the opinions and judgments of those about them. The speaker who suggests without much evidence that "most good students" support his point of view is employing a subtle persuasive factor; the listener should be on guard.

f. PROPAGANDISTIC DEVICES. Sort them out, label them, ignore them. *Opinion* is not fact; *assertion* is not evidence. *Repeating a lie* does not make it honest. *Making the lie bigger* does not make it more truthful. *Calling names* is not logical argument. *Testimonials* of actresses, socialites, do not make the product better.

g. DEFINITION. Be on the lookout for terms that are undefined or that are defined loosely. One speaker quoted a medical authority to the effect that "tobacco in any form is not harmful when used sensibly by a reasonable man." This statement seemed wise until one listener inquired, "How do you define 'sensibly'? Who is a 'reasonable man'?" Although the speaker made a spirited defense of the medical man's statement, most listeners decided that the advice was too general to be truly helpful.

On the positive side, look for the exact, accurate statement; note the willingness to consider both sides, even though the speaker favors one side; detect the perceptive limitation of the subject that shows the speaker is not biting off more than he can chew; test the evidence for internal consistency and listen with wisdom and judgment; try to sense the speaker's basic sincerity and integrity; appraise him by the quality of his ideas, by his sympathy, considerateness, understanding, range of information. (See also pages 137-140.)

4. *The subject.* The quotation from Epictetus on the first page of this chapter raised the pertinent question: "On what subject are you able to hear me?" Whether the speaker's topic is one of your favorites or something new or strange, listen to learn.

5. *The critique.* Listen to be able to answer the question: "How could this topic have been presented more effectively?" The 24-year-old Thomas Erskine once listened to the barristers in an English courtroom, thinking to himself that he perceived ways of presenting the evidence more effectively; in the years to follow he became perhaps the greatest of all English courtroom pleaders. The 20-year-old William Pitt once discussed arguments heard in the House of Commons with his older friend, Charles Fox: "But surely, Mr. Fox, his argument might be met thus." The 20-year-old Henry Clay attended a debate, listening attentively; after the speeches heard the chairman call for the vote; Clay quietly observed that the topic was not exhausted; the

chairman invited him to present his views, and thus Kentucky began to become aware of the eloquence of one of its famous senators. Listen therefore not merely to pass judgment on what the speaker said or did but also to answer questions like: "How would I have handled this topic" or "What suggestions can I give this speaker for presenting this topic more effectively?" Under this heading you can review his choice of topic and ways in which he has limited it and adapted it to his audience; his organization; the reasons, evidence, and examples that make up the body of his speech; factors of delivery such as voice, articulation, bodily action; the total impact that the speech appears to make upon the listeners.

Questions for Classroom Discussion

1. Discuss the place of good listening in:
   a. Social conversation.
   b. Interviewing an applicant for a position.
   c. A physician's consultation with a patient.
   d. A lawyer's consultation with a client.
   e. A teacher's conference with a student.
   f. A supervisor's conference with an employee who has a grievance.
2. Is a poor listener necessarily an unintelligent person?
3. What steps can you take to improve your ability as a listener?

Speech-Related Projects

1. Hand in a Listening Report of approximately . . . . pages on a significant speaker. Consider his choice of subject, choice of material, organization, language, method of presentation, delivery, general effectiveness. What would you consider his strong points as a speaker? Assuming that he sought your advice about possible ways of improvement, what would you urge him to consider first?

2. Make a similar report on a TV speaker. In your critique, in addition to the suggestions under "1" above, keep in mind that the opening part of a TV speech is of special importance to help make sure that the viewer does not change stations. Comment also on the use of visual aids, if any; and on such features of delivery as facial expression.

Speaking Assignment 4

A Speech About Listening and Listeners

Make a speech of .... minutes in which you report on your observations about listening and listeners. Consider yourself and others in social, classroom, and other situations. What listening faults did you observe? What good listeners did you see in action?

REFERENCES ON LISTENING

A. Craig Baird and Franklin H. Knower, Chapter 14, "Informational and Critical Listening," in *General Speech*, 2nd ed. (New York, McGraw-Hill Book Company, Inc., 1957).

Giles Wilkeson Gray and Claude Merton Wise, pages 60-65, in *The Bases of Speech*, 3rd ed. (New York, Harper and Brothers, 1959).

Robert T. Oliver, Harold P. Zelko, Chapter 10, and Paul D. Holtzman, "Listening," in *Communicative Speech*, 3d ed. (New York, Holt, Rinehart, and Winston, 1962).

Eugene E. White, Chapter 8, "Listening and Observing," in *Practical Speech Fundamentals* (New York, The Macmillan Company, 1960).

William H. Whyte, Jr., *Is Anybody Listening?* (New York, Simon and Schuster, 1952).

Organizing:
The Short Speech

The short speech, often used as a classroom exercise to develop skill in organizing, has a counterpart in life wherever a brief, to-the-point talk is necessary. ■ *It may be narrative, expository, persuasive, or stimulating in purpose.*

A SPEAKER MAY FIRMLY SEIZE two handles to pull himself to higher levels of achievement.

One is to perfect the organization of the ideas making up the speech. This kind of planned structure, helping the speaker to keep his train of thought in mind, and the listener to follow and remember, is discussed in this chapter.

Two is to use specific example and illustration; these are part of the narrative method, explained in the following chapter.

I. The History of Speech Structure

That a speech should have a well-planned form or structure including a beginning and an ending is ancient wisdom handed down through 25 centuries of speaking experience.

CORAX (fifth century B.C.) taught that a speech should have five parts: introduction, narration, argument, refutation of opposing ideas, conclusion.[1] He thus showed the civilized world how to organize a speech. Although he lived and taught in Sicily, his notions quickly

---

[1] He called the introduction a *proem*. His *narration* was a brief account of what the speech was about. As he was primarily concerned with courtroom speeches, the narration would be the part in which the speaker explained what the *case* was about. The *argument* consisted of the points suporting the case, and the refutation (his *subsidiary remarks*) commented on opposing evidence. His term for conclusion was *peroration*, a term still used today to suggest a formal, somewhat eloquent, ending for a speech.

Note. Shakespeare's foolish constable, Dogberry, should be named as the patron saint of all rambling, repetitious, disorganized speakers. In *Much Ado About*

spread to Athens, and became embodied in the instruction of later rhetoricians. He firmly believed that public speaking was teachable. He also clearly saw that sound thinking about probabilities can accompany the presentation of demonstrable facts.

PLATO (late fifth and early fourth centuries B.C.) said that a speech should have a beginning, a middle, and an end. A speech should be put together like "a living creature," he declared in a famous analogy, having a body, and not lacking head nor foot, all put together in suitable fashion. He was a great seeker-after-truth, but he realized that "the man who knows the actual truth of things," unless he possesses also the art of speaking, "is not thereby a whit the nearer to a mastery of persuasion."

ARISTOTLE (fourth century B.C.) asserted that, ideally, a speaker should have only two parts in his speech. "You must (1) state your case, and (2) prove it." He quickly added, however, that since hearers are not ideal, the speaker should open with an introduction, and end with a conclusion. The order of the four parts then becomes (1) introduction, (2) statement of the case, (3) proof, (4) conclusion. These parallel the modern technique of (1) introduction, (2) central idea, (3) body, (4) conclusion.

CICERO (first century B.C.) and QUINTILIAN (first century A.D.) developed the classical Roman seven-part type of speech structure, consisting of (1) an exordium or introduction, (2) a narration or actual background, (3) a statement or central idea, (4) a partition or listing of main points, (5) proof, (6) refutation, and (7) peroration or conclusion. If a speaker stated his central idea, then enumerated the main points he proposed to establish, and then discussed them one by one, his procedure would recall a part of the structure advocated by speakers and pleaders of classical Rome. Both believed in the most thorough preparation for speech making, advising continual reading and study.

MODERN AUTHORITIES (twentieth century A.D.) recommend a simple type of speech structure, resembling that advocated by Greek rhetoricians (Plato, Aristotle) rather than that by Roman rhetoricians. Many favor a four-part structure: (1) introduction, (2) central idea, (3) body, (4) conclusion. Other teachers prefer to consider the central idea as a part of the introduction. And on occasion the central idea may be stated *after* the body of the speech has been developed, the plan

---

Nothing when asked to tell the Prince with what offense certain culprits are charged, Dogberry's classic rejoinder is: "They have committed false report; moreover, they have spoken untruths; secondarily, they are slanders; sixth and lastly, they have belied a lady; thirdly, they have verified unjust things: and to conclude, they are lying knaves" (Act V, Scene 1).

being to present the evidence first, *then* reveal the speaker's purpose. This chapter, however, will discuss the introduction-central idea-body-conclusion type of organization, as being useful in the short speech, and as a good way for the beginning speaker to develop habits of clear thinking.

II. Principal Parts of a Speech

The *introduction* is the opening part of the speech; its function is to arouse interest in what is to follow. Many ways of opening a speech will be found discussed in Chapter 12. The introduction to a short speech, like those illustrated in this chapter, often consists of only two or three sentences. Examples of these introductions will be given a few pages further on.

The *central idea,* sometimes called the "purpose sentence," is a brief statement of what the speech is about. Although it is brief, it represents much thought on the part of the speaker. Here are sample central ideas, informally stated, as worded by adult students in a business man's public speaking class:

I want to draw your attention to two new developments in air transport.

I'd like to tell you about a speech that made a deep impression on me.

My thoughts on the present crime wave fall into two areas.

It occurred to me that there are two ways of discouraging the passing of bad checks.

I want to point out things to look for when you inspect the safety practices of a plant.

I'd like to tell about an incident that occurred when I was checking the oil pressure on a B-47.

I do not want to be either Red or Dead, and here are two courses of action we must take in order to make democracy survive.

I dreamed up a couple of reasons why we should support the Red Cross in its current drive for funds.

Here is a central idea more formally stated:

Today I plan to discuss the viewpoint of the informed American taxpayer on three issues: (1) more government—or less? (2) more redistribution of income—or less? (3) more centralization of government—or less?[2]

---

[2] Adapted from a speech to the Tax Seminar by Roger A. Freeman, research director, Institute for Studies in Federalism, Claremont Men's College, Claremont, Calif. In *Vital Speeches,* XXVII (August 15, 1961), 649.

Whether the speech is short or long, the central idea is of the utmost importance. A clearly-stated central idea is the beginning of accurate thinking. Often adult speakers of experience lessen their effectiveness because they do not master the central idea. Remember the statement of the famous stone-cutter who was asked how to carve an elephant. "Just get a block of stone, a chisel, and a mallet," he replied, "and carve away everything that is not elephant." So the speaker gets a good central idea in mind, and then chisels away everything that does not support it. Determining the central idea is the beginning of good thinking about the subject. Oliver Wendell Holmes put it, "strike the jugular and let the rest go." Disraeli, using a different figure, advised speakers not to chase a subject all the way from the steam engine to the kettle.

Ordinarily the central idea follows the introduction. Your instructor will explain to you, however, that although the order introduction-central idea-body-conclusion is an effective arrangement for the first speeches in a speech course, exceptions arise. For the time being however, follow the normal order as explained in this chapter.

The *body* is the main part of the speech, in which the speaker develops the theme stated in the central idea. In planning the body of your speech, keep these principles in mind:

Main points should not overlap. "What kind of president is Lyndon B. Johnson turning out to be?" asked one speaker at the opening of his talk. "Let's examine his performance from three points of view: business, foreign policy, and leadership." Actually this speaker had only two points of view: first, the President's handling of business (or domestic) problems, and second, his handling of problems of foreign policy. The promised third point overlapped the other two.

The main points should follow a carefully-considered order. The arrangement may be self-determining, like a time-order plan or a space-order plan. Or the speaker may open with what he thinks is the least-controversial argument and close with what he thinks is the most-controversial argument. Use your best judgment in determining the order of your points. To read further about different methods of development, turn to pages 114-117 in Chapter 9 and to pages 132-142 in Chapter 10. To read further about the central idea, transition, and related ideas, see pages 226-228 in Chapter 16.

The *conclusion* is the summary, application, appeal, or restatement with which the speech ends. Many ways of concluding a speech may be found in Chapter 12. The conclusion to a short speech may consist of a single sentence or two.

Many teachers of public speaking make use of *short speeches* to teach basic principles of organization. Especially at the beginning of a course, you should practice the short speech until you gain a sense of structure. You should, moreover, *say something*, even though the time allowed is brief. In this way you will get solidly in your bones a feeling for a well-planned speech.

Our day has given every preference to the concise utterance over lengthy, diffuse, rambling remarks.[3] Before you can do good thinking in front of an audience, you must do good thinking while planning your speech for that audience.

No one should scorn the opportunity to make a short speech, either in class or out of it. Judge Florence E. Allen has written that early in life she was trained to state her points briefly and with emphasis and then sit down. (See footnote 10, page 276.) As a young woman in her 20's she participated actively in the woman suffrage movement in 1912. Of this experience she writes:

> On countless occasions I was given five, four, three, or only one minute to speak on behalf of woman's suffrage before some important meeting. I did just that and no more. As a result I have had the honor of speaking at highly important bodies, such as the International Bar Association at the Hague. I was asked to speak at the plenary session of that great meeting representing the women, but limited to three minutes. I timed my speech again and again and put it through on schedule.[4]

III. Short Speech: Examples

A. EXAMPLE 1

The following short speech is built around a single example.

WHEN YOU INVEST, DIVERSIFY

I read in the paper this morning that forty million Americans own stocks and bonds, which reminds me that forty million Americans are learning the rules of investing in the market.

---

[3] Although authorities from Quintilian onward may be cited in connection with the making of short speeches, Professor John P. Ryan of Grinnell College was one of those who placed stress on this kind of assignment both in college and university classes and in courses for business and professional people. See the author's article, "John P. Ryan's Art of Teaching," in *Speech Teacher*, VIII (November, 1959), 288-299. Professor Ryan is also mentioned on page 39.

[4] Judge Allen responded to the author's request to write about her speech making experiences in order to lend her encouragement to the young people who are studying public speaking. She has addressed students on many campuses; one appearance was at the commencement ceremony of the university of her native state, the University of Utah, in the summer of 1960. This speech appears in *Representative American Speeches, 1960-1961*, ed. Lester Thonssen (New York, The H. W. Wilson Company, 1961), 100-114.

In investments class we are taught that an important rule is to diversify your holdings; don't put all your eggs in one basket. Suppose Jim Hawkins has $25.00 a month to invest, and each month buys stock in the Slippery Oil Company. All business today is highly competitive, and if Slippery goes up, Hawkins profits; if Slippery has a bad year, Hawkins will see part of his savings vanish. It will not diversify much to invest half of the savings in Slippery, and the other half in another oil company, such as Waxy Petroleum. This is because the whole oil industry can have a bad year.

The idea is to pick not simply different companies, but different industries. Diversification in this situation means that if one of your industries in oil, the other should be an entirely different industry—for example, food. So having bought a few shares of Slippery Oil, Hawkins next tries Eastern Supermarkets.

If you ever decide to join this group of Forty Million Americans Who Owns Stocks, first understand this basic rule.

The outline:

(Title) WHEN YOU INVEST, DIVERSIFY

Introduction
Forty million Americans own stocks and bonds.

Central Idea
An important rule of investing is to buy stocks in different industries.

Body
I. Jim Hawkins is an example of a wise investor who diversifies.
A. He first buys stock in Slippery Oil Co.
B. He next buys stock in Eastern Supermarkets.

Conclusion
If you ever decide to join the Forty Million Who Own Stocks, first understand this basic rule.

Note that the foregoing outline consists of *complete sentences.* You can test your reasoning better with complete sentences than with fragments. This type of outline is different from the notes that the speaker takes to the platform. *Speaker's notes* might look like the following:

Hawkins $25.00

Slippery Oil

Waxy Petroleum

Eastern Supermarkets

To emphasize and repeat:

The *speech outline* is a special way of setting down ideas, first to help you organize your thinking, and second to hand in to your instructor so that he can see whether your thinking is clear or hazy. Its complete sentences and its system of lettering and numbering help him to see what *you* have in mind and what *your* purpose is.

Speaker's notes are something you write to take to the speaker's stand to guide you while you make your speech. As they are designed for nobody but you, you can put them in whatever form you choose. Your instructor will advise you about keeping these notes *brief*—and when or whether to abandon them altogether.[5]

As you progress through a speech course, your *speech outlines* will get longer and more detailed because you will gradually talk on subjects of increasing significance, packed with information and reasoning. Your speaker's notes will get more brief because your memory becomes more sure; you are less likely to get rattled. Ideally you should soon find yourself making excellently-organized speeches of modest length with no notes whatever.

B. EXAMPLE 2

The short speech with two or more supporting statements introduces the problem of division (*partition* or *analysis*). In this kind of speech the central idea is worded so as to be capable of being divided into supporting ideas.

[5] For interesting photographs of actual speaker's notes, consult Waldo W. Braden and Mary Louise Gehring, *Speech Practices: A Resource Book for the Student of Public Speaking* (New York, Harper & Brothers, 1958).

PROFIT FROM YOUR MILITARY CAREER

Nowadays every young man has to prepare himself mentally for the time when he will need to interrupt his education and spend a period of months or years in the armed forces.

Several of us were talking about military service last week, and we decided that recruits would profit more from their military careers if they would keep two rules in mind.

Rule One is that you must not expect every moment in the armed forces to be productive. You may have to report on a Friday, and nothing happens until Monday. You may have to show up at seven a.m., and the officers do not arrive until nine, and do not start work until ten. You will find yourself working on a weapon for a solid week, so intensively that you can take it apart and put it back together with one hand, or in your sleep, or both. Then, the next week, a new set of officers appears, and you do the same thing over again. Now: if you realize that things like this happen, instead of cracking up when they do happen you will say to yourself, "Well— here I am again, standing around doing nothing—just as my good friend in Public Speaking 10 said it would be." So in these situations I urge you to be patient.

Rule Two is: Try to learn from every experience that *does* come your way. You will have a chance to know many different kinds of people. Learn to appreciate every human being for his own worth, and you may find yourself developing new qualities of leadership. You will find no better place than the armed services for learning to do a wide variety of tasks. Do each of these as well as you can, whether it is to police the barracks, scour pots and pans on K. P., or improve your marksmanship on the range.

These two rules will help anyone develop the proper attitude so that he will get more out of his military career. I hope you will follow them and persuade others to do so also.

The outline:

(Title) PROFIT FROM YOUR MILITARY CAREER

Introduction

Every young man has to prepare himself mentally for a period of months or years in the armed forces.

Central Idea

To learn more from their military careers, recruits should keep two rules in mind.

Body

I. Be patient when nothing much seems to happen.
   A. You may have to report days before you are actually assigned to duty.
   B. You may have to wait hours on some assignment or detail.
   C. You may find yourself needlessly repeating some duty.

II. Be an active learner when different kinds of situations come your way.
   A. Some experiences teach you about people.
   B. Other experiences help you develop qualities of leadership.
   C. Still other experiences teach you skill in a variety of tasks.

Conclusion

These two rules will help one profit from his military career.

The central idea sums up the speech in a single sentence. Teachers of writing sometimes frown upon the candid announcement, illustrated in the example above, that *two supporting ideas follow,* but speakers have found this frank labelling of points to be of advantage to the listener. (The listener, unlike the reader, can not go back and reread; he has to get the point accurately *as the speaker utters it.*) So long as listening differs from reading in this regard, listeners will generally commend speakers who announce, "there are *two* reasons," "this problem has *two* facets," "so much for the *first* question; let us turn to the *second.*" So when the speaker said, "Recruits will learn more from their military careers if they will keep two rules in mind," he was applying a time-tested principle of good speaking.

A central idea may be divided into two or more supporting statements according to various principles: the one illustrated is a simple *series of reasons.* This speech has a series of two main reasons, but it could have had three or more. The two reasons given could be presented in reverse order, although psychologically it is probably better to have the stronger reason last.

In a short speech the conclusion is necessarily brief; here it is a simple restatement of the central idea.

C. EXAMPLE 3

Even a short speech can be impressive and memorable. In the closing days of August, 1864, three hundred-day regiments of Ohio militia were about to be mustered out. President Abraham Lincoln made short talks to each: the 148th, the 164th, and the 166th. The talk to the 166th is the briefest and most appealing.

SPEECH TO THE 166TH OHIO REGIMENT
ABRAHAM LINCOLN

Soldiers: I suppose you are going home to see your families and friends. For the services you have done in this great struggle in which we are engaged I present you sincere thanks for myself and the country.

I almost always feel inclined, when I happen to say anything to soldiers, to impress upon them in a few brief remarks the importance of success in this contest.

It is not merely for today, but for all time to come that we should perpetuate for our children's children that great and free government which we have enjoyed all our lives. I beg you to remember this, not merely for my sake, but for yours. I happen temporarily to occupy this big White House. I am a living witness that any one of your children may look to come here as my father's child has. It is in order that each one of you may have through this free government which we have enjoyed, an open field and a fair chance for your industry, enterprise and intelligence; that you may all have equal privileges in the race of life, with all its desirable human aspirations.

It is for this the struggle should be maintained, that we may not lose our birthright—not only for one, but for two or three years. The nation is worth fighting for, to secure such an inestimable jewel.[6]

You will notice many interesting features of this short address, which must have taken less than two minutes to deliver. The first two sentences constitute the introduction; here the audience is uppermost in the speaker's thoughts, as is seen by the use of *you* and *your*. The central idea is stated in the second paragraph; here the speaker tells his listeners that he wants to impress upon them "the importance of success in this contest." The body of the speech is in the third paragraph. The opening part of it reminds listeners of their children's children, with a promise that any one of them may some day occupy the White House; the remaining part impresses listeners with the advantages of a free government to each of them personally. The concluding sentence recalls the speaker's purpose, again reminding the audience the struggle should be maintained.

[6] The text originally appeared in the *New York Herald and Tribune* for August 23, 1864, and is reprinted in *The Collected Works of Abraham Lincoln* (New Brunswick, Rutgers University Press, 1953), VII, 512.
Although the text was at first printed in one paragraph, the author has divided the material into four paragraphs to suggest the four parts of a well-organized speech.

C. OTHER TYPES OF DESIGN

Here are other simple ways of subdividing a *central idea* into *two supporting statements:*

1. *List of topics*

As just stated, a central idea may be subdivided into a series of supporting *reasons*. When the purpose is to explain, the supporting statements are better termed *topics* than *reasons:*

(Title) A TRIBUTE TO LINCOLN

Introduction

During these centennial years of the Civil War period we are reading much about Abraham Lincoln.

Central Idea

Abraham Lincoln had two outstanding traits of personality.

Body

I. He was witty.
- A. He used humor in courtroom and campaign speeches.
  1. He said his talk would be short like an old lady's dance.
  2. He won a jury by joking about the city lawyer's fancy shirt.
- B. He used humor in conversation and in conference.
  1. Once he read a humorous essay of Artemus Ward's to his cabinet.
  2. On another occasion he told the story of the little steamboat with the big whistle.

II. He was humble.
- A. He was easily approached by all kinds of people.
  1. Mothers of soldiers asked him to protect their sons.
  2. Job hunters took their pleas to him personally.
  3. Old friends were as welcome after he was President as before.
- B. He did not claim to know it all.
  1. In 1855 he wrote that the slave problem "is too mighty for me. May God, in his mercy, superintend the solution."
  2. In 1860 he said: "I do not think I am fit for the Presidency."
  3. He gratefully accepted Seward's help with his speeches.

Conclusion

These two qualities of wit and humility are as valued in these days as they were a hundred years ago.

2. *Classification*

Sometimes the supporting statements suggest a grouping, or *classification*:

(Title) ADVANTAGES OF FRATERNITY MEMBERSHIP

Introduction

Every once in a while fraternities find themselves under fire.

Central Idea

Membership in a fraternity offers two distinct kinds of advantages.

Body

I. Educational advantages are of immediate usefulness.
   A. Members have the opportunity to study with others taking the same course.
   B. Members have the opportunity to take their problems to others in the house who are majoring in their field.

II. Business and professional advantages are especially useful in later years.
   A. You have a better chance of doing business with a person if you can meet him through a mutual friend.
   B. Local alumni chapters of your fraternity afford you an opportunity to broaden your acquaintance.

Conclusion

When you hear criticism of fraternity membership, recall these advantages to help offset the unfavorable criticisms.

3. *Other methods*

Additional ways of subdividing a central idea are discussed in later chapters dealing with specific kinds of speeches. If you wish to look ahead, turn to the two following chapters.

D. THE OUTLINE

Note that outlines should be composed of complete sentences. If your instructor asks you to turn in an outline, use complete sentences. DO NOT turn in something like the following:

HIGHER EDUCATION (Vague title.)

Central Idea

The two kinds of final exams. (Not a complete sentence.)

Body

I. Graded by a reader.   (Not complete sentences.)
II. Students left in ignorance.

This central idea contains merely a faint notion about two kinds of final exams; it is not clear whether the speaker is for them or against them; the supporting statements, moreover, suggest only that the speaker in some unfathomable way is unhappy about the examination situation. The title is vague. Better say:

(Title) IMPROVE FINAL EXAMINATIONS

Introduction

Students give much thought to possible methods of improving the final examination system.

Central Idea

Professors should correct two serious faults in the examination system.

Body

I. Each professor should review all final papers scored by student graders.
  A. He can assure himself that the grader understood each question.
  B. He can review the grades proposed by the grader.
  C. He can give suggestions that will help the grader to become a better teacher himself.
II. Each student should have a chance to study the mistakes marked on his final examination.
  A. He will learn how well he got facts in proper perspective.
  B. He may determine whether he is improving his ability to think and write clearly.

Conclusion

If professors would remedy these two faults, their final examinations would be a better way of helping us learn.

IV. A Specific Problem in Organizing

The foregoing discussion suggests that in his preparation the speaker searches for a central idea, and then for some main points or sup-

WORK SHEET: HOW TO PREPARE A SHORT SPEECH
(Think With a Pencil)

I. Make a list of POSSIBLE TOPICS and choose the one the audience
will like best.

1.

2.

3.

II. Write the topic you choose in the form of a "central idea."

III. JOT DOWN supporting ideas, good or fair.

IV. Write below the two BEST of these ideas. Across from each idea jot
down a possible example or statistic to use with it.

    Ideas here   Examples, statistics here

1.

2.

This is your talk in the rough.
Next: Plan a conclusion. Last: Plan an introduction. Finally: Rehearse.

porting ideas that logically develop that central idea. **Let us examine this process more closely by considering a specific problem.** Suppose you decide you want to talk about seat belts and have limited your subject as follows:

CENTRAL IDEA: My purpose today is to urge you to have seat belts installed in the car you operate.

You may then make a *trial list* of ideas that might some way fit into the speech:

Belts are required equipment on the 1700 cars owned by Allstate Insurance.

In the event of an accident you are safer if you are not thrown from the car.

A French race car went out of control, left the course, turned end over end four times; the driver unhooked his safety belt, got out of the car unassisted, and ran half a mile to tell his wife he was all right.

Belts are widely used by the highway patrols of at least 26 states.

John Moore, director of the Cornell studies on crash injury, who has seven children, has his 9-passenger station wagon equipped with 9 seat belts.

Belts are installed on all cars operated by the U. S. Department of Health, Education, and Welfare.

In the event of an accident your chances of injury are reduced if you are not thrown into the windshield.

Dr. R. Arnold Griswold, chairman of the American College of Surgeons' Committee on Trauma, has seat belts installed in his car.

The fear of being trapped in a wreck is ill-founded.

What this speaker has done is to review his note cards and put down ideas that seem to bear on his speech. The foregoing list is scattered, disjointed, and even contains contradictory statements, but is a step in your thinking. Writing statements down helps your concentration; remember the saying, "Think with a pencil."

Now that your ideas are in front of you, your next step is to review them critically. How can they be arranged? A few of the ideas can be grouped together. For example:

In the event of an accident you are nearly five times safer if you are not thrown from the car.

In the event of an accident your chances of injury are reduced if you are not thrown into the windshield.

12.8 per cent of car occupants ejected through open doors are killed as compared to 2.6 per cent of those who remain in the car.

These statements can be arranged as supporting details for what might be a main point in your outline. You write down a main point and put them under it:

  I. Seat belts increase your chances of surviving an accident.
     A. In the event of an accident you are nearly five times safer if you are not thrown from the car.
        1. 12.8 per cent of car occupants ejected through open doors are killed, as compared to 2.6 per cent of those who remain in the car.
     B. In the event of an accident your chances of injury are reduced if you are not thrown into the windshield.

This material tends to prove that seat belts do the things they are supposed to do. Your item "A" needs still more evidence. Your item "B" as it now stands, moreover, is an assertion without proof, so you will need to do further reading to find the evidence that will determine whether or not it is true.

Another group of items can be grouped as follows:

  II. Many firms and organizations use seat belts.
     A. Belts are required equipment on the 1700 cars owned by Allstate Insurance.
     B. Belts are widely used by the highway patrols of at least 26 states.
     C. Belts are installed on all cars operated by the U. S. Department of Health, Education, and Welfare.

With this part of your trial outline worked out, you can, as you continue your reading, look for additional proof to support your growing conviction that every one should see that the cars he operates are equipped with seat belts.

Another important aspect of outlining now suggests itself. Are these two ideas the most convincing that you can assemble? Is there anything lacking? On your trial list you note the following:

The fear of being trapped in a wreck is ill-founded.

This statement confirms your suspicion that a few people may object to seat belts; listeners in your class room may also harbor secret doubts or fears. You will not have to read widely, however, to find evidence to support an argument that "commonly-heard objections to seat belts are not justified," since, for example, fire breaks out in only 2/10 of 1 per cent of injury-producing auto accidents, and, moreover, if your belt will help you keep from being knocked unconscious, you will have a better chance to escape than if you wore no belt and were unconscious.

Again, looking over your list, you see an item like this:

A French race car went out of control, left the course, turned end over end four times; the driver unhooked his seat belt, got out of the car unassisted, and ran half a mile to tell his wife he was all right.

In your reading you will come across many unusual, dramatic examples of escape; no single one of them offers proof of consequence, but the cumulative effect has persuasive impact. You could put this incident under "A" of main point "I" above ("Seat belts increase your chances of surviving an accident"); it does, however, have a certain entertaining, interest-holding value, so you consider using it at the opening of your speech. An even better introduction could be to describe an accident that you knew about first-hand; it may not be so sensational but it might seem more real and therefore more plausible to your listeners.

The item about John Moore and his 9-passenger station wagon equipped with 9 seat belts does not have a place in your outline as developed thus far, though, like the French race car item, it has interest value. You keep it at hand for possible further use.

You can now go back to the library for further reading (or over to the police station to talk to the chief), confident that your speech is progressing in good shape.

What has been outlined above is a composite of student speeches about traffic accidents. The subject is vital, since the advice of the speakers could save the lives of those who listen and heed. Statistical evidence is steadily accumulating, both from investigations of the famous Cornell University crash injury research program, and from observations of highway patrol officers and like groups. If you wish to see a more complete outline on this topic, turn to pages 263-265.

Questions for Classroom Discussion

1. Complete this statement: "Unless one is an experienced speaker, he should never speak in public longer than ——— minutes."

2. Amplify: "A supporting statement may take the form of a quotation from an authority; a reason; a statistic; an illustration, an example; a comparison."

Speaking Assignment 5

A Short Speech

Make a one-point speech, ... minutes in length.

Use a work sheet, the one on page 107 or one similar to it, to list possible topics.

Note that your *purpose* may be to inform, to entertain, to persuade, to impress or stimulate.

Write the topic you choose in the form of a central idea. Use a complete sentence, thus: "The compact car should have its engine in the rear." "Featherbedding in work agreements should be deplored." "Camera fans should save their money for a zoom lens." "Here is the one minimum essential in babysitting." "Railroads are doomed, unless . . ."

Develop your central idea by a single well-chosen example, illustration, reason, testimony from an authority, selected group of statistics.

Plan a conclusion. A simple summary or restatement of your central idea will serve.

Last of all: plan an introduction. A single sentence that will catch attention will add to the effectiveness of your talk.

Rehearse—several times. Do not try to memorize anything word for word. Get a *sequence of ideas* in mind; if you use different language each rehearsal, don't worry. Time yourself (most people at first try to say too much).

Hand in an outline in the form prescribed by your instructor. Short outlines appear in this chapter; longer outlines appear on pages 143-144 and 263-265.

Speaking Assignment 6

A Short Speech with Two Supporting Ideas

Make a speech with *two supporting ideas*, ... minutes in length.

Your purpose may be to inform, to entertain, to persuade, to impress or stimulate.

In planning this speech, follow the suggestions given under Speaking Assignment 5 above. Your central idea will be developed by *two* supporting points. Select and word these supporting points so that they do not overlap, but rather represent a natural division of the central idea.

Rehearse several times, as suggested above.

Hand in an outline in the form prescribed by your instructor.

REFERENCES ON THE SHORT SPEECH

A. Craig Baird and Franklin H. Knower, Chapter 6, "Supporting Details," in *General Speech*, 2nd ed. (New York, McGraw-Hill Book Company, Inc., 1957). Discusses definition and explanation, particulars, instances, figures and statistics, comparisons and contrasts, cause-and-effect sequences, testimony of authority, quotation, incident and anecdote, questions.

W. Norwood Brigance, Chapter 3, "First Steps in Managing Ideas," in *Speech Communication*, 2nd ed. (New York, Appleton-Century-Crofts, Inc., 1955). Discusses facts and figures, specific instances, illustrations, comparisons, testimony.

Alan H. Monroe, Chapter 4, "How to Support One Point," in *Principles of Speech*, 4th ed. (Chicago, Scott, Foresman and Company, 1958). Discusses explanation, analogy, illustration, specific instance, statistics, testimony.

Paul L. Soper, Chapter 6, "Supporting Materials," in *Basic Public Speaking*, 2nd ed. (New York, Oxford University Press, 1956). Discusses definition, comparison and contrast, examples, authority, statistics.

CHAPTER 9

Development By Narrative Methods

Narrative materials may open a speech, develop an idea within a speech, close a speech; occasionally an entire speech is narrative. ■ *Through narrative materials the speaker capitalizes on his own experience; their use, by introducing an element of variety, may help improve delivery.* ■ *In building a narrative speech, plan the opening, develop the complications, build to a climax.* ■ *Humor, dialog, dialect, specific names and details, heighten the interestingness of a narrative.*

LEARNING TO OUTLINE a speech, discussed in the last chapter, is one of the first steps in improving one's speaking. You have seen that your outline requires you to determine your central idea, and to decide upon the divisions and subdivisions. Often you want to expand one of these divisions or subdivisions through the use of a short *narrative*; learning to use the narrative method is therefore another important step in improving speaking. The whole speech, or most of it, may be cast in narrative form; or the introduction, or the conclusion, or both, may be narrative.

This chapter therefore explains principles of preparing the *narrative* speech, and of using narrative materials in speeches that are primarily *expository, persuasive,* or *impressive* in purpose.

I. Planning a Narrative Speech

Assume that your instructor has assigned a narrative speech—a typical assignment in present-day public speaking courses—to your class. Obviously it is a better starting point for developing you as a speaker to let you talk about ideas easy to keep in mind than to send you to the library to research a controversial issue. Such an assignment is also of high value, but comes later.

The counterpart in later life of the classroom narrative speech is the trip speech ("My Summer in Paris," given to the Rotary Club) or the story of an experience of an individual, or of a community, or an industry, told in personal terms for its entertainment value. The student who today tells a story about getting a sudden interest in religion (he was stationed overseas and signed up for a ten-day religious retreat in Vienna primarily to get away from the barracks) may tomorrow, as an assistant minister, find himself telling a congregation about his experiences with underprivileged children.

Your preparation of the narrative speech may follow these steps:

A. PLAN THE OPENING

A narrative speech follows a chronological outline; your task is to relate the story as it happened. The opening should move briskly, with enough details to set the stage. Here is an example from a California speaker:

> In December, 1941, I was in the U. S. Navy, stationed at Pearl Harbor. On the morning of December 7 I was on my way to the ship in my '36 Ford to try to overhaul the starter. As I drove down the highway I saw four civilians running across a field.[1]

Students in the class were impressed by the quiet authority of the speaker as he unfolded his narrative. As he had only five or six minutes to tell the story of that morning at Pearl Harbor, he lost no time in preliminaries. Moreover, and this principle is important, listeners learned about what went on in the same order that the speaker himself found out. *He avoided the temptation to give the plot away.* The listeners, of course, were aware that they were hearing an eye-witness account of a disaster, and they realized that the situation being described would quickly become serious.

Magazine editors who have needed to revise scores of manuscripts say that most stories can be improved by lopping off the first two or three paragraphs. Many writers take too long to get their plots off the ground. Speakers may profit by this advice. Discover the high point of your story, and build your speech around it.

---

[1] By Gerald Pease, student at San Diego State College in the summer of 1954.

B. INTRODUCE THE COMPLICATIONS

A good narrative has a *complication* in the plot. If the story progresses so matter-of-factly that participants face no difficulties or complexities, it may not arouse the interest of listeners.

It would not be easy to create a rousing speech about the average first ride in an aircraft. The personal excitement of the takeoff, the thrill of rising into the air the first time, the pleasure of recognizing familiar sights from high above them, are by now commonplace. In short, there seem to be no *complications.*

One student, however, making a speech about an airplane ride, said that when his plane started to land, a mechanic suddenly ran out and waved the aircraft back up into the sky. This detail introduced a *complication,* and showed the audience this plane ride was no routine trip. The pilot circled, leaned out of the window to inspect his landing gear, and saw that the wheels had dropped off. Meanwhile he received confirming word over the plane's radio. The pilot explained the predicament to the passenger, offering him a choice between bailing out and riding the plane down for a belly landing. The aircraft continued to circle while the passenger deliberated these two unpleasant choices. This situation the speaker dwelled on for a sentence or two; then he asked the pilot, yelling to make himself heard: "What do you think we'd better do?" The pilot shouted back, "I think we'd better try to land." By now the complication was developed, and the interest of listeners aroused.

The Pearl Harbor narrative introduced complications swiftly:

> As I drove down the highway I saw four civilians running across a field. As I drove near them, they climbed on my running boards. I asked them, "What is the matter?" "The Japs are attacking," they replied.
>
> I could not believe them; and when we arrived at Pearl, I let them off and drove down to the pier. I asked a marine, "What's the score?" Since I didn't have much use for marines then, I didn't believe him either when he said, "The Japs are attacking us."

The outcome of these narratives will appear later.

C. PLAN THE CLIMAX

After the speaker has laid the groundwork for his narrative and has introduced the complications, he moves steadily along until the *climax,* the high point, is reached.

The speaker telling about his first ride in an airplane swiftly narrated the events of the story that transpired after the pilot and passenger had agreed to attempt a landing. After a few sharply-worded instructions about how to brace for a crash, the speaker provided details about the final approach to the landing strip, and the landing itself, with its shrieking and grinding and bouncing, pilot and passenger badly shaken but not injured.

Here is the climactic part of the Pearl Harbor speech:

I decided it was time to go down to my ship and see what I could do. The only ammunition on ship was some rifle ammunition that we used for abandon ship drill. I took it and a rifle out on the pier, got behind a group of boxes, and was shooting at the planes as if they were ducks. The Captain came aboard, gave me a pat on the back for doing a good job, and sent me down to the USS *Indianapolis*, which was short of gunners' mates.

I reported aboard there for duty. I was told to man a .50 caliber machine gun. This gun had just been rolled out on deck and had not been readied for firing. I wiped the grease off with my shirt, loaded it and fired it without water. The grease flew everywhere but between waves we managed to get some salt water to fill the water jacket; then when I fired, the corks flew out because of the steam that was generated.

The situation was further complicated because of the recruits that were on the ship. They would get excited and dive under the turrets when each new attack took place, leaving me with the job of firing the gun and loading it, too. But finally the attack ended, about ten o'clock in the morning, as I seem to remember it.

D. PLAN THE CONCLUSION

The conclusion of a narrative speech is not long; the speaker gathers up the loose ends and rounds the story out.

The ending to the airplane ride was brief, but satisfying. At the end of the runway the aircraft came to rest, pilot and passenger unharmed. A few details about the condition of the plane, and a brief comment by the passenger-speaker that today, when riding in a plane, he is attentive to all the auditory and visual cues that tell him that the landing is proceeding in routine fashion, brought the talk to a conclusion.

The sailor concluded his narrative with a few sentences telling how he spent that December 7 after the Japs left: he helped unload mines and drove an ammunition truck. His last sentence was:

I know you have heard the historians' report on Pearl Harbor but I thought you would like to know how it looked from the eyes of one individual who went through it.

This excellent conclusion not only brought the narrative to a close, but reaffirmed the point of view of the whole speech—to unfold December 7 as one onlooker experienced it.

A speaker may plant an idea in the beginning of his speech, or even in the middle of it, and, in the conclusion, refer to it. This artistic device is used in fiction: a mention of a squeaking gate is planted in the opening chapters; at the end the accidental rediscovery of the squeaking gate helps the amnesia victim recover his memory. At the beginning of the following speech, a current event is used to open the talk and is again referred to in the conclusion. As you read the speech, note also the complications and the climax.

PARACHUTING FOR A LIVING[2]

A little more than a week ago, the Sunday *Cedar Rapids Gazette* carried the headline announcing the death of Captain Iven Kincheloe, the test pilot, the man proposed to make the first manned flight into outer space. Every time I read in newspapers of the crash of one of our Air Force planes, I think how wonderful it could have been if the men killed in the crash could have had a chance to save their lives. Captain Kincheloe was not given the chance to use his parachute or ejection seat, whichever the case may be, and as a result of this today he is no longer with us. At the same time when I read these newspaper accounts, I recall an incident I experienced during World War II in which it was necessary to bail out of a plane.

In July, 1944, I was a radio operator on a B-17 Flying Fortress on my 18th mission over occupied Europe and Germany. Our target was Vienna, Austria, and we were to bomb the oil refineries in that beautiful city.

We were directly over the target at approximately 26,500 feet and had just dropped our bombs. At the same time we were in a heavy flak barrage and received a direct hit between number 3 and 4 engines, setting our plane on fire. I would like to explain that 3 and 4 engines are on the right wing. As a result of this severe flak our plane went into a flat spin which looks something

[2] By John F. Red, student at the State University of Iowa, summer of 1958.

like this [gesturing], not a spin such as this [gesturing], which could have been fatal.

As we got hit, the interphone became clogged with a mass of exclamations and orders. I heard out of these mixed calls an order from the pilot, "Pilot to crew! Pilot to crew! Prepare to bail out!" As we had just dropped our bombs, the bomb-bay doors were still open and I started to climb out on the catwalk in the bomb bay, my assigned exit. I hesitated a moment, but just then I saw the engineer, and he made a thumbs-down motion. I took his hint and jumped from the plane.

The first sensation I had was feeling the air pressure change from a heavy pressure to a lighter one. This change is caused by the slip stream from the engines and the air feels lighter as you get farther away from the ship. I instinctively knew I was clear of the plane. It is difficult to relate the exact sequence of events as much happened in a matter of seconds. When I pulled my rip-cord, however, I must have been falling head down, flat on my back. The next sensation was a feeling of terrific shock as the chute opened. Up to this point I hadn't had time to be scared. But after the chute opened, I began to pray.

The next sensation was a realization of being suspended in mid-air, accompanied by an oscillation back and forth. It is impossible to tell that you are falling because at such a height you are unable to judge the distance to the ground. The chute oscillation is a frightening thing. You are swinging back and forth and there are times when you swing so far in one direction that you think the chute will spill and you will go plummeting to the ground. I didn't try to direct my chute because I was afraid I would pull the wrong line. I thought I had better leave well enough alone.

As I was hanging in mid-air I saw six other members of my crew floating in the dark sky. Over to my left I saw a large form that had to be our co-pilot, a man six feet three inches tall who weighed more than 200 pounds. As we hung there in the sky he yelled over to me, "Who are you?" I identified myself and he yelled back, "Let's stick together!" There we were, carrying on a conversation, such as it was, at 20,000 feet. But the co-pilot, even though he had bailed out after me, was falling at a much more rapid pace. In a few moments he passed me as if I were standing still. But soon I realized that I was falling rapidly.

Soon I felt another sensation of bailing out of an airplane. At about 800 to 1000 feet, instead of feeling that I was falling toward the ground, I felt that the ground was speeding up to meet me. Luckily I made a good landing in a back yard of a residential section in Vienna. Our crew was quickly rounded up and captured. I learned that the co-pilot had landed feet first on the tile roof of a large building, and that the fall injured both of his legs severely.

Afterwards we spent some time in a war prison in East Germany. But I do not want to set myself up as telling a war story. I simply want to give you some idea of the experience of bailing out of an airplane. It is something I wouldn't want to do every day. I would like at this time, however, to pay tribute to Captain Kincheloe and the thousands of young men who were never given a chance to use their chutes. I also hope that next Memorial Day, when we again honor our nation's war dead, that you will pause in reverence as I will, to all of the airmen, not so lucky as me, who have given their lives for our country.

E. SUSPENSE, POINT OF VIEW

The speaker can borrow from the techniques of the writer in developing his narrative speech.

One key word is *suspense*. Consider the two aircraft stories: in one a navigator bailed out, in another a passenger undertook to ride in on a crash landing. What will be the outcome? Don't reveal the answer until you have developed the suspense in the situation. Recall Oscar Wilde: "The suspense is terrible. I hope it will last."

Don't begin by saying, "I want to tell you about the time I won first prize in a beauty contest." If you do, your only chance for creating suspense is in the story of *how* you did it. Unfold the story as it happened: "I was a little surprised to find a note on my typewriter, 'See Mr. Phelps at once,' and, like any employee, I wondered if I was in for a bawling out. Even when I was in his office, he must have talked a full two minutes before I realized that instead of scolding me he was nominating me as the firm's entry in the city-wide 'Miss Greater Chattanooga' beauty contest." Develop your speech so that none of your listeners will know until you have finished whether you eventually won first, or were disqualified; or perhaps you were announced as second, but through a mistake in adding the scores, you later learned that you were first.

Still another key phrase is *point of view*. An interesting feature of the Pearl Harbor speech was that the speaker kept the point of view of the seaman who only gradually realized what was happening. He did not try to be an official historian of the event. If you are an old employee, and your point of view, for the purpose of the narrative, is to be that of a new employee, don't unexpectedly revert to being an old hand. If your point of view is to tell the story as it unfolded, don't bring in advance knowledge; or if you feel the advance knowledge will help, tell us you are shifting your point of view ("I found out the next day what actually had happened").

II. Heightening the Narrative Effect

What has just preceded has stressed the longer, single-incident, narrative speech. Another use of the narrative method, as mentioned at the beginning of this chapter, is to introduce, develop, or conclude other types of speeches. Here the advice is two-fold:

1. *Build a storehouse of narrative materials.* Recall the discussion in Chapter 2 of *recording*. Use cards, slips, or loose-leaf sheets to write down stories, illustrations, anecdotes, examples.

If you will turn to Chapter 12, pages 162-172, you will see a discussion of the use of narrative materials in beginning and ending a speech (begin with an illustration, end with an illustration).

2. *Watch opportunities to use narrative materials.* Ask yourself whether a narrative (illustration, anecdote, short story, example) will add interest to some part of your speech to inform, persuade, or stimulate. Variety is important: if you have been giving a series of reasons or statistics, a story or example affords a change of pace.

The short narrative, like the long, should introduce a complication followed by a satisfying solution. About 1931 Henry Ford decided to put a V-8 motor in his popular-priced car. To gain the advantages of economy and efficiency, he wanted to cast the engine block in a single piece. His experts assured him that this was impossible. Not discouraged, he proceeded anyway; he spent time with his engineers making drawing after drawing, and finally evolved a solution to his problem. Since then, more than 30,000,000 one-piece castings have been made.[3] This short narrative is a satisfying one, and could be used

---

[3] Details supplied by Henry E. Edmunds, Manager, Research and Information Department, Ford Motor Company. The story was released in December, 1957, and was, according to Mr. Edmunds, carried by several hundred newspapers and magazines at that time. He wrote the author: "There is more to the story, of course. . . . When engineers and foundrymen came to Mr. Ford repeatedly and said, 'Mr. Ford, it can't be done; it's impossible,' he is reported to have said, 'I know it's impossible, but do it anyway.' Regardless of whether this version is literally true, it demonstrates Mr. Ford's stubborn belief that anything that could be visualized could be achieved." (Letter of December 4, 1961.)

to illustrate a variety of situations. But suppose you told a story of an automobile magnate who wanted to design an engine block cast in a single piece; the engineers declared this could not be done; the magnate said, "By George, you're right!" and abandoned his project! Now the complication is gone, this narrative loses its interest.

Most of the following devices are also associated with the narrative method, and may be used to heighten the effect.

A. HUMOR

A principal ingredient of humor is *incongruity*: something out of place. When a fine young male tells about enrolling in Girls' Cooking I and later in Girls' Cooking II, the audience quietly enjoys the incongruity of the situation. In a national cherry-pie baking contest he found himself, as state winner, competing against girls from 49 states. The presence of a lone male entrant presented the judges with a problem: each contestant, said the rules, must wear a simple white dress, white apron, white cap. After consultation, the judges allowed the contest to proceed with one entry wearing white slacks. This entry turned out to be one of the winners.

A Moslem student from India entertained a class of American students by talking about some observations made in this country. "At first I had a bitter prejudice against Christians," he said. This would seem incongruous to all who feel that true Christians should be beloved of everyone. He went on to say that he found their habits of eating and drinking objectionable, and many of their religious beliefs untenable. "But," he continued with a twinkle, "as I got to know a few Christians well, I decided they were a high-type, entirely moral lot."

Another ingredient of humor is *spontaneity*. The colorful phrase or the vivid detail that grows naturally out of the situation can be delightfully entertaining. The casual comment of the former sailor, "Since I didn't have much use for Marines then, I didn't believe him either when he said, 'The Japs are attacking us,'" illustrates spontaneous humor. Additional humor also grows out of the incongruity of this kind of remark in a narrative dealing with a national disaster.

Humor also takes the form of *overstatement* and *understatement*. The speaker narrating a day in the life of a student at a university that was building fifty million dollars' worth of new buildings employed overstatement as he told in heartily exaggerated fashion of the dangers of overhead cranes, unexpected tunnels, blocked streets, holes in the ground where parking lots formerly stood, and professors' lectures punctuated by riveting machines. Another student observed: "Five times in the last three weeks I have found myself in the second-floor shower of Knox Hall, covered with soap—when suddenly the water was turned off." Another speaker, narrating a simulated strafing attack, included the detail of a 300 pound sergeant hiding under a Volkswagen. *Understatement* appeared in the speech of a student who found himself with his fraternity brothers in a gang fight with another group; when the police suddenly appeared, the speaker said he decided to stroll home. *Stroll* is certainly an understatement for the word the audience might have expected: *ran, dashed, scurried, rushed.*

Unusually specific words add humor to a statement. Although much of the humor of the following incident grows out of the incongruity of seeing an advertising sign in the Holy Land, part lies in the specific language of the last sentence:

> On a trip to Old Jerusalem three years ago, I made my way to the Via Dolorosa as every Christian tourist must, and started up the narrow pathway, following the fourteen stations of the Cross. As I plodded along my head was bowed . . . and I was lost in contemplation of how things must have been in that very place, two millennia past. Suddenly on an impulse I looked up. There above me a huge banner was stretched between the buildings on either side of the busy lane. Its message brought me sharply back to modern times.
>
> "The Great Sioux Uprising," it said, "with Jeff Chandler."[4]

Every speaker needs to make his own collection of humorous material, and to learn from experience what sorts are best suited to his style.

When former Senator Kenneth B. Keating accepted the annual brotherhood award of the Chapel of the Four Chaplains, in Philadelphia, he related a short narrative:

> I have come up from Washington, a very social city. . . . Sometimes a chance whisper . . . becomes the policy statement you read next morning in the *New York Times,* so you have to keep your antennae ever on the alert.

---

[4] Harlan Cleveland, assistant secretary of state, delivered the speech at the Colgate Foreign Policy Conference, Hamilton, New York, July 3, 1958. From a copy of the speech furnished by Dr. Cleveland. Answering an inquiry, he wrote that he had made some 61 speeches in the preceding 10 months, most of them off the university campus. He was an undergraduate at Princeton University. Like many speakers today, he was active in debating; for two years he was vice-president of Princeton's political and debating society. The complete speech may be seen in *Vital Speeches,* XXIV (September, 1958), 686-690.

I recall, for instance, a White House reception last spring. Near the cluster of friends I was talking with was a distinguished group that included the Vice President, the Secretary of the Treasury, the Chairman of the Securities and Exchange Commission and the Budget Director, all with their charming wives. The entire group was listening intently to a man I had not met. I got enough snatches of his conversation, though, to realize that a high level financial discussion must be in progress. I strained my ears and I heard the stranger say, "This much I can tell you. It would be fatal, a national catastrophe, to raise it any higher. . . . So much is at stake, financially, and so many people are involved when we tinker with even a slight rise or drop. What I do foresee is a possibility that pressures will be such—all over the nation—that an eventual lowering—perhaps by the first of the year—is to be anticipated."

I turned to the lady next to me, who, I could tell by her expression, was also tuned in on the stranger's words and I said, "I wonder if you heard that. It looks like the interest rate is scheduled to go down."

"The interest rate," she said, and her eyes made me feel like a fourth grader. "Oh, my dear Senator, it's not the interest rate that Mr. Cassini is discussing. It's the hemline."

The Senator then turned to the main theme of his address—the total war "between a society that would maintain the freedom of man, and a sociey that would destroy that freedom."[5]

The narrative does not have to be funny; often its appeal grows out of its human interest or its suspense. In his talk, "How to Make a Hit With the Boss," Henry B. du Pont emphasizes an important point with this thoughtful narrative:

A man I know who is a successful manager once told me a story about one of his pet peeves. This, he said, is the employee who came in with the following question: "Where do you think I will be ten years from now?"

My friend's answer was this: "Don't ask *me* to tell you where you will be. Tell me where you *want* to be. If you've got the qualifications, I'll help you make the grade. If you haven't, I'll tell you what's wrong so you can try to do something about it. But don't

[5] Delivered on October 18, 1961. Text of the speech furnished this book by Senator Keating.

ask me to chart your future for you. It's your property and it's up to you to decide it for yourself."[6]

George Romney addresses many civic and business groups each year. He often uses a short narrative to illustrate a point, as he did in this speech to the Better Business Bureau in Atlanta, when he wanted to show that the Communists were determined to convince the world that they are more idealistic than we are:

When Khrushchev was here on his first visit, he talked at the National Press Club. . . . He did one of those deliberate things that he is very skillful at doing, as one of the world's great propagandists. He addressed the assembled Washington correspondents by saying: "Comrades." Then he stopped. "Oh," he said, "forgive me. You don't consider yourselves 'Comrades.' You consider yourselves 'Gentlemen.' I'll start over. Gentlemen."

This was very deliberate—to create the idea that the relationship in their society on a comrade basis is greater than ours on the basis of being gentlemen; where actually, our relationship is one of brotherhood.[7]

A student often wonders whether *he* or *she* can develop a sense of narrative; this desire may develop after hearing speeches in which talented students hold forth, or after a social gathering at which the life of the party is a good story-teller. Our wishful student then suddenly realizes that he (or she) doesn't know any stories: of those heard, all have been forgotten. This realization stresses the necessity of *writing down* and *compiling*. Then comes practice—many a story fails from a simple lack of fluency in handling details. The experienced speaker has had to work at it. Giving special attention to the use of narrative material, however, can result in improvement.

[6] From a commencement address given to graduates and friends of La Salle College June 8, 1955. Mr. du Pont, vice president of E. I. du Pont de Nemours and Company, wrote the author that he makes talks each year both to company and non-company groups. Outside groups include a divisional meeting of the Association of Land-Grant Colleges and Universities in Washington; an annual meeting of the Virginia State Chamber of Commerce in Richmond; the Instrument Society of America in Philadelphia; the Academic Deans of Southern States in Miami Beach; the Rotary Club at Louisville; and others. Talks to company groups "cover a variety of subjects ranging from remarks at safety awards, retirement dinners, and similar events, to talks of a more serious nature on company activities and problems."

These details are cited to illustrate the kind of speech making that many company executives find themselves engaged in. Mr. du Pont observed that he had "no formal training in public speaking or debating in school or college. I wish I had had such training. I believe public speaking and debating should be a required course in both Liberal Arts and Engineering education." (Letter of December 10, 1959.)

[7] Delivered September 6, 1961. Text of the speech furnished this book by Mr. Romney.

B. DIALOG

Interest in a narrative is heightened by the use of dialog. Instead of saying, "The pilot told us to bail out!" say, "I heard the order from the pilot, 'Pilot to crew! Pilot to crew! Prepare to bail out!'" A moment later this speaker described the descent:

I saw six other members of my crew floating in the dark sky. Over to my left I saw a large form that had to be our co-pilot, a man six feet three inches tall who weighed more than 200 pounds. As we hung there in the sky he yelled over to me, "Who are you?" I identified myself and he yelled back, "Let's stick together!"

The dialog helps the listeners to recreate the scene and relive it with the speaker.

Scientist Willy Ley used dialog to show how the space age began for him:

Let me tell you a little personal story of how this date [October 4, 1957] shaped up for me. On that evening I attended a small private dinner at the Harvard Club in New York, and around 10:30 the waiter came in and said, "Which of you gentlemen is Professor Ley?" I got up and he said, "You are wanted on the telephone." I went to the telephone . . . picked up the receiver and said, "Yes, dear?" (I could do this with impunity because only Mrs. Ley knew where I could be found that evening.) "You'd better brace yourself," my wife said, "The first Russian satellite is in orbit." After a moment of speechlessness on my part, I said, "But they are late." "Yes, I know," my wife answered, "but they are in orbit now."[8]

Here is an example of a use of the narrative method in which dialog is prominent:

Keep awake, then; for you do not know on what day your Lord is to come. . . . [On that day] the kingdom of Heaven will be like

---

[8] Delivered at the Summer Lecture Series of the Popular Science Workshop at the Rocky Mountain Writers' Conference, August 3, 1960. The speech appeared in *The Colorado Quarterly*, Winter, 1961, and is copyrighted by that publication. It is reprinted here through the courtesy of that publication and of Dr. Ley. It appears in *Representative American Speeches, 1960-1961*, pages 115-116.

Dr. Ley writes the author that he delivers an average of two dozen lectures every season, to college assemblies, city forums, and men's clubs. "As a speaker I am self-taught; as you know I grew up in Germany and German universities, at least in my time, did not have any such courses. . . . My 'speaking career' began with discussions in small circles, then presentations in small clubs" (letter of January 24, 1962).

this. There were ten girls, who took their lamps and went out to meet the bridegroom. Five of them were foolish, and five prudent; when the foolish ones took their lamps, they took no oil with them, but the others took flasks of oil with their lamps. As the bridegroom was late in coming they all dozed off to sleep. But at midnight a cry was heard: "Here is the bridegroom! Come to meet him." With that the girls all got up and trimmed their lamps. The foolish said to the prudent, "Our lamps are going out; give us some of your oil." "No," they said, "there will never be enough for us both. You had better go to the shop and buy some for yourselves." While they were away the bridegroom arrived; those who were ready went in with him to the wedding; and the door was shut. And then the other five came back. "Sir, sir," they cried, "open the door for us." But he answered, "I declare, I do not know you." Keep awake then; for you never know the day or the hour.[9]

C. DIALECT

On occasion the use of dialog gives the speaker a chance to use dialect, and thus gain additional interest and variety. Said Benjamin F. Fairless:

> You people in Detroit remind me a lot of the old Swedish prospector who went out to California and struck it very, very rich. Every time he disappeared into the hills he came up with a new vein of ore that was even bigger and better than the last one; and his envious companions were trying desperately to learn his secret. Finally, one day, he broke down and told them how he did it:
> "Boys," he said, "I yoost keep digging holes."

Mr. Fairless went on to tell his audience that that was also the secret of Detroit's success: the auto makers "yoost keep making cars!"[10]

The skillful use of dialect is highly entrancing to an audience; some speakers make it a point to develop a German dialect, a Swedish dialect, a Southern dialect, or some other—preferably one that they grew up with. A former New York alderman in his campaign talks

---

[9] Matthew 25: 1-13. The translation is that of *The New English Bible*, published in 1961 jointly by the Oxford and Cambridge university presses. The purpose of the distinguished committee which produced this translation of the New Testament was to render "the best available Greek text into the current speech of our own time" (p. vii).

[10] Benjamin F. Fairless gave this talk, "What Kind of America," September 21, 1953. The text is supplied by the speaker. The complete address may be found in A. Craig Baird, ed. *Representative American Speeches: 1953-1954*. The audience was The Economic Club of Detroit, and the speech is a provocative analysis of business conditions then confronting the Detroit industrial community. Mr. Fair-

told Polish stories in the Polish sector, Yiddish stories in the Jewish sector, and Spanish stories in the Puerto Rican sector—always to the delight of his constituents. Even a novice, with dialect, can gain effectiveness by *suggesting* a dialect. He does not need to *imitate* it. "Yoost" for *just* would suffice in the story just related, even if the speaker knew no other characteristics of Swedish dialect. And don't overlook this speaker's skill in making his point: success consists largely in yoost keeping on the job.

Former governor Arthur M. Hyde was aware of his rural American dialect and was frank to admit his small-town, Missouri background:

> I once heard the governor of one of our western States introduced to an audience by an enthusiastic friend who regretted that, since the governor had been born in the old country, he was not eligible to the Presidency. The governor said, "I vas glad dot der Chairman told you dot I vas in der old country born, oderwise you might not have known it."[11]

D. NAMES

If the narrative is short, "old Swedish prospector" is identification enough. If the narrative is longer, identify your characters by name. Otherwise you will hear yourself awkwardly saying "this first girl" and "the second girl." The usual names like *John* and *Mary* are not so colorful as others you can select; and identifications like *Mr. X* and *Mr. Y* are sometimes improvable. For suggestions, search the telephone directory.

E. THE NOVEL

An unusual detail heightens interest. The president of the New York Stock Exchange, discussing the difficulty Americans have in understanding the problems of the new, young nations, included this comment:

> In another country I visited, women sometimes wear high-heeled shoes around their necks as they walk barefooted to market. Such

less, long chairman of the Board of U. S. Steel, later special adviser to the Board, had an active career as a speaker in connection with his distinguished career in business. He wrote the author that he made about eight formal talks a year, and numerous informal talks. In business and industrial circles he was known as a defender of business and free enterprise.

To study the characteristics of commonly-spoken dialects, consult Claude M. Wise, *Applied Phonetics* (Englewood Cliffs, N. J., Prentice-Hall, Inc., 1957). Other books about dialect may be available in your library.

11 From a manuscript in the Hyde papers, Trenton, Mo. Quoted by Robert P. Friedman, *The Public Speaking of Arthur M. Hyde* (University of Missouri Ph.D. dissertation, 1954), p. 406.

shoes are "status symbols." And even though they aren't a bit practical, a woman carries them just to show that she is one of the elite.

He then resumed the more serious thread of his discussion: that in some parts of the world the facts of life are harsh indeed, and the people have a critical need for better educational and vocational opportunity.[12]

The student who described the plans being formulated to save the statues and temples that now border the Nile from being flooded when the High Dam at Aswan is completed chose a novel subject for his talk. One of the more spectacular proposals, he explained, is to lift the four 67-foot-high statues of Ramses II, through the wizardry of modern engineering, 195 feet above their present site; a feat roughly equivalent to the elevating of a big section of a stadium to a level 20 stories higher.

F. OTHER DETAILS

The Pearl Harbor speech started with a ride in a 1936 Ford. This specific name makes plausible the later detail, "climbed on my running boards." The details that follow give a clear picture of the Pearl Harbor morning as seen by one of the defenders:

I went down to the water's edge, near the Officers' Club, between Battleship Row and the Liberty Landing. I saw a fighter plane, with the Rising Sun insignia, flying in a parallel course with the liberty boats that were taking sailors to church or to a baseball game. As the plane neared the boat it strafed it, causing the men to jump into the water. Then a machine gun from a submarine, tied up at the submarine base, opened fire on the plane and it turned into a ball of fire and plunged into the water.

I then looked down the channel where the preceding wave of planes had gone just in time to see the *Arizona* blow up and the *Oklahoma* turn over. It happened so close together that I thought it was one ship, but found out the next day what actually had happened. I decided it was time to go down to my ship and see what I could do.

A speaker needs to choose between details that will make the narrative more vivid to the listener, and details that slow up the story.

12 "Sharing the American Dream," an address by G. Keith Funston to the Trinity College Alumni Association of Western Connecticut, April 14, 1961. Text furnished by the speaker.

Your listeners will be eager to follow your story if you keep it clear, *and* if you keep it moving. Obviously this speaker did not want to spend time on the sailors who had to jump out of the boat to save their lives. But if *he* had been one of the sailors, he would have had an exciting story to tell about *his* friends frantically swimming about, the *Arizona* blowing up and the *Oklahoma* turning over in *their* background. The main part of our speaker's story is what *he* did on *his* ship.

Questions for Classroom Discussion

1. Comment: "A speech is more than a string of stories."
2. Discuss: In what situations is a narrative speech appropriate?
3. What suggestions can you give about the use of humor?
4. Formulate simple rules to help a speaker build suspense.
5. What talents of the actor are helpful to a speaker who plans to give a narrative speech? How can a speaker without any special dramatic ability nevertheless improve his skill in the use of the narrative method?

Speech-Related Project

Survey recent issues of *Vital Speeches,* the *Congressional Record, The Listener, Congressional Digest, U. S. News and World Report,* the *New York Times,* or current volumes of *Representative American Speeches,* and decide for yourself what use speakers make of examples, illustration, anecdote, dialog, complication, climax, specific details, and other narrative techniques.

Speaking Assignment 7

A Narrative Speech

Make a narrative speech of . . . minutes (your instructor will suggest time limit).

Review your experiences or adventures, and select one that you think your audience will enjoy. Choose a point of view, and follow it consistently; let your narrative unfold as it actually happened, in order to generate suspense; remember that conflict and complications heighten interest. Added vividness may usually be gained through dialog, selection of concrete details, use of specific places and names.

Practice your speech so you will not exceed the time limit. In rehearsal try to imagine that you are conversing with actual listeners. If you go overtime, cut out less essential details and practice further. Opening sentences are important, so select these words with care. Concluding sentences are also important; perhaps your narrative will suggest an application, warning, or interpretation.

REFERENCES ON THE NARRATIVE SPEECH

Waldo W. Braden and Mary Louise Gehring, first part of Chapter 5, "The Speaker Supports His Proposition," pages 70-75, in *Speech Practices* (New York, Harper and Brothers, 1958).

Wilbur E. Gilman, Bower Aly and Loren Reid, Chapter 13, "Entertaining," in *The Fundamentals of Speaking* (New York, The Macmillan Company, 1951). Understatement, overstatement, irony, ridicule, raillery, the striking, the unusual, dialogue, timing.

Alan H. Monroe, Chapter 19, "The Speech to Entertain," in *Principles and Types of Speech,* 4th ed. (Chicago, Scott, Foresman and Company, 1955). Exaggeration, puns, poking fun at authority, irony, burlesque, unexpected turns, peculiar traits of people; with examples.

Paul L. Soper, Chapter 6, section on "Examples," pages 94-103, in *Basic Public Speaking* (New York, Oxford University Press, 1956). Instance and extended illustration; factual, fictional, humorous examples; rules for the use of examples.

CHAPTER 10

Development By Expository Methods

A description of exposition and a few of the methods it employs: ▪ *classification and division, time order, space order, comparison and contrast, definition, analysis, example.*

SPEAKERS USE THE EXPOSITORY METHOD when their purpose is to *explain* or *inform*. Through exposition a speaker *simplifies* what is complex, *makes clear* what is obscure. When you tell how the Peace Corps is organized or how the point-system of licensing drivers operates, when you demonstrate a method of self-defense or a Geiger counter, when you explain the duties of a highway commission or the theory of people's capitalism, you are using principles of exposition.

In making an expository speech, convey to your listeners *significant* information. The student who explained the operation of a pencil sharpener had nothing to communicate that was vital or all-absorbing. His listeners knew in advance everything he could possibly say. You do not need to go to the other extreme and select a topic of formidable complexity, but you should choose one that will command your interest and that of the class.

The expository method may also be employed when the speaker's purpose is to *persuade*. Thus he can tell how the Peace Corps is organized simply to give information about it, or in order to persuade listeners to join it; in the latter instance he may follow the information with an appeal to join. Again, he may explain the duties of the highway commission to inform listeners about an important state agency, or to persuade them to increase appropriations for it.

I. Kinds of Exposition

To distinguish the concept of *exposition* from the concept of *narration*, recall that narration grows out of such principles as *suspense, humor, dialog, complication, climax*. The concept of *exposition* is explained through different principles; among them are *classification and division, time order, space order, comparison and contrast, definition, analysis, example.* Let the word *inform* suggest that to make an idea *clear,* you should put it IN A FORM; reveal its shape, dimension, "form"; study it until you arrive at a "form" or plan of arrangement that best sets it forth.

A. CLASSIFICATION AND DIVISION

Classification and division are closely-related methods of explaining. A speaker employs *classification* as an informatory device when he arranges his materials in groups or classes: *kinds* of sports, *types* of blood, *classes* of insurance salesmen. An object is said to be *divided* when it is analyzed into its parts: philosophy may be separated into *ethics, logic, aesthetics, epistemology;* an automobile may be regarded as consisting of *chassis* and *body.* A speaker employs *division* as an informatory plan when he breaks his subject into units or individuals.

Certain rules govern the use of either classification or division.

Rule One is that *the same principle of classifying or dividing be used throughout.* Consider the following classification:

> Principal vocational groups in this community
>> Retired farmers
>> Employees of Cooperative Mutual Insurance Company
>> Employees of American Can Company
>> Methodists
>> Catholics

Here the basis of classification is confused. At first the speaker decided to list community groups according to vocational status: hence "retired farmers," "employees of Cooperative Mutual." Then he decided, "Methodists and Catholics are influential groups in this community," thus suddenly abandoning his listing according to vocation and substituting a classification according to religion. "Methodists" is a long way from "retired farmers"; one is an organized, religious denomination and the other a loose-knit vocational group. Moreover, many individuals belong under both of these headings. The speaker should make a choice: list groups according to a principle of classification by vocation, OR religion, OR some other principle.

Consider this list:

> Automobile design
>> the body
>> the chassis
>> the driver

Here the basis of division is confused. The last item belongs with a list in which the supporting ideas are divided according to a different principle. The following is better:

Automobile design
    designer
    engineer
    cost accountant
    dealer
    mechanic
    driver

The principle of division is: *people who influence automobile design.*

Rule Two is that *groups should be mutually exclusive.* The foregoing list would be faulty if it read:

Automobile design
    designer
    engineer
    factory personnel
    dealer
    mechanic
    driver

The term *factory personnel* overlaps *designer* and *engineer.*

Rule Three is that *the classification or division should be complete.* As the speaker prepares his speech, he needs to assure himself that his plan is logically defensible. He need not, however—and this principle is of the *highest importance—discuss the entire scheme.* He does not even have to *reveal the entire scheme* in his prepared speech —though he should have it in mind in the event that after the speech questions are directed to him about it.

Limiting a subject is an excellent procedure. A speaker may say:

"As you realize, a good automobile designer must take into consideration not only his own artistic preferences; he must also consider the requirements of the factory engineers and cost accountants, of the dealer and service mechanics, and of the ultimate purchaser, the driver. I would like to explain how driver preferences influence automobile design."

Dr. Louis H. Evans offered this division in a sermon:

There are two kinds of "death." There is that physical death that takes place when the soul is separated from the body. That none of us can escape. Then there is that spiritual death that takes place when the soul is separated from God by unforgiven sin. He who can remove that sin and bring God and man together again can restore life.[1]

B. TIME ORDER

Certain processes, methods, procedures, or historical movements can best be explained in chronological sequence. *Time order* thus becomes the basis of the exposition.

The student who explained the mouth-to-mouth system of artificial respiration used *time order* in her development. First she explained the preliminary steps: getting the body out of the water and getting it in the proper position, with mouth open, tongue and jaw forward. Second, she explained the mouth-to-mouth breathing process. Third, she explained how to care for the patient once he started breathing again. Time order is also a logical plan for discussing topics like "How to Fight Forest Fires," "How to Sell Encyclopedias," "The Origin of the Democratic Party," "Using the New Voting Machines," "How to Turn a Prospect Into a Customer."

In a talk, "Massacre at Sharpville," an air policeman began by relating an incident in which a mob got out of control and a massacre resulted. This opening led to his exposition on methods of riot prevention. The speech may be briefly outlined thus:

MASSACRE AT SHARPVILLE

Introduction

The frightful massacre in the African village of Sharpville shows what happens when police are poorly trained in techniques of handling a mob.

Central Idea

My talk today is to suggest the steps in preventing a riot, a procedure with which members of the Air Police are familiar as a part of their training.

---

[1] *Ibid., 1953-1954,* 181. Delivered at an Easter sunrise service, Hollywood Bowl, California, April 5, 1953.

Dr. Evans, minister-at-large for the Board of National Missions of the United Presbyterian Church, former all-conference and all-state end in football (Occidental College) was once chosen by *Life* as one of the twelve outstanding religious leaders of America. Of his speaking, his secretary, Anna Laurie Paulus, wrote: "He does not prepare a manuscript of his addresses, but speaks extemporaneously from brief notes of single words or short phrases. . . . In a typical year he will visit as many as 20-25 states, fulfill an average of 60 engagements, averaging two addresses per day." (Letter of November 18, 1959).

Body

I. The police should, by loud speakers or otherwise, call upon the mob to disperse.
II. The police should, by massing or by mounting heavy weapons, make a show of force.
III. The police should, if necessary, use smoke bombs to fog up the situation.
IV. Only when absolutely necessary should the police employ its full fire power.

Conclusion

If the police at Sharpville had followed the first three steps, the mob would very likely have dispersed, and the massacre would have been averted.

C. SPACE ORDER

The central idea can be developed by areas or regions: east side, north side, west side, south side; inside the city, outside the city; the approach to the State Capitol, the Capitol itself; or as in the following partly-outlined plan for a talk on "An Ideal Classroom Building":

Central Idea

Here is my blueprint for an ideal classroom building.

Body

I. The ground floor should contain special facilities for recreation.
II. Well-equipped classrooms should be located on the first and second floors.
III. Open-shelf reading rooms should be located on the third floor.

On a lecture tour, Adlai E. Stevenson discussed his trip to Africa, explaining the political situation in various African countries. He discussed them country by country: Union of South Africa, Rhodesia, the Belgian Congo, and Liberia. As he spoke, he unfolded the space-order plan of his address; starting with the southern tip of Africa, he proceeded up the center and continued toward the West. He had previously explained that he would not discuss the countries on the northern coast.

D. COMPARISON AND CONTRAST

Abraham Lincoln explained his position on slavery by using the principle of comparison in a famous speech delivered to a New England audience:

If I saw a venomous snake crawling in the road, any man would say I might seize the nearest stick and kill it; but if I found that snake in bed with my children, that would be still another question. [Laughter.] I might hurt the children more than the snake, and it might bite them. [Applause.] Much more, if I found it in bed with my neighbor's children, and I had bound myself by a solemn compact not to meddle with his children under any circumstances, it would become me to let that particular mode of getting rid of the gentleman alone. [Greater laughter.] But if there was a bed newly made up, to which the children were to be taken, and it was proposed to take a batch of young snakes and put them there with them, I take it no man would say there was any question how I ought to decide. [Prolonged applause and cheers.]

That is just the case. The new Territories are the newly made bed to which our children are to go, and it lies with the nation to say whether they shall have snakes mixed up with them or not.[2]

Often a difficult topic can be made more clear by comparing or contrasting it with something familiar. The British or German system of education can be compared and contrasted with the American system. Marriage or funeral customs of one race are made understandable by comparison with familiar customs. Sometimes the comparison is *figurative,* as in the Lincoln example above, or as when Roosevelt compared aggression with disease, and declared that we should *quarantine* the aggressor nations. At other times the comparison is *literal,* like comparing two systems of education, two methods of taxation, two literary or nationalistic movements.

When Paul G. Hoffman wanted to explain the phenomenal growth of education in this country, he compared figures for 1900 and 1950. He said:

Particularly during the past fifty years there has been a spectacular growth of intellectual opportunities for the individual. At the end of the last century only 7 per cent of all children in the United States of high school age were still in school. By 1950 this figure had increased to 80 per cent. In 1900 we had 7200 college and university professors. Today we have more than ten times that number—more than 72,000. Since the turn of the century the number of our college graduates has increased six times as fast as the population.

[2] Speech at New Haven, Conn., March 6, 1860. From Roy P. Basler, ed. *The Collected Works of Abraham Lincoln,* IV (New Brunswick, Rutgers University Press, 1953), 18.

Later in the speech he declared:

A totalitarian society differs sharply from a free society in almost every particular. I shall mention only two.[3]

This idea he developed by contrast, singling out two sharp differences.

Roger M. Blough, speaking on "Compete or Die" at the annual meeting of the Cleveland Chamber of Commerce, subtitled his address, "A Talk of Two Towns." He began by describing the similarities between Cleveland, Ohio, and Dusseldorf, Germany: both of them rapidly-growing industrial centers in which the major industry is steelmaking. Because, however, the weekly wage of a Cleveland steelworker is more than three times that of a Dusseldorf steelworker, the cost of producing steel products there is substantially lower than it is here. The speaker said:

Now, what does all this mean to you in Cleveland? What does Dusseldorf mean to you?

Well, let me give you just one example which concerns a spool of barbed wire. . . . It was manufactured by our American Steel & Wire Division, and it was delivered to a jobber whose warehouse is right here in Cleveland.

But in the jobber's warehouse it was placed alongside another spool of barbed wire that had been manufactured in Dusseldorf. That German wire was of exactly the same type, and it had come from a mill many thousands of miles away. It had been shipped from Dusseldorf to the sea, and across the ocean to New York. It had been freighted to Cleveland by rail, and hauled from the freight-yards to the warehouse by truck. Yet, delivered to that warehouse, it still cost the jobber $40 a ton *less* than the spool of wire we sold right here in Cleveland.[4]

E. DEFINITION

Exposition by definition consists of telling what the subject of the speech *is*. This method would seem applicable in speeches like

[3] *Representative American Speeches, 1951-1952*, 79, 81. Says the editor of this volume, Professor A. Craig Baird, in his preface: "Hoffman delivered the speech with energy and with challenging tones. . . . [He] is a lively and rapid speaker, with clear articulation and excellent radio voice" (p. 77).

[4] Delivered April 17, 1958. Text supplied through the courtesy of Phelps H. Adams of the United States Steel Corporation.

This address, which appeared in *Vital Speeches*, XXIV (July 15, 1958), is an interesting exposition of the problem of growing competition from overseas. Roger M. Blough, chairman of the board of U. S. Steel (his last name rhymes with "now"), is, as a lawyer, "accustomed to speaking before groups, and does so either extemporaneously, or from text, as the situation requires." (Letter from Mr. Adams.) Blough, described as "a strong voice for U. S. business," is featured in a cover story in *Newsweek*, LIX (January 22, 1962), 69-74.

"What is a Liberal," "What is a Conservative," "What is an Intellectual," "Are You a Conformist."

Burglary is defined as being characterized by (1) breaking and entering (2) a dwelling (3) in the night time (4) with intent to commit a felony. One who wishes to make a speech on this subject could discuss these four parts, showing how the courts had interpreted what is meant by each item. The same formality of definition is shown in the following:

> Our real problem now, as it has always been, in medicine, in law, in the natural and social sciences, as well as in engineering, is to produce an adequate supply of high quality people and utilize them properly.
>
> By "adequate supply," I do not mean the largest number of engineers we can create quickly, but a variable number determined by . . . the ever-changing needs of our economy and of society.
>
> By "proper utilization," I do not mean the use of engineers in positions which require routine skills, . . . but in positions which demand the highest level of thought, ability, and performance, of which the engineer is capable.[5]

The president of the New York Stock Exchange defined, largely by illustrative detail, what he termed *people's capitalism:*

> It is the growth of a new kind of capitalism—a People's Capitalism. In it, men and women from every walk of life have begun to invest directly in the ownership of our great businesses. Today, more than 8.5 million people—two thirds of them with incomes under $7,500 a year—are the owners of our publicly-held companies. This is a 33 per cent jump over 1952. And if owners of private corporations are added, the stockholder family would swell to over 10 million.[6]

---

[5] Speech by Henry T. Heald at the annual dinner of the Engineers Joint Council, January, 1957. *Representative American Speeches, 1956-1957,* 175.

A copy of the original text of this speech was supplied by Dr. Heald, formerly president of the Illinois Institute of Technology and chancellor of New York University, now president of the Ford Foundation. Dr. Heald wrote: "At the present time I make about 15 formal speeches a year. When I was a college and university head, I made many more." He added this sentence: "The demands of the posts I have held would seem to govern the number of speeches I make rather than any desire of my own to make a speech." (Letter of January 13, 1960.) Most men in business and professional life report that this is so; as they accept posts of increasing responsibility, they find themselves required to make increasing numbers of formal and informal speeches.

[6] From "Memo to the Class of '57: Our Economic World—and You," by G. Keith Funston. Occasion: University of Maryland commencement exercises, College Park, Maryland, 1957.

Dr. Funston, formerly president of Trinity College, dates his speaking ex-

In a talk to the Toledo Chamber of Commerce on the topic, "What Should We do About Margins?" he explained that margin buying gave *liquidity* to the stock market. He defined and illustrated:

Liquidity is a word, I must confess, that is easier to illustrate than to define. And the most dramatic illustration I can think of is the impressive performance of the New York Stock Exchange in 1959 . . . [when] 820 million shares of stock changed hands on the floor. Each and every transaction had to find its own bid and offer. What was the result? Seventy-two per cent of all trades were made either at no change in price from the last sale, or within . . . 12½c from the last price!

That degree of price continuity which is a clear mirror of liquidity is something we are prone to take for granted. But think for a moment what the market would be like *without* this liquidity. Prices might fluctuate wildly from sale to sale. Consider how this would affect *the hundreds* of companies planning to issue new shares . . . or *the millions* of Americans—now one out of every eight adults—who invest part of their savings in stocks.[7]

Defining real Americanism, former president Harry S. Truman said:

Real Americanism means that we will protect freedom of speech. . . .

Real Americanism means freedom of religion. It means that we will not discriminate against a man because of his religious faith. . . .

Real Americanism means fair play. It means that a man who is accused of a crime shall be considered innocent until he has been proved guilty. . . .

perience back to a third-year English course in Washington High School, Sioux Falls, South Dakota. The school's debate coach heard him making a talk in class, and asked him to join the debating team. Wrote Dr. Funston: "As I recall it, the interscholastic debating competition was pretty strenuous but our team won all except one of the debates during my two years on the team. That's the only chance I ever had for any formal training in speaking since Trinity College had no public speaking course or active debating society. When I became president there in 1945, however, one of the first activities I stimulated was debating. It has since become a very successful undergraduate activity.

"I give a half dozen to ten major speeches each year before a variety of audiences. Most are based on extensive research by the Exchange staff so that I usually have some new material in an effort to make each one different and interesting. In addition, I make perhaps twenty or thirty informal talks to smaller groups. These are usually extemporaneous about the Exchange and its work." (Letter of November 18, 1959).

7 Dr. Funston continued his illustration by showing the relation between margins and liquidity ("when margins are raised sharply, volume tends to fall off—that is, liquidity is lessened"). The speech was delivered on January 10, 1961. Text furnished this book by the speaker.

Real Americanism means also that liberty is not license. There is no freedom to injure others. The Constitution does not protect free speech to the extent of permitting conspiracies to overthrow the Government. Neither does the right of free speech authorize slander or character assassination. . . .[8]

F. ANALYSIS

Complex ideas may be explained by subjecting them to an analysis that reveals different aspects of the idea. Abraham Lincoln was often called upon to explain his position on the Union and on the institution of slavery. Many thought he could not at the same time be *for* the Union and *against* slavery. He therefore found it necessary to explain *what* he was for and *what* he was against, and at the same time to distinguish between his official duty and his personal belief. Here is his analysis:

My paramount object in this struggle *is* to save the Union, and it is *not* either to save or to destroy slavery.

If I could save the Union without freeing *any* slave, I would do it, and if I could save it by freeing *all* the slaves, I would do it; and if I could save it by freeing some and leaving others alone I would also do that.

What I do about slavery, and the colored race, I do because I believe it helps to save the Union; and what I forbear, I forbear because I do *not* believe it would help to save the Union.

I shall do *less* whenever I shall believe that what I am doing hurts the cause, and I shall do *more* whenever I shall believe doing more will help the cause.

I shall try to correct errors when shown to be errors; and I shall adopt new views as fast as they shall appear to be true views.

I have here stated my purpose according to my view of *official*

[8] Address in Washington, D. C., to the American Legion, August, 1951. *Representative American Speeches, 1951-1952*, 68.

Former president Harry S. Truman invariably gives a stimulating and often provocative speech. He has frequently spoken on the campus of the university of his native state, always in an auditorium packed with students, faculty, and townspeople. His interest in students has been shown by visits to many campuses. The most comprehensive study of his speech making is that of Edward A. Rogge, *The Speechmaking of Harry S. Truman* (Ph.D. dissertation, University of Missouri, 1958). And see also: Eugene E. White and Clair Henderlider, "What Harry S. Truman Told Us About His Speaking," *Quarterly Journal of Speech*, XL (February, 1954), 37-42.

duty; and I intend no modification of my oft-expressed *personal* wish that all men every where could be free.[9]

What Lincoln has done here is to state clearly not only what he would do but what he would not do; and to restate the basic issue, with variations, about six different times.

In your speeches you may take a difficult concept and put it in your own words; you may explain not only what it is, but what it is not; you may point out situations when your concept is applicable, and when it is not; and you may restate your concept from different points of view. If you wanted to explain *fluoridation, euthanasia, business ethics, segregation* or *resegregation, the right to strike, libel, oil depletion allowances, most-favored-nation, immigration quotas,* or any other complex, easily-misunderstood, social, political, or economic problem, you could employ methods of analysis to make the concept understandable.

G. EXAMPLES

Exposition may use *examples* in order to make an idea clear. An example may answer the question, "What is this?" and thus serve as a form of definition. Or it may answer, "How does this work?" and thus support some form of analysis.

In 1957 Ben W. Heineman, chairman of the board of the Chicago & North Western Railway Company, delivered an address, "Railroads: A Revolution in the Making," at the annual meeting of the Illinois State Chamber of Commerce. The speech was printed by *U. S. News and World Report* and later by the *Reader's Digest.* The central idea of the speech may be found in these paragraphs:

Just what is the matter with the railroads?

The answer, I believe, is relatively simple.

The railroads as an industry set an example of sheer economic waste that is, in my opinion, without parallel in the economic history of our country. . . .

[9] These thoughts were expressed in a letter to Horace Greeley, August 22, 1862. Paragraphing has been altered, but the italics are Lincoln's, and reinforce his desire to be clear. *Collected Works of Abraham Lincoln,* V, 388-389.

As to his consummate ability as a speaker, Lincoln is said to have delivered the greatest five-minute speech ever made, the Gettysburg address; the greatest twenty-minute speech, the Second Inaugural; and the greatest hour lecture, the Cooper Union address.

This central idea was developed largely by examples:

> Now let me give you some specific examples of what I mean by waste. We run fast passenger trains to Minneapolis, a distance of just over 400 miles. We run them with six-man crews—two men in the engine crew, and four in the train crew. We run the distance in approximately seven hours. In that seven hours, we use three engine crews, and each time we change engine crews we pay that crew approximately a full day's pay, and, in the case of one crew, two days' pay. . . . Put somewhat differently, we are paying the equivalent of four days' pay to our engine crews for seven hours' work.

Later in the speech Mr. Heineman made this observation, always helpful to make when dealing with *examples* as speech materials:

> These are examples only. They are not exceptional; they are typical.[10]

II. Presenting the Expository Speech

Although the expository speech is factual, the presentation need not be matter of fact.

Information can be of the highest importance, Some one's life may depend upon it. It may guide an individual, shape a career. It may save time or money. It may open up an intellectual adventure, a new line of thought. It may touch on community welfare or national security. It may add to enjoyment, improve leisure time.

If the assignment in class, or the speaking situation in later life, calls for an expository speech, make your purpose clearly to inform— not to persuade. Even so, if you feel your information is important and worth while, let your voice, your facial expression, your choice of words, reflect that feeling. "Note this step especially" . . . "This discovery was the key to the whole situation" . . . "This is of the highest importance" . . . "I want to underline the idea that . . ." and so on are typical of the kind of comment reflecting the speaker's conviction that what he is explaining is meaningful, valid, authoritative, dependable, *worth remembering.*

[10] *See U. S. News and World Report,* XLIII, 25 (December 20, 1957), 95-96; *Reader's Digest,* LXXII (March, 1958), 32-34. The text for this book was supplied by Mr. Heineman, who wrote that his interest in speaking came mostly "from twenty years of advocacy in the trial courts, before administrative agencies, and in appellate and other courts." (Letter of March 17, 1958.)

III. A Sample Expository Outline

A sample outline follows:

TWO EUROPEAN TRADE GROUPS

Introduction

I. European nations are grouped into two competitive economic units.

    A. The European Economic Community is generally known as the Common Market, or the Inner Six.

    B. The European Free Trade Association is generally known as the Outer Seven.

Central Idea

My purpose is to explain the organization and the functioning of these two economic groups.

Body

I. The two groups have certain similarities in organization.

    A. Both groups were created by mutual agreement.

        1. The Common Market was founded in 1957 by the Treaty of Rome.

        2. The Outer Seven was founded in 1959 by the Treaty of Stockholm.

    B. Together the two groups include most of Free Europe.

        1. The Common Market consists of 168 million people from Belgium, France, Italy, Luxembourg, Netherlands, West Germany.[11]

        2. The Outer Seven consists of 90 million people from Austria, Denmark, Great Britain, Norway, Portugal, Sweden, Switzerland.

    C. The two groups have extensive European and non-European trade.

        1. The Common Market transacts about 44% of its imports with European markets, 56% with the outside world. (*Fortune,* Oct. 1959, p. 148.)

        2. The Outer Seven transacts about 46% of its imports with European markets, 54% with the outside world. (*Ibid.,* p. 149.)

---

[11] Although these countries constituted the original membership of the Common Market, other countries are in process of applying for admission.

   II. The two groups differ in their functioning.

      A. The Common Market maintains a common tariff wall against outsiders.

         1. Example: France assesses a 31% duty against electric motors manufactured either by Outer Seven nations or by the United States.

      B. The Outer Seven is free to negotiate tariffs independently.

         1. Example: Britain could reduce tariffs toward Norway, assess a higher rate against Germany, and a still higher rate against the United States.

Conclusion

   I. American business men are following these developments closely in order to meet foreign competition.

  II. Americans generally will feel the influence of these agreements.

      A. Wages, prices, and employment may be affected in this country.

      B. Our European friends will become stronger politically as they work out solutions of their domestic differences.

This sample expository outline is printed to illustrate matters of form (I, A, 1, etc.; margins; use of complete sentences; the four parts of the speech).

The conclusion suggests an attempt on the part of the speaker to relate his materials to his listeners.

The outline could be developed in further detail by the use of additional examples. The speaker could compare and contrast the previous confusion of tariff schedules with the present, more orderly, arrangement. He could mention particular situations growing out of manufactured goods and commodities like beef, butter, watches, jet planes, small cars, and the like. He could use a map to show the geographical relationships of the two groups.

Note also that this subject suggests other possibilities for speeches about the European Coal and Steel Community, Euratom (nuclear agreements), and various attempts to unite politically the European nations. Most of all, since the Common Market may absorb part or all of the nations now in the Outer Seven, since other common-market areas may be established (e.g. Southeastern Asia, Latin America), since tariffs and schedules are continually changing, and since U. S. trade agreements will react in one way or another to the intensified competition that will result, students may want to discuss various topics growing out of the free-trade-vs.-tariffs issue.

Above: United Press International (both photos)

Below: Fay Foto Service; American Motors Corporation

POSITIONS OF RESPONSIBILITY CALL FOR SPEECHES

Above are Roger M. Blough and Richard M. Nixon; *below* are John F. Kennedy and George Romney. Men and women in responsible positions in business, industry, and the professions find themselves addressing a wide variety of audiences. The photos above show four speakers, each in his own way actively communicating with his listeners.

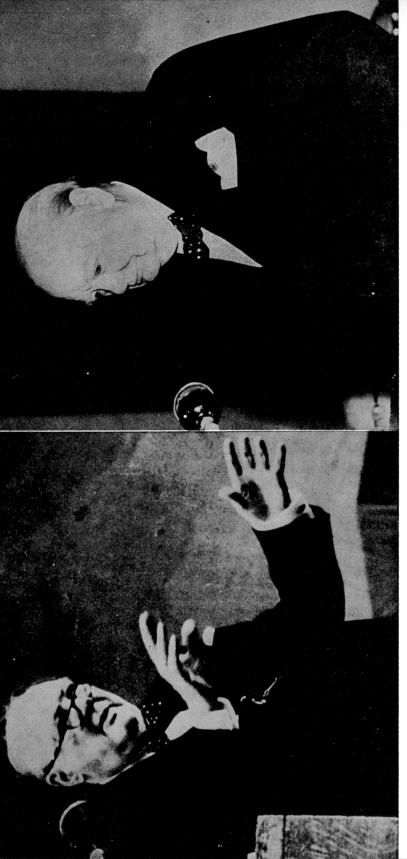

SIR WINSTON CHURCHILL

"I have nothing to offer but blood, toil, tears, and sweat." . . . "We shall not flag or fail. We shall go on to the end. . . . We shall de-fend our island whatever the cost may be; we shall fight on beaches, landing grounds, in streets and in the hills." . . "Never in the field of human conflict was so much owed by so many to so few". . . "From Stettin in the Baltic to Trieste in the Adriatic an iron curtain has descended across the continent."

Questions for Classroom Discussion

1. Sometimes we can not *inform* our listeners because:
   a. We can not catch the interest of the listener.
   b. The listener does not think he *needs* the information.
   c. The listener feels that the speaker does not *understand* what he is trying to explain.
   d. The speaker uses unfamiliar or technical words.
   e. The speaker has no plan: he backtracks, omits essential details, rambles or repeats unnecessarily.

Discuss each of these, showing how the speaker can make the right sort of preparation to avoid each fault.

2. General Electric installed a communications program and reported results for the years 1946-1951. Average weekly dollar output per employee more than doubled; labor required per unit was cut in half; waste was reduced two-thirds; spoilage was reduced two-thirds; absenteeism fell from nearly 10 per cent to slightly more than 2 per cent. Explain how such a program (conference, discussion, clear exposition, freedom to offer suggestions) could account for this result. See the charts in David C. Phillips, *Oral Communication in Business* (New York, McGraw-Hill Book Company, Inc., 1955), 4-5.

Speaking Assignment 8

A Speech to Inform

Make a speech of . . . . minutes, the purpose of which is *to inform*. Your intent will therefore be to make an idea, concept, principle, or method *clear;* you are not trying to persuade us, or sell us, but you do wish to have us *understand*.

See the lists of topics on pages 45-47, 68. For further lists, see the references at the end of Chapter 4.

Choose a topic about which you have first-hand information. You may not need to go beyond your own experience; or you may find it advisable to do observing, interviewing, or reading to secure needed details.

1. You may explain a process, a procedure, a method, a device, a technique, an art, a craft, a skill, a game, a sport.

2. You may explain a theory, a principle, an invention, a discovery.

3. You may explain a historical, economic, social, literary, or artistic movement, period, custom.

4. You may interpret a personality, a group, an organization. (Avoid a purely *descriptive* character sketch; *explain* the greatness or the significance of this person or group.)

Limit your subject; you will probably not be able to tell everything you know.

One of the suggested plans may help you select, arrange, and order your materials. Consider the possibilities of time order, space order, comparison and contrast, definition, analysis, example.

Hand in an outline in the form required by the instructor.

REFERENCES ON THE EXPOSITORY METHOD

A. Craig Baird and Franklin H. Knower, Chapter 15, "Informative Speaking," in *General Speech,* 2nd ed. (New York, McGraw-Hill Book Company, Inc., 1957).

W. Norwood Brigance, Chapter 13, "Supporting the Ideas," in *Speech: Its Techniques and Disciplines in a Free Society,* 2nd ed. (New York, Appleton-Century-Crofts, Inc., 1960).

Donald C. Bryant and Karl R. Wallace, Chapter 7, "Amplification in Informative Speaking," in *Fundamentals of Public Speaking,* 3d ed. (New York, Appleton-Century-Crofts, Inc., 1960).

Milton Dickens, Chapter 17, "Presenting Information," in *Speech: Dynamic Communication* (New York, Harcourt, Brace and Company, Inc., 1954).

John E. Dietrich and Keith Brooks, Chapter 7, "Make Your Information Clear," and Chapter 8, "Make Your Information Interesting," in *Practical Speaking for the Technical Man* (Englewood Cliffs, N. J., Prentice-Hall, Inc., 1958).

Giles Wilkeson Gray and Waldo W. Braden, Chapter 8, "The Informative Speech," in *Public Speaking: Principles and Practice* (New York, Harper and Brothers, 1951).

James H. McBurney and Ernest J. Wrage, Chapter 15, "Inquiry," and Chapter 16, "Reporting," in *Guide to Good Speech* (Englewood Cliffs, N. J., Prentice-Hall, Inc., 1955). For a fuller treatment, see the corresponding chapters in their longer work, *The Art of Good Speech* (New York, Prentice-Hall, Inc., 1953).

Alan H. Monroe, Chapter 6, "How to Develop Talks to Inform or Instruct," in *Principles of Speech,* 4th ed. (Chicago, Scott, Foresman and Company, 1958).

W. P. Sandford and W. Hayes Yeager, Chapter 9, "Speeches to Explain, Instruct, and Report," in *Effective Business Speech,* 4th ed. (New York, McGraw-Hill Book Co., Inc., 1960).

Paul L. Soper, Chapter 10, "Planning the Informative Speech," in *Basic Public Speaking,* 2nd ed. (New York, Oxford University Press, 1956).

CHAPTER 11

Using Visual Aids

To present information so that it will be quickly grasped, consider blackboard diagrams, charts and maps, actual objects, slides, moving pictures. ■ Orient your visual aid; talk to audience, not to aid; during your speech, let everyone look at the same aid at the same time; use a variety of aids.

THE USE OF VISUAL AIDS has been stimulated by the training procedures devised by the armed forces as they have undertaken the job of instructing civilian recruits in military practices. Business and industry have also given attention to graphic methods. This is a natural outcome in a nation that has rapidly developed TV, cinema, advertising, and other visual arts.

Particularly in explaining complicated devices or complex relationships or concepts, you should raise the question, "Will a visual aid make my speech more effective?" The speaker who attempted to explain the use of the slide rule to extract square root, without employing any visual aid, was doomed to failure at the outset.

I. Kinds of Visual Aids

The following kinds of aids are available to speakers:

A. BLACKBOARD DIAGRAMS AND SKETCHES

This type of visual aid is the most frequently used in classroom speaking. A good diagram or sketch may rescue a talk from mediocrity and give it a clarity that will make it more easily remembered.

An obvious advantage of the blackboard is its readiness. Since, however, it is immediately at hand, the speaker is tempted to improvise. At times he may do this effectively, but at other times he finds himself erasing and re-erasing, drawing parts too small or too large, or out of position or proportion.

Unless the diagrams and sketches are simple, the speaker should make a preliminary drawing as a part of his preparation, to reassure himself that he can handle the chalk effectively *while in front of an audience.* He should, moreover, experiment with different designs, arrangements, shadings, and the like, in order to make the result as striking as possible; the blackboard method otherwise is open to the charge of being commonplace. Imaginative or not, you should at least be accurate. During the last war large-scale models of beaches to be assaulted or targets to be bombed were prepared by intelligence officers. The men preparing for these missions were to study the models, retire to another room, *draw a diagram of what they had seen,* and then compare their diagram with the original to see if their learning was accurate. Similarly, a speaker planning a blackboard presentation should draw a diagram of what he wants to present and compare it with his source to see if *his* learning has been accurate.

MAP ILLUSTRATING A SPEECH ENTITLED "A TALK OF TWO TOWNS"

Roger M. Blough, chairman of the Board, United States Steel Corporation, compared and contrasted costs of making steel in Dusseldorf, Germany, and Cleveland, Ohio (see page 137). From the cover of a pamphlet containing the text of the speech. (Courtesy, U. S. Steel Corporation.)

A second important advantage of the blackboard is that it makes possible a step-by-step animated presentation of the drawing. If this inherent advantage is to be exploited, the speaker should develop his sketch or diagram in *the presence of the listeners.* If he is explaining, for example, the trade arrangements between the nations of the European Common Market and other nations, he can draw a large outline map of Europe on the blackboard, indicate the member nations of the Common Market, and draw x's and arrows to show the important manufacturing areas and the flow of their manufactured goods. If a girl is describing new ideas in fall styles, she can sketch on the blackboard a new frock, commenting upon each style feature as she draws it in.

You may be able to devise an original way of varying or supplementing the blackboard sketch. Colored chalks, for example, are striking. Colored industrial tapes are easily stuck into place, and do not leave adhesive on the blackboard. Your sketch may be used with cut-outs on colored paper; or you may use two blackboards, one sliding in front of the other. A blackboard that can be reversed, bringing the other side into sudden view, may make it possible for you to achieve a bold effect.

B. PREPARED CHARTS AND MAPS

Charts and maps, less frequently used than blackboard sketches, are consequently more novel. The speaker may mount his chart or map on an easel and refer to it with a pointer as he develops his talk. He may have a series of charts, turning the sheets from time to time.

If the chart is a large one and he wishes to explain it in parts, he may have each part covered with a strip of paper, held in place with a piece of tape so it can easily be detached. Thus the speaker detaches one strip, explains the part of the chart that is revealed, detaches a second strip, explains that part of the chart, and so on.

Sometimes a chart consists of a series of catchy words or phrases. A talk on counterfeiting, given by a speaker who wanted to point out why counterfeit money was inferior in appearance to good money, could be based on these points:

    I. Counterfeit money is made from defective plates.
    II. Counterfeit money is printed with cheap ink.
    III. Counterfeit money is printed on cheap paper.
    IV. Counterfeit money is made by poor workmen.

His chart might contain these phrases:

> DEFECTIVE PLATES
>
> CHEAP INK
>
> CHEAP PAPER
>
> POOR WORKMEN

To expose this chart to the audience all at once would blunt the effectiveness of his speech, as some listeners would look at one line while he was talking about another. To avoid this eye-wandering, the speaker covers each line with a horizontal slip of paper. While he makes his opening comments, the entire chart is covered. As he begins his first point, he pulls off one of the slips, and the audience sees the phrase:

```
┌─────────────────────────┐
│                         │
│   DEFECTIVE PLATES      │
│                         │
└─────────────────────────┘
```

When he begins his second point and removes the second slip, the listeners then see

```
┌─────────────────────────┐
│                         │
│   DEFECTIVE PLATES      │
│                         │
│      CHEAP INK          │
│                         │
└─────────────────────────┘
```

and so the speech unfolds before them visually as the speaker develops it. This method is used so frequently by military instructors in their lectures to officers and men that it has acquired a special name: *the strip tease.* The method may also be used with maps. If you wanted to show an audience how the United States grew across the continent, you could prepare a large map showing the successive additions to U. S. territory; the Louisiana purchase, the purchase of Florida from Spain, the annexation of Texas, the acquisition of the Oregon country, the Mexican cession, the Gadsden purchase. Each of these *areas* would be hidden by a paper cutout the size and shape of the area it covered. As the speaker progressed he would detach the cutouts in chronological order, thus demonstrating the dramatic story of America's territorial growth.

You may draw pictures or sketches; or, as one student did who wanted to explain the growing use of modern conveniences in rural homes, use colored pictures cut out of magazines. Colored tapes can be used to fashion letters, or as edgings and borders for maps. If, for example, you wanted to show on a state map where the new freeway would be constructed, you could stick a strip of narrow black tape on the map to show the route. If you need areas of solid color, use crayons, or cut out pieces of colored paper and paste them in place. For novel effects, such as "before and after," prepare a part of your chart in layers; as you peel off one layer you reveal another.

Overlays, made of cellophane or other transparent material, may be used with forceful effect. Suppose, displaying a map of your state, you wish to discuss the future highway construction program. After identifying principal cities, you may attach to the map the cellophane overlay on which you have previously traced, with a grease or marking pencil, the route of the proposed throughways. You may also have second or third overlays on which are traced routes of new secondary or farm-to-market roads. An electrical engineer, interested in a specialty described as bio-electric medical technician, explained various types of pacemaker that have been designed to regulate the heart action of patients with heart disorders. He drew on a sheet of white cardboard an outline of the chest with a large red heart in the appropriate place. On a sheet of Saranwrap he drew a schematic diagram of one type of pacemaker; this sheet he wrapped around a cardboard mailing tube. At the proper point in his speech he rolled the mailing tube over the white cardboard and the Saranwrap overlay stuck in place without need for further attachment.

You may use *cutouts:* arrows, squares, stars, etc., in bright colors, to be stuck on a map or chart during a demonstration, to identify special features or locations. For a simple adhesive, fashion a small loop of masking tape with adhesive on the outside; attach this loop to the back of the cutout, leaving an exposed section of sticky loop, so that the cutout remains in place when it is pressed against the map or chart. Charts may be constructed with windows or flaps that can be opened, circular discs that can be revolved, sections that can be adjusted or removed. If the speaker keeps reminding himself that his purpose is to be clear, he may devise other special means to help his explanation.

If your talk contains figures, consider the possibility of constructing a *bar graph* or *pie graph*. Suppose you want to explain to college students the high cost of owning and operating a car. Your research reveals that a low-priced automobile with a 6-cylinder engine and a manual gearshift costs $1,260 a year. This figure is divided into: depreciation, $635; insurance, $257; gasoline, $208; other expenses, $160. These last four figures could be represented by four tall bars of proportionate lengths; or the total sum could be represented by a circle, the wedges, like pieces of pie, being of proportionate sizes. You could go on to explain that these estimates are based on 10,000 miles of driving per year. With the bar graph or the pie graph clearly before your listeners, you could point out several amazing facts: for example, most people are surprised to learn that insurance costs more than gasoline, and that depreciation more than three times as much as gasoline.

Do not make any chart too involved: the chart is, after all, a means to an end, not an end in itself. Make letters and figures large, so that the student in the rear row can see. Letters and figures only an

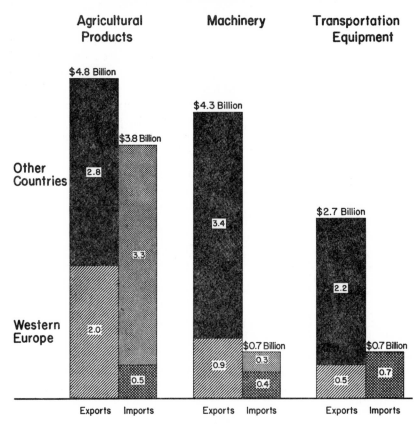

EXPORTS FAR EXCEED IMPORTS FOR MAJOR COMMODITY GROUPS

A BAR GRAPH

One of a set of charts used by President Kennedy in 1962 in briefing various individuals and groups in regard to the trade program. The actual charts were about four by six feet in size. Supplied this book through the courtesy of Andrew T. Hatcher, associate press secretary, The White House.

inch high may be too small. Use plenty of white space, and a variety of bold and striking colors: pale pinks, light yellows, and feeble greens do not have much impact at the back of the room.

Listeners often realize and often appreciate the special pains that a speaker takes to prepare his material for them. This preparation may take the form of locating or constructing visual aids—or any other kind of helpful investigation and research.

See the photos of Reuther and York, opposite, and of Truman, facing page 281, for illustrations of speakers using visual aids.

VISUAL AIDS HELP MAKE AN IDEA CLEAR

The use of charts, graphs, and other visual aids may almost be called a twentieth century contribution to speech making. Although they have been used for centuries, it is at least true that today they are employed in greater numbers and varieties than ever before.

Above, Walter P. Reuther, president of the United Auto Workers Union, uses a chart to make a point clear. *Below*, Dr. Herbert York, then director of Research and Engineering at the Defense Department, uses blackboard notations to illuminate his talk.

Both speakers are looking at their listeners; a fault in the use of visual aids is to look too much of the time at the aid and thus seem to ignore the audience.

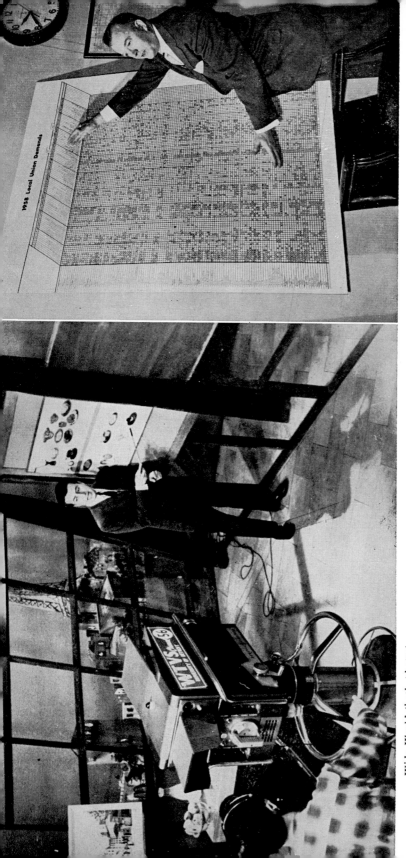

Wide World (both photos)

VISUAL AIDS ARE USED IN A WIDE VARIETY OF SITUATIONS

Left: In a Detroit TV studio, an instructor of French reviews the day's vocabulary lesson, indicating the objects as he pronounces the French names. *Right:* A General Motors executive uses this chart at a press conference to emphasize the large number of demands being made upon the company by local unions.

C. ACTUAL OBJECTS

Actual objects or replicas may be demonstrated with compelling effect. Don't be content to *talk* about the slide trombone—bring it to class. Manipulate it in the presence of the audience, so your listeners can see how it works; give them a sample of your sweet tones. Every one has seen a slide trombone, but in your hands it may be an exciting and imposing instrument. If you collect native beetles, as one student did, bring a few cards of them to class and display them—pick out the large ones with shiny wing-cases and big pincers. If you want to explain the operation of a transit, use an actual transit to help you. A photographer brought to class 20 cut-film holders and 20 sets of negatives in order to teach his listeners how to load a cut-film holder of the type used in press cameras. With the actual materials in front of him, each member of the audience learned to perform the operation by watching the speaker and going through the procedure step by step as he explained and demonstrated. A policeman used toy busses, cars, and traffic lights to demonstrate an automobile accident. An electrical engineer mounted on a large board a distributor, coil, and spark plug, all properly connected to a storage battery, to demonstrate an ignition system. Many groups have probably not yet heard a speech about new kinds of typewriters, copying machines, portable calculators, gas turbines, teaching machines—all new products in the field of industrial research.

If the actual mechanism is too small to demonstrate—for example, the valve of an aerosol container—you may need to make a large model of it, or use a picture or diagram. The figures on a slide-rule are too small for listeners to see, but you could construct a dummy slide-rule six feet long, and thus confidently proceed to explain how square root is extracted. If the object is well known, the small size may not be so objectionable. In a talk on how to use a first-aid kit, a surgeon held up a safety pin and talked about it so impressively that listeners quickly felt that, small and commonplace though it was, it had an important role in first-aid treatment.

Industrial concerns sometimes prepare special exhibits, called *mock-ups*, for demonstration or instructional purposes, made of plywood or other materials. Often the mock-up is prepared so that a side or top can be removed, exposing what is within with startling effect. Nearly every one has seen these devices at fairs and expositions. Sometimes they are modified versions of the real thing itself—as for example a demonstration version of a new type missile, with the outer wall cut away and the inner mechanism exposed, to show the operation of valves, chambers, and firing devices. You would not be able to secure one of these for a classroom speech, but you can easily imagine an officer, his men grouped around him, using one of the models to give a stirring talk about the features of the new weapon and how it is superior to all earlier models.

At times a speaker can use a helper from the audience in order to demonstrate a point: he may need a victim for a demonstration of artificial respiration or a thug on whom to practice the art of self-defense. The policeman who demonstrated ways of breaking a choke hold used a listener to show the exact holds and the best defenses.

One speaker used his audience as a kind of visual aid. The cost of production, he said, takes 35 per cent of the consumer's dollar: here he indicated with his outstretched hands a 35 per cent segment of his audience; distribution takes 55 per cent: here he moved his hands to take in 55 per cent more of the group; profit is only 10 per cent: here he indicated with his hands the thin slice of the audience that remained.

An old campaign trick—and a novel use of a visual aid—is for a candidate, when his opponent has refused to debate the issues with him, to stage debates with an empty chair.

D. SLIDES, FILM STRIPS, MOVING PICTURES

Slides, film strips, and moving pictures are also used in present-day speeches. They may not be suitable for a short talk as they themselves may consume so many minutes that not much opportunity is left for the talk; if time permits, however, they have much to recommend them. A physician, after preparing an elaborate set of charts for a medical convention, realized his charts would be too small for the expected audience of a thousand people; so he had slides made from the charts, and thus his pictures could be projected on a large screen. If you plan to use mechanical gadgets of this sort, do not overlook pointers, extension cords, alternating and direct current, ways of darkening the room, the advisability of using an assistant, getting your slides turned the proper way, and the like.[1] In fact any sort of visual presentation needs attention to details like easels, colored chalk,

---

[1] This advice may be superfluous, however:

1. A woman drove thirty miles to give an illustrated lecture on girl scouts, and arrived at the scene fully equipped with projector and screen—but had left the slides home. Her husband drove back after them.

2. A college conferred a signal honor upon a distinguished alumnus. This scientist gave a speech illustrated with 40 dazzlingly beautiful color slides—but during the talk he said, "Oh, that one is out of order—however, what I want to show is," or "That one I intended to omit—so let's go on," etc.

thumb tacks, and tape. The speaker needs to bring all his supplies with him. These items are almost never to be found in the room where the speech is to be given.

Special projectors are made today in a variety of designs; new models are coming out all the time. One popular type allows the speaker to stand behind the machine, either at the back or the front of the room, and show pictures, newspaper clippings, music scores, and similar materials. Or he may insert a sheet of blank paper into the proper receptacle, and as he speaks draw a chart, sketch, or diagram, which is simultaneously projected on the screen.

Auditory aids may be helpful. One girl used a phonograph to play snatches from tunes to illustrate various musical idioms.

E. IMAGINARY VISUAL AIDS

Occasionally a speaker will *imagine* the presence of a visual aid. "If we had a blackboard," he will say, "we would write over here a list of all the members of the class who can not swim." This statement is accompanied by an appropriate gesture, to help the listener visualize the imaginary blackboard. "Over here," he would continue, indicating, "we would write a list of those who can swim." He might then go on to explain what the people on the first list need to do in order to have their names written on the second list. Or he might say, "I want you to imagine four statues, one in each corner of this room, representing four great virtues. Over here in this corner is a statue representing *health*." The speaker then continues by describing and exemplifying health. Strictly speaking the examples illustrate visual *imagery*, but the speaker leads the audience to imagine that the actual *object* is in the room.

II. Basic Principles

These suggestions will help you use visual aids effectively:

A. ORIENT YOUR VISUAL AIDS

If you are using a chart, tell what it is: "This is a cross section of the human heart, viewed from the front—here is the right side, here is the left." If it is a map, identify it: "This is a map of Memphis and its suburbs—this is north, this is the Mississippi River, here is Arkansas, etc." Some orientation is always necessary unless the diagram or chart is immediately self-explanatory. Otherwise the speaker will begin his explanation, and some listeners, instead of following his words, will still be puzzling over the diagram wondering literally which end is up.

As an officer who rose to the position of Supreme Commander and later to the post of Chief of Staff, Dwight D. Eisenhower made countless speeches on military matters in which he employed maps and charts. Accordingly, when as President of the United States he gave an address on a nation-wide TV hookup, and wanted to use a map to help him explain a point, he oriented it in this simple but highly professional manner:

> Here in my office is a map of Germany. The light portion of the map is West Germany—the darker portion is East Germany. The lighter gray lines are the air corridors to Berlin—and the dotted lines show both the main roads and railroads that give access to the city.[2]

B. TALK TO AUDIENCE, NOT VISUAL AID

Make your talk to the audience, not to the visual aid. If you are explaining a blackboard drawing, look at your audience as much as you can. To be sure you will need to glance now and then at the blackboard, but look at your listeners most of the time. If you are exhibiting a magazine, hold it boldly out to them, saying, "This is a copy of the November *Harper's*"—don't hold it at your side, saying "This is a copy of the—" (quick peek) "—November—" (another quick peek) "—*Harper's*." Perhaps you have had teachers who wrote on the board, sometimes mumbling so you could not hear what they said; sometimes standing so you could not see what they were writing; sometimes hiding completely what they were writing, which they would quickly erase before turning around to face the class. Honor them for other virtues, but do not imitate their method of using visual aids. In short, *be sure everybody can see*. Charts are often too tiny. Exhibits are set up in positions impossible for some listeners to view. So: think of the listener in the back row or at the extreme side of the room.

C. MAKE YOUR PRESENTATIONS LIVELY

Use the visual aid in a lively, animated fashion. If you are demonstrating a steering wheel incorporating a new safety principle, hold it up so all can see it; demonstrate this feature and that; ask your audience questions like, "Can you see?" "See how this

---

[2] *Vital Speeches*, XXV (April 1, 1959), 354. President Kennedy has also used maps and other visual aids in his press conferences and TV reports to the nation.

works?" "Isn't that ingenious?" and the like. You may even walk across the front of the room, to make sure everyone gets a good view. Good speaking requires a concern that everyone present has a fair opportunity to understand. If you put the steering wheel down to demonstrate a chart or make a sketch on the blackboard, you may want to pick it up again when you review or summarize. You may need to invite people sitting in the back of the room to come down closer; or you may have the whole class gather around you, if the group is not too large or the situation too formal. Or you may need to stand on the platform, or on a bench.

D. WHEN USING HANDOUTS

It is not a good idea to pass around a photograph, folder, book, Indian wampum, wire puzzle, or other articles for listeners to examine during the course of a speech. If you are describing your trip West and pass around a photograph of your camping outfit, the attention of each listener will be momentarily distracted from what you are saying as the photograph reaches him. If all need to see the photograph, it may be better for you to walk around the room and display it to everybody and then return to the front of the room and resume your speech. This solution is awkward, but possible.

Students planning careers in business and industry will be interested in a study by Dahle at Purdue. Experts in management know that a paramount problem is to transmit information from manager to employee. An employee who is kept fully informed, who is given a chance to express his opinion, not only has better morale but will produce more and spoil less. (See the quotation from Phillips on page 145.) Dahle asked the question, "What is the best way to transmit information?" Should one let it travel by the grapevine? post it on the bulletin board? put the information in writing and hand it out? call the group together, explain the information, and at the same time distribute material containing the information? A thousand and thirty Purdue students, 84 employees of a nearby industrial plant, and 528 employees of a Chicago department store participated in the experiments, which clearly showed the superiority of the oral explanation plus handout method.[3]

---

[3] Thomas L. Dahle, ". . . Five Methods of Transmitting Information to Business and Industrial Employees," *Speech Monographs*, XXI (March, 1954), 21-28. Consult the study for other details of the experiment and for the statistical computations.

E. USE A VARIETY OF VISUAL AIDS

Use different kinds of visual aids, whenever practicable, in order to make a point vivid. Use charts, maps, graphs, blackboard diagrams, models, actual objects—in any combination that is feasible. A student explaining the refining of crude oil used charts, blackboard sketches, and actual samples of the material in various stages of the process. A student explaining methods of straightening teeth used blackboard drawings, a skull, and plaster casts of teeth before and after. A girl who wanted to teach her classmates to make good chocolate fudge began by handing them a mimeographed copy of the recipe; then she mixed the ingredients before their eyes, showing how the recipe was followed step by step; then she passed around samples.

III. Use Suitable Aids

Not every speech requires visual devices. No record exists that Jesus on the Mount used charts reading "Blessed are the meek" and the like. Abraham Lincoln argued that the Union could not be divided into North and South as long as the great Mississippi separated it into East and West, but he conveyed that idea by words and gesture, not by a blackboard and crayon or a projected slide. Undoubtedly the greatest speeches ever made employed no visual devices however.

On the other hand, visual devices are centuries old. Mark Antony's funeral oration with Caesar's torn and rent gown, Chatham's crutch and Burke's dagger, lawyers who have used an "exhibit" to further the case for prosecution or defense, all swell the long list of speeches that have employed visuals. A visual aid in a speech is as helpful as an illustration in a book. When the purpose is not so much *to impress* as it is *to inform* or *to persuade,* when the subject is complex, when exact comprehension and complete grasp are sought, wisely-selected and competently-employed visual aids have wide usefulness.

Simple materials may be used with impressive result. To make a pie graph, use a string-and-pencil compass or a large dinner plate to draw the circle, and a ruler to draw the wedges. Ordinary colored crayons may be used to shade the various areas. To construct a bar graph, use colored tape; contrasting colors may be employed for striking effects. To letter, make lightly-pencilled parallel lines, and draw the letters between the lines; for bold letters, use a colored crayon, india-ink with a special wide pen-point, or the special drawing pens on sale at nearly any bookstore. The paper or cardboard you need may be purchased in various sizes in any bookstore or other place where art supplies are sold. You may also buy devices or special alphabets to help you design different styles of lettering.

Do not apologize for your early attempts at constructing visual aids. Sometimes a home-made effort, by showing that the speaker has given personal thought to his subject, is highly effective. When you have become a professional speaker and are called upon to make presentations to critical groups, then you may seek expert artistic advice in preparing your visual aids.

Questions for Classroom Discussion

1. Under what conditions will a visual or auditory aid make a speech *worse* instead of *better?*

2. Recall speeches where the novelty of the visual aid or the *variety of kinds of visual aids employed* added to the effectiveness of the speech.

3. What advice would you give some one who was going to give a travelog illustrated with color slides? Consider possibilities for novelty and variety. List some do's and don'ts.

Speech-Related Project

Appoint a committee to visit your art department, or art-supply stores, secure samples of available materials that seem promising for use by speakers, and demonstrate them to the class.

Speaking Assignment 9

A Speech Using Visual Aids

Make a speech to inform of .... minutes in which you employ visual or auditory aids.

You may:

Demonstrate an object: musical instrument, chain saw, sporting good items—new vs. old type of helmet, etc., mechanical device, chemistry experiment, magic trick.

Use a map—actual map, or one drawn on the blackboard: a part of the world that is in the news; a sketch of a military or naval battle.

Use statistics: employ a line graph, bar graph, pie graph.

Demonstrate a process: how to make home-made ice cream, how to string a racket, how to fence.

Use your body to demonstrate a skill: how to model a dress, how to jump the low hurdles, how to tap or rhumba, how to improve posture. Variation: ask a classmate to assist you in demonstrating a dance step, a wrestling hold, a football play.

Use a diagram or chart—either previously prepared, or drawn on the blackboard: how air conditioning works, the Van Allen radiation zone, problems in orbiting a satellite or space station.

For further suggestions, consult the list of topics on pages 45-47, 68.

REFERENCES ON USING VISUAL AIDS

Donald C. Bryant and Karl R. Wallace, Chapter 8, "Visual Aids to Amplification," in *Fundamentals of Speaking,* 3d. ed. (New York, Appleton-Century-Crofts, Inc., 1960). A well-illustrated chapter.

Glenn M. Loney, Section II, "Audio-Visual Aids for Speakers" in *Briefing and Conference Techniques* (New York, McGraw-Hill Book Company, Inc., 1959). Complete, well-illustrated section discussing both visual and auditory aids.

Robert T. Oliver, Harold P. Zelko, and Paul D. Holtzman, Chap. 11, "Using Visual Aids," in *Communicative Speech* (New York, Holt, Rinehart, and Winston, 1962). Helpful discussion and illustrations.

CHAPTER 12

Beginning and Ending the Speech

Speeches may open with (1) an illustration, (2) a quotation, (3) a striking statement, (4) a personal reference, (5) other methods. ■ *Speeches may end with (1) a summary, (2) summary plus appeal, (3) an application, (4) a quotation, (5) an illustration.*

IN MAKING BRIEF SPEECHES like those described in Chapter 8, the speaker does not have much time to expend on preliminary information or removing prejudice. Neither does he bother with a formal conclusion: summary or review seem less necessary when the hearer's mind has been taxed only a minute or so. When, however, a speaker attempts longer talks, he needs to give much thought to the beginning and ending of the speech. The reason is psychological: the *first* impression of the speaker and the *last* impression are highly important. Furthermore, because audiences are visibly responsive to a good introduction and a good conclusion, the speaker *sees* that he has been more than usually effective. This realization adds to his confidence; he can tell that he is growing in stature as a speech maker.

I. Planning the Introduction

An experienced speaker would probably disapprove beginning the talk with a blunt statement of the central idea:

I want to give you three reasons why you should contribute to the Community Chest.

Such a speaker would very properly wonder whether this abrupt language would put the listener on the defensive and make him unreceptive to what is to follow. Nearly always there must be a paving of the way through the *introduction*.[1]

Actually, many speeches have *two* introductions, the first consisting of *preliminary remarks,* or informal comment, and the second the *introduction proper.* Quite likely the use of what is here casually labelled "preliminary remarks" may be an important technique that distinguishes the experienced speaker from the beginner. Certainly experience develops a sense of timing in the speaker that advises him when to shorten the preliminaries, when to eliminate them altogether.

In most real-life situations, the speech is only part of the occasion. The speech may follow a dinner, a business meeting, a musical number, or other speeches. The speaker has only a general idea of what will be said or done before his turn comes to speak. All he can do is to look sharply and listen carefully, and formulate his few preliminary remarks—*when they are advisable*—out of what he sees and hears. Chapter 9 pointed out that spontaneity was an essential ingredient of humor; these preliminary remarks give you opportunity to make a spontaneous, and cordial, adaptation to the occasion.

What sorts of introductions, then, may a speaker devise in order to avoid blunt openings like:

> Ladies and gentlemen: I should like to give you my views about hot-rods and why we should condemn those who drive them.

Or:

> Fellow classmates: School spirit around here is dead.

Many kinds of introductions have been listed, but the following have generally proved successful:

A. BEGIN WITH AN ILLUSTRATION

Often an introduction may effectively lead off with informal and disarming words like "the other day," or "last week," or:

> As I was coming across the campus on my way to class, I met a young lady, a good friend of mine, and noticed the tears streaming down her face.

Or:

> Yesterday when I pulled the mail out of my box at the dormitory I found a long envelope with this ominous inscription in the upper-

---

[1] Many teachers urge, as did Cicero long ago, that a speaker *not* prepare his introduction until after the rest of his speech is planned. Only then are you sure what you want to introduce. Order of preparation—(1) central idea, (2) body, (3) conclusion, (4) introduction; Order of speaking—(1) introduction, (2) central idea, (3) body, (4) conclusion. For your ease of reading, however, this chapter presents the material on *introducing* before the material on *concluding.*

left-hand corner: "Office of the Dean of Men." My hand trembled as I ripped it open and unfolded the letter inside. It began: "My dear Mr. Harrison: It has just come to my attention . . ."

Opening with a pertinent illustration that can lead into your central idea helps the speaker gain attention from the first.

Many thoughtful Americans have speculated about what would happen to the country in the event of a disabling illness to the President. In a talk on "Presidential Inability: The Constitutional Problem," George Cochran Doub began as follows:

On March 4, 1881, James A. Garfield, who as a boy drove the mule team of a canal boat on the Ohio Canal, became President of the United States. Only four months later, Garfield drove in his carriage from the White House down Pennsylvania Avenue to the Baltimore and Potomac Railroad depot on Sixth Street intending to take a train to New England. As he walked through the station arm-in-arm with Secretary of State James G. Blaine, an assassin stepped forward with a cocked revolver and fired two shots at Garfield striking him in the arm and side. . . .

Here is a masterful introduction, its concrete detail showing that it was taken from the pages of history, immediately inviting attention to what could have been a forbiddingly dry legal discussion. Interest in the topic, however, does not have to be forcibly whipped up; the facts are there, awaiting the researcher. Let us listen to this speaker a little further:

. . . striking him in the arm and side. When the lunatic, Charles J. Guiteau, was seized and dragged through the crowd, he cried, "Arthur is President of the United States now."

Garfield lay in a coma for 80 days completely unable to perform the duties of President. During that period, he performed only one official act—the signing of an extradition paper. The total incapacity of the President during this period, we are told, had a harmful effect on the country. . . . Only routine business was handled by Department heads.

Yet, nothing was done. There was criticism that Secretary of State Blaine was attempting to usurp the President's duties and there were insistent demands that Vice President Chester A. Arthur act. After 60 days, a Cabinet meeting was held in which it was unanimously voted that Vice President Arthur should assume the powers of the presidential office. But would he become President and thus preclude Garfield from returning to office? Opinions were divided.[2]

After you prepare your outline, *look over the examples* you have planned to employ. Perhaps you can extract one of them from its *logical* place in the outline and put it at the *beginning* of your speech to use as an interest-arousing device.

B. BEGIN WITH A QUOTATION

A speech may begin with a quotation. John F. Kennedy, speaking at a Harvard commencement, opened with:

> Prince Bismarck once remarked that one third of German students broke down from overwork; another third broke down from dissipation; and the other third ruled Germany. As I look about this campus today, I would hesitate to predict which third attends reunions . . . but I am confident I am looking at "rulers" of America in the sense that all active informed citizens rule.[3]

The Secretary of Labor opened with a quotation: "Those who forget the past, said Santayana, are doomed to repeat it. Are we today for-

[2] Mr. Doub gave this talk as Assistant Attorney General of the United States to the Maine Bar Association, Rockland, August 27, 1959. The text was supplied for this book. An earlier version of the address, given to the Federal Bar Association in Denver, appears in *Vital Speeches*, XXV (September 1, 1959). In the address the speaker goes on to narrate a similar crisis in the Wilson administration, and proposes a constitutional amendment to meet future emergencies.

Mr. Doub wrote (December 2, 1959): "I suppose that I have to make about ten speeches a year outside of the courtroom and I attempt to limit them as to content to legal, constitutional or governmental problems. On many occasions, when in private practice, I was called on to make political speeches in election years."

The author will use the striking introduction to Mr. Doub's speech as an occasion to observe that specific details like those he uses (Garfield's assassination, Wilson's critical illness) are not ordinarily to be found in the history texts usually written for beginning college and university courses. These writers must necessarily cover tremendous ground, and therefore they have to omit much illustrative detail. At this point the history instructor often expands the text he uses. The speaker similarly finds his historical examples and illustrations not from highly-compact texts but from biographies, memoirs, correspondence, journals—and thus the closer he gets to *source* materials, the more fascinating his research becomes, and the better his chance of locating interesting materials for speeches.

[3] A copy of the text appears in the *Congressional Record* for June 22, 1956, and was supplied this book.

John F. Kennedy is the author of *Profiles in Courage*, a series of essays about courageous Americans, many of them speakers. He wrote (December 3, 1959), then U.S. Senator: "I have never had any formal training in public speaking except that which has come from a career in politics. Currently I average approximately 50 Senate speeches and 100 speeches off the Senate floor per year." See his inaugural address in the Appendix.

getting the past?"[4] The president of the American Institute of Co-operation opened his talk to an audience of farmers with famous words from the other side: "Khrushchev has said to us, 'We will bury you—your grandchildren will be Communists.' This best weapon we have pointed against him is our overabundance of food—this is even more important than any missile in the long run."[5]

C. BEGIN WITH A STRIKING STATEMENT

You may perhaps arouse the interest of others by opening with sentences like these:

Every year we have about a million acres of farm land going out of production.

One-third of the people in this town are in one way or another reached by the services of the Community Chest.

There are so many cars in California that at any given moment everyone in the state could ride in the front seat.

It is no longer true that a straight line is the shortest distance between two points.

Last week, in the lives of each of you, opportunity knocked not once but five separate, distinct times.

This type of opening promises much, so be sure to live up to the expectations you arouse.

D. BEGIN WITH A PERSONAL REFERENCE

Although we are sometimes admonished to avoid personal experiences, in most situations this taboo is not warranted. A good introduction to your speech may be a brief statement of why you selected this topic. Pointing out that one session you were a page in the Senate may explain your choice of a political topic. Mentioning that you nursed a favorite aunt through a long illness with arthritis will help explain your concern about that ailment. Stating that you visit a mental hospital each week with a group of YWCA workers gives you some authority to discuss the problems of the mentally ill. Without such a statement the listener may feel that you are merely summarizing a magazine article.

Surprisingly enough, perhaps from a sense of false modesty or

---

[4] Arthur J. Goldberg, speaking before the School of Social Service Administration, University of Chicago, June 9, 1961. Quoted in *Vital Speeches*, XXVII (July 15, 1961), 595.

[5] J. K. Stern, at Farmer's Night Program, Roaring Spring, Pa., March 30, 1961. Quoted in *Vital Speeches*, XXVII (May 15, 1961), 469.

because of a failure to appreciate to the full the natural curiosity of listeners, speakers sometimes omit a highly-important detail. Thus a colonel told a story about a general's unusual skill at presiding over staff conferences; only accidentally, during a questioning period, did the colonel reveal that the general was George Patton, by far the most colorful military personality of World War II. The listeners were pleased to discover that their speaker had been on Patton's staff.

If you have a striking personal reason for choosing a topic, you may reveal it in the introduction. A speaker from out of town will often open with a reference to the place he is visiting: "I well remember my stay in Cincinnati five years ago," or "Our company operates a division office right here on State Street," or "My parents both came from northwest Kentucky."

E. OTHER TYPES OF INTRODUCTIONS

These samples by no means exhaust the list. Instances, incidents, examples, humorous stories, striking statements, quotations, analogies, comparisons and contrasts, proverbs, anecdotes, questions and answers, and other devices are useful ways of beginning a speech or theme. So you can now quite possibly find a way of avoiding:

Fellow classmates: School spirit around here is dead.

This opening might be better:

Fellow classmates: I am here today to solicit contributions for a funeral.

Before I tell you whom or what I want to bury, I want to describe the kind of funeral services that I think would be appropriate.

In the mourners' bench I want to seat Coach McJohnson. He has done more sobbing recently than anyone else I know. Behind him, clothed in black and gold, I want to group the entire football squad.

I have a good place for all of you, too. As you are good friends of the deceased, in fact have been constantly in the company of the deceased, I want you as honorary pallbearers. . . .

F. FAULTY INTRODUCTIONS

Don't make undue explanations. The public platform is not the place to confess your shortcomings as a speaker. Don't say that you are not qualified, that you are not well prepared, that you have mislaid your notes, that the preceding speaker stole your thunder. Don't express your regrets that you are not so funny, or so well-informed, as another speaker. Don't say that you wish the president of the company had come instead of sending you. If the occasion to speak arrives and you have a headache, you will be tempted to tell the audience of your illness so listeners will not expect much from you. Don't do it.

In these and similar circumstances, *do the best you can.* Generally speaking, audiences are more sympathetic and less critical than many novices realize. At least, *omit unnecessary apologies.*[6]

Extend courtesies and pay respects to the occasion as seems warranted and as this chapter has urged, but don't *overdo* the preliminaries; make the first impression one that suggests you are mindful of your real purpose for being there.

II. Planning the Conclusion

A good conclusion is of the highest importance, as with it you make your final impression upon the listener.

A. END WITH A SUMMARY

Consider these examples:

Let me repeat the four significant events in the life of Moses: the incident of the burning bush; the adventures in the wilderness; the reception of the ten commandments; and the arrival at the promised land.

Or:

If, therefore, you wish to improve your academic standing, you must first of all make specific preparation for each day's assignment; and, more important, you must look for opportunities to show that you are developing a mastery of your materials. The habit of preparing carefully each day's assignment will, in itself, bring you to the teacher's attention; but the special opportunities you will have of writing term papers, making reports, and participating in projects and the like, let you show what you really can do.

Former Prime Minister Harold Macmillan summarized an address given at the annual conference of the Conservative party:

To sum up: here at home, we seek a balanced society, in which our prosperity as individuals is reflected in the standard of the things we do together. . . . In our Colonial territories we seek to place new nations on a true course. In Europe and the Common-

---

[6] If you unexpectedly showed up to make a speech with head swathed in bandages or leg in a cast your listeners would be entitled to enough of an explanation so that, their curiosity satisfied, they could listen attentively to your talk.

wealth, we seek to add a new relationship to old ties and to find a greater common strength in the face of the greatest common challenge. In all the world, we seek to help poorer nations, to preserve freedom and to promote peace. These are exciting opportunities for all of us in the next ten years.[7]

The summary is so useful a device that many speeches should contain one. The speaker should make his summary as clear as possible; he may use the obvious milestones of "first, second, . . . finally," etc., as well as connectives like *therefore, in addition, moreover, consequently.* Ofttimes beginning students of public speaking are surprised to learn that this obvious labeling is as effective as it is. The speaker is usually not asked to go back and repeat; he therefore must assume that since he may not be clear to every listener he should summarize and review.

B. END WITH SUMMARY PLUS APPEAL

Often the conclusion becomes more effective if it contains *not only a summary but an appeal as well. Summarize* your points so the listener will grasp your point of view; then *appeal* to him to support your belief or plea for action. Hence, in the example above giving two ways to improve one's scholarship, the speaker may continue by *appealing* to the student to adopt the scholarly life, to increase his intellectual exertions, to recall that the college years offer one of the great chances of a lifetime to do serious thinking.

A variation is to end with a summary plus a *re-emphasis.* Summarizing three attitudes of the British toward American military forces in England, one speaker reviewed that the British are fearful of war; they feel America is primarily interested in its own self-preservation; they are resentful of American prosperity. But, the speaker re-emphasized, the primary characteristic of the British is their deep-seated fear of another war.

C. END WITH AN APPLICATION

At times the speaker can lift a thought to a higher plane by giving it a special application at the end.

A student whose home was in the Eastern mountains, and whose family had for generations amplified its income by merchandising a superior brand of moonshine, once entertained a class by describing in detail methods used in selecting the grain, preparing the

---

[7] Delivered on October 14, 1961. Text of this speech is provided by courtesy of the Prime Minister's office.

mash, distilling the liquor, and aging the final product. His listeners were amused as he told about skirmishes with revenue agents, and as he described how he personally had made deliveries to well-known families in the big cities. As he approached the end of his talk, he said that the Korean War had interrupted his moonshining career; during his years in the service, he learned a different set of values; when he was discharged, he found himself with a GI income that encouraged him to get an education. "I want you to know," he concluded, "that although I honor my folks, I have received an opportunity they never had. I will be the first of my family ever to get a university education. I am going to get a B.A. degree, and then enter law school; and when I leave this campus with my LL.B., I will be the first member of my family to be on the side of the law instead of opposed to it." This comment made a deep impression. What achieved this result was the good-humored discussion of the steps involved in making moonshine, followed by the contrast of his announcement that he was dedicating himself to the life of a law-abiding citizen.

You have heard this principle exemplified in sermons, when the pastor talked twenty minutes on a modest plane, and then, at the end, applied his thought to a present-day problem in a way that gripped your interest. Or you have seen motion pictures or plays which, after a slow opening, moved to a striking climax. If a speech, a sermon, or a drama has a powerful conclusion, we are impressed even though the beginning and the middle are only average.

D. END WITH A QUOTATION

At times a conclusion can be further strengthened with a literary quotation. For such an ending you may search a book of quotations, found in the reference division of the library, to locate one that is appropriate. Books of quotations usually have excerpts classified under appropriate headings like *courage, education, fidelity, war,* and the like.

Speaking of the need for education in the current crisis, Senator J. William Fulbright concluded with:

Do we have time? We will never have more time. Long years ago it was said: "Civilization is a race between education and catastrophe."[8]

Former president Herbert Hoover thus ended a tribute to Benjamin Franklin:

[8] *Representative American Speeches: 1957-1958,* 161.

It was Joseph Choate who said, "When the spirit of Franklin decays the sun of America will have begun to set."[9]

When Senator Paul H. Douglas paid tribute to five great Americans, he ended with two quotations:

In the words of George Eliot, they have joined the choir invisible of those immortal dead, who live in minds made better by their presence. But at times one hopes that mankind can recognize such men while they are living and not merely after they have died. I shall close, therefore, with the final words of Bernard Shaw in his play, *Saint Joan:* "O God that made this beautiful earth, when will it be ready to receive Thy saints? How long, O Lord, how long?"[10]

E. END WITH AN ILLUSTRATION

Mark Twain used an illustration to close a famous after-dinner speech:

There was a presumptuous little self-important skipper in a coasting sloop . . . always hailing every ship that came in sight. He did it just to hear himself talk and to air his small grandeur. One day a majestic Indiaman came ploughing by with course on course of canvas towering into the sky. . . . It was a noble spectacle, a sublime spectacle! Of course, the little skipper popped into the shrouds and squeaked out a hail, "Ship ahoy! What ship is that? And whence and whither?" In a deep and thunderous bass the answer came back through the speaking trumpet, "The *Begum,* of

[9] *Ibid., 1953-1954,* 85.

[10] From a copy of the speech supplied for this book by Senator Douglas.

Douglas is an important name in the long record of American public speaking: witness Stephen A., the Little Giant, and in this decade U. S. Supreme Court Justice William O. and Senator Paul H. (Dem., Illinois). The Senator is the subject of a master's essay by Arno Hill, written at the University of Illinois ("The 1948 Douglas-Brooks Campaign"). Senator Douglas's secretary, Jane Carey Enger, wrote that in 1958 he made approximately 135 addresses. "These included speeches on 'The Current Economic, Political and Diplomatic Position of the United States,' political speeches before Democratic groups, and speeches on civil rights, unemployment problems, ethics in government, area redevelopment and foreign policy. Mainly these were given before college groups, and management groups." (Letter of November 18, 1959.)

Senator Douglas is a former professor of economics and labor relations (he may be addressed as Dr. Douglas) who also had a period of military service (Col. Douglas). The topics listed above grow naturally out of this background of experience plus his career in politics.

This speech on "Five Great Americans" has been a favorite of public speaking classes. It appeared in *Representative American Speeches, 1951-1952,* and is used as a speech for study in W. Norwood Brigance, *Speech Communication,* 2nd ed. (New York, Appleton-Century-Crofts, Inc., 1955).

Bengal, one hundred and forty-two days out from Canton, home-ward bound! What ship is that?" Well, it just crushed the poor little creature's vanity flat! and he squeaked back most humbly, "Only the *Mary Ann*—fourteen hours out from Boston . . . !"

That is just my case. During just one hour in the twenty-four—not more—I pause and reflect in the stillness of the night with the echoes of your English welcome still lingering in my ears, and then I am humble. Then I am properly meek, and for that little while I am only the *Mary Ann,* fourteen hours out, cargoed with vegetables and tinware; but during all the twenty-three hours my vain self-complacency rides high on the white crest of your approval, and then I am a stately Indiaman, ploughing the great seas under a cloud of canvas and laden with the kindest words that have ever been vouchsafed to any wandering alien in this world, I think; then my twenty-six fortunate days on this old mother soil seem to be multiplied by six, and *I* am the *Begum* of Bengal, one hundred and forty-two days out from Canton, homeward bound![11]

F. IMPORTANCE OF THE CONCLUSION

An audience is usually aware that the end of a speech is at hand, and hates to hear a speaker go past a natural, forceful ending.

When you have completed your last point, summon your energies for an appropriate ending: summary, summary plus appeal, illustration, application, or quotation; then stop.

Don't end with a mechanical formula like "I thank you." Ordinarily speakers end with a smile and slight nod to the listeners. If you do want to thank the audience—and remember, this is not the usual custom of speakers—put your appreciation in a sentence of your own wording instead of the routine "I thank you" or "Thank you very much." Note the comment on page 31.

Speakers are more likely to neglect the preparation of their conclusions than they are any other part of the speech. Often when they finish the presentation of their last supporting idea, they apparently suddenly realize that they have devised no good way of ending the speech. Knowing they must have some kind of ending, they close with a lamely-worded sentence. The remedy is to work out in advance the best conclusion you can prepare.

Undoubtedly this best conclusion is one that will remind your audience again of the meaning and purpose of your talk. The more

11 *Mark Twain's Speeches* (New York, Harper and Brothers, 1923), p. 374.

specific and pointed your appeals and recommendations, the more likely the listeners will respond as you wish.

Wiebe examined several successful and unsuccessful radio campaigns, coming to the conclusion that those which sugggested specific action were more successful than those which suggested vague action. A radio documentary that urged listeners to form neighborhood councils to combat juvenile delinquency was in effect too vague to be helpful; not knowing what to do first in order to form such a council, listeners generally failed to make any response at all.[12]

Klapper reports an experiment in which 700 U. S. Air Force recruits listened to tape recordings designed to convince hearers that the United States was right to participate in the Korean war. In two versions of the recording, *well-stated conclusions* were drawn and in two versions they were not. Clear organization was used in certain versions, not in others. The versions with well-stated conclusions and clearly-defined organization were better comprehended, particularly among the less intelligent. Quite obviously a well-organized talk with a specific conclusion will reach more people than an unorganized talk with a vague ending; although the more intelligent listeners can perform the necessary operations of mentally rearranging and interpreting the speaker's materials, other listeners may find these materials "actually inaccessible" to them.[13]

William Jennings Bryan admitted, long after the famous "Cross of Gold" speech, that he felt nervous on that occasion; he added, however, the knowledge that he had a good conclusion "kept him going." The knowledge that you have a good conclusion will add to your self-assurance, also.

Questions for Classroom Discussion

1. After a round of classroom speeches, discuss the *introductions* and *conclusions*. Which were outstanding? Which can be strengthened? *and how?*

2. If you were to give an entertaining speech, and wanted to begin with one funny story and end with another, in which spot—

---

[12] G. D. Wiebe, "Merchandising Commodities and Citizenship on Television," in *Public Opinion Quarterly*, XV (1951), 679-691. Quoted in Elihu Katz and Paul F. Lazarsfeld, *Personal Influence: The Part Played by People in the Flow of Mass Communications* (Glencoe, Ill., The Free Press, 1955), p. 29. See also the Hovland and Mandell study, p. 288.

[13] See Joseph T. Klapper, *The Effects of Mass Communication* (Glencoe, Ill., The Free Press, 1960), pp. 87-88.

beginning or ending—would you put the *funnier* of the two stories? If you were to give a sermon and had an extremely impressive story that summed up the central point of your speech, would you *begin* with it, *close* with it, or put it in the *middle?*

3. You are to give a pep talk before the student body on the evening before the homecoming game with an extremely formidable opponent. In your talk you want to include a story that describes how an inspired team that refused to give up came from far behind to defeat what ordinarily was a superior team. Would you open with this talk, put it in the middle of your speech, or close with it?

Speech-Related Project

Inspect speeches in the annual volumes of *Representative American Speeches* and in the semi-monthly issues of *Vital Speeches* for examples of introductions and conclusions that catch your attention.

Speaking Assignment 10

An Introduction for a Longer Talk

Prepare an introduction of . . . minutes for a twenty-minute talk. The chairman will present you, announcing the title of the talk, but you are to give the introduction only, followed by a sentence or two to suggest the direction the main part of your talk would take if you gave it. Your introduction should show how you would arouse interest in your topic, or remove any prejudice or misunderstanding that might exist about it.

You may select any general purpose for the speech; to entertain, to inform, to persuade, to stimulate.

Speaking Assignment 11

A Conclusion for a Longer Talk

Prepare a conclusion of . . . . minutes for a twenty-minute talk. The chairman will present you, announcing the title of your talk. Open with a sentence or two summarizing what you would have said in the body of the talk; then deliver an appropriate conclusion for it. Select an effective type of conclusion: *summary, summary plus appeal, application, quotation, illustration.*

You may select any general purpose for the speech: to entertain, to inform, to persuade, to stimulate.

REFERENCES ON INTRODUCTIONS AND CONCLUSIONS

As nearly every public speaking text contains selected examples of introductions and conclusions, you will find your concept of the theory and practice of beginning and ending speeches broadened by studying the following references.

W. Norwood Brigance, Chapter 12, "Beginning and Ending the Speech," in *Speech: Its Techniques and Disciplines in a Free Society*, 2nd ed. (New York, Appleton-Century-Crofts, Inc., 1960).

Milton Dickens, Chapter 15, "Conclusions, Introductions, and Transitions," in *Speech: Dynamic Communication* (New York, Harcourt, Brace and Company, Inc., 1954).

Giles Wilkeson Gray and Waldo W. Braden, Chapter 13, "The Introduction" and Chapter 15, "The Conclusion," in *Public Speaking: Principles and Practice* (New York, Harper and Brothers, 1951).

Raymond G. Smith, Chapter 14, "Concluding, Beginning, and Bridging," in *Principles of Speaking* (New York, The Ronald Press Company, 1958).

Paul L. Soper, Chapter 10, "Planning the Informative Speech," sections on planning the introduction and on planning the conclusion, and Chapter 12, "Planning the Persuasive Speech," sections on introduction and conclusion, in *Basic Public Speaking*, 2nd ed. (New York, Oxford University Press, 1956).

Eugene E. White and Clair R. Henderlider, Chapter 7, "Developing the Introduction" and Chapter 8, "Developing the Conclusion," in *Practical Public Speaking* (New York, The Macmillan Company, 1954).

CHAPTER 13

The Body in Speech Making

Speakers use action to feel more at ease, to aid expressiveness of voice, to help communicate both attitudes and ideas. ■ *The term action includes gestures, facial expression, poise and bearing, position and movement on the platform. Some gestures emphasize, others describe.* ■ *Good gestures involve the whole body, are properly motivated, timed, varied.*

DISPLAYING CHARTS AND DEMONSTRATING objects gives experience in managing the body purposefully. This chapter will give further suggestions about gesture and other forms of action. It will also answer questions about what to do with your hands, how to stand, when to move around.

Action is the term generally employed to include hand gesture, facial expression, shruggings of the shoulder or motions of the head, posture, and movement about the platform. Teachers of public speaking usually reserve their detailed instruction in these matters until after the speaker has gained experience in selecting and organizing speech materials. The use of voice and action represent what is meant by the *delivery* of a speech—an important aspect of effective speaking.

I. The Significance of Action

And why study action? Keep these points in mind as you try to improve your own effectiveness:

A. MAKES SPEAKER MORE AT EASE

Speakers like to be comfortable while speaking and to be assured that they *appear* all right. They need to know where to look and what to do with their hands. Perhaps they have learned to do simple things, like standing at ease behind a lectern, or resting a hand lightly on a table or chair back, but they may be able to make further improvement. When a speaker can put his whole body at work in helping him speak effectively, he feels more at ease.

B. HELPS COMMUNICATE ATTITUDE

Your facial expression, posture, and gesture help show how you *feel* about your subject. If you want to communicate to your listeners your strong belief that nuclear fallout is a problem of the *utmost* seriousness, you can communicate your attitude not only with words but also with bodily action.

Speakers who sense that they are too reserved and that they do not have enough enthusiasm in their voices may improve the situation by learning to use the body more effectively. Say "This is very important" with your hands hanging quietly at your side; then repeat the words, clenching your fist and shaking it as you utter *very;* quite likely your gesture will encourage you to speak that word with more vigor and meaning. In this way *action* can add to variety of voice.

Nothing stated here should be taken to imply that action can communicate an attitude that the speaker does *not* experience; listeners are probably able to detect strained enthusiasm or forced concern. The real loss to an individual comes when he is so restrained and inhibited that he cannot communicate an attitude that he deeply feels.

C. HELPS COMMUNICATE IDEAS

Action *by itself* can communicate ideas. Gestures and postures can say "yes" or "no" with differing degrees of positiveness. Pictorial gestures can convey accurate impressions of size, shape, slope, direction and the like. When the actor George Arliss first read the play, *Disraeli,* he advised the author to delete two pages. "I can say all that with a look," he said. "What look?" asked the author. Arliss demonstrated, and the pages came out. Speaking and gesturing accompany each other continually. Recall your own use of gesture, movement, and facial expression when you are in active conversation. Some people seem as if they would find it exceptionally difficult to speak with hands tied. Obviously a certain amount of animation needs to accompany speaking if ideas are to be fully communicated.

D. INFLUENCES AUDIENCE RECEPTIVITY

Experimental studies in listening show that members of an audience may develop an initial prejudice against a speaker who has a mannerism or who in some way does not measure up to their ideal of what a speaker should *look like* while speaking. You may notice that a few of your classmates, in their critiques of speeches, seem overly concerned with gesture and other aspects of action. If your classmates and others mean what they say, you should capitalize upon their general interest in action by improving your own.

Effective speaking is lively and animated. Although listeners are willing to listen to one who is restrained, they are more responsive, other things being equal, to speakers who radiate vitality and who are stirred up about what they are saying. This quality, not to be mistaken for restlessness, grows out of a strong impulse to communicate an idea or a feeling to some one else.

A speaker may wish to enter this phase of his development slowly, trying himself as he goes along. He may feel he wants to move around as little as possible, and may especially feel shy about gesturing. In other words he may hesitate to do anything that suggests he is trying to lead or command the situation. You may be right to approach cautiously the problem of vigorous and expressive bodily action, but do not be any more timid than you can help. Make a *genuine effort* to use action—if you are awkward at first, no harm is done.

II. Using the Hands

What to do with the hands is a problem of many a beginning speaker. Clutching the lectern or toying with articles on it, holding hands behind back or putting hands in pockets, adjusting clothing, ties, collars, or hair-do, all reflect a lack of ease. For random movement of these sorts, substitute positive, purposive movement that helps you with the job of communicating. Primarily the hands can be used in two kinds of gesture, described below.

A. GESTURES THAT DESCRIBE

A type of action with which to begin is the simple descriptive gesture employing one or both hands. If you want to describe shape, size, or length, use the hands to demonstrate what shape, size, or length. If a hand grenade is the size of an orange, or a hari-kari dagger is eight inches long, or a jet bomber has a swept-back wing of so many degrees, make these facts vivid by picturing them with simple hand gestures. *Show* an audience, just as you would show a friend, how to hold a tennis racket for a forehand drive, or the length of a cricket bat as compared with a baseball bat. Simple gestures help the listener contrast, for example, Gothic lines as compared with Greek lines.

Visualize an appropriate descriptive gesture for the following assertions:

Our ignorance is like a vast jungle.

What causes this inner cohesion of our society?

Airplanes fly fifteen hundred miles an hour in this shrunken world.

Hang this picture in the corner of your room.

In majestic isolation each star travels through the darkness of endless space.

I do not see our country huddled in a paralysis of fear.[1]

Although a few people may use their hands too much in conversing, giving the impression of nervousness, most people add liveliness to their conversing by a few gestures; and this kind of descriptive action can well be carried over into speaking. A speaker seems restrained if his *words* call for illustrative gesture but his *hands* hang motionless at his side. Descriptive gestures are so natural that almost any speaker can use them in moderation. The drill sentences above show that they may be used not only with literal dimensions or directions but also with imaginative concepts.

B. GESTURES THAT EMPHASIZE

The hands may also be used to emphasize ideas.

1. *The index finger gesture*

The index finger or pointing gesture may accompany ideas like "This fact is the key to the problem," or "Here is the idea I want you to grasp," or "The one most important export is cotton." The gesture clearly says that *one idea* is singled out for emphasis. If the speaker says, "Remember this one thought as you leave," and accompanies the words *one thought* with a vigorous, index finger gesture, he gives the sentence an emphasis that he could not make with his hands held, for example, behind his back.

Practice an appropriate index finger gesture for each of the following:

Let us first briefly glance at our military power.

He argued for freedom of speech in his very first law lecture.

I will start predicting from the housetops that hard times are on their way.

---

[1] The illustrative sentences in this chapter are taken from speeches by Kennedy, Johnson, Eisenhower, Nixon, Truman, and others active in contemporary speaking. In a few instances slight changes in wording have been made to heighten the illustration.

This nation is the world's foremost manufacturer, farmer, banker, consumer, and exporter.

There is another side of the picture.[2]

Use either hand in making this gesture. You can not use the two index fingers at the same time, however, or you will defeat the idea of trying to emphasize *one* thing.

As with all gestures, the index finger movement accompanies the word or phrase emphasized by the voice: "Let us *first* briefly glance at our military power" or "Let us first briefly glance at our *military* power."

Don't waggle the finger at the audience if you are using this as a serious gesture; give the gesture a dignity compatible with the idea it is emphasizing.

(Note: There is a sense in which the index finger gesture is *descriptive,* as when the speaker says, "Look at California, and what do you find," pointing in the direction of an imaginary California.)

2. *The counting gesture*

Just as we emphasize an idea by using the index finger to show its singleness, we can emphasize groups of ideas by simple counting gestures. Thus the speaker may hold up two fingers when he says, "Only *two* objections to the sales tax really concern us." You have seen speakers make an imposing gesture out of this, letting the audience see that one finger stands for one objection and the other represents the second objection, at times using a finger of the other hand to point to the one or two fingers of the first. This gesture can be overworked, but naturally fits certain groups of ideas and helps to single them out for special attention by the listener.

3. *The palm up gesture*

The palm up gesture may be used with thoughts like "We want to do everything we can to reduce the smoke menace," or "I appeal to you to join me in the campaign to put an end to the pollution of our streams." Simply extend a hand toward the audience, the palm slanted about half way between the horizontal and the vertical, much as if you were offering to shake hands with a listener. This is one of the most gracious and most restrained of the emphatic gestures. Women may use it as freely as men. You may use either or both hands. It sug-

---

[2] A useful practice exercise is to read aloud the illustrative sentences in this chapter practicing suitable gestures. Try two or three different gestures or combinations of gestures on each sentence.

Additional sentences will be found at the end of the chapter.

gests emphasis, reconsideration, or appeal. Here are other sentences which conceivably a palm up gesture could accompany:

> Five precious weeks have already been lost.
> I know your hearts are troubled.
> A belief in liberty was his greatest contribution to the American people.
> We need a new law—a wholly new approach—a bold new instrument of American trade policy.
> We are living in the most fateful period of world history.
> Why should we be saved?

Let the palm up gesture—one hand or two—accompany the word or phrase that is also emphasized by the voice: *"Five precious weeks* have already been lost." "I know *your hearts are troubled"* (or *"I know* your hearts are troubled").

4. *The palm down gesture*

Essentially the opposite in effect and meaning of the palm up gesture, the palm down gesture is a sideward or downward thrust of the hand, as if the speaker is rejecting or disapproving an idea. "We should *abandon* the idea of economy in time of war," declares the speaker, the vigorous down-thrust palm accompanying *abandon;* or "We have *too many* required courses."

No one needs to ask what attitude is conveyed by this vigorous movement of disapproval; the meaning is clear to all. In each of the following sentences also is a notion of viewing with disfavor:

> His advice about early rising was especially objectionable.
> Communism is repugnant to the people.
> It is important to see that nothing is wasted on non-essentials.
> This most respected historian says the West is not worth saving.
> This republic was not established by cowards; and cowards will not preserve it.
> Let me say that I am no economist.

This gesture may be made with either or both hands, and it may be as forceful as your feelings honestly warrant.

A motion picture film taken of Winston Churchill addressing the Canadian parliament in 1941 shows him speaking these words:

> These gangs of bandits . . . shall themselves be cast into the pit of death and shame, and only when the earth has been *cleansed and purged* of their crimes and their villainy shall we turn from the task which they have forced upon us.

When he uttered the words in italics not only did his voice reflect his grim determination but he used a sweeping, palm down gesture to reenforce his meaning.

5. *The clenched fist*

Clenching the fist shows that the speaker is ready to do battle for his belief. It has the utmost emphasis. "We *can not trifle* with this scheme any longer," says the speaker, shaking his fist vigorously on the phrase in italics. "We must put our plans into *immediate effect*."

Read these sentences, using a clenched fist gesture to accompany what seems to you to be the emphatic phrase.

Our party's fortunes must suddenly improve.

He waged an unrelenting war on all forms of tyranny over the minds of men.

We have proved the dynamic character of the principle of competition.

I believe profoundly that this country needs more of what your organization stands for.

Liberty—not Communism—is the most contagious force in the world.

You will find that sentences under (4) above may also be appropriately emphasized with a clenched fist gesture if the speaker's conviction is strong.

College women sometimes feel that the clenched fist gesture is not for them. If a woman speaker finds that other gestures, like the index finger, palm up, palm down, etc., are sufficiently emphatic, those may be sufficient for her speaking career. Women who frequently speak, however, use the clenched fist gesture, like the others, with conviction.

III. Other Types of Gesture

Effective action also involves the use of other parts of the body. Head, face, eyes, may be employed; the speaker may move around on the platform as occasion warrants.

A. USING THE BODY TO SUGGEST AN ATTITUDE

By a shrug of the shoulders, a twinkle of the eye, a lift of the eyebrow, or a toss of the head a speaker may suggest attitudes like indifference, contempt, hopelessness, or resignation. A slight gesture of the hands may or may not accompany the other movements. Consider these statements:

I shall not attempt here to catalog all of the many broken promises of the Communists.

A typical student agony is, "What shall I do? Where am I headed?"

Let us stop this senseless exchange of abuse.

My captain continually gave the impression of being an exceedingly pious and sanctimonious person.

So far as posture is concerned, the ideal toward which to work is a physical bearing that suggests ease, self-assurance, and competence. Stand with your feet far enough apart so that you do not sway, but not so far apart that you are too immovable. Stand erect, but not at attention. Do not bend over too far forward, nor incline too far backward. You may practice a variety of stances until you find one that feels comfortable; check it with your instructor or classmates.

B. USING THE BODY TO DEMONSTRATE

A speaker may use his hands to describe simple concepts of size or shape, but will employ his whole body if the description becomes complicated. In explaining the semaphore alphabet, a golf stance or grip, a football referee's signals, or other complicated procedures or processes, he may use his body to make the exposition clear. Other relationships can also be demonstrated to the listener: over on this side of the room (walking and pointing) is Longstreet Hill, over on the other side is Cemetery Ridge, and here is Little Round Top; thus the stage is set for a retelling of Pickett's famous charge at Gettysburg.

A speaker may effectively puctuate his remarks with vigorous noddings or shakings of the head. The late President Roosevelt, being crippled, needed to support himself while speaking by holding to the lectern; since his hands were therefore not free to gesture, his emphatic nodding of the head became a trademark.

C. USING FACE AND EYES

Facial expression is in itself an important agent of communication. Speakers are sometimes too doll-faced or poker-visaged. If you will refer to the photographs of Eisenhower, Truman, Kennedy, and others, you can study a variety of facial expressions: serious, thoughtful, determined, friendly, playful. Individuals of your acquaintance add to their interestingness as persons by facial expression—their quizzical, astonished, reflective, anguished, surprised, warning, or playful glances add to your delight in their conversation.

The eyes are the focal point of an expression of the face. Contrast, for example, the downcast glance at the floor with the clear, direct, level gaze of the speaker who looks each member of his classroom audience in the eyes. Contrast the sparkle and brilliance of the eyes of a speaker who feels on sure ground with the tense stare of one who is trying to explain a topic too deep for him. But no extended argument for facial expression is necessary to readers today who have watched successful actors in closeups on cinemascope and TV screens. Occasionally a speaker needs to be advised not to overwork the facial muscles—too much hamming can get in the way of an idea—but many need to put themselves more into the speech by using a variety of motivated, purposeful expressions of the face.

In a critiquing session, one perceptive student made this comment about one of the good speakers of the class: "He has a speaker's face." This sentence caught the fancy of the class: it was decided that a speaker's face was mobile, sincere, earnest—in short, *communicative*.

D. USING THE FEET

Random pacing during speaking is distracting, but a speaker may properly move from one part of the platform to another to emphasize ideas or to indicate the major divisions of the speech. Stepping forward tends to emphasize an idea; stepping backward suggests review or reconsideration. If you are standing behind a lectern during the first supporting idea of your speech, you may step to one side as you begin the second supporting idea, and cross to the opposite side for the third supporting idea. If you move while you are speaking your transition sentence, your movement will seem less mechanical. If, however, you are speaking over a fixed microphone, you may not be able to move around at all. In classroom speeches it may help to shift your position a bit between main points.

IV. Basic Principles

To help you counter any feeling of awkwardness, study the three suggestions that follow.

A. USE THE WHOLE BODY

Although the chapter has spoken of gestures of different parts of the body, actually the whole body is employed to some extent in all gesturing. A simple index finger gesture involves not only the hand, but the forearm, upper arm, shoulders, and back. Even the weight shifts to give the movement added vigor. If a given gesture seems awkward to you, a reason may be that only part of the body is working and part is holding back.

B. USE PROPER TIMING

The essence of good action lies in its *timing*. Consider for example the index finger gesture. Part of the gesture may be called the *approach,* as you lift your hand and forearm upward into gesturing position; part of the gesture is the *stroke,* which is the gesture proper, the shake of the finger; a third part is the *return,* during which you bring your hand back to your side. The *stroke* of the gesture accompanies—or precedes—the key word or phrase that carries most of the meaning. Suppose that in saying "I do not know what course others may take," you choose to emphasize *others.* Some may want to do one thing, you are saying in effect, some may prefer another: "I do not know what course *others* may take." The stroke of your gesture firmly accompanies *others.*

A gesture may *precede* the key phrase, and this principle you should practice for yourself: "I do not know what course (short pause, during which you make two or three emphatic, vigorous strokes of your clenched fist) *others* may take." Or the fist-shaking may accompany *others.* But if the gesture is delayed until *after* you have uttered that word, it may have a distracting or even ludicrous effect.

Although hand gestures must be accurately timed, timing of other action, such as a facial expression, is looser. A broad smile may accompany several sentences if it is appropriate to the passage. Even so, the smiling should be suited to the words being uttered; if your language suddenly becomes somber, your smile must be replaced by a serious gaze. This "rapid play of expression," to quote an old phrase, is highly communicative.

Another aspect of timing is that the gesture should be truly vigorous, forceful, expressive. A weak, flabby hand gesture is worth little. A feeble smile or a timid scowl is not impressive. Think of the enigmatic Bob Hope smile that says so much. Think of the broad Eisenhower smile, or of William Jennings Bryan, whose smile was equally broad; he could whisper in his own ear, his fans alleged.

C. USE VARIETY

Good speakers use a variety of gesture: sometimes one kind, sometimes another. They are skillful with either hand; they use head, eyes, face; they move around the platform; they employ informal or unconventional types of gesture.

Repetition of a single gesture, even a good one, becomes monotonous. The palm up gesture is wonderfully effective, but you would be unwise to repeat it constantly. Some sentences may call for two different kinds of gesture. An index finger gesture may be immediately followed by a palm down gesture or clenched fist. These combinations seem natural with longer statements, like: "America was built by men of *courage and daring* who had confidence in themselves, and who were willing to risk their fortunes and their lives for *what they wanted*." Try this and similar sentences with two or three different kinds of gesture, letting one flow into the other. Think also of what facial expression would be appropriate.

V. Have a Strong Desire to Communicate

We save for the latter part of the chapter one of the important requirements of good bodily action.

In all speech making you must have confidence in your subject; you must have a strong feeling that what you have planned to say *will be* interesting, and *will be* effective. You therefore should do enough preparation, and over long enough time, so that you have located the materials you need and have them well in mind. You must have rehearsal practice, so that you will feel confident of your ability to command words and phrases with adequate fluency. You may not be able to say to yourself, "Today I am really going to shake the world with this talk," but perhaps you can reassure yourself with the thought, "This subject is worth while; this information should be shared; what I have to say may prove some day to be important to my listeners."

Moreover, deliver the talk with the thought in the back of your mind, "I want to get this idea across *to these people*"; "I want to explain this concept *to these listeners in front of me*"; "I want to talk *to you*"; "I want *you* to understand and believe me." Some of this resolution and determination will make it seem *more natural* for you to gesture, and to gesture *forcefully* and *convincingly*.

The philosopher-humorist Abe Martin once said, "There's more difference between a professional and an amateur than between anything else on earth." Posture, bearing, eye contact, facial expression, gesture, movement, truly help distinguish the professional—a *speaker with a strong desire to communicate*—from the amateur—one who is simply *saying words*. Start with this strong desire to communicate, and let it flow to your listeners with all your resources of language, voice, and action.

Questions for Classroom Discussion

1. Comment: A business man who does considerable speaking was asked whether he ever consciously attempted to use gesture in speaking for emphasis. He replied, "Never; if I tried to gesture I would become artificial, and therefore less effective."

2. Students at times say "I do not use gesture because I do not feel natural." Often they are right; their gestures *do* seem awkward. How would you advise them? Sometimes they are wrong; their gestures are entirely natural. How would you advise them?

3. Students sometimes use vigorous, forceful convincing gestures in conversation even while they are saying they can not gesture in speaking. How would you advise them?

Speech-Related Project

Study each of the following sentences for meaning: note emphatic words, words or phrases that are echoed, repeated, or contrasted. Say each sentence aloud, giving the words suitable vocal emphasis, accompanied by appropriate gesture. Try different kinds of gesture with each sentence. A variety of good interpretations is possible; seek one that best represents you as a *concerned, energetic, forceful, thoughtful* speaker.

Here is exposed the naked, calculated cruelty of official Kremlin policy.

I have not been asked to speak about political matters but rather about trade and economics.

If two diplomats have the same amount of native ability, the one who has the most facts about a given situation is likely to prove the better officer.

It is not our objective to sell America, or American policy, or even the American way of life.

We are here today to examine the role that education has played in world progress.

Make no mistake about it—the diesel engine brought about the biggest single advance in railroad economics in this country.

A driver who is in a drunken condition when he operates a motor vehicle is in possession of a deadly weapon.

Last year for the first time in 15 years oil men failed to discover as much new oil as the nation used.

I need not stress that these are days of hard decisions.

It is time to penetrate deeper and to see what goes on in the very soul of the mathematician.

The first men to reach the moon will discover a world of magnificent dilapidation.

To say that Omaha has the same rules as Rome or Florence does not mean that it is like Rome or Florence.

America was the first country to teach nearly everybody to read.

Is this simply a way of saying that man will always be eager to investigate any thing that appears new?

The one all-important law of human conduct—the deepest principle in human nature—the standard guiding all behavior—is the need to feel appreciated.

Take my advice, young man: choose your pleasures for yourself, and do not let them be chosen for you.

Is a week too much to spend in the search of a brand new method?

Academic freedom may be defined as a three-fold right or privilege.

There is no fundamental cure except better teaching of English by all teachers, in all classes, and in all schools.

Speaking Assignment 12

A Speech Demonstrating Bodily Action

Plan a speech of .... minutes in which you present an idea about which you are concerned. Make a special effort to use a number and a variety of gestures. You may use more than you ordinarily would, largely for the purpose of trying various kinds of gestures.

In rehearsing this speech, give attention not only to the idea but also to the *voice* and the accompanying *action*. Be experimental in your approach; try two or three different gestures on each idea to be emphasized. Speak the same line in two or three different ways. This assignment is frankly an exercise to loosen you up so that you will feel more free to use action in speaking.

The instructor may interrupt you during your talk to offer suggestions, or he may ask you at the end of your talk to go back over certain parts of the talk.

REFERENCES ON THE BODY IN SPEECH MAKING

John W. Black and Wilbur E. Moore, Chapter 11, "The Speaker's Gestures and Bearing," in *Speech: Code, Meaning, and Communication* (New York, Mc-Graw-Hill Book Company, Inc., 1955). Reflective discussion, plus experimental findings, about the nature of gesture.

W. Norwood Brigance, Chapter 4, "Being Seen," in *Speech Communication,* 2nd ed. (New York, Appleton-Century-Crofts, Inc., 1955). "Visible action is an older code of communication than spoken language, and is more basic."

Milton Dickens, Chapter 7, "Bodily Communication," in *Speech: Dynamic Communication* (New York, Harcourt, Brace and Company, Inc., 1954). Stages of learning to gesture: the distracting stage, the neutral stage, the awkward stage, the skillful stage, with illustrations and suggestions.

John E. Dietrich and Keith Brooks, Chapter 10, "Be Visually Forceful and Direct," in *Practical Speaking for the Technical Man* (Englewood Cliffs, N. J., Prentice-Hall, Inc., 1958). "Make first impressions count . . . move forcefully and with a purpose."

Robert T. Oliver, Harold P. Zelko, Paul D. Holtzman, Chapter 9, "Delivering the Speech," in *Communicative Speech,* 3d ed. (New York, Holt, Rinehart, and Winston, 1962). Discusses the visual code; empathy; the auditory code.

Raymond G. Smith, Chapter 17, "Communicating by Body," in *Principles of Speaking* (New York, The Ronald Press Company, 1958). Kinds and types of gesture; practice sentences.

CHAPTER 14

Improving the Speaking Voice

A good voice reflects the speaker's energy and general responsiveness. ■ *The process of sound production involves (1) breathing, (2) phonation, (3) resonance.* ■ *You may seek vocal improvement through (1) pitch, (2) loudness, (3) duration, (4) quality.*

BY THE TIME YOUR CLASS has met a few weeks, you will have begun to make observations about the voices of your fellow speakers. You will have noticed that although most voices are adequate and serviceable and that each has its own individuality, a few hold your attention better than others. You will have noticed also that voices improve as speakers become more accustomed to speech making and thereby lose a part of their nervousness.

So that you may move along another avenue of progress, you should become familiar with methods of improving voice.

I. Can the Voice be Improved?

Let us answer this question first, in the event you have misgivings about the feasibility of developing your own voice,

An old story is that of Demosthenes, who went to the seashore and practiced speech making in a loud voice that could be heard against the beating and splashing of the waves. By this procedure, according to tradition, he developed a strong voice. One student who read this decided that if it would work for Demosthenes, it would work for him. He did not have a surf handy, but he did spend evenings feeding noisy newspaper presses, and practiced his speeches in a strong voice that could be heard above the clatter of the machinery. A few weeks of this vocal exercise convinced him that both Demosthenes and he were on the right track.

Henry Clay practiced speaking as he plowed corn behind a team of oxen; this extended rehearsal strengthened his voice. William Jennings Bryan rehearsed speeches in a grove of trees. Winston Churchill in his early days practiced speech making in his bedroom; members of the family had to accustom themselves to hearing his baritone sounds reverberating through the walls. These men developed voices of flexibility and power while still young. Student debaters have such an opportunity today; after practice sessions and tournament debates they find their voices have become more vigorous. As voice is produced by the operation of vocal muscles, they, like all muscles, are strengthened by proper exercise.

Look at the matter another way: the good voices among your acquaintances belong to students who have probably done considerable speaking or singing in earlier days. Much of this activity may have been informal: reciting in class, taking a lively interest in conversation, appearing on church, club, or assembly programs. Weak voices among your acquaintances belong to students who have done pitifully little of this, just as frail bodies belong to people who have had a lifelong disinterest in participating in sports, games, exercises, or physical labor. Still, a delicate voice or a fragile body can be made stronger once the owner's concern is aroused.

By the thousands, students in speech classes have observed the kind and the degree of the improvement of their voices. Tape recordings made of speeches both at the beginning and at the end of the course show that the student is rare who demonstrates no improvement at all. If you have access to a tape recorder, make a recording of one of your own speeches (and believe the recorder when it plays the speech back to you), or solicit comments from your instructor (and believe him, also), and work out a routine of practice. Meanwhile, study this chapter to learn for what to listen and what methods are available.

II. Observations About the Speaking Voice

A beginning may be made by gaining more insight into the problem. For example:

A. A GOOD VOICE IS ENERGETIC

Listen to recordings by Roosevelt, Churchill, Truman, Murrow, and men and women in public life who speak frequently, and you will observe that they expend a good deal of *energy*. The amazing variety of voices recorded on the *I Can Hear It Now* series reflects vitality.

The simple fact is that more energy is required to talk to a room full of people—and this statement is true whether there are fifteen in the room or five hundred—than to talk to one lone individual.

B. A GOOD VOICE IS RESPONSIVE

A good voice responds to the varying emotions of the speaker.

Enthusiasm, for instance, is one of the priceless virtues—not the enthusiasm of the shallow, easily-put-on-and-quickly-taken-off variety, but the sustained enthusiasm that grows out of an honest conviction, a keen appreciation, a fine sensitivity. Says Emerson in a famous quotation: "Nothing great is ever achieved without enthusiasm." *Earnestness, warmth,* and *spiritedness* are other associated qualities. The voice quickly reacts to these inner states. When a woman talks about the profession of nursing, for example, and has a profound belief in the social importance of nursing, some of that belief will show in her *voice,* over and above what her words express; and thus a part of her interest in her profession will rub off on her listeners.

One way to make your voice convey your attitudes, feelings, and convictions is to use care in the selection of your speech material. You may have a growing belief that the *new drugs are wonderful.* You have read this, you have heard others say so, and you recently made a speedy recovery from once-baffling pneumonia. This experience is certainly enough to start you out making a speech on the subject. Get facts: for example, "in 10 years the fearful diseases of childhood— scarlet fever, diphtheria, whooping cough, and measles—have dropped 90 per cent." An imposing, armor-plated fact like *90 per cent* ought to have effect upon your voice if you utter it with the importance it deserves. Somehow manage to say it more forcefully: perhaps louder, perhaps slower, perhaps both. Thus your realization of the significance of your statistic can put more vitality in your speaking voice. You explain that twenty years ago, an average pneumonia case like the one from which you just recovered cost $300 to $400 for hospitalized care, and if the victim didn't die, he lost five weeks from work or school.[1] This fact should bring a little joy into your voice as you contrast this experience with your own two-day stay in the student clinic. Perhaps you can work in a little of the dialog between you and the physician when he broke the news to you that your ailment was pneumonia. In Chapter 9 you were encouraged to use dialog; this device should also add flexibility to your voice.

[1] These facts come principally from "How Revolution in Drugs Saves Millions of Lives," by John G. Searle, in the *Chicago Tribune,* July 19, 1959.

Thus the use of specific example and other forms of narrative can intensify your own belief and conviction, and lead you to voice your ideas with more assurance than if you gave a vague, somewhat generalized, talk that *new drugs are wonderful. Wonderful* doesn't begin to say it; the new drugs are *miraculous;* the treatment of disease in our own decade has, to use the words of your source, undergone a *revolution.* You will read more about words in Chapter 16.

Specific ways of studying and improving the voice are available to us, and it is to some of these that your attention is now turned.

III. The Production of Sound

Begin by learning about this flexible and complicated wind instrument called the human voice.

A. BREATHING

A starting point is to learn to manage the air you breathe. Normal breathing consists of a cycle of inhalation followed by exhalation, the cycle being repeated every three to five seconds (twelve to twenty times a minute).

Inhalation for ordinary quiet breathing is an active process. The ribs and breastbone move upward and outward, as you can see for yourself by taking a moderate breath. The diaphragm, a muscle between the chest cavity and the stomach cavity, moves downward. These muscle movements increase the size of the chest cavity, and air flows into the lungs.

Exhalation in quiet breathing is a fairly passive process. The muscles of inhalation relax, partly because of their weight, partly because of their elasticity; this process decreases the size of the chest cavity and forces air out of the lungs. By contracting certain chest and abdominal muscles, you can exhale additional air.

This cycle of inhalation-exhalation is then repeated, every three to five seconds, during normal, quiet breathing.

Breathing for speaking causes changes in the aforementioned procedure. Air is inhaled more quickly, in a second or less. As this air is exhaled, it sets the *vocal cords* (often called *vocal bands, vocal folds*) into vibration (see *phonation,* below). The speaker will use this outgoing breath to utter words, phrases, or sentences.

Ordinarily even a beginning speaker does not need to give much attention to his breathing. He should, of course, inhale quickly but noiselessly. He should control exhalation so he can speak the words in his thought group without gasping for a new breath. At times a speaker needs to learn to inhale more quietly; or to utter more words on one breath; or to use exhaled air efficiently, so the vocal tone itself will be full rather than breathy.

Demonstrate for yourself the relation between breathing and speaking by reading the lines below. Inhale at the slash marks. Inhale just enough air at each break to see you comfortably to the end of the phrase. Keep the last word in each unit sufficiently loud; a common fault is to speak the final words or syllables of thought units too weakly.

> Four score and seven years ago /
> our fathers brought forth on this continent /
> a new nation /
> conceived in liberty /
> and dedicated to the proposition /
> that all men are created equal.

If this arrangement of breath intervals does not suit your lung power, rearrange them, avoiding, however, inhaling in the middle of a thought unit.

B. PHONATION

As the exhaled air leaves the lungs it passes into the trachea, or windpipe, and then into the larynx. Housed in the larynx are the two vocal cords (folds), about an inch long in adult males, shorter and less massive in adult females. The vocal cords are located at the point of the Adam's apple. To produce sound, they are brought together and are set into vibration by the outgoing air. Combinations and adjustments of unbelievably complex muscles alter the length, mass, elasticity, and hardness of the cords so that changes in pitch and loudness may be produced.

C. RESONANCE

Passing through the upper larynx, the vocal sound enters the cavities of the throat, mouth, and nose. Here it is modified and amplified in a process called *resonance*. Since the throat, mouth, and nose cavities of different individuals are of varying sizes and shapes, and are lined with membranes of different degrees of firmness and moisture content, human beings can produce a wide variety of sounds. As the size and shape of most of these cavities is adjustable, one can learn to modify the tone of his voice.

IV. Studying Your Own Voice

You may improve voice in four different ways: (1) pitch, (2) loudness, (3) duration, (4) quality. These terms are the *four attributes of sound.*

A. IMPROVING PITCH

Pitch is the highness or lowness of the voice. If you can call to mind how a piano works, you know the keys at one end produce high-pitched notes, and the keys at the other bring forth low-

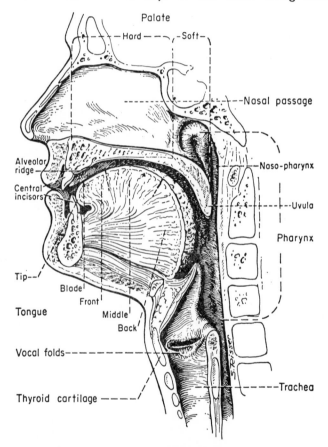

DIAGRAM OF THE SPEECH MECHANISM

Trace the passage of the exhaled air through the *trachea*, between the *vocal folds*, into the *pharynx*. Locate also the *tongue, hard palate, soft palate, alveolar ridge, nasal passage*. By permission from *Phonetics: Theory and Application to Speech Improvement*, by James Carrell and William R. Tiffany. Copyright 1960 by McGraw-Hill Book Company, Inc.

pitched sounds. If you are an average male, you will find the average pitch of your voice in the neighborhood of C below middle C on the keyboard. If you are an average female, your average pitch will be about G sharp below middle C. Individuals vary, however, and if your average pitch is within two or three tones, either higher or lower, of the foregoing, you are within normal limits.

You know that male voices vary in pitch and that some of these voices carry better than others. As voices go up in pitch they tend to carry better, other things being equal, than voices pitched too low; these latter voices sometimes become muffled. Voices that get too high, however, become unpleasant. Voices that get too low become throaty or breathy and consequently more difficult to hear. Between the limits of high and low is a broad, comfortable region of vocal pitch acceptable to everybody.

You will find it difficult to judge your own voice. Your voice sounds different to you than it does to other listeners. The reason is that when you speak the sound you hear is accompanied by vibrations that travel from your vocal cords to your ears by way of bones, cartilage, and tissue. To the listener, on the other hand, your voice is entirely airborne. It is a little like listening to the piano, first with your ear pressed against the sounding board, and then standing a few feet away. Since tape recorders are found almost everywhere, you may have already discovered that, when you first heard your recorded voice played back to you, you were surprised that you could not recognize it. On the same occasion you also noted that your friends could not recognize themselves, either.

So far as pitch is concerned, you may note two kinds of suggestions. First, is the pitch of your voice about right? Is it within normal limits—not too close to the high or to the low end of the scale? And second, does your vocal pitch have enough flexibility and variety? Poor control of pitch leads to monotonous or chant-like effects, which make it difficult for the listener to hear you with pleasure. Speakers rely largely on pitch changes to make thoughts clear and emphatic and also to suggest emotional attitudes. A difference between the mild "this is very important" and the emphatic "this is *very* important" is the difference in pitch with which the word *very* is uttered in the two statements. It would, moreover, be impossible to express one's earnestness, conviction, sympathy, kindliness, approval, or anger, without appropriate pitch changes.

These pitch changes are called *inflections,* and may be classified as *rising, falling,* or *circumflex.* Rising inflections may be used to express questioning, surprise: You *are?* She *did?* In this *way?* Falling inflections express certainty, approval, finality, and the like: It can't be *done.* I'm *sure.* Come this *way.* Circumflex inflections may rise, fall, and rise—or fall, rise, and fall—as in expressions of unusual hesitation, reflection, or doubt: *Ye-e-es. No-o-o.* English inflection, however, is too complicated a subject to dispose of in a single paragraph; one can take a single word, like *oh, yes, no, hello, goodbye, forever, always, never,* or your own first name, and say it with different kinds of inflections to suggest different meanings.

Read the following, using pitch changes as effectively as you can:

An automobile manufacturer has to plan not one, not two, not three, but ten and fifteen years ahead.

Ninety per cent of the drugs prescribed today were not even known to your physician fifteen years ago.

You ask me what my program for the company is? I say it is to make the Acme Box Corporation known all over the country, from the Atlantic to the Pacific.

You can not call yourself a good citizen unless you cast an intelligent ballot in every election.

Even if the plan will save only one life—one single life—I would say it will be worth all the trouble it takes.

What the world needs today even more than a giant leap into outer space, is a giant leap toward peace.—DWIGHT D. EISENHOWER.

B. IMPROVING LOUDNESS

Possibly you have a better insight into the loudness or softness of your voice than you have into its pitch. Perhaps your friends have complimented you on your vigorous voice and have called upon you when announcements were to be made to large assemblies. Or perhaps they have said, "Speak up. Back here we can't hear you." Another possibility, however, exists: perhaps you speak just barely loud enough so that people can hear you if they make effort; they may miss a few words, but not many; and thus it has happened that you have developed a level of loudness adequate only for small conversational situations. You now need information about whether your voice is loud enough for making talks, because speech making calls for more energy than does carrying on a conversation. You can be guided by seeing whether listeners in the back row are hearing you comfortably, and by asking them, later, if you made yourself heard—not just barely heard, but easily heard. You may be advised to talk louder—so much louder that what is right for them seems like shouting to you. In this circumstance you need to be guided by the listener, because you can be as deceived about the loudness of your own voice as you can about its pitch.

Once you learn to use a good loudness level, you need also to consider using *variety* of loudness. Although most monotones and singsongs are caused by sameness of pitch, or sameness of inflections, loudness may contribute to the fault. Some ideas need to be expressed with more vigor than others. To emphasize the word *very* in "This is *very* important," you raise the pitch of the voice as stated above; you also need to say *very* a little louder. Speakers of unusual force and power sometimes achieve striking effects by using different degrees of loudness: one idea may be expressed with great energy, and a contrasting idea may be spoken somewhat softly. When you feel determined and positive, when you have a conviction that much is at stake, when you are sure your course is right, when you know your facts are correct, you may communicate your sincerity, your conviction, and your high purpose by suiting the energy in your voice to the importance of the idea. The Book says, "For if the trumpet give an uncertain sound, who shall prepare himself for the battle?" If, similarly, the speaker's voice seems uncertain, his listeners are not going to leap into action.

Emphasize the important words in the following passages by changes in loudness. You may, of course, hear yourself making some pitch changes also. In studying these sentences, first decide which words should be spoken more loudly. Inhale deeply enough so you can generate enough vocal energy.

> Each night one-third of the world's population goes to bed hungry.

> I did not say simply that freedom was valuable—I said it was the most priceless gift we had in our possession.

> Of all the nations of recorded history, the United States has proved itself to be the most generous, the most selfless, the most willing to share its vast wealth to alleviate human suffering.

> I remember how the excitement in his voice increased as he started the count-down: Five—four—three—two—one—FIRE!

> I say this in all honesty—and I mean every word of it—we are doomed if we do not act now.

C. IMPROVING DURATION

Duration is a third term used to describe the voice. It refers to the length of time a certain sound is prolonged. One can say "Vote n-o-w," the prolonging of the second word serving to make it more urgent. So also a person could say "This is *v-e-r-y* important," not changing the pitch or loudness of the key word much, but so prolonging it that its effectiveness is increased. "Time marches rapidly past us; tomorrows become todays, and then yesterdays; before we realize it, a *w-h-o-l-e* semester is *g-o-n-e*."

Nearly every one has heard a classmate reproved for speaking too rapidly. The universal admonition of parents and teachers is *slow down; make the sounds distinct; don't run words together*. What the elders are saying, assuming for the moment that their impressions are well founded, is that students should improve their duration by stretching out the main words. Whereas the average rate of experienced speakers is 100 to 150 words a minute, many beginners try for 175 or 200. Ultimately your rate of speaking depends upon the way you are built, and the kind of nervous and muscular systems you have; 100 words a minute may be all right for a deliberate speaker, but far too slow for you. Perhaps you are one of those who can slow down with profit to yourself and your listeners.

A point which all speakers may well consider is the use of *pause*. American observers have reported that British speakers use pauses frequently and effectively; it is with them a compelling and dramatic device. Utter an idea and then pause; let the idea soak in. The sign in the boiler factory is reputed to say, "In case of emergency, there will be a five-second blast of silence, followed by two thunderous intervals of quiet." You, too, can punctuate your boiler-factory flow of words with blasts of silence now and then.

The pause helps the speaker combat the tendency to talk too hurriedly; it also gives the listener opportunity to reflect upon what the speaker has uttered. "Does anyone in this audience really think that our school spirit is as good this year as it was last? (PAUSE) Has anyone here been impressed by the attendance at our home games? (PAUSE) Has anyone recently heard praise for the present student government administration?" (PAUSE) Obviously these questions are less forceful when read *without* the pauses than when read *with* them. Pauses therefore not only slow down the speaker's rate of utterance but also add emphasis to the ideas they follow. Vary your rate to suit the idea. At times speak slowly and deliberately, at other times eagerly and rapidly. Whether your rate is fast or slow, however, you should not forget the value of the pause.

No stretch of the imagination is needed to visualize even a beginning speaker, sure of his facts and personally deeply concerned, utter something like the following:

What has been the record for traffic safety in Collegetown the last six months? (PAUSE) I asked the chief of police that question yesterday. (LONGER PAUSE) This is what I discovered. (PAUSE) There are eight new graves in the city cemetery (SHORT PAUSE) five of them from a single accident. (LONG PAUSE) The number of accidents requiring hospitalization increased from 34 to 47. (PAUSE)

In the following sentences, seek opportunities to vary the rate by prolonging a key word, or by pausing.[2] (You will also note opportunities for varying *pitch* and *loudness.*)

Labor racketeering—no matter how limited—smears all labor with the foul taint of corruption.—JAMES B. CAREY.

I am not here to justify the past, to gloss over the problems of the present, or to propose any easy solutions for the future.— DWIGHT D. EISENHOWER.

It is not enough to prove that despotism is bad. It is equally necessary to go on—and on—proving that freedom is good.— JOHN FOSTER DULLES.

We hope to show the entire world the value of the philosophy that has led to our prosperity. I do not have a name which adequately describes it. It has been called the new capitalism; the people's capitalism, or consumer capitalism. . . . Whatever it is, it is something new and far better than anything the world has ever seen before.—RICHARD M. NIXON.

D. IMPROVING QUALITY

Thus far the chapter has discussed pitch, loudness, and duration. That these are three separate aspects of voice may be shown visually when speech is recorded, by mechanical or electronic devices, as a graph. On such a graph sounds appear as a series of waves of varying shapes and patterns. *Pitch* is shown by the *number* of waves per second—the faster the waves are created, the higher the pitch. *Loudness* is shown by the *size* of the waves—the higher or taller they appear, the greater the loudness. *Duration* is shown by the *number* of waves required to make one sound: more sound waves go into *n-o-o-o* than into *no.*

---

[2] For an impressive demonstration of the use of pause, listen to the Hal Holbrook recording, "Mark Twain Tonight," mentioned at the end of this chapter.

Of course the pause is not so all-important as appeared to the saucy English girl who attended her first political meeting and heard John Morley speak. "I know the secret of how to be a great orator," she declared. "You say two or three sentences very slowly and then wait for the applause." Joseph O. Baylen and Patrick G. Hogan, "W. T. Stead on the Art of Public Speaking," in *Quarterly Journal of Speech,* XLIII (April, 1957), 132.

The fourth aspect of voice is *quality,* a characteristic of vocal sound more difficult to describe than the others. On the recorded sound wave described in the foregoing paragraph, quality is indicated by the *complexity* of the wave pattern. Quality refers not to pitch, loudness, nor duration, but to the basic tone itself. Whereas pitch can be described by *high* or *low,* loudness by *loud* or *soft,* and duration by *short* or *prolonged,* quality is described by words like *hoarse, harsh, shrill, muffled, nasal, breathy, infantile, dull, rasping,* or by *resonant, melodious, brilliant, musical,* and the like. Tom, Dick, and Harry can say the phrase, "Oh, no, sir," almost identically so far as pitch, loudness, and duration are concerned—but something basic in their tones will enable you to tell, without looking, which was Tom, which Dick, and which Harry. These are differences in *quality:* Tom may have a voice that is fuller and richer (quality): Dick is shrill and nasal (quality): Harry's voice was breathy and muffled (again, quality). Yet the three may have used identical inflections, made the tones equally loud, and required the same length of time to utter the phrase.

A speaker may use changes in quality when he makes his voice more breathy (as in excitement), more tense (when suspense or expectation is involved), more harsh, hoarse, or nasal (as when depicting different characters in a dialog), more full or resonant (as when quoting the Bible or when using solemn language). In the "I Can Hear It Now" records, Winston Churchill uses changes in quality especially in the conclusions of his speeches; Harry S. Truman changes quality when he imitates Kaltenborn, newscasting on election night, assuredly predicting a Truman defeat; Herbert Morrison of WLS, Chicago, beginning a description of a routine landing of the dirigible *von Hindenberg,* suddenly noticing that the airship is on fire and falling apart, describes the scene with almost uncontrollable changes in quality (also pitch, rate, and loudness). And in an earlier day, Senator "Fighting Bob" La Follette, probably the greatest speaker and campaigner the state of Wisconsin has yet produced, frequently used the device, in the middle of a campaign speech, of "calling the roll," in which he imitated the voice of the clerk calling the names of members of the Senate (or others) and then, in a variety of voices, their answering "yea" or "nay."[3]

Changes in quality represent a sophisticated use of the voice. But they are not beyond your reach. Try the following (attempt to get a little extra seriousness or solemnity into the quality of your voice):

[3] See Gordon F. Hostettler's discussion of "The Political Speaking of Robert M. La Follette" in *American Public Address: Studies in Honor of A. Craig Baird* (Columbia, University of Missouri Press, 1961), pp. 127-128.

For the complete dimension of the Christian faith is contained, on the one hand in the petition, "Give us this day our daily bread," and on the other, in the observance, "man does not live by bread alone."—REINHOLD NIEBUHR.

And perhaps if we ask what is the innermost nature of solitude, we should answer: It is the presence of the eternal upon the crowded roads of the temporal. It is the experience of being alone but not lonely, in view of the eternal presence which shines through the face of the Christ and which includes everybody and everything from which we are separated. Let us dare to have solitude: to face the eternal, to find others, to see ourselves. Amen.—PAUL J. TILLICH.

E. GENERAL IMPROVEMENT OF VOCAL VARIETY

As would be expected, people can use their voices to express their feelings with wide variations in effectiveness. In a Teachers College, Columbia, experiment, in which individuals tape-recorded the alphabet in such a way as to express feelings like anger, happiness, sadness, and seven other emotions, followed by listening sessions in which selected listeners noted the emotion they thought each speaker was attempting to convey, the most effective speaker communicated his feelings accurately a total of 161 times—the least effective 70 times.[4] Although a speaker can choose words, or use facial expression, to communicate to listeners how earnest, or sincere, or determined, he is, in the last analysis much of this earnestness, sincerity, or determination must be communicated by the voice.

For many years the two best speakers in the House of Commons were Charles Fox and William Pitt. "Fox," said an observer, "always speaks to the House; Pitt speaks as if he were speaking to himself." The contrast between the two men is overstated, but quite obviously Fox is being commended for his strong sense of communication to the listener.

A good speaking voice has a *communicative* quality as opposed to one that sounds *dull, feeble, withdrawn, monotonous.*

Choose materials that you strongly wish to communicate about. You may find it easier if you include in your speech sentences that show you are thinking about the listener. You have heard examples like these: *"This point is especially important . . . Here's the root of the whole difficulty . . . I hope you agree with what I've said thus far*

4 See the study by Joel R. Davitz and Lois Jean Davitz in *The Journal of Communication,* IX (March, 1959), 6-13.

. . . You may want to question me on this later . . . These were his exact words . . . You remember that Helen made this argument last Monday . . . What follows is complex but let me see if I can make it clear . . ." The use of *you* helps to bring the listener into your speech and into your thinking, and may perhaps help you project more of your meaning to him.

At times you may use a striking variation in quality, loudness, pitch, or duration to enhance your communicativeness.

This book has mentioned previously that using dialog to suggest the vocal manner of another person adds variety and interest. One speaker imitated the mobs in Africa chanting "free-dom, free-dom, free-dom." Perhaps your narrative calls for a slow count: *one—two— three—four,* or a countdown: *seven—six—five.* Maybe you would like to suggest the chant of the spectators at the Madrid bullfight: *olay—olay—olay* (*olé*). Or use a special sound (these come from student speeches): "As the Arab leaped into the air his cape made a big *whoosh.*" "We made a sudden stop and *smack!* the car behind plowed into us." A student explaining the procedures used by the National Rifle Association in pistol competition called off the commands heard on the firing range: "Ready on the right (PAUSE) ready on the left (PAUSE) ready on the firing line (PAUSE) FIRE!" These commands, spoken in an authoritative tone, spaced with the long, ten-second pauses used in competition, made the description highly realistic.

An example of the effective use of all attributes of voice is a sentence from a speech of William Jennings Bryan, heard in Des Moines, Iowa, one hot, summer afternoon. During the speech he quoted what is everywhere known as the great commandment, "Thou shalt love the Lord thy God with all thy heart, and with all thy soul, and with all thy mind." The speaker continued:

> Jesus did not say, Thou shalt love the Lord thy God with a PART of thy heart, and a PART of thy soul, and a PART of thy mind: what he did say, thou shalt love the Lord thy God with ALL thy heart, and with ALL thy soul, and with ALL thy mind.

An obvious scorn was revealed in the pitch and quality of the speaker's voice as he repeated each PART; and when he came to each ALL, he uttered these words with notable increase of loudness and duration: A-L-L. This example is cited from the memory of an incident that happened some forty years ago; and that it is remembered is explained in part by the simple and vivid choice of words and in part by the tremendous force and power of the speaker's voice.

Questions for Classroom Discussion

1. What demands do radio and TV make upon the speaker?

2. Distinguish between *voice* and *voice control*.

3. Read the illustrative sentences included in the foregoing chapter for drill purposes. After each sentence, ask yourself this question: Exactly what is communicated by the *words* in the sentence, and exactly what is communicated by the *voice?* Demonstrate to the satisfaction of the class that you can, through changes of *voice,* make the message more forceful, convincing, and emphatic.

Speech-Related Projects

1. Listen to any of the three issues of the *I Can Hear It Now* series (Columbia Record; Edward R. Murrow, narrator). Volume I contains the voices, among others, of Roosevelt, Churchill, Arthur Godfrey, Elmer Davis, John L. Lewis, Wendell Willkie. Volume II contains H. V. Kaltenborn, Harry S. Truman, James Petrillo, David E. Lilienthal, Howard Hughes, Walter Winchell. Volume III, which goes back to the 1919 to 1932 period, introduces Woodrow Wilson, Warren G. Harding, Herbert Hoover, Calvin Coolidge, William Jennings Bryan, Clarence Darrow (but note the foreword on the jacket which indicates that some of the recordings were made by actors or non-professionals whose voices and manner of speaking best resembled the fragments heard on the old records).

2. Listen to Hal Holbrook's recording, *Mark Twain Tonight* (Columbia Record). Here is an example of a young actor, in his thirties, presenting his impression of Mark Twain's delivery, based upon his study and his interviewing of people who actually heard Mark Twain. The result is an impressive demonstration of the importance of *vocal variety* and especially of *pause.* You can apply to your own speaking the lessons you learn from this album.

Speaking Assignment 13

A Speech Demonstrating Vocal Variety

Make a speech of .... minutes in which you attempt to demonstrate something different in the way of vocal variety.

Treat this assignment in the spirit of trial, experiment, venture. No attempt is being made to introduce unnatural inflections in your voice—yet every one needs to try to extend the range, the flexibility, and the power of his speaking voice—along lines that are natural to him. To achieve this result, you may go through an awkward stage.

For example: In your talk, introduce a bit of dialog, which will give you an opportunity to *suggest* different characterizations. Or you may make a talk giving some of your favorite passages from poetry—and in reading these short passages, try to bring out the deeper meanings. The reading of poetry has always been considered an extremely useful way of developing vocal variety, just as the writing of poetry is one of the best ways of increasing your vocabulary and general sensitivity to language. Or you may describe two or three professors, or ministers, or salespeople (with characterizations). Or make a talk on a subject close to your heart, and try to show us something arresting in *force*. Or describe a battle between you and your conscience (perhaps on the order of Eugene O'Neill), with you speaking in one voice and your conscience in a slightly different one. Or talk about some business or profession that requires a good voice; demonstrate the voice of command of an officer; the volume and endurance needed by a tour conductor, an executive, an auctioneer.

REFERENCES ON IMPROVING VOICE

Johnnye Akin, *And So We Speak: Voice and Articulation* (Englewood Cliffs, N. J., Prentice-Hall, Inc., 1958).

Virgil A. Anderson, *Training the Speaking Voice*, 2nd ed. (New York, Oxford University Press, 1961).

A. Craig Baird and Franklin H. Knower, Chapter 10, "The Speaking Voice," in *General Speech*, 2nd ed. (New York, McGraw-Hill Book Company, Inc., 1957).

James Carrell and William R. Tiffany, *Phonetics: Theory and Application to Speech Improvement* (New York, McGraw-Hill Book Company, Inc., 1960).

Milton Dickens, Chapter 8, "Vocal Communication," in *Speech: Dynamic Communication* (New York, Harcourt, Brace and Company, 1954).

Giles Wilkeson Gray and Waldo W. Braden, Chapter 21, "Vocal Aspects of Delivery," in *Public Speaking: Principles and Practice* (New York, Harper and Brothers, 1951).

Elise Hahn, Charles W. Lomas, Donald E. Hargis and Daniel Vandraegen, *Basic Voice Training for Speech*, 2nd ed. (New York, McGraw-Hill Book Company, Inc., 1957).

Alan H. Monroe, Chapter 4, "Improving Voice Quality" and Chapter 5, "Developing Vocal Variety," in *Principles and Types of Speech*, 4th ed. (Chicago, Scott, Foresman and Company, 1955).

Paul L. Soper, Chapter 8, "Voice," in *Basic Public Speaking*, 2nd ed. (New York, Oxford University Press, 1956).

Charles Van Riper and John Irwin, *Voice and Articulation* (Englewood Cliffs, N. J., Prentice-Hall, Inc., 1958).

CHAPTER 15

Improving Articulation and Pronunciation

Distinct articulation is an asset to a speaker throughout his speech, but note especially (1) the opening, (2) ends of sentences, (3) proper nouns, (4) unusual or technical terms, (5) key words, (6) quotations, (7) close of the speech. ▪ Study (1) vowels, (2) diphthongs, (3) consonants. ▪ Pronunciation varies with (1) standards, (2) the passing of time. Names in the news and foreign words present a special problem.

BY ARTICULATION IS MEANT the *precision* and *clearness* with which sounds of speech are uttered. A synonym is *enunciation*. Mumbling and indistinctness, therefore, as when a speaker says "puhtikly" for *particularly* and "govment" for *government,* are forms of faulty articulation.

By *pronunciation* is meant the traditional or customary utterance of words. *Acoustic* is spoken with the second syllable as "koo"; to utter it as *cow* is a fault of pronunciation. *Nuclear* pronounced as "nucular" is similarly a fault of pronunciation; so also is *perspiration* pronounced as "prespiration," *fragment* with the *a* of *hate* instead of the *a* of *hat, bestial* as "beestial."

You know how quickly your ear notes the wrong utterance of your home town or other familiar proper name (like *Illinois, Des Moines,* or *Louisville,* with an s or z sound), or expressions like "fillum" for *film,* "deef" for *deaf,* "drownded" for *drowned.* Others in the audience also note faults and are momentarily distracted from the speaker's message. In nearly every audience, moreover, a few at least will be aware of even slight deviations from standard (prescribed) articulation and pronunciation. When appearing in public, therefore, you will feel more at ease if you can employ the sort of articulation and pronunciation that become an educated person.

I. Improving Articulation

Good articulation, like good use of voice and body, requires the expenditure of muscular *energy*, and necessitates precise operation of the speech mechanism. You need to give the same attention to being distinct that you would display in lively, animated conversation—plus additional care to make sure you are easily understood by everybody in the room. You do not want to overdo the matter, or you will sound artificial or pedantic; this fault, however, is rare. Speakers are more likely to mumble, to slur words or run them together, or to utter sounds too feebly, than they are to be overly precise. Part of their laxity grows out of their not fully realizing what listeners expect.

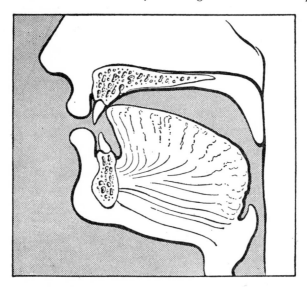

NOTE POSITION OF TONGUE TIP FOR [t] AND [d]
Lips are slightly parted, tip of tongue rests on gum ridge (alveolar ridge). Opening to nasal passage is closed. By permission from *Phonetics: Theory and Application to Speech Improvement,* by James Carrell and William R. Tiffany. Copyright 1960 by McGraw-Hill Book Company, Inc.

Sounds of speech are produced by operating the vocal cords in combination with adjustments of the size and shape of the throat, mouth, and nasal cavities, along with changes of position of lips, teeth, and tongue. This is a marvellous and complex procedure which we will not pause to wonder at, or even to describe, other than to offer examples to show how the mechanism works.

If you look into a mirror while you say *we, fee,* and *see,* you will notice that your tongue and lips behave in different ways. In *we* the lips are active; in *fee* the upper teeth touch the lower lip; in *see* the tongue tip is so placed as to allow the air to hiss past the front teeth. Now if you again say *we, fee,* and *see,* this time allowing the lips and the tongue to become sluggish, the three words are no longer so clear. Obviously, therefore, clear articulation calls for precise adjustment of the speech mechanism. To explore the matter further: if you say *oo* as in *boot, a* as in *calm* and *i* as in *police,* you will see that the lips are rounded for *oo,* parted and relaxed for *a,* unrounded for *i.* You may also be able to tell that your tongue takes a different position for each sound. If you again say *oo, a,* and *i* in a sluggish fashion, with less lip and tongue action, your three vowels will tend to resemble one another. What you have done is to demonstrate to yourself that certain exact movements of lips, tongue, and teeth are necessary to articulate (1) clear consonants and (2) clear vowels. Certain other muscular activity also takes place, i.e. of jaw and soft palate, of the vocal cords, of breathing muscles.

Below are crucial points in a speech where clear articulation is essential.

A. OPENING OF THE SPEECH

Good first impressions are important. Clear articulation suggests poise and self-assurance. Say "Mr. Chairman," or "Madame Chairman," or speak the name of your presiding officer, distinctly. Don't hurry, and don't mumble. Abraham Lincoln is reputed to have said "Mr. Cheerman," which amused his listeners from the big cities and momentarily distracted them. You can say "Friends" or "Ladies and gentlemen" (not "la'ies and gennulmun") with clarity and distinctness (and with cordiality). Then launch into your opening sentences. Counteract your tendency to be nervous by taking extra care to make yourself heard. Here it must be admitted that certain great speakers stumbled and hesitated at the opening—among them Patrick Henry of Williamsburg and Charles Fox of London—but you can improve on this fault.

Don't forget what you learned about using your voice—keep level of loudness strong enough so that listeners will hear easily.

B. ENDS OF SENTENCES

English sentences have a pitch or melody pattern that calls for a falling inflection at the end of a sentence (unless it is a question); in this way a speaker shows he has come to a full stop. Use enough loudness and enough clarity of articulation on those last words so that the audience will hear them. If your sentence is, "I want to pay a special tribute to the three most distinguished speakers in our class this year," make those last words *distinct;* do not let them sound like "in our class susseer."

C. PROPER NOUNS

We can not tell whether you said *Johnson* or *Jensen* by the context of your sentence—our only clue is the way you pronounce the first vowel in the name. Be careful of all proper nouns: *Bunsen* burner, *Van Allen's* belt, *Doppler* effect, *Grimm's* law, *Broca's* area, *Von Braun's* statement, *Lewis* and *Clark* expedition, *Robert Penn Warren's* new book, *Monroe's* administration, a new play by *Gristlethwaite* and *Oppensteiner,* the trial was held at *Ipswich.* If the name is unusual, you will confer a favor on your listeners by repeating it, or spelling it, or even writing it on the blackboard.

D. UNUSUAL OR TECHNICAL WORDS

Gaiter, retrorocket, laparotomy, monitor, turbine, vault, launching pad, cornering, enfillade, trajectory, placket, placebo, may not be so familiar to your listeners as to you. Speak technical terms distinctly; you may also need to spell them and perhaps define them.

E. OTHER IMPORTANT WORDS

Any word that carries a special burden of meaning must be distinctly spoken. Listeners may mis-hear or misunderstand unless the speaker is careful. Any teacher or speaker of experience would quickly see why a group of children showed up at the Smithsonian Institute asking to see *Dinah Shore's bones,* or why *Dentist the Menace* appeared in a composition written during class. The punch line of a narrative must be articulated with clarity, or listeners will miss the point of the humor. Imagine a three-minute story ending with the line "Oh, you've *shot* him!" The total effect of the story, the fate of the joke, hinges on the single word "shot"; any faltering here, and the effect is destroyed. A half-*shod* tramp is different from a half-*shot* tramp.

If your utterance of *foreign policy* sounds like *farm policy,* your listener may be confused for the dozen following sentences. If you talk about *The Hunchback of Notre Dame* and the *hunch* is gargled and swallowed, don't be surprised if some listener gets set to hear a football story about a Notre Dame halfback. Your *visibility unlimited* may be heard as *visibility limited* if you do not speak the all im-

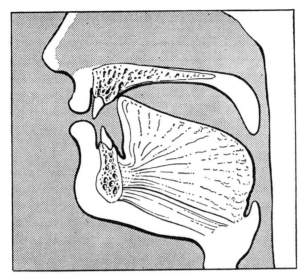

NOTE POSITION OF TONGUE TIP FOR [n]

Lips are slightly parted, tip of tongue rests on gum ridge (alveolar ridge). Sound escapes through nasal passage. By permission from *Phonetics: Theory and Application to Speech Improvement,* by James Carrell and William R. Tiffany. Copyright 1960 by McGraw-Hill Book Company, Inc.

portant "un" with precision. Perhaps you have sometimes said, "This isn't difficult," and your listener has said, "Did you say *is* or *isn't?*" And "green pebbles" can sound like "green petals" if the speaker half-way mumbles and the listener half-way listens.

F. QUOTATIONS

Quotations should be uttered distinctly. "The chief thing in art" (this is you, now, quoting Cicero) "is that what you do shall be fitting." Nearly all these words are important to understanding: *chief thing, art, what you do, fitting.* What meaning can the listener wring from "The chief glub in art is that whaddadoo shall be fliffglmp," originally uttered, you go on to say, by Sestero. ("What did he say?" mumble the listeners.)

G. ENDING OF THE SPEECH

Don't weaken the important last impression. "We should all get behind the drive to raise funds for the student union." Make the words *distinct.* This is the give me liberty or give me death part of your talk, the appeal to give us the tools and we will finish the job.

Don't leave the platform until after you have spoken your last word, and have paused a moment; then nod at the audience to show that you have finished. A cluttered ending makes a poor closing.

H. SPECIAL PROBLEMS WITH VOWELS

English has at least fourteen different vowels and all are important to understanding. It makes a difference whether you say "Give me a pen" or "give me a pin." *Sing* should be spoken with the vowel of *it*, not of *ate* (technically the *a* is a diphthong). *Wish* has the vowel of *it*, not of *put*. *Poor* should not sound like *pore*. Some of these examples may illustrate faulty pronunciation, rather than faulty articulation; the point here is to utter each sound with precision.

In excessively rapid speech, vowel production suffers. This fault is regrettable, since most of the music and melody of the voice is expressed in the vowels. A word like *shot* begins with a slushy noise and ends with a click, but the vowel of the word is acoustically pleasant. Some speakers may be able to dwell on their vowels more than is habitual; this practice will result in an agreeable slowing down of the rate. But don't overdo this.

I. SPECIAL PROBLEMS WITH DIPHTHONGS

The way one utters his diphthongs (as in *oil, tire, few, cow, say, go*) is often a clue to his regional dialect. If you find you are (1) distorting diphthongs, as "kee-ow" for *cow* or (2) omitting a part of the diphthong, as *tar* for *tire* or *all* for *oil*, you may need special drill on these sounds. Speakers of foreign language background who habitually speak the first and last sounds in *okay* as pure vowels will need to learn the English pronunciation of these sounds as diphthongs.

J. SPECIAL PROBLEMS WITH CONSONANTS

One summer a college student interested in radio and television was given a news program by a Chicago station. His first assignment was to broadcast election returns: he was to speak a series of names, followed by the number of votes cast for each. After a few moments, however, he was taken out of the studio and a regular newscaster took over. "You were misspeaking *thousand*," the student was told; "you kept saying *thousan'*, not *thousand*." After a little drill, he was allowed to go back and continue. Another announcer who pronounced *for* like *four* confused his listeners by reading statements like "four hundred and twenty for Johnson," which sounded, in his dialect, like "four hundred and twenty-four, Johnson."

Radio and TV announcers take pride in distinct *articulation*. All speakers, however, should avoid the tendency to drop *final consonants*. *Rah* and *rock* should be spoken differently; *rate* should not sound like *ray*. The consonants *r* and *l* are at times weakened in combinations like *pray* and *blame* resulting in something like "pway" and "bwame." Unless awkward combinations like the *sts* in *ghosts*, *sps* in *wasps*, and *shr* in *shrimp* are handled skillfully, the pronunciations may be overly simplified and sound respectively like "ghos," "wass," and "srimp." If a speaker has a defective consonant, such as a lisp, or a foreign accent that makes it difficult for him to pronounce the *th* or other English sounds, he needs a special speech course or individual help from his instructor or from a speech clinician.

II. Improving Pronunciation

In addition to uttering individual sounds of speech distinctly, the speaker must also pronounce the words themselves in acceptable fashion. Any one who uses words like *alias, façade, protégé* and **marital** immediately suggests that he is a person of some schooling; but if he pronounces the second syllable of *alias* as *lye*, the *c* of *façade* like *k*, *protégé* in two syllables instead of three, and confuses *marital* with *martial*, listeners just as immediately realize that he is not so well schooled as they at first assumed. Rightly or wrongly, we tend to agree that if a person mispronounces a word, he knows little about the idea represented by that word. One who has spent years in musical circles will utter words like *concerto, pianissimo, fugue, aria*, and *ensemble* with accuracy and sureness; conversely, one who fumbles over these terms will be assumed to know little about the finer points of music.

English is not a phonetic language; that is, the spelling of English words does not give an unfailing clue to the pronunciation of those words. *Cough, through, though, enough*, and *hiccough* look as if they should rhyme. *Read* can be pronounced two ways; *need, kneed, knead* are pronounced identically. The letter *c* is pronounced as *s* in *fleece*, but as *k* in *cat, crew*, and *close*. *Ch* is pronounced as *k* in *Christmas* and *chrome*, but differently in *chew, choice*, and *itch*, and still differently in *Chicago*. One who had not seen *pneumonia, ghost, women, busy, gnat, one* in print would never guess, from the pronunciation, how to spell them. The upshot is that we must give special study to the mastery of pronunciation.

III. Standards of Pronunciation

The old belief dies hard that each word should have, or does have, only one pronunciation. Although each italicized word in the preceding paragraph has one single, acceptable pronunciation,[1] many words, on the other hand, have two or more pronunciations. Teachers of speech at times hesitate to use the phrase "correct pronunciation"; the term suggests a single, inflexible standard. They prefer to speak of "acceptable pronunciation"; this term better describes the variety that exists.

A. DIFFERENCES IN REGION

A pronunciation may be acceptable in one part of the country, but less acceptable in another. "Idear" is acceptable to educated Easterners, but jars the Western ear. A Westerner's "Aunt Nan," with the same vowel in both words, sounds rustic to the Eastern ear that prefers to hear *ant* and *aunt* pronounced differently. Former President Roosevelt's "I hate wah" was long mimicked in many parts of the country. These and hundreds of other examples illustrate why "acceptable" is better than "correct" in describing pronunciation. Regional differences should be taken as a matter of course.

If you were to make a pronunciation map of the continental United States, you would divide the country into three major regions.[2]

One region is that part of New England east of the Connecticut River and the ridges of the Green Mountains, plus the eastern part of New York state; you may label that section "Eastern American" speech. Here speakers tend to drop their r's in words like *farm, clear, sailor*; they use a variety of the vowel of *ah* in words like *class, dance,* and *half*; occasionally the "ei" in the first syllables of *either* and *neither* is pronounced like *eye*.

Another is a group of southern states: Virginia, North Carolina, South Carolina, Georgia, Florida, Mississippi, Louisiana, Alabama, east Texas, Arkansas, Tennessee, and Kentucky; you may label that section "Southern American" speech. Speakers in this region also drop their r's, in this characteristic resembling speakers of Eastern American. They do, however, use the vowel of *at* in words like *class* and *half*.

---

[1] This statement is broadly true, but the instructor if he wishes may suggest minor, acceptable variations.

[2] Many pages would be required to develop this section in detail. For accurate particularization of these broad generalizations, consult one or more of the following, all reasonably sure to be in your college library: Giles W. Gray and Claude M. Wise, *The Bases of Speech* (any edition, but the latest is the third, published in New York in 1959 by Harper and Brothers); Claude M. Wise, *Applied Phonetics,* published at Englewood, New Jersey, in 1957 by Prentice-Hall, Inc., or his briefer version, *Introduction to Phonetics,* published by the same company in 1958; C. K. Thomas, *An Introduction to the Phonetics of American English,* 2nd ed. (New York: The Ronald Press Company, 1958); Arthur J. Bronstein, *The Pronunciation of American English* (New York, Appleton-Century-Crofts, Inc., 1960).

The remaining states constitute that large section known as "General American." This region, stretching across the country from western New York and Pennsylvania to the Pacific shore, contains more speakers than the other two regions combined. Here is the home of most of the speakers of English who sound the r's in words like *farm, clear, butter, sailor*. Here, too, *aunt* is pronounced the same as *ant*, and *dance* rhymes with *ants;* the "ei" in the first syllables of *either* and *neither* is the same as the vowel of *see*. A few phoneticians subdivide this large area into other dialect regions, but the characteristics mentioned prevail throughout. You could extend this zone to Alaska, most of which was settled by western people, and perhaps also to Hawaii. In Honolulu, however, you would find a wide variety of special foreign accent or dialect problems, as you would note also in New York, Boston, Chicago, New Orleans, San Francisco, or other metropolitan areas.

If you wanted to make your map truly representative, you would not try to draw sharp boundary lines. You may also locate special dialect areas like those of tidewater Virginia or the Ozarks. And as suggested, you would be puzzled by metropolitan sections where people gather from all over. You would note areas where French, Spanish, German, Italian, Polish, Japanese, or some other language colors the speech.

These lesser distinctions, however, are of more importance to the phonetician than to the speaker. So far as standards of pronunciation are concerned, the current practice is to label the speech of all three regions as equally acceptable. One American president omitted his r's, another pronounced them. One who speaks standard Southern, standard Eastern, or standard General American is accepted by audiences outside his region with not more than a momentary pause now and then for dialect identification.

Occasions calling for a speaker to adopt the dialect of another *region* are few indeed. If, however, he speaks a *mediocre* or *substandard version* of his own regional dialect, he should improve that.

B. DIFFERENCES IN TIME

Pronunciations change with the passing of time. American English is a growing, dynamic language and what is acceptable today may be less acceptable tomorrow. The first syllable of *ration* has the vowel of *hat* in the speech of most people. Before World War II, the "ay" of *ray* was frequently heard. More people today pronounce the first syllable of *bouquet* like *beau* instead of *boo*. Not too many years ago *boo* was preferable. College students who have spent a period of service in the Navy report that *quay* is no longer *key* but "kway." *Apparatus* with the third syllable as *rat* seems to be rapidly supplanting *rate*. Before you condemn the pronunciation of *sacrilegious* as "sacreligious," look at the dictionary, which now gives both "—rileg—" and "—relig—." For generations dictionaries said that the pronunciation of *conversant* was "CONversant," but "conVERsant" is now well established.

When a majority of educated people in a linguistic community shows preference for a given pronunciation, that pronunciation becomes accepted and eventually may drive out entirely the older form. If after graduation you continue speaking in public, you will need to be sensitive to changes in pronunciation wrought by time. You should then take note of the new standard; you can not appeal to an outdated usage to sustain you. *Webster's Third New International Dictionary*, published in 1961, reflects the exceptionally liberal attitude of modern scholars towards pronunciation.

C. NAMES IN THE NEWS

What standard of pronunciation governs names in the news, or, for that matter, any proper name? The first president Roosevelt reputedly preferred his last name pronounced in two syllables, ROSE-velt; the second president Roosevelt preferred three, ROSE-uh-velt. To pronounce "Roose" to rhyme with *moose*, in either instance, is not acceptable. We try to pronounce a person's name as he pronounces it himself. If the name is that of a community, we accept the prevailing usage of the citizens of the community wherever it is made clear. The city of *Cairo*, in Illinois, rhymes with *Karo*; it is not pronounced like the Egyptian city. Good usage may be divided, as in *Missouri, Los Angeles, Louisiana*; here we may side with either camp, but may encounter discussion from partisans of the other.

D. WORDS OF FOREIGN ORIGIN

What standards govern the pronunciation of words of foreign origin? This problem, too, confronts speakers.

Foreign words are quickly given an American equivalent that gains currency in American speech. Undoubtedly radio and TV announcers set the pattern; since they are deservedly reputed to be studious about these matters, their decisions are followed without much question. When the Korean city of Seoul made the news, radio and TV people at first differed among themselves, then settled on the simplified *sole;* this pronunciation became standard. The Russian word *sputnik* became Anglicized with "sput" pronounced as in *sputter*, but now that the skies are filled with American satellites the Russian word has faded. The German *Volkswagen* is pronounced much as spelled, disregarding German practice in which initial *v* is pronounced *f* and initial *w* pronounced *v* ("folksvagen"). A compromise pronunciation, often heard, is "volksvagen." Similarly, thousands of Air Force personnel stationed in the German city of *Wiesbaden* pronounce the first syllable "weese," though in German it is "vees." Yet we respect the German pronunciations of *Wagner, Beethoven,* and *Bach,* since these pronunciations are in the custody of cultured and educated classes; to Anglicize them as "wagner, bee-thoven, and batch" would stamp a speaker as intellectually beyond repair. (The *ch* in *Bach* calls for a German sound that does not exist in English; professional musicians at times employ that sound, though others pronounce *Bach* like *bock* with no ill effects.)

Unless therefore, the foreign pronunciation, or one close to it, seems to prevail, the speaker will be in good standing if he adopts any widely-used Americanized form (our pronunciation of *pizza* is close enough to the Italian to satisfy us, but would not fool a native).

E. TECHNICAL TERMS

In pronouncing technical terms, select the pronunciation used by the industry. Some of the older dictionaries were once in an untenable position when they gave the pronunciation of *automobile* as "autoMOble" when the industry and most people were saying "autoMO-beel." Some pedants were saying *oleomargarine* with the *g* of *go,* after the industry and others much preferred the *g* of *gem.* That issue was resolved, however, when the long word dropped almost completely out of spoken usage in favor of the short *oleo.* If the experts pronounce *transister* as "tranzister," use that instead of "transister." If they prefer "hellicopter" to "heelicopter," follow their guidance.

F. OTHER INFLUENCES

Other factors, some of them subtle, also influence one's standards of pronunciation.

The stress given a word in a sentence affects its pronunciation. The conjunction *and* may be variously pronounced as *an, 'n',* etc., in informal expressions ("bread 'n' butter," not "bread AND butter"). The preposition *of* in a strongly stressed position (like "government OF the people") may be variously pronounced with the vowel of *love* or *sod. On* is heard with the vowel of *love* (very informal), *sod,* or *awe.* But most speakers would much prefer *what* with the vowel of *ah,* not of *uh,* and *get* and *just* not as "git" or "jist."

Many words have more than one acceptable pronunciation, regardless of the regional standard. *Abdomen* may be accented on either the first or the second syllable. *Advertisement* may have the primary accent on *-tise-*, to rhyme with *flies,* or on *-ver-* to rhyme with *sir.* Some speakers say "MonDAY," "TuesDAY," etc., although "Mundy," "Tuesdy," etc. may be preferable. *Calm, palm, walk* are preferably pronounced without the *l,* though in every group of students a few elect the pronunciation with the *l.* This is another kind of situation in which the notion of "one correct pronunciation" must give way to "acceptable pronunciation." If alternate pronunciations are acceptable within your region, you need to make a choice as to which you prefer to use. You may adopt the pronunciation first given in the dictionary until your own judgment has matured by observation, remembering, however, that the second pronunciation is also acceptable.

The theory underlying choice of pronunciation is simple. A speaker's responsibility is to communicate a message to listeners. He seeks a standard of pronunciation that will further that message, not distract from it. When he speaks to listeners from some other dialect region, or when he speaks to national audiences made up of listeners from all regions, his dialect may arouse a momentary curiosity, but he will need to rely on the strength of his message to outweigh a possible distraction. He may, in fact, be able to capitalize on his dialect; we enjoy a British speaker none the less because of his British speech. What a speaker should not do is to employ a substandard version of the speech of his region.

IV. Use a Dictionary

Keep a college-level dictionary on your desk. Make it a part of your preparation to look up the pronunciation of words about which you have the least doubt.

Students who feel insecure about their pronunciation at times find that a principal difficulty is to manage long words. Read the following aloud, giving each syllable its proper value. Consult a source like the Kenyon-Knott *Pronouncing Dictionary of American English,* or any collegiate level dictionary, to learn acceptable pronunciations: the syllables written in capital letters will give you a clue. Although in several instances other pronunciations are acceptable, if you find yourself accenting a word differently from the pronunciation given below, better check your pronunciation in a dictionary for **acceptability**. **Repeat combinations that are bothersome, and group several words in** drill sentences: "The repercussions of those formidable archaelogical findings are peculiarly lamentable."

abDOMinal	disINterestedly	perseVERance
acCOMpaniment	FORmidable	pronunciAtion
ADmirable	HOSpitable	reperCUSsion
APplicable	imMEdiately	sacriLEgious
apPROXimately	inQUIRy	scienTIFically
archaeoLOGical	inCOMparable	simultaNEity
arguMENtative	inDISputable	subsidiZAtion
aristoCRATic	inEXplicable	sucCINCT
arTICulatory	intelLECtualize	superinTENdent
arTIStically	INtricacy	surPRISing
asPIRant	irREParable	SUStenance
authoriTAtively	LAMentable	unQUEStionably
BARbarous	manuFACturer	VEGetable
characterIStic	oleoMARgarine	VEhemence
civiliZAtion	parenTHETically	verBAtim
conTEMplative	parTICularly	VETerinary
deTEriorate	peCULiarly	zoOLogy

Questions for Classroom Discussion

1. What are characteristics of the articulation of speakers in your region? Which characteristics are desirable? Which should be modified or changed?

2. Differentiate, with examples, between articulation and pronunciation.

3. From the point of view of articulation and pronunciation, what responsibility does a speaker have to his listeners? Formulate standards of (a) good articulation, (b) good pronunciation.

4. Study and read aloud this list of commonly mispronounced words:

arctic	column	genuine
address	condolence	gesture
alias	comparable	government
ally	coupon	height
bade	despicable	heinous
because	dour	homage
bouquet	electoral	humor
clique	exquisite	impotent

inquiry	precedence	secretive
irrelevant	presentation	superfluous
larynx	program	statistics
library	rationale	status
maintenance	research	toward
mischievous	respite	tremendous
often	ribald	vehement
orgy	robot	victuals

Speaking Assignment 14

A Speech About Articulation and Pronunciation

Make a speech of . . . . minutes entitled "A Report on My Investigation of the Articulation and Pronunciation of Campus and Community Speakers."

Listen to the articulation and pronunciation of your teachers, your pastor, visiting speakers to the campus and community, students who give reports or speeches—all kinds of situations in which one person is addressing a group of others. Your talk may include samples of both good and bad practices that you observed.

REFERENCES ON IMPROVING ARTICULATION

W. Norwood Brigance and Florence Henderson, *Drill Manual for Improving Speech*, 3rd ed. (Chicago, J. B. Lippincott, 1955).

Fairbanks, Grant, *Voice and Articulation Drillbook* (New York, Harper and Brothers, 1960).

Alan H. Monroe, Chapter 6, "Making the Voice More Intelligible," in *Principles and Types of Speech*, 4th ed. (Chicago, Scott, Foresman and Company, 1955).

C. K. Thomas, *Handbook of Speech Improvement* (New York, The Ronald Press Company, 1956).

(See also the references at the end of Chapter 14 by *Akin, Anderson, Brigance, Dickens, Gray and Braden, Hahn, Van Riper.*)

CHAPTER 16

Improving Your Use of Words

A first important quality of language is clarity, achieved by (1) accurate data, (2) specific instead of general words, (3) awareness of the limitations of technical or unusual words, (4) utilization of preview, enumeration, transition, summary. ■ *A second important quality is vividness, achieved by (1) epigrammatic phrases, (2) repetition, (3) parallelism, (4) rhetorical question, (5) figurative language.* ■ *Tools for improving language are (1) dictionaries, (2) wordbooks, (3) books of quotations.*

AN EARLIER CHAPTER in this book explains visual aids; useful as that chapter is, the speaker should realize that the ability to paint pictures with words is, for many types of speeches, an even greater talent. One always wishes to be *clear,* so that listeners will understand what he says; one should strive also to put ideas in *striking, forceful* language, so that listeners will remember what he says.

I. Good Qualities of Language

For centuries it has been established that the language of the speaker should meet two qualifications. The first is described by words like *clarity, simplicity, accuracy;* this aim of language grows out of the desire of every speaker, beginner or expert, to be *understood.* The second is described by words like *striking, forceful, lively, vivid;* this aim shows that speakers have invariably yearned not only to have the listener understand but to remember.

These qualities of language are illustrated in the career of a truly illustrious American speaker, Abraham Lincoln. Early in life Lincoln became interested in speaking: possibly because he disliked hard physical work, possibly because he saw that good speech making would help him enter politics, possibly because he was encouraged from the outset to develop his latent talent. The text of his first political speech has been handed down to us as follows:

> Gentlemen and fellow citizens: I presume you all know who I am. I am humble Abraham Lincoln. I have been solicited by many friends to become a candidate for the legislature. My politics are short and sweet, like the old woman's dance. I am in favor of a national bank. I am in favor of the internal improvements system and a high protective tariff. These are my sentiments and political principles. If elected, I shall be thankful; if not, it will be all the same.[1]

This speech is a humble beginning, and may not fairly represent Lincoln's ability to express himself even at that youthful age. At any rate, early in life Lincoln became impressed with the clear reasoning of Euclid's geometry: the geometrician began with a well-defined problem to prove, and then demonstrated the solution step by step. Lincoln thought a speaker should strive for this same clarity; his idea was that a speech should be a demonstration, the speaker's main idea being supported by clearly stated reasons.

When Lincoln was elected President, however, and began to think about what he should say in his inaugural address, he began to realize that *clearness* alone was not enough; when citizens of a nation are troubled, they need to be reached through their hearts and souls as well as through their reason. Perhaps he got the impetus from reading speeches by his great hero Henry Clay, and by Andrew Jackson and Daniel Webster, all of which he reviewed before he undertook to write his speech. A first draft of his first inaugural reads as follows:

> The mystic chords which, proceeding from so many battlefields and so many patriot graves, pass through all the hearts and all the hearths in this broad continent of ours, will yet harmonize in their ancient music when breathed upon by the guardian angel of the nation.

Language like "mystic chords" and "the guardian angel of the nation" may well have been inspired by Webster, who knew more literature than many a professor.

---

[1] Carl Sandburg, *Abraham Lincoln: The Prairie Years* (New York, Harcourt, Brace and Company, 1926), I, 160-161.

Because the times were so critical that Lincoln wanted his inaugural address to strike exactly the right note, he showed this draft to his secretary of state, William H. Seward. Seward thought Lincoln's composition should have more *vigor* and *vividness*. Terms like these describe the *second imperative quality of the effective spoken word* mentioned at the outset of this chapter. Seward, an earnest and conscientious critic, suggested revision of the Lincoln prose; Lincoln did not adopt all of Seward's ideas, but he did respond to the thought of making his manuscript more eloquent, and he rewrote the paragraph as follows:

> The mystic chords of memory, stretching from every battlefield, and patriot grave, to every living heart and hearthstone, all over this broad land, will yet swell the chorus of the Union, when again touched, as surely they will be, by the better angels of our nature.[2]

This final version is an improvement upon its predecessor; the speaker is earnestly trying for a striking, lively, colorful, quality.

When Carl Sandburg speaks about Lincoln, the result is an example of one genius with words discussing the art of another: Says Sandburg:

> His words at Gettysburg were sacred, yet strange with a color of the familiar:
> We cannot consecrate—we cannot hallow—this ground. The brave men, living and dead, who struggled here, have consecrated it, far beyond our poor power to add or detract.
> He could have said "the brave Union men." Did he have a purpose in omitting the word "Union"? Was he keeping himself and his utterance clear of the passion that would not be good to look back on when the time came for peace and reconciliation? Did he mean to leave an implication that there were brave Union men and brave Confederate men, living and dead, who had struggled there? We do not know, of a certainty. Was he thinking of the Kentucky father whose two sons died in battle, one in Union blue, the other in Confederate gray, the father inscribing on the stone over their double grave, "God knows which was right?" We do not know.[3]

---

[2] This incident is based upon Earl W. Wiley's "Abraham Lincoln: His Emergence as the Voice of the People," in W. Norwood Brigance, ed. *History and Criticism of American Public Address* (New York, McGraw-Hill Book Co., Inc., 1943), II, 866-868.

[3] Delivered to a joint session of the United States Congress, Washington, D. C., February 12, 1959. Mr. Sandburg wrote the author: "You are welcome to quote from my Joint Session speech of February 12, 1959." He added: "I had a good elocution teacher in college." (Letter of December 22, 1959.)

A. MAKING IDEAS CLEAR

But let us leave the presidential level and come down to the every-day level in search of usable suggestions: ways to raise your mark from *average* to *good*, or higher.

1. *Use figures*

Expressions like "a few," "several," "a whole lot," or "millions" lead away from Euclidian clarity to a vague and fuzzy picture for the mind's eye. Often these terms show simply that the speaker has not taken the trouble to get exact information.

Suppose you want to say that there were "a whole lot" of auto-mobile accidents in your home county. Why not get the precise figure? To say that in 1960, in your home county, 87 automobile accidents were recorded by the sheriff's office, is accurate and there-fore more convincing. Instead of saying that old age pensions have greatly increased, why not use the exact statement: "Since 1950, old age pensions have *doubled*." Maybe you can draw directly on your own observation; to say "I know personally six students who went to the student clinic because of the strain of final examinations" is more convincing than to say "several students."

Nearly always a figure has to be interpreted before it is as mean-ingful as the speaker wants it to be. To say that your home county had "87 automobile accidents" seems to be about as specific as a speaker can get, but you can add to the impact of the idea by continuing, "This is a fifteen per cent increase over last year," and the further interpretation, "And my home county has the best record (poor as it is) in the state" (or has "one of the best records") (or is "one of the ten best counties"). Skin diving is one of our most popular sports? you were about to say. Not specific enough; a million skin divers bought three times as much gear in 1960 as in 1957.

Developing the thought that the world needs young leaders, one speaker said:

> Our greatest lack we share with all the rest of the world— we have too few young, alert, and devoted leaders. . . . Mac-millan is 65, DeGaulle and Franco are 68. Mao Tse-tung is 66. Every major world leader today is old enough for social security! . . . The people born in the 20th century have not yet taken over from the people born in the 19th century. The whole world is being led by men who would have been retired

by any sound American corporation as overaged. This is no indictment of the oldsters—but of all of us who have never tried hard
enough to relieve them.[4]

During the 1960 national election many editors commented on the
closeness of the vote; one of the more striking observations, however,
was that *one vote more per precinct* would have put the loser ahead
of the winner. This statistic will be useful in the future to a political
speaker seeking to urge each listener that his single vote is important.
Sometimes the interpretation of a statistic is quite casual: "Norman
Thomas ran six times for the presidency, which is two times more
than Franklin D. Roosevelt"; sometimes it is more scholarly, as when
the professor in his lecture observes that during the years of the
French Revolution "more people were hanged for petty crimes in
England than were guillotined for treason in Paris."

The following is a novel interpretation of statistical material. The
speaker is describing what this country must do to "equal" the Soviet
Union:

> In order to enjoy the glories of the present Soviet system, we
> would have to abandon three fifths of our steel capacity, two thirds
> of our petroleum capacity, 95 percent of our electric-motor output,
> destroy two of every three of our hydroelectric plants, and get along
> on a tenth of our present volume of natural gas.
>
> We would have to rip up 14 out of every 15 miles of our paved
> highways and two out of every three miles of our main-line railway
> tracks. We'd sink eight out of every nine ocean-going ships, scrap
> 19 out of every 20 cars and trucks, and shrink our civilian air fleet
> to a shadow of its present size.
>
> We would have to cut our living standard by three fourths,
> destroy 40 million TV sets, nine out of every ten telephones, and
> seven out of every ten houses; and we would have to put about 60
> million of our people back on the farm.[5]

[4] Charles H. Brower, president of Batten, Barton, Durstine & Osborn, Inc., gave
this speech, entitled "The Packaged People," to the Los Angeles Rotary Club,
May 29, 1959. Text furnished by Mr. Brower. The entire speech may be con-
veniently found in *Vital Speeches*, XXV (August 15, 1959).

Mr. Brower, who took public speaking while a freshman at Rutgers, wrote: "I
am sure that whatever small ability I may have in this area has its roots in
Rutgers." His speeches reflect wide reading, the use of vivid example, and good
counsel. He gives about a speech a month "before various groups in advertising,
marketing, sales, banking, etc., on a variety of subjects usually pertinent to each
group's interest." (Letter of November 17, 1959.) Says *Time*, speaking of Mr.
Brower's high reputation among business speakers: "He could easily make a speech
a week, but likes to limit himself to one a month—and writes every word himself" LXXV (February 8, 1960), 84.

[5] The speaker is Bryce N. Harlow, addressing the Southwest Electric Conference,
Chandler, Ariz., March 29, 1960. Mr. Harlow, then Deputy Assistant to the President, later a Procter & Gamble executive, wrote the following about his speech

Anything described in numbers can often be made more striking by restating the idea in other language. To say that the Hawaiian Islands have an area of 6,435 square miles conveys a certain amount of information to most people. But to add that they are larger than Connecticut (5,009 square miles) conveys more meaning. To say that in area they are midway between Delaware (2,057) and Maryland (10,577) suggests that they constitute quite a respectable body of land (certainly large enough to be welcomed into the Union as the fiftieth state). An audience is probably surprised to learn that four million babies are born in the United States each year, but perhaps more amazed to learn that one baby is born every seven seconds. If you have spent ten minutes reading this chapter to this point, 85 babies have been born since you started.

So: get exact figures, but don't stop there; explain, compare, contrast, interpret, illuminate, amplify. A year's gasoline costs $208, says the statistic; a year's insurance costs $257. Say you: "My goodness! the insurance costs *more* than the gas! I must certainly put *that* in my speech!"

2. *Use specific words*

Specific words add interest to language. *Chevrolet, Ford, Jag* say more than the colorless "automobile." An adventure in an old "1941 Plymouth" sounds more awe-inspiring than one in "the family car." "I am puzzled nowadays about what kinds of toothpaste to buy," said a student. "Each one contains a mysterious ingredient. Just as I am about to buy Crest, with fluoristan, I note Brisk with fluoride, Pepsodent with irium and I.M.P., and all-new super-white Kolynos with three modern cleansing ingredients." Some one talks about cameras, and makes references to *Leica, Retina, Exacta,* and the like. If his speech contains these and similar specific terms, you quietly conclude that he knows what he is talking about. In your speaking try to drive out the soft, mushy words and substitute those that conjure up a bright, diamond-sharp image.

One beginning speaker had the usual difficulty in seeing the edge of specific words over abstract terms, but when the concept finally gripped and seized him, he made a striking speech about Liz, who

training: "I had some formal work in speech at the University of Oklahoma as well as practical application of public speaking there in connection with numerous campus organizations. Later, in various governmental positions, both in the Congress and in the Executive Branch, as well as in private business in Oklahoma City, I have had numerous occasions to speak publicly on many matters." (Letter of November 14, 1961.) Text of the speech supplied by Mr. Harlow and reprinted with his permission.

went through the double crisis of getting a divorce and then rebuilding her social life:

She had just finished twenty years of unsuccessful marriage. She was afraid of what life held for her.

I helped Liz dry her tears, and yelled for Betty, the third-floor neighbor, who loved Liz also. We decided that Liz needed a rejuvenation—and the time to start was now.

First stop was the hairdresser's. Liz's long brown hair had always been worn in a big, braided fashion. So Liz was taught how to wave and wind and comb her hair in a stylish way.

Clothes were next. Liz always used to wear conservative suits and dark colors. Now we bought her wide-flared skirts, a genuine horsehair petticoat, sweaters and low-cut blouses. Her laced oxfords were discarded for black, high-heeled opera pumps.[6]

Whereas a speaker might have said, "Liz bought herself a lot of new clothes," this speaker spelled out, in specific language, what the new clothes consisted of. Both men and women in the class enjoyed hearing him describe his venture into the woman's world of (that particular season) *wide flared skirts,* a *genuine horsehair petticoat, black, high-heeled opera pumps.*

3. *Explain technical or unusual words*

You will need to develop an understanding of kinds of terms that are familiar to listeners and of kinds that are unfamiliar. People like to be exposed to new ideas or new concepts if these can be made clear. If you introduce an unfamiliar word into your speech, casually explain it, and then go ahead and use it. So you might say, "Engine number 3 was on fire (that's the first one on your right)." "My home town is Poplar, ten miles south of Springfield."

Often young men who have completed a tour of military duty use so many technical terms, talking about military topics to civilian listeners, that the audience misses part of the meaning of the speech. More than 50 million Americans must still not know what *TDY* or *MATS* means ("temporary duty," "Military Air Transport Service"). Too much technical language, to borrow a phrase from Jacques Barzun, has a toxic effect upon the listener.

4. *Use enumeration, transition, summary*

Language achieves clarity when it follows order, plan, method. The discussion in this text about speech organization has already suggested the following principles, but they are here reviewed.

---

[6] From a speech by Louis Rittmaster, student at the University of Missouri.

The formal statement of the *central idea* prepares the listener for what is to come. Certainly it adds clarity to the speech. It has the force of a *preview*, and thus, by orienting the listener, helps him to follow the speaker's reasoning as it unfolds. The Secretary of State, speaking to a group of foreign ministers of other American states, said, early in his speech:

> Our agenda contains two items: the first deals with the Caribbean situation as a whole, the second with the more general problem of human rights and democracy.[7]

At times in his central idea the speaker may also add what he is *not* going to discuss: this procedure is especially good. Thus:

> I would like to discuss the general problem of substitutes for steel. I am not going to talk about the ways in which the plastics industry is encroaching upon the steel market, and I am not going to say anything about concrete or copper, though these materials are important. My purpose today is to comment on three markets where aluminum is today displacing steel.

Speakers frequently use the device of *enumerating*, or numbering their points: this feature adds to clarity. Often a speaker also wishes to make a clear transition between one point and the next. Suppose the *central idea* is: "If you would like to achieve social success, make three personal rules for yourself." Suppose, further, the three rules are stated as follows:

I. Don't join an organization just for the sake of belonging.

II. Develop to the fullest your resources as an individual.

III. Make an effort to reach out to other people whose character you admire and respect.

After discussing Point I, and showing the folly of belonging to groups just to trade on the reputation of the group, and of getting into the social whirl just to be a part of the whirl, he might introduce a transition between Points I and II as follows:

> So you see that if you join various organizations just for the sake of belonging, you may defeat your own purpose. A second rule to follow, if you want to achieve success in your social life, is: Develop to the fullest your resources as an individual.

These two sentences (a) review Point I, (b) remind the listener

---

[7] Christian A. Herter, at Santiago, Chile, August 13, 1959. In *Vital Speeches*, XXV (September 15, 1959), 714.

of the *central idea,* and (c) introduce Point II. A good transition sentence will fill each of these three functions.

When you finish Point II, you may say:

If you want to achieve social success in the finest sense of the term, you will find it still is not enough to develop your resources as an individual. Important though this step is, you must do one further thing: you must reach out to other people whose character you admire and respect.

Experienced speakers use this device freely and easily. Former Prime Minister Harold Macmillan, in a nation-wide broadcast in England, said:

There are two ways to preserve the peace of the world and two only. . . . The first is to maintain the full strength of our alliances.

The speaker proceeded to discuss this thought, and concluded:

That is the first way, then, to keep the alliances together.

But there is a second way to preserve world peace that is just as important, the way of negotiation, of conciliation.[8]

Paul G. Hoffman wanted to explain to a large audience something of the importance of smaller, undeveloped nations to the UN. He observed that many who had seen the UN grow from a membership of 60 to 100 and more were afraid that the new, small nations would prove a source of weakness rather than of strength. The following parts of his speech contain well-worded enumeration and transition sentences:

As a matter of fact, for a number of reasons the smaller nations are an underlying source of strength for the United Nations. First, the people and governments of these nations are passionately dedicated to the cause of peace . . .

---

[8] Broadcast January 4, 1958. Text supplied through the courtesy of the staff of the Prime Minister, and used with his permission.

Former Prime Minister Harold Macmillan, who like Winston Churchill, has one American-born and one English-born parent, is a former Oxford Union debater who became a principal spokesman for Great Britain. The author addressed an inquiry to 10 Downing Street to learn about the kinds of speeches made by the Prime Minister, and received this reply from his secretary, Harold Evans:

"It is impossible to say what is a typical year. For example, this year was an election year and the Prime Minister made many speeches during the campaign up and down the country. In a non-election year he would obviously make a smaller number of political speeches, though it could certainly be expected that there would be five or six major speeches on Party political platforms up and down the country. In addition, there would be perhaps 15-20 major speeches on various public occasions. [In addition] during his visit to Commonwealth countries in Asia and Australia early in 1958 he made some 30 major speeches within five weeks." (Letter of December 3, 1959.)

That is the beginning of an enumeration. Other sentences illustrate transitional words:

> Another way in which the UN is strengthened by the presence of the smaller nations is the quality of the men who come as their representatives. Big countries have no monopoly on big men. . . .
> There is a further advantage in having these new nations as members. Again and again their voices have been joined with those of the overwhelming majority of the older members in re-affirming their faith in the United Nations. . . .[9]

He concludes this well-organized speech, filled with facts and figures, with eight numbered, specific suggestions for developing the smaller nations.

To achieve clarity, use freely the structural devices of enumeration and transition. The importance of *summary* has already been mentioned in Chapter 12 as a way of *ending* the speech; you may also incorporate, in the *body* of your speech, *internal summaries* of what you have discussed up to that point.

B. MAKING IDEAS STRIKING

Speakers use various methods to make ideas vivid and memorable.

1. *Epigrammatic phrases*

At times a speaker succeeds in compressing much into few words; the result is a phrase or epigram that becomes famous. Theodore Roosevelt's "big stick"; Wilson's "make the world safe for democracy"; Franklin D. Roosevelt's "We have nothing to fear but fear itself"; Newton Minow's "vast wasteland" are familiar instances.

The history of public speaking is filled with similar examples. Edmund Burke, whose speech on "Conciliation With the Colonies" was once required reading in most American high schools, earnestly asserted: "I do not know the method of drawing up an indictment against a whole people." This eloquence is recalled whenever tyrannies attempt to exterminate racial minorities. You may at times be able to put an idea into a short, striking statement.

2. *Repetition*

The advertising experts know that the repetition of a slogan has a powerful effect. A good slogan, they say, may be used a year and

---

[9] Delivered on October 24, 1961, to the Women's American ORT (Organization for Rehabilitation and Training) Convention, Philadelphia. Text supplied this book through the courtesy of Mr. Hoffman. For another reference to this speaker, see pp. 136-137.

a half—or longer—before it loses its force. Beginning speakers, too, can use this method, as when one asked, "Is it, then, so smart to drink and drive?" and then repeated it, alternating it with vivid examples showing that it was not smart to drink and drive. Ministers use repetition with compelling impact. Bishop Gerald Kennedy of Los Angeles, selected by *Newsweek* as one of the ten greatest ministers in America, preached a text during the Christmas season, 1955, on "I will awake the dawn." His concluding words, also, were "I will awake the dawn." In the body of his speech he repeated, "I will awake the dawn." Moreover, he contrasted the true dawn with the false dawn. No one could have missed the speaker's message.[10]

Harry Emerson Fosdick has observed that repetition has a climactic effect. "Climax is achieved," said he, "by showing [listeners] the Manterhorn in the beginning, reshowing it, reshowing it, and each time the Matterhorn gets bigger.[11]

3. Parallelism

Parallelism is repetition with a variation; some of the words of the phrase or sentence may be repeated, but other words are altered. This method is popular today with scores of competent speakers.

Whenever you hear parallelism you know that the speaker has given thought to phrasing his ideas; parallelism is not usually improvised on the spur of the moment.

Sir Winston Churchill was an acknowledged master of English style. When preparing his speeches, he walked up and down the

[10] *Representative American Speeches, 1956-1957*, ed. A. Craig Baird (New York: The H. W. Wilson Company, 1957), 181-190. The sermon also appeared in the *Christian Century Pulpit*, January, 1957.

Bishop Kennedy wrote in answer to the author's inquiry: "I took public speaking and debating in high school and college. I think the most valuable training I had was in debating and the best teacher I ever had was in high school. I would urge every young man who intends to do some speaking to take debating especially and also training in public speech.

"I make a good many different speeches a year, of course, and I give them to different audiences. However, I consider myself a preacher and I make it clear that I will speak in terms of religious and moral values always. I believe that when religion is seen truly it deals always with life. It is, therefore, always appropriate on every occasion." (Letter of November 25, 1959.)

The student who has been reading these footnote commentaries will have observed that each speaker selects certain kinds of subjects and *sticks to those*. With experience his range of subjects broadens and deepens. The audiences of a given speaker, however, show infinite variety. The principal problem is therefore to adapt a topic in the field of the speaker's competence to all kinds of listeners.

Bishop Kennedy's support of debating is solidly endorsed by the experience of scores of eminent American and British speakers. Webster, Clay, Calhoun, Bryan, Wilson, Burke, Fox, Pitt, Bright, Lloyd George, and many others, had training in public speaking and *debating* while young men.

[11] Roy C. McCall, "Harry Emerson Fosdick: A Study in Sources of Effectiveness," in *American Public Address: Studies in Honor of A. Craig Baird* (Columbia, University of Missouri Press, 1961), p. 66.

room, mumbling words to himself as if trying them for sound before dictating them to his secretary. In the course of preparing one of his memorable speeches he wished to pay tribute to the airmen of the Royal Air Force who saved the nation during the Battle of Britain. Looking back at the speech itself, and at the volume of *Memoirs* in which he describes the events of that fall, one can recreate the bare statistics underlying the fight of some 600 British airmen, flying Hurricanes and Spitfires, against 1200 single- and twin-engine bombers sent over by Hermann Goering.[12] As Churchill thought about this struggle, he could have composed something like this to himself:

All of us owe a great deal to these few airmen.

This however, would have been pale and colorless; what he actually declared was:

Never in the field of human conflict was so much owed by so many to so few.

"Never" at the head of the sentence gives it dramatic emphasis; "in the field of human conflict" departs from the trite "in all history"; and the parallelism of

was so much
owed by so many
to so few

is striking indeed. Two months earlier Churchill had declared:

We shall not flag or fail.
We shall go on to the end.
We shall fight in France and on the seas and oceans.
We shall fight with growing confidence and growing strength in the air.
We shall defend our island whatever the cost may be.
We shall fight on beaches, landing grounds, in streets and in the hills.
We shall never surrender. . . .

Parallelism is not the exclusive property of genius; speakers who make no claim to be professionals can employ it, as when a captain warned his troops: "Under this regulation your stripes can be torn off your sleeve, your money can be taken out of your pocket, your accumulated leave can be wiped away." An audience seems to notice

12 See Winston Churchill, *The Second World War* (Boston, Houghton Mifflin Company, 1949), II, 717.

a series of three or more statements. Two statements are insufficient to develop the effect. A student who had spent many summers as a salesman on a used-car lot wanted to warn his listeners about unscrupulous practices of some dealers. "Stay away from the lot filled with gaudy banners; stay away from the lot with the suspicious come-ons," he concluded, and sat down. If he had added one or two additional "stay aways"—and he was sufficiently informed to do so—he would have heightened the force of his ending.

4. *Rhetorical question*

The speaker may state his ideas as questions addressed to the listeners. The president of the Standard Oil Company of California, speaking on oil problems growing out of the Middle East, asked his audience:

> Why should these oil resources, thousands of miles from America and its western allies, particularly concern us? Why should America, the world's largest oil producer, be disturbed by the loss of access to any oil beyond its own continent?

Later in his talk he developed the structure of his speech again with questions:

> How serious then is the situation in the Middle East today? How much cause do we and our allies have for alarm?[13]

5. *Figurative language*

When a speaker uses words in a figurative sense—and here you will recall your previous exposure in English classes to *simile, metaphor,* and the like—he achieves a striking effect.

In March, 1946, Churchill uttered these words at Fulton, Missouri: "From Stettin in the Baltic to Trieste in the Adriatic, an iron curtain has descended across the continent." *Iron curtain* is the famous metaphor of our day.

Adlai E. Stevenson was one of the colorful speakers on the American scene. At a commencement address in 1951, he selected a text from Shakespeare's *King Henry IV,* Part I, where Hotspur says: "But I tell you, my lord fool, out of this nettle, danger, we pluck this

---

[13] T. S. Petersen, speaking to the Executives' Club of Chicago, October 3, 1958. The text of this speech was supplied through the courtesy of the speaker, who makes five or six prepared addresses a year plus various speeches to company employees and stockholders. He wrote that he had a brief course in public speaking. The Standard Oil Company of California has a policy, wrote S. Z. Natcher of the Public Relations Department, of encouraging employees to study public speaking.

flower, safety." Developing this metaphor in a way that might apply to the graduating seniors present, Stevenson said:

> Can we identify the nettle? the flower? Can we agree what the danger is; can we agree what safety is; can we agree where it lies? Perhaps it has never been more difficult. But we must try, and keep on trying to identify our dangers and our goals.

He went on to describe the nettles that confront good citizens.[14]

Figurative language occurs in one of Eisenhower's most eloquent statements: "In the final choice, a soldier's pack is not so heavy a burden as a prisoner's chains." Roosevelt said, in a famous fireside chat: "When you see a rattlesnake poised to strike, you do not wait until he has struck before you crush him. These Nazi submarines . . . are the rattlesnakes of the Atlantic."

Classroom speakers use figurative language; again, experts hold no monopoly of the process. One student argued: "If during your years at school you discover a shortcoming, *don't sweep it under the rug.* Hold this shortcoming up in full view, and examine it. Ask yourself what you can do about it. Maybe an activity will help, or a special course." Another student, intrigued by the discussion in newspapers about the labor union practice of featherbedding (*made* work—i.e., unnecessary or useless work), discussed featherbedding in fraternities and in classrooms. Other current expressions like "hard sell," "soft sell," "hold the line," "breakthrough," and "fallout" are also used in a figurative sense. A professor urging a group of young teachers to use clear, vivid language in their lectures to beginning classes, declared: "Don't put the fodder too high for the calves."

Here is another example of a concept illuminated by effective language. The subject is Abraham Lincoln:

> It is common knowledge that when one stands too close to a mountain range, one cannot see which mountain is higher and towers above the rest. . . . So it was that some who lived close to Lincoln could not see his greatness. . . .
>
> Why was he so great? Why does the poet say that his deep spirit broods over this nation? Why, a few short years, after the most bitter of partisan struggles, was he accepted as a nonpartisan and unifying figure? Let me share with you my poor analysis, in

---

[14] *Representative American Speeches, 1951-1952,* 172-180.
Stevenson was well known as one of the outstanding speakers of the decade. He is remembered for his speaking presence, his use of language, his pervasive sense of humor, his wisdom and humility. One of those who believed in thinking with a pencil, his method was, having gathered his facts, to get a big tablet and a pencil with a soft lead and start to work.

which I have been helped by other men, and ask that you continue it in your own thoughts.[15]

6. *Improper language*

If you have any doubt about the propriety of a word or expression, *don't use it.* Indecent, profane language *has no place in public speaking.*

II. Tools for Improving Language

Familiarize yourself with sources that speakers consult to improve their use of language.

A. DICTIONARIES

When he was a young man, the British orator, William Pitt, after whom Pittsburgh is named, read Bailey's *Dictionary* through three times from A to Z in order to increase his vocabulary. It was said of him at the height of his oratorical career that he never lacked for a suitable word. You may not care to repeat his arduous exercise, but you should own a good dictionary of collegiate grade, and use it to look up meaning, pronunciation, spelling, usage, origin.

B. WORDBOOKS

Roget's *Thesaurus*, available in a paper bound edition for less than fifty cents, lists under appropriate headings words of similar meaning. Instead of saying "A *good* argument is . . ." you might prefer one of these (see Roget, under *reasoning*): *just* argument, *sound* argument, *valid* argument, *cogent* argument, *logical* argument, *forcible* argument, *persuasive* argument. Instead of *agreeing* (see Roget under *consent*)

---

[15] From a speech, "The Greatness of Lincoln," delivered by Bishop Richard S. Emrich, in Washington Cathedral, Washington, D. C., observing the Lincoln sesquicentennial, January 11, 1959. Text supplied by Bishop Emrich. The speech also appeared in the *Congressional Record* for February 2, 1959, and in *Representative American Speeches, 1958-1959*. The entire speech deserves careful study.

Bishop Emrich wrote these observations about public speaking in answer to the author's inquiry:

1. One should, of course, study public speaking and its general rules. One cannot, for example, listen to an address which does not have unity and does not progress in a logical fashion.

2. One should study his subject thoroughly and have something to say.

3. One should sit under, and gather inspiration from, a great public speaker. I have always been grateful to God that for two years I listened every other Sunday to the preaching of Harry Emerson Fosdick.

He added that *one must continue all one's life studying and reading.* (Letter of November 30, 1959.)

one may *admit, allow, concede, grant, yield, give in to, comply with, acquiesce, accede, accept.* Suppose you are inclined to overwork *great.* Would you prefer *eminent, famous, celebrated?* or *large, bulky, ample, huge, mighty, massive?* or *abundance, sufficiency, multitude?* One of these may be more accurate for your purpose than *great,* although *great* may, on review of possibilities, be the exact word you wish.

Crabb, Webster, and other dictionaries of synonyms supply definitions and examples. As an illustration, *Webster's Dictionary of Synonyms* defines *aggressive, militant, assertive, self-assertive,* and *pushing,* and shows the differences among them (*aggressive* often suggests self-seeking, *militant* usually implies extreme devotion to some cause, movement, or institution, etc.).

C. BOOKS OF QUOTATIONS

At times a speaker wishes to use an apt quotation about *duty, patriotism, woman, success, teachers,* or any of a thousand other themes or topics. This quotation might suggest a title, a central idea, an opening comment, a concluding remark, or an illuminating phrase somewhere in the middle of the discourse. Therefore, as a part of your preparation ask yourself: "Could I effectively use a quotation in this speech?" If you can, look through several volumes until you locate the quotation that best fits. This is a simpler task than you may think, since the volumes classify the quotations under subjects and have various indexing helps.

Among well-known books of quotations are:

John Bartlett, ed. *Familiar Quotations,* 13th ed. (Boston, Little, Brown and Company, 1955).

Clifton Fadiman and Charles van Doren, eds. *The American Treasury* (New York, Harper and Brothers, 1955).

Rudolf F. Flesch, ed. *The Book of Unusual Quotations* (New York, Harper and Brothers, 1957).

Henry L. Mencken, ed. *A New Dictionary of Quotations on Historical Principles* (New York, A. A. Knopf, 1942).

Oxford Dictionary of Quotations, 2nd ed. (London, Oxford University Press, 1953).

Burton E. Stevenson, ed. *The Home Book of Quotations,* 8th ed. (New York, Dodd, Mead and Company, 1956).

As each editor reflects his own taste in selecting his few thousand quotations from countless available items, each collection has its own contribution to make to the speaker. Perhaps the freshest and most unusual quotations are found in the Fadiman, Flesch, and Mencken volumes.

Questions for Classroom Discussion

1. Recall striking phrases from your knowledge of great speeches, or from speeches you have heard in and out of class. Contrast these phrases with more ordinary ways of expressing the same idea. Starters:

> "an iron curtain"
> "give me liberty or give me death"
> "I have but one lamp by which my feet are guided,
>   and that is the lamp of experience"
> "make the world safe for democracy"
> "the power to tax is the power to destroy"
> "nothing to offer but blood, toil, tears, and sweat"
> "quarantine the aggressor nations"
> "liberty and union, now and forever, one and inseparable"
> "you shall not crucify mankind upon a cross of gold"
> "speak softly, and carry a big stick"
> "the only thing we have to fear is fear itself"

2. Consider the famous sentence, "These are the times that try men's souls," by Thomas Paine. Do you like any of these versions better:

   a. Times like these try men's souls.
   b. How trying it is to live in these times!
   c. These are trying times for men's souls.
   d. Soulwise, these are trying times.

3. Comment on: "The line between the fancy and the plain, between the atrocious and the felicitous, is sometimes alarmingly fine. The opening phrase of the Gettysburg address is close to the line, at least by our standards today, and Mr. Lincoln, knowingly or unknowingly, was flirting with disaster when he wrote 'Four score and seven years ago.' The President could have got into his sentence with plain 'Eighty-seven,' a saving of two words and less of a strain on the listeners' powers of multiplication. But Lincoln's ear must have told him to go ahead with four score and seven. By doing so, he achieved cadence while skirting the edge of fanciness. Suppose he had blun-

dered over the line and written, 'In the year of our lord seventeen hundred and seventy-six.' His speech would have sustained a heavy blow. Or suppose he had settled for 'Eighty-seven.' In that case he would have got into his introductory sentence too quickly; the timing would have been bad." Questions 2 and 3 are taken from a most excellent treatment of style: William Strunk, Jr. and E. B. White, *The Elements of Style* (New York, The Macmillan Company, 1959), 53, 63.

Speech-Related Projects

1. Interpret and thereby make more striking each of the following statistics:

a. Trade with Russia should total five billion dollars annually.

b. For every ten people who entered teaching last year, only eight planned a second year, and only five planned to make it a continuous, life-time career.

c. Seventy per cent of the age 16 group in America is in school; in England and France only 10 per cent is in school. About twenty-five per cent of American college-age students attends college in America; about 5 or 6 per cent of college-age students in Europe attends college in Europe.

d. The income of three-fifths of all the aged is under $1000 a year.

e. Total crime in the U. S. was up 8 per cent in 1958 over 1957; 3,020,112 major crimes compared with 2,796,400. Murder was up 5 per cent (from 6,920 to 7,266); robbery was up 14 per cent—the greatest increase of all.

f. Seven per cent of all Americans over 20 now have college degrees.

g. Twenty-one million men and women, 13 per cent of the American population, have lost all their teeth, according to the U. S. Public Health Service.

h. Doctors are curing more cancers than they could ten years ago. In fact, 800,000 Americans are alive and well today, cured of cancer—all of them because they went to their doctors in time.

i. Sixty-nine per cent of all American children now under 18 will go to college, if parental ambitions are realized, says a 1959 Elmer Roper poll. In 1958 the percentage of Americans aged 18 to 21 *actually* in college was 21.4 per cent.

j. Ninety per cent of all the scientists who ever lived are alive right now.

k. The average family's bill for the funeral of a relative is $1,000. This expenditure is the third largest that a family ever makes.

2. Consult Roget's *Thesaurus* and compile a list of words having meanings similar to each word given below:

Example: *conventional* (ordinary, common, habitual, usual, strict, rigid, uncompromising).

bad man	*loud* (adj.)
change (n.)	*love* (n.)
cold	*mistake*
commentator	*move slowly* (v.)
concealed	*persevere*
courage	*plan* (n.)
courtesy	*poor* (adj.)
cunning (n.)	*prayer*
dilemma	*question* (n.)
easygoing	*restoration*
energetic	*severe* (adj.)
exciting	*shorten*
frighten	*supposition*
humorist	*willing*
innocent (adj.)	*work hard*

3. Discuss *usage,* with respect to the following examples:

a. Each of the speakers used *(his, their)* own notes.

b. *(This, these)* data *(is, are)* out of date.

c. Between you and *(I, me)* . . .

d. At the debate tournament, prizes were awarded to Joseph and *(me, myself)*.

e. The *(consensus)* *(consensus of opinion)* of the group is . . .

f. The *(policeman, policeman's)* arresting me was embarrassing.

g. This book is stimulating, *(like, as)* a book should be.

h. The reason is *(that, because)* the whole line participated in every play.

i. None of us *(is, are)* perfect.

j. To make a good talk, it helps *(to inquire diligently, to diligently inquire)* among experts.

k. You *(can hardly, can't hardly)* imagine *(it, its)* being done **better.**

l. I will *accept* your brother. I will *except* your brother. (Explain the difference in meaning.)

m. (*Most, almost*) everybody has trouble with English.

n. (*Over, more than*) 500 people were present.

o. He lives (*further, farther*) from school than you do.

Speaking Assignment 15

A Speech Based on a Famous Quotation

Make a speech of . . . . minutes about a famous quotation, preferably one that has influenced you. This may be a quotation often heard in your home; perhaps it is a favorite of your father, your mother, a teacher, an acquaintance. Use illustration and example to impress your listeners with its significance.

Use these quotations primarily as an exercise in improving your own use of *language*. These speeches will give you an opportunity to be *stimulating, inspirational, appreciative, reflective*. They therefore call for attention to *words*. Avoiding any attempt either to be preachy or patronizing, try through your sincerity and choice of language to make a talk that listeners may remember.

Suggested quotations:
The race is not alone to the swift.
A penny saved is a penny earned.
A rolling stone gathers no moss.
Don't swap horses in the middle of a stream.
None so blind as those who will not see.
No answer is also an answer.
Necessity is the mother of invention.
A barber learns to shave by shaving fools.
A bird in the hand is worth two in the bush.
A burnt child dreads the fire.
A drowning man will catch at a straw.
A good beginning is half the battle.
A light purse makes a heavy heart.
A miss is as good as a mile.
All is not gold that glistens.
All work and no play makes Jack a dull boy.
Any stick is good to beat a dog.
An open door may tempt a saint.
The best is cheapest.
Birds of a feather flock together.
Brevity is the soul of wit.
Don't burn your house to scare the mice.
Do not keep a dog and bark yourself.
Every horse thinks his own load heaviest.

Fools rush in where wise men fear to tread.
Good company on the road is the shortest cut.
Early to bed and early to rise
Makes a man healthy, wealthy, and wise.

Speaking Assignment 16

A Speech About a Distinguished Person

Make a speech of .... minutes about a distinguished person (see list below), *or* about some one in your community whose life has influenced or impressed you (father, mother, brother, sister, other relative, teacher, minister, storekeeper).

The following list may give you a suggestion:

ARTISTS: ARCHITECTS, PAINTERS, SCULPTORS

Thomas Hart Benton	Raphael
Leonardo da Vinci	Vincent van Gogh
Michelangelo	Frank Lloyd Wright

or your favorite among impressionists, realists, futurists

BUILDERS, ENGINEERS

George W. Goethals	W. A. Roebling

ACTORS, ACTRESSES

Ethel, John, or Lionel Barrymore	Helen Hayes
Sarah Bernhardt	Helena Modjeska
Katharine Cornell	Sir Laurence Olivier
John Gielgud	Sarah Siddons

or your favorite cinema or TV actor or actress

ENTERTAINERS

Phineas T. Barnum	Harry Houdini
Blackstone	

EXPLORERS, SCOUTS

Daniel Boone	David Crockett
Richard E. Byrd	Vasco da Gama
Meriwether Lewis, William Clark	Hernando de Soto
Buffalo Bill Cody	Charles A. Lindbergh
Christopher Columbus	Fernando Magellan

your interest in an astronaut might assert itself here

HUMORISTS

Fred Allen	Bill Nye
Finley Peter Dunne	Will Rogers
Ring Lardner	Mark Twain
Groucho Marx	Artemus Ward

SPEAKING ASSIGNMENT 16 (Continued)

LAWYERS

Rufus Choate
Clarence Darrow
Thomas Erskine

Abraham Lincoln
Lord Mansfield
Daniel Webster

NOVELISTS

Willa Cather
Charles Dickens
Feodor Dostoevski
Theodore Dreiser
William Faulkner
Ernest Hemingway
Sinclair Lewis

W. Somerset Maugham
John Dos Passos
Sir Walter Scott
Leo Tolstoy
Mark Twain
Robert Penn Warren
Rebecca West

POETS AND PLAYWRIGHTS

Maxwell Anderson
Sir James M. Barrie
Robert Frost
Vachel Lindsay
Amy Lowell
Arthur Miller

Eugene O'Neill
Edwin Arlington Robinson
Carl Sandburg
William Shakespeare
George Bernard Shaw
Tennessee Williams

PREACHERS, SPIRITUAL LEADERS

Thomas à Becket
Buddha
John Calvin
Confucius
Harry Emerson Fosdick
Billy Graham
Jesus

Martin Luther
Mohammed
Norman Vincent Peale
Savonarola
Ralph W. Sockman
John Wesley
Ulrich Zwingli

SCIENTISTS, INVENTORS

Marie and Pierre Curie
Thomas A. Edison
Albert Einstein
Enrico Fermi
Sir Alexander Fleming
Robert Fulton

Charles Goodyear
Samuel F. B. Morse
Isaac Newton
Louis Pasteur
Jonas E. Salk
Gottfried Wilhelm von Leibnitz

SPEAKERS, STATESMEN

William J. Bryan
Edmund Burke
John C. Calhoun
Sir Winston Churchill
Henry Clay
Benjamin Disraeli
Charles James Fox
William Ewart Gladstone

Patrick Henry
Abraham Lincoln
David Lloyd George
William Pitt
Franklin D. Roosevelt
Theodore Roosevelt
Richard Brinsley Sheridan
Woodrow Wilson

SPEAKING ASSIGNMENT 16 (Continued)

SPORTS: PLAYERS, COACHES

Eddie Arcaro	Tom Harmon
Yogi Berra	Nile Kinnick
Roy Campanella	Connie Mack
Citation, Man o' War	Satchel Paige
Dizzy Dean	Knute Rockne
Jack Dempsey	Babe Ruth
Don Faurot	Alonzo A. Stagg
Lou Gehrig	James M. Tatum
Harold Grange	Charles B. ("Bud") Wilkinson

*the list is so endless your own favorite may not be here
For records, statistics, consult the latest World Almanac*

NOTE: The list of categories is far from exhausted: business men and industrialists like Armour, Carnegie, du Pont, Rockefeller; editors like Greeley, White, Pulitzer; musicians like Paderweski, Rachmaninoff; physicians, nurses, surgeons like the Mayo brothers, Carrell, Nightingale, Schweitzer; social workers and humanists like Jane Addams, Father Flanagan; teachers like Hopkins, Dewey, Pestalozzi. For a check list of more than 2,000 additional names, consult the current issue of *World Almanac* under "Personalities Noted."

REFERENCES ON USING WORDS

John W. Black and Wilbur E. Moore, Chapter 6, "The Speaker's Meanings: Speech and Evaluation," in *Speech: Code, Meaning, and Communication* (New York, McGraw-Hill Book Company, Inc., 1955). Evaluating and abstracting; different levels of abstraction.

W. Norwood Brigance, Chapter 15, "Using Words," in *Speech: Its Techniques and Disciplines in a Free Society,* 2nd ed. (New York, Appleton-Century-Crofts, Inc., 1960). Specific advice: suggestions, examples.

Lionel Crocker, Chapter 19, "Effective Language in Speech," in *Public Speaking,* 3rd ed. (New York, American Book Company, 1956). Study of words, use of phrases, gaining variety in sentence structure, figures of speech.

Milton Dickens, Chapter 9, "Language and Fluency," in *Speech: Dynamic Communication* (New York, Harcourt, Brace and Company, 1954). Clarity, interest, appropriateness; helpful section on usage.

James H. McBurney and Ernest J. Wrage, Chapter 17, "Language and Style," in *The Art of Good Speech* (New York, Prentice-Hall, Inc., 1953). Reflective discussion; suggestions, examples.

Paul H. Soper, Chapter 13, "Language," in *Basic Public Speaking,* 2nd ed. (New York, Oxford University Press, 1956). Exactness, appropriateness, economy; special attention to usage.

Persuading Through Argument

Three ways of persuading a listener: through logical argument, through emotional appeal, through the confidence he has in your personal character. This chapter deals with the first. ■ Formal patterns of argument: deduction, induction, causal reasoning. ■ Ways of developing an argument: (1) assumptions, (2) examples, (3) instances, (4) authority, (5) analogy, (6) statistics, (7) reasoning. ■ Principles of refuting.

THE TERM "PERSUASION" has very nearly come to mean a word designating the outcome of all speaking. We can not be positive even when "entertaining" or "informing" that we may not change somebody's belief or arouse him to do something.

As used in this text, persuasion is a form of oral communication in which a speaker seeks to influence the belief or the conduct of his listeners.

A speaker has three ways of persuading listeners. He may influence their belief or their conduct through appeals to their emotions (affections, fears, hopes, loyalties, sense of duty). He may also influence belief or conduct through the force of his personal character (his sincerity, his integrity, his sense and judgment, his fairness and unselfishness). The next chapter will discuss these two methods. The third way of persuading listeners is through logical argument (reasons, examples, testimony of authority, analogy). This chapter discusses these last-named factors.

If a speaker's persuasive speech is well supported by facts, reasons, logic, he will be on solid ground indeed. The great philosopher and rhetorician, Aristotle, wrote 2300 years ago: "We must know the facts about the subject on which we are to speak. How could we advise the

Athenians, for instance, whether they should go to war or not, if we did not know their strength, whether it was naval or military or both, and how great it is, and what their resources are?"[1] Disraeli, twice prime minister of Britain, rightly declared that a speaker should be "completely master of the subject."

When your public speaking teacher uses the word *argument* he does not mean the heated, contentious type of dispute often associated with "arguing." To him an argument is a form of reasoning: *orderly, objective, logical*. It can be carried on in lively and spirited fashion, but it should focus on issues, not personalities.

I. Importance of Logical Argument

Since repeated experiment has shown that listeners can be persuaded to change or modify a belief, it is entirely worth while to undertake the research necessary to give a well-reasoned speech. On many subjects, a part of your audience will hold a neutral position; this group of listeners especially will be open-minded toward your proposal. Others may be favorably disposed, and these should have their belief strengthened by your arguments. Some may be strongly opposed; these you may not be able to sway, although you may get them to see why others hold a different opinion from theirs.

On each topic the members of your audience probably align themselves differently. Some topics involve more deep-seated prejudice or preference than others.[2] You may plan to vote a straight Republican ticket the rest of your days, and your neighbor may be equally loyal to Democratic candidates. But perhaps neither of you has given thought to the twenty-second amendment, which forbids a President from holding office longer than two terms. On this issue neither of you has firm convictions one way or the other. If a speaker in discussing this amendment took the moderate position that, although it seemed wise at the time of its adoption, experience is beginning to show that it should be repealed, both of you might find yourselves in agreement.

The impelling value of logical argument is that when its method is calm, deliberate, and objective, the listener is given a chance to *reason for himself*. This statement is not designed to minimize, however, the well-founded observation that what appears calm, deliberate, and reasonable to most of the group may seem slanted or biased to some of those present—or vice versa. Yet every one *should learn to speak as*

---

[1] From the *Rhetoric*, Bk. II, Chap. 22; adapted from the translation by W. Rhys Roberts. Copyright 1924 by Oxford University Press.
[2] See the discussion of topic-bound predispositions in Carl I. Hovland and Irving L. Janis, eds. *Personality and Persuasibility*, vol. 2 of *Yale Studies in Attitude and Communication* (New Haven, Yale University Press, 1959), Chap. 1.

objectively as he can. The speaker's responsibility is to present the evidence fairly; it is the listeners' responsibility to weigh this evidence and thus check the speaker's reasoning.

Suppose, however, that in discussing the twenty-second amendment, the speaker got involved in politics; this amendment was a *Republican* measure, aimed at avoiding the calamity of having another *Democrat* in office for four terms. You can see that you and your Democratic friend would find it more difficult to agree upon the issue involved. Or suppose he used language describing the amendment as ridiculous, calamitous, and beetle-brained; a listener with conservative tendencies would hesitate to accept the speaker's reasoning. Or even suppose the speaker, a little tactless, gave the impression that he was going to hurry the listener to a conclusion; the listener would quietly resent being prodded, and would be less likely to agree with the speaker.

The statement is sometimes heard that *good persuasive speaking allows the listener to persuade himself.* "A fool convinces me with his reasons, a wise man convinces me with my reasons." Although this is a perceptive insight, let us not take away too much of the speaker's responsibility. Your classmate may never have given thought to the twenty-second amendment until you called it to his attention. You stirred him with reasons for developing an attitude against it. You reminded him of incidents which he may have noted only casually; you started him thinking about national emergencies where the 22nd would be disadvantageous. Even so, however, your best approach is often to *remind, suggest, point out*: you should not *force* your conclusions upon him.

The effective speaker, therefore, will likely *not* say, either in word or manner, "I am determined to convince you," or, "any one who disagrees with me is seriously in the wrong"; or, "this is one of those rare questions that has only one side." He will be more likely to say "it seems possible that" or "a good many people agree." He will make a concession to the other side, now and then: "although the American people *could* reelect a weak executive two or three times, it is more reasonable to conclude that in this country, as in Great Britain, . . ." and so on.

What a wonderful achievement it is for a beginning speaker to take a controversial issue and present his point of view in a well-reasoned manner. Such a speech will have a good effect: favorable and neutral listeners will lean toward the speaker's viewpoint, and even opposing listeners may better appreciate why some one else disagrees with them. It has been observed that business men and technical experts especially should heighten their persuasive skill; otherwise when pressed they will take refuge in the technical details with which they are familiar and thus fail to gain the listener's agreement and support.

II. Start With a Specific Question

Following are controversial issues put in the form of questions:

1. What should be done to make labor unions more responsible?
2. Should we recognize the government of Red China?
3. Should federal aid scholarships be based entirely on need?
4. Should the national budget be balanced?
5. Should billboards be allowed on federal highways?
6. Should this state adopt (increase) (repeal) the sales tax?
7. Should capital punishment be abolished?
8. Should the lame-duck amendment be repealed?
9. Should colleges adopt a learn-now, pay-later, tuition and fees plan?
10. Should early marriages be encouraged?
11. Should teachers have scheduled salary increases plus merit increases?
12. How can juvenile delinquency be lessened?
13. Should this state adopt a right to work law?
14. Should we strengthen this institution's extra-curricular activity program?
15. Should we raise standards of admission to this institution?
16. Should the legislature of this state be redistricted?
17. Should this country join the Common Market?
18. Should agricultural price supports be drastically reduced?

And see other topics on pages 347-348.

Your first step in considering a proposition like one of the foregoing is to study the question and decide what your own attitude or belief is. After your study, you may emerge with a statement like this:

We should not now recognize the government of Red China.

Or: Capital punishment should be abolished in this state.

Or: The 22nd amendment, limiting presidential terms of office, should be repealed.

Such a *central idea* gives you a specific job of persuasion to accomplish. The supporting statements in the body of your speech should help establish the central idea. Please note, however, that these questions can be answered in more than one way. If the proposition is, "What can be done to make labor unions more responsible," some speakers will suggest one plan, some another. Still a third may take a position that labor unions are *now* responsible, and provide examples. If the proposition is "Should we give the president greater authority to regulate tariffs," some will say "Yes," others "No."

Many vital questions present us with a choice of solutions. No almanac or statesman's guide provides the one correct answer. We must weigh probabilities. First, however, we must get what facts we can. Should you become a merchant or a teacher? Inquire as best you can into income, duties, rewards, hazards; the information itself will not answer the question, but it will give you a better basis for deciding. You are a health official, and learn that markets are selling certain fruits and vegetables with residues of allegedly harmful sprays. Find the facts: are the residues present? are they harmful? and *then* decide upon policy. Traffic accidents are increasing in a college town. Some one proposes that students no longer be allowed to have cars. Again, find the facts; then decide upon policy. The facts may not tell the whole, necessary story, but they will point a direction.

III. Formal Patterns of Argument

Important kinds of argument are *deductive* and *inductive,* and a combination, *causal reasoning.* You have met these terms in freshman English, in logic, in science; we review them here briefly.

A. DEDUCTIVE

The speaker uses *deductive argument* when he begins with a general statement and applies it to a specific instance. If this general statement is a *certainty,* he may develop it in the form of a *syllogism.* The world's most famous syllogism is:

> All men are mortal.
> Socrates is a man.
> Therefore Socrates is mortal.

Since all men must some day die, the syllogism reasons, and since Socrates is a man, he, too, must some day die. A speaker, discussing the need for life insurance, might put his syllogism in a shortened form: "Since we are all human, we must give thought to what our family will do when we die." Or: "Of course we'll die; we're human, aren't we?"

The general statements from which a speaker reasons are, however, more likely to be *probabilities* than *certainties*.

All men are mortal.

is a certainty. But consider this general statement:

All citizens should vote.

This statement is highly probable: the *should* in the sentence shows that exceptions may exist. Starting with a probability, deductive reasoning may proceed as follows:

All good citizens should vote for the hospital bonds.
John Jones is a good citizen.
John Jones should vote for the hospital bonds.

The word *good* gives the statement emotional appeal, but even so, the speaker can marshal logical reasons. A listener should note that although the statement leaves room for exceptions (some other good citizen may vote against the hospital bonds because he feels the interest rate is unnecessarily high), the speaker may still sensibly conclude that the *best* step for the community to take is to pass the bonds.

Further examples:

From the *general statement* "Those who want to protect themselves against radiation should build a shelter" the speaker makes a *specific application*: "You should build a shelter."

From the *general statement* "Those who want to avoid lung cancer should give up smoking" the speaker makes a *specific application:* "Young smokers should give up smoking."

Whenever a speaker reasons from a general statement—either a certainty like "All men are mortal" or a probability like "All who want to protect themselves against radiation should build a shelter"—to a specific conclusion, he is employing deductive reasoning.

B. INDUCTIVE

The speaker uses *inductive argument* when he mentions *specific instances* and from them arrives at a *general conclusion*.

Instance 1: A Buick overturned at Mill Road corner last week.

Instance 2: An oil truck hit a Chevrolet convertible at Mill Road corner Monday.

Instance 3: Two out-of-town drivers had a bad side-swiping accident at Mill Road corner yesterday.

General conclusion: *Mill Road corner is dangerous.* The conclusion would be even stronger if the speaker cited a statistic: "Last year, according to police records, there were 22 accidents at Mill Road corner." Statistics are compilations of *specific instances*.

This kind of argument is persuasive, provided that the speaker gives *enough* instances, that his instances are *typical*, and that no important evidence conflicts (negative instances). Similarly, a speaker may collect specific instances to show that *tax loopholes are being plugged*, that *alumni are increasing their financial support to colleges*, that *the scholarship of athletes is improving*, that *unmarried male drivers under 25 are a traffic hazard*. In dealing with topics of this kind, the speaker needs to take into account exceptions and contrary evidence; he can then argue the high probability that his position is tenable.

C. CAUSAL

When a speaker attempts to analyze the multifold *causes* of a complex social, political, or economic event, or when he urges that if a certain reform be adopted desirable effects will take place, he will employ either inductive or deductive reasoning, or both, in order to persuade his listeners.

Causal reasoning, therefore, though related to other forms of reasoning, is here considered separately. One type of causal reasoning is *cause to effect;* a better way of describing it is to call it *known*-cause to *probable*-effect. In its January meeting, the National Collegiate Athletic Association (NCAA) introduces changes in the football rules. A speaker reasons that these changes (*known* cause) will produce a faster game (*probable* effect).

Another type of causal reasoning is *effect to cause;* in other language, *known*-effect to *probable*-cause. "The Federal budget is not balanced," says the speaker. This is a *known*-effect that can be demonstrated. What caused this effect? Here the causes are probable or speculative, but the speaker reasons about what he thinks they are, and then proposes to remove them. Again: "Zenith has a higher tax structure than Afton," says the speaker; this is a *known*-effect that can be demonstrated by comparing the tax rates. "Why should this be?" he continues; "the two cities are of equal size, and have comparable resources, yet Afton has better streets, more parking, better lighting, a better municipal library. Afton citizens are therefore getting more for their tax dollar than are Zenith citizens. Now the (*probable*) cause is, Zenith has an unwieldy, mayor-and-council system and Afton has a city manager." So he reasons in favor of the city manager system.

As you listen to speeches, and as you prepare your own, give thought to the use of these different kinds of argument to influence belief and action. Experimental studies conducted by teachers of

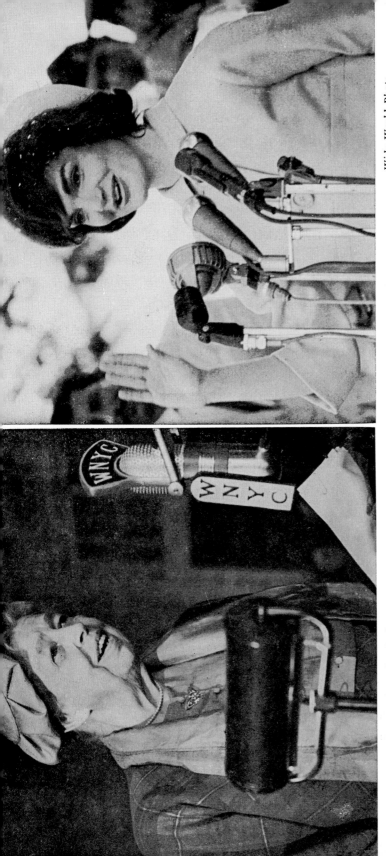

United Press International Photo

Wide World Photo

WOMEN IN PUBLIC LIFE ARE ACTIVE AS SPEECH MAKERS

Mrs. Eleanor Roosevelt, the former First Lady of the land, is shown here speaking at the New York City Hall. Mrs. Roosevelt had a long and distinguished career as a lecturer on the public platform. Mrs. John F. Kennedy through her speeches makes contributions to national solidarity and to international good will. In Caracas, in 1961, she addressed Venezuelans in Spanish, and, according to press dispatches, was received with great cordiality. Since then she has made speeches of greeting and good will on many occasions and in many lands.

AUDIENCES MAY BE SMALL AS WELL AS LARGE

Above, executives of an advertising agency meet with clients in a new, TV-equipped, conference room. *Below*, apprentices in a steel plant listen to a lecture-demonstration in the proper use of electrical switches.

In both instances the speaking is informal, yet principles of selection of material, organization, adaptation to audience and occasion, and good delivery are still valid if these clients are to be persuaded and if these students are to be in-**formed.**

speech suggest that knowing the forms of argument and faults of reasoning improve critical thinking.[3]

IV. Ways of Developing an Argument

The following can be used to develop an *argument* in the reflective, orderly, logical sense in which the term should be used:

A. BASIC ASSUMPTIONS

Good argument proceeds from sound basic assumptions, which may or may not be stated. One assumption of the Hoover plan of reorganizing the federal government was that *government should not compete with private industry.* If this assumption is accepted, then it follows that the branches of government should *buy* their supplies, not *manufacture* them. Accordingly, many changes recommended by the Hoover plan were designed to keep the government from competing with private industry. If the basic assumption had been that government should procure its supplies in the cheapest possible way, the Hoover commission would have made a different series of recommendations.

E. S. Fields, president of the Cincinnati Gas and Electric Company, speaking to the graduating class of Indiana Technical College, attempting to describe the world of 15 or 20 years hence in which these graduates would live, specifically stated his premises:

> There are two basic premises underlying these forecasts: First, that the population of the country will continue to grow at a rapid pace; and second, that the people of this country will continue to exert their efforts, skills, and ingenuities to raise their standard of living.[4]

If those listening to Mr. Fields' speech agreed with these premises—and most people would—they would be more willing to follow his reasoning than would a listener who thought the premises were faulty. In arguing educational, social, and political problems, you need to be sure in your own mind what your basic assumptions are. Whether you state them or not, they guide your selections of materials.

Former Senator Barry Goldwater has given serious and continued attention to issues of foreign and domestic policy confronting Americans. In an address to the Air War College at Maxwell Air Force Base, he began with this candid statement:

[3] Winston L. Brembeck, "The Effects of a Course in Argumentation on Critical Thinking Ability," *Speech Monographs*, XVI (September, 1949), 188.
[4] From a text supplied by Mr. Fields. This address appeared in *Vital Speeches*, XXV (April 15, 1959), 409.

Gentlemen, I begin by making some assumptions with regard to our national objectives.

He then proceeded to state three assumptions on which he based his speech on "National Objectives in American Foreign Policy." The first one was:

Assumption 1. The ultimate objective of American policy is to help establish a world in which there is the largest possible measure of freedom and justice and peace and material prosperity; and in particular—since this is our special responsibility—that these conditions be enjoyed by the people of the United States. I speak of "the largest possible measure" because any person who supposes that these conditions can be universally and perfectly achieved—ever—reckons without the inherent imperfectibility of himself and his fellow human beings, and is therefore a dangerous man to have around.[5]

In arguing education, social, and political problems, be sure in your own mind what your basic assumptions are. Whether you state them formally, as Mr. Fields and Senator Goldwater did, or not, you need to have them in mind to guide your selection of materials.

B. EXAMPLES

Inductive reasoning, of course, leans heavily on *examples,* described below, and on *instances,* described in section C following.

When Ford Motor Company's Ernest R. Breech wanted to show his listeners, members of the Pittsburgh Chamber of Commerce, how difficult it was to sell automobiles abroad, he used a specific example:

Consider a 1959 Ford Fairlane 500 Fordor Hardtop, with full optional equipment, delivered in Pittsburgh. The suggested list price is about $3,600, including state and federal taxes. . . . If you wanted to buy the same car in France, England or Italy, you would have to hurdle barriers of severe quota restrictions and heavy cost penalties.

In France, the delivered price of that car is about $8,200. It includes no less than $3,200 of duties. . . . In Italy, it would cost

[5] Delivered November 14, 1960. Quoted through the courtesy of Senator Goldwater. The complete speech may be read in Lester Thonssen, ed. *Representative American Speeches: 1960-1961* (New York, The H. W. Wilson Co., 1961), 83-99.

Senator Goldwater wrote the author: "My speaking schedule for 1962 is completely filled and my guess is that at the present time I have between 100 and 105 speaking commitments through June of this year." (Letter of February 7, 1962.)

$5,800, with a penalty of $1,400, plus an annual use tax as high as $302.50. In England, the price would be about $8,000.[6]

Lionel B. Moses, of *Parade* magazine, wanted to convince his listeners at the De Paul University College of Commerce that the "pearl of great price" in any field of business was the *new idea:*

Let me give you an illustration from my territory—marketing.

About 50 years ago a group of California orange growers decided to try something never attempted before. They decided to put a brand name on something that grows out of the ground. The money they were getting for their oranges barely paid the production costs—and they wanted a profit. So they gave their oranges a rigid inspection and the 20 or 25 per cent that passed their very strict requirements as to size, color, juice content, etc., were branded "Sunkist," to be sold at a premium price.

This called for advertising, so they raised a budget of $40,000, then went to Lord and Thomas . . . and asked them to handle the account. Lord and Thomas sent a young man named Albert Lasker to discuss the problem with them. . . .

Lasker advised them to run a 12 month newspaper campaign in one state. They picked Iowa, and orange sales in Iowa showed a 40 per cent increase that year. Lasker went back to Los Angeles and was surprised to learn that the orange growers were pleased.

"The campaign was a complete flop," he told them. "Sales in Iowa should have doubled or tripled. What we need is an idea. . . ."

A month or two later he wired them "I have the idea you need. Leaving for Los Angeles today." They had their meeting, and Lasker said:

"We are going to teach people to drink oranges instead of eating them." . . .

With Albert Lasker's idea a great new industry was born. Not just the citrus industry of California, Florida, Louisiana, Texas, New Mexico, and Arizona; the entire juice industry was created by that idea.[7]

[6] From "A New Challenge from the Old World," given December 1, 1958.
Answering an inquiry, Mr. Breech supplied a copy of the speech and wrote that he had no courses in public speaking, although in high school he participated in speaking activities. "Since those days," he added, "I have studied various books on the subject, but have obtained any speaking ability that I may have mainly through the experience of having been called upon to make speeches or to act as toastmaster on many occasions. I should like to say that I regretted I did not have formal training, because I realize how much this could add to one's effectiveness, although I do not feel that formal training in itself will make a public speaker out of one." (Letter of December 10, 1959.)
[7] *Vital Speeches,* XXV (April 1, 1959), 373. Mr. Moses wrote in answer to an inquiry that he gained his experience beginning at the age of 16 when he became

Lieut. Gen. Ira C. Eaker addressed students and faculty at Air University on "Some Observations on Leadership." After developing the observation that "a real leader must really want the job; there are no reluctant leaders," he turned to another division of his speech:

An interesting fact associated with leadership needs to be recognized. When the crown is placed on a head, when a general gets his stars, when a marshal is handed his baton, by a strange alchemy the recipient seems to grow in stature. There is also a corresponding change of attitude among his subjects, troops or followers. They show new respect; they accord new and often exaggerated powers to their new leader. Everyone prays and hopes he will succeed. They put new emphasis in their own effort to see that he succeeds. They want to share in his success.

Only last week I saw an excellent example. A man came into a crowded room at a reception; he was followed by an eager retinue, reporters crowded around, flash bulbs popped, autographs were sought, all wanted to grasp his hand.

Less than two years ago at a similar party this same young man stood in a corner quietly viewing the scene. He was alone, no reporters sought him out, no pictures were taken, no autographs requested. He was not then, as now, the President of the United States.

Wise leaders know how to use the symbols of the office; they recognize the great psychological impact of their flag, their crown, their stars, the physical trappings or badge of office.[8]

chairman of the Democratic Central Committee in Colorado back in 1892. His present field is merchandising, and he has addressed many meetings of advertisers' salesmen. His suggestion: *"Understand the problems your audience faces, and make some constructive suggestions for meeting those problems."* (Letter of December 21, 1959.)

This principle of effective speaking is of the utmost significance. Harry Emerson Fosdick, an eminent preacher—I once heard him give chapel lectures at Grinnell College on religious themes: the students *ran* to chapel each morning in order to be sure to get a seat—declared that he never *really* began to preach until he tried to *visualize the problems* that members of his congregation might be facing.

[8] Delivered on March 17, 1961. General Eaker (Lt. Gen. USAF, Retired) kindly furnished a copy of this speech for use in this text. A famous short speech of his ("I do not intend to do any talking until we have done some fighting . . .") appears in the Appendix.

In response to an inquiry, General Eaker wrote the author as follows:

"My first interest in public speaking was probably inspired by membership on the debating team at Southeastern State College at Durant, Oklahoma. I had the rare privilege of being coached by Dr. A. Linschied, one of the finest public speakers I have known, and who was later president of East Central State College in Oklahoma.

"In my own speech writing since that time I have endeavored to follow his injunctions and precepts. These included brevity, careful assembling of all pertinent facts, and enlivening the whole with homely incidents and historical example." (Letter of May 9, 1961.)

Students and professors in a college of liberal arts like to feel that the "theory" and "pure research" of today may eventually have a practical application. When the president of the Standard Oil Company of California addressed the students of Occidental College on "An Oilman Looks at Science and Liberal Education," he used an example to stress the superiority of liberal education in science to vocational education in the technologies:

In the transportation of petroleum products, we move great volumes through underground pipe lines. These lines as a rule are filled continuously, from one end to the other, with one product being pumped in at the point of origin and different products, perhaps, being drawn off along the way . . .

For instance, at a given moment in the operation of our company's pipe line from Salt Lake City to Spokane, Washington, we may be pumping premium gasoline into the start of the line at Salt Lake, drawing off heating oil at Boise, and taking off regular grade gasoline at the Spokane terminal.

Obviously, it's essential to know the location of all these different product shipments at any given moment. . . . The solution? Each time a new product goes into the line, a small amount of radioactive tracer fluid is injected at the beginning of the shipment. As this tracer proceeds through the line, Geiger counters pick up its signal and transmit it to our control stations. This tells us how far the shipment has progressed. . . .

What was the origin of this ingenious application of atomic energy? Again, pure research in the laboratory. No one ever set out to find a way to identify pipe line shipments with atomic energy. The basic facts were discovered first; the application followed.[9]

If you select convincing examples and can accurately say, *"These are typical . . . I could give others,"* your listener will find it difficult to refute your argument. If, however, your example is in some way not typical, he may sense that it is not fairly chosen and may even have at hand one proving the opposite.

C. INSTANCES

An instance is a shortened example: often as short as a single sentence. Speakers often present them in clusters of five or six or more.

Henry B. du Pont, vice president of E. I. du Pont de Nemours and Company, delivering the annual Budd lecture at the Franklin Insti-

[9] Delivered on September 29, 1960, by T. S. Petersen. Text furnished this book through the courtesy of the speaker.

tute in Philadelphia, wanted to convince his listeners that communication was important to science: that "poor communication led to frequent duplication of effort, with the result that many things were invented several times by different people who were ignorant of each other's work." This thought will be of obvious interest to all who speak and write. Mr. du Pont clinched his point with a swift series of instances:

When Eli Whitney set up his factory to make guns with interchangeable parts, he spent a large amount of time working out machine tools which already had been developed, or at least anticipated, in other countries. He had no way of knowing that they even existed. Fitch worked for years on a double-acting steam engine, apparently ignorant of the fact that James Watt and Matthew Boulton had already solved many of the problems he faced. Oliver Evans started from scratch, and had no access to technical books, although many had been written in the fields in which he worked. Henry worked for six years on magnetism and electric currents before discovering that Faraday, an ocean away, was doing the same research.[10]

Here four instances are presented in one sentence each.

Vice Admiral H. G. Rickover has made many speeches on significant issues of the day. He wanted to remind his audience at a meeting sponsored by the Yale Club and the Yale Law School Association in Washington that we owed a great debt to European scientists. Here are a few *specific instances* he cited:

Steam and diesel-driven locomotives, refrigerator cars, and the automobile—all came from Europe. Among means of communication, wireless, radar, and sonar were invented abroad. Most of our great medical discoveries came from there—more vaccines and inoculations are European than American; more antibiotics, too—such as the sulphas and penicillin. Reading the list of Nobel prize winners in physics and chemistry is a sobering experience. During the first half-century that these awards were made, England received in proportion to population $2\frac{1}{2}$ times; Germany, 3 times; Holland, 4 times; and Switzerland, 5 times as many awards as we.[11]

Imagine yourself using instances to support your argument that students should take a greater part in the intellectual life of the campus. "Only two hundred students attended the Hungarian Quartet last week," you may say. You continue, with instance after instance:

[10] From a copy of the speech supplied by Mr. du Pont. Another excerpt from a speech by this speaker may be found on pages 123-124.
[11] *Vital Speeches,* XXV (April 15, 1959), 402-403. The speech also appears in his *Education and Freedom* (New York, E. P. Dutton & Co., 1959).

But the Ringling Trio filled the auditorium twice—1800 each time. Seventy-two students—I counted them—attended the debate with Wesleyan. But the gymnasium was full when the basketball team met Tech in the conference playoff. At the library last night I counted 161 students: eight in the reference room, 32 in the reserved book room, 14 in the stacks and around the card catalog, and 107 chatting in the halls and on the steps. We started a literary magazine last semester, but the first issue did not pay out and we had to abandon the project. We wanted to invite Carl Sandburg to give a public lecture, but couldn't raise the guarantee.

Each of these items could be expanded into an *example*. The method of specific instances, however, is one of the best ways *in which much evidence* can be presented in brief compass. If you find yourself wanting to give a 10-minute speech when the time limit is only five, employ this method of using instances.

D. TESTIMONY OF AN AUTHORITY

Sometimes listeners become more willing to accept your belief if you can support your position with the testimony of a well-known authority. The student who presented a carefully-reasoned speech to show that women drivers, contrary to popular belief, had good traffic records, secured a statement from the city's chief of police supporting her position. The president of the Allegheny Ludlum Steel Corporation of Pittsburgh quoted a well-known American sage:

The warning against inflation is being sounded now almost daily. Bernard Baruch, the famous "adviser to presidents," said recently: ". . . Inflation is a cancer which is eating away at our economic and financial health. . . . It is responsible for much of the burden of taxation we bear; for the swollen prices we pay; for the debt with which our government is saddled; for the devalued savings of the little people who suffer most from it. Allow this malady to run unchecked and it will impoverish a people and destroy a nation."[12]

This language is strong, but it carries weight since it quotes an American famed for his judgment about and insight into economic matters.

[12] A copy of this address, "Keeping the Store Open," was supplied the author of this text by the speaker, E. J. Hanley. The speech discussed, in well-organized fashion, three forces most likely to influence business in the future: big labor, inflation, and growing foreign competition. The speaker wrote that he makes three or four prepared speeches a year of this type, and does a great deal of extemporaneous speaking to Allegheny Ludlum Steel Corporation employees at various meetings on company matters. (Letter of December 9, 1959.)

Ask yourself, as you prepare your persuasive speech, whether a quotation from a recognized authority will strengthen your argument. If your authority is not known to your listeners, insert a few words to identify him for them.

E. ANALOGY

An analogy is a comparison. You may well reason that an honor system which worked at Liberal Arts College A and Liberal Arts College B will work at Liberal Arts College C. Or you may reason that because socialized medicine faces serious difficulties in Great Britain, it is likely to run into similar problems here. Your analogy is valid to the extent that conditions in the liberal arts colleges, or in Great Britain and the United States, are comparable. When the items being compared are similar in kind—two colleges, two medical systems—the analogy is termed *literal*. In the speech below Henry B. du Pont uses a literal analogy to compare two kinds of problems—those of management and those of the scientist:

> . . . Few ventures of lasting significance are totally free from risk, and where there are risks there will always be some failures. On this score, I think that the attitude of the scientists could well be applied to our problem [the problem of management]. The scientists discovered long ago that man learns most rapidly by pushing his way into unexplored territory, even though he may stumble and lose his way from time to time. . . .

> There is a valid parallel between the scientist and the manager in the modern world. The manager, too, must travel across some unmapped ground. . . . The executive who is always right is, by definition, a man pursuing only the safest and most predictable of projects. That attitude, in the long run, will only take his company downhill. The business firm which never makes a move without a chart to guide it . . . is, in my opinion, in an advanced state of managerial decay.[13]

At times a speaker achieves an almost unexplainable effectiveness through a device termed *figurative analogy*. Here the objects being compared bear a resemblance only in an imaginative way, as when Lincoln compared slavery to a poisonous snake (see page 136). Jesus used *figurative* analogies when he preached about the sower of the seed (some of which fell on rocky ground), the house built on the sand, the feast prepared at the return of the prodigal son.

[13] Delivered to the Midwest Management Faculty Conference, Bowling Green State University, Bowling Green, Ohio, April 28, 1961. Used by permission.

F. STATISTICS

You may support your argument by statistics.

A Stanford University professor of geography used these statistics to illuminate the problem of world population and world hunger:

In the year 1800 there were in the entire world only 900,000,000 people. In 1959 the figure is roughly 2,760,000,000. By 1975 most authorities roughly estimate the figure will stand at 3,800,000,000. . . . Some authorities suggest that by the year 2050, the world will have a population of 16,000,000,000 persons!

Henry Pratt Fairchild believes these figures are "the most important statistics in the world, for all human interests have meaning only as they are projected against the encompassing background of population and its growth. All others are mere embroideries upon this great central pattern."[14]

Beginning speakers should invariably give the *source* of their statistics: "the *World Almanac* says," "the police blotter shows," "the director of admissions told me." And avoid the well-known weakness of statistics; one is revealed in this story:

I had a very good friend once, who was a platoon leader and he was in strange country, and he wanted to cross a river with his platoon, and he got out the guide book he'd been given, and he saw that this river had an average depth of 24 inches and he started across.

The guide book was right: from its source to the sea the river had an average depth of 2 feet—but where he tried to cross it was 15 feet deep.[15]

The president of Allegheny Ludlum Steel Corporation used these statistics in an address entitled "Opportunities (and Problems) Unlimited":

[14] *Vital Speeches*, XXV (May 15, 1959). The speaker was C. Langdon White, professor of geography at Sanford University. Professor White wrote in answer to a query: "Yes, I did have formal training in speech when I was in college and I regard such training as extremely valuable for any one going into the teaching profession. I do give a number of lectures each year. These deal with: (1) world population; (2) underdeveloped lands; (3) Latin America, and (4) industrialization (particularly the scientific location of types of industrial plants). When I was younger . . . I belonged over a five year period to two different lecture bureaus. I traveled for weeks at a time over the entire country. I enjoyed the work very much." (Letter of November 11, 1959.)

[15] *Vital Speeches*, XXV (July 1, 1959), 557. The speaker was John M. Seabrook, at public hearings on farm labor, Washington, February 5, 1959.

Mr. Seabrook answered a query by stating that the speech was not written out but delivered from notes; this text was therefore secured from a tape recording.

Since the end of World War II we have added more people to the U. S. than in the entire preceding two decades of the Twenties and Thirties, plus half of the 1940's. Some 4½ million babies were born in America last year; in 1975 the number of births is estimated at six million.

There will be 55 million more citizens in the U. S. 15 years hence. This is an increase equal *to almost all the people now living west of the Mississippi River*. It means that for every three consumers in the American marketplace today, there will be four by 1975. . . .

By 1975 the number of young adults in America, age 18 to 24, will have gone up to 28 millions, a 70% increase from today. These young people provide an unusually strong market stimulus—and much of it in areas where you and I can profit.

It will take 23 million more homes to provide the additional space needed by a total population of 240 million Americans in 1975. More houses will have to be built in the next 15 years than were built during the last 30.[16]

Speaking at the Congress of the American Correctional Association, Dr. Leo K. Bishop, vice president of the National Conference of Christians and Jews used statistics to describe an attitude of young people today:

In spite of all that America has done for her youth . . . today's youth do not cherish the heritage which we want to hand on to them. . . . The Purdue University attitude survey of high school students gives us a glimpse of the wide gap between our heritage and present day attitudes. Purdue observers reported in their study:

—Half of the teenagers questioned are ready to dispense with freedom of the press.

A graduate in chemical engineering from Princeton, he took a course in public speaking as a freshman. He writes: "I have always urged much more work in English and learning to express thoughts both in the spoken and written word. I think I was always a good engineer, but I believe I have been successful in business more because of my ability to express my thoughts than because of my ability to solve engineering problems.

"Most of the speeches that I am called on to make have one central problem. I am usually trying to explain a complex subject to a group of lay people whose interest is at the best fleeting and who are not going to take the trouble to understand it unless it is interestingly presented. . . .

"When I talk to the sales department of one of my companies, I know that an effort to drive them on with a pep talk will have only a temporary effect. But if I can get them to understand the company problems and what we are trying to do with our sales campaign, they will be better salesmen all year long."

16 E. J. Hanley, speaking at the annual luncheon of the National Association of Manufacturers, New York, April 11, 1961. The preceding week he had received the 1961 "Man of the Year" award of the Duquesne University Society for the Advancement of Management. Text supplied by Mr. Hanley.

—One quarter of the students say police should be free to search your home or your person without a warrant.

—A third of those responding to the test believe that free speech should be denied to some people when it is convenient to do so.

—Sixty per cent approve censorship of books, newspapers, magazines. . . .

Obviously, these young people have escaped all training, all understanding, and all the basic concepts which would enable them to appreciate our democratic heritage.[17]

V. Common Faults

What are faults to avoid in planning a speech to influence belief?

A. DON'T EXAGGERATE

Don't say *all* when you mean *most;* don't say *nearly all* when *a good majority* is more accurate; distinguish among *many, several, a few,* and *often, occasionally, never.* A listener may challenge you on your statement, and you will find yourself unable to defend your language.

Don't say "I have absolutely proved" when the most a speaker can

[17] Delivered in Chicago on September 28, 1961. Quoted in *Vital Speeches,* XXVIII (November 15, 1961), 91-95.

Dr. Bishop, graduate of Phillips University, recipient of a Junior Chamber of Commerce "most useful citizen award" in 1937, delegate to the Conference on World Brotherhood, Paris, 1950, wrote the author that he gives 15 to 20 major speeches a year before a wide variety of audiences: business men at Chamber of Commerce, Rotary, Kiwanis, and similar meetings, state and national conventions of various professional associations, occasionally a college convocation.

His letter (February 7, 1962) continued: "It was my good fortune to have a very excellent speech teacher in my high school days—my college did not afford a formal training in speech, but we had an extracurricular group that met and studied platform work. Another significant influence was a professor who was a stickler for careful outlining. He taught me that you must not only have something to say, but it must be outlined carefully or the audience would not long remember what was said."

The effectiveness of a speaker, Dr. Bishop believes, depends on four factors:

1. "*Content*—he must have something significant to say; something in which he believes; something that is important to the audience with which he is trying to communicate. . . ."

2. "His material must be *well-organized* . . ."

3. "The material must be *presented in a vocabulary* which the audience understands . . ."

4. He must have skill in delivery. "The most brilliant concepts and the most valid ideas are often lost because the speaker has not paid the price to develop *platform skill.* The manner of presentation, . . . the projection of the speaker's personality, are of equal importance to the content and the organization. Diction, enunciation, changing one's pace, gestures, . . . personal mannerisms, are all a part of effective platform work. Skills in these areas are achieved through long years of self-criticism, discipline, and a humble approach to effective public speaking."

do, especially when he deals with future events, is to suggest. Most listeners will be more receptive to hear you say, "I believe I have shown that," "It seems extremely likely that," or whatever judicious statement you think applies.

If a speaker quotes a fact that is incorrect or out of date, any expert in his audience will find it easy to correct him. Note how often letters to the editors of national magazines accurately point out that the experts have slipped. A good many years of reading, learning, and observing experience is found in any audience.

Remember Lincoln: "You can fool part of the people all of the time, and all of the people part of the time, but you can not fool all the people all of the time."

B. AVOID HASTY GENERALIZING

This is a common fault in inductive reasoning. If Team A in the Southwestern Conference is strong and Team B is strong, it does not follow that all teams in this conference are strong, or even that it is a strong conference. One of your listeners may have observations to offer about mediocre Team C. If Law School Graduate A gets his first position at $500 a month and Law School Graduate B gets $550, whereas Engineer A commands $475 and Engineer B $480, it does not follow that law school graduates start at higher salaries than engineers. Note that a listener does not have to be informed about starting salaries to see that the reasoning here is faulty: all he needs to do is to reflect, "You can't prove anything with two examples."

If a speaker has time for only two examples, he takes care to suggest that these are typical of additional evidence that he can produce on request.

C. AVOID IMPROPER CAUSAL RELATION

Much speaking attempts to show that a certain effect was produced by a given cause: the Democrats lost the election because too many Democrats stayed home. If this reasoning is to be valid, the speaker will need to show that the *alleged* reason (too many Democrats stayed home) is the *actual* reason. Much speaking also attempts to show that, if certain steps are taken, certain other steps will follow. If we regulate labor unions, the speakers argue, certain irresponsible practices will stop. If we build a throughway north of town, the town will grow. Facts are needed to show that in similar instances these things actually happened, and that the towns being compared are actually comparable in important respects.

D. DON'T PROVE TOO MUCH BY ANALOGY

This suggestion grows out of the sentence just above. If Coach Throckmorton had good seasons from 1958-1960 at Desert State College, and good seasons from 1960-1962 at Mountain State College, a speaker can state that *there is every likelihood* that he will have a good season in 1962-1963 at Valley State. The speaker would not be wise to say *he is sure to have a good season* in 1962-1963. If conditions in the three schools are similar, the speaker can strengthen his reasoning by pointing this out. If Valley State has different conditions— poorer material, more difficult schedule, shattered morale, and the like—the speaker will be wise to admit this. Some one in the audience is *likely to spot this flaw in the reasoning* if the speaker does not.

You will recall that one of the reasons for studying public speaking was to learn to amass facts and reasons so that one could make decisions that looked to the future. Obviously whenever a speaker declares that because something happened in the past, a certain other thing is going to happen in the future, or whenever he reasons that because something worked out one way one time it will work out the same way next time, he is taking a leap beyond the facts into the realm of conjecture and uncertainty. Since we need to take this leap if we are to make long-range plans, our listeners will be more certain to accept our conclusions about what will likely happen next year if they are convinced we are in possession of the available evidence about what has happened in the past and about what is happening at the moment.

VI. Refutation

When speeches are made on persuasive topics, opportunities for disagreement arise. In your speech you may wish to express a different opinion from one you have heard. Here are suggestions:

1. Begin by stating, fairly, the opposing argument. State this argument clearly, accurately, courteously. Avoid misquoting another speaker—some one in your audience may recognize that you are unfairly representing him. State the argument so clearly that the other speaker himself can admit, "Yes, that is exactly what I said."

2. Show the importance of this opposing argument. Don't minimize or belittle it; if the speaker's conclusion largely hangs on this argument, say so: "This is probably the strongest argument in Mr. Goodson's speech."

3. Keep your language fair and objective. Probably you should not use language like, "I disagree with you," "This is inaccurate," or "This is stupid." The trouble with "I disagree with you" is that it draws the lines hard and fast; you then make it difficult to convert the other person to your way of thinking. Phrases like "This is inaccurate," or "this is stupid," refer to conclusions which the *listener should draw for himself.* You can show by careful reasoning or use of evidence that an argument is inaccurate, or outdated, or fallacious, without calling it by these labels.

Often, instead of saying "I disagree," a more persuasive tactic is not to refute the other person's argument, but to reemphasize your own. Suppose he says, "I am opposed to the new city library tax; taxes are too high already." Instead of saying, "I disagree that taxes are too high already," keep the argument on *your ground.* "Ten years ago the population of the city was 30,000; now, you say, it is 45,000. Ten years ago the library circulated 141,000 pieces of material a year; now the circulation is 274,000. The children's department needs many more titles; if the young people of the community are to have a chance to develop the habit of reading good literature, we must strengthen the juvenile collection." And so on. Let him argue *cost;* you argue *need.*

But certainly every student has learned this in his own experience. You need a new coat (suit, car). Your sire says, "I can't afford it." Do you say, "Of *course* you can afford it! Look at all the money *you* spent last year on golf (fishing gear, club dues, trip West)." No; this kind of rebuttal centers the argument upon an issue that you are likely to lose. Better say, "I know we are hard pressed, but—" and, if you have a case for a new coat (suit, car), put it forward. If this point seems labored, it is because novice speakers forget their own experiences of this sort and flatly announce, in their speeches, "I disagree," or "The trouble with you is," or "That's a stupid argument," and the like— and thus the door to persuasion is solidly slammed shut.

Refute evidence with evidence: "Mr. Hammell gave us strong reasons why we should continue capital punishment. He pointed out that capital crimes increased in this state from 107 in 1960 to 154 in 1962. This increase is of course alarming, and it worries me, as it does Mr. Hammell. His argument is that we should continue capital punishment, or crime will increase even more rapidly. Now you will have to judge for yourself whether this will happen. Let us look at five states that have abolished capital punishment. Here the number of capital crimes *has steadily decreased.* (Quote figures.) I have also studied the opinions of three criminologists on this matter. Professor Young states that capital punishment is no deterrent (quote him)."

And so on. If you handle evidence skillfully, you can lead your listeners to persuade themselves that *capital punishment should be abolished.* And this you can do without using discourteous language ("This is stupid") or gratuitous labelling ("This is inaccurate"). Just answer the argument with better reasons, better evidence, better interpretations.

Although the material in this chapter has stressed content—the speaker's use of evidence and of valid reasoning processes—the student needs to be reminded that good *delivery* also has strong persuasive impact. An experiment of Bettinghaus records that four speakers were chosen to prepare speeches on persuasive subjects: "Drinking Regulations," "Grading Curves," "Parking Regulations," and "The Eighteen Year Old Vote," each speaker being assigned one subject. After practice each speaker was able to present his speech (a) with good delivery and (b) with bad delivery, to different, although matched, audiences. The general conclusion, says Bettinghaus, "confirms what rhetorical theorists have said for centuries . . . the speaker with better delivery is more persuasive than the speaker with poorer delivery."[18]

VII. Sample Outline

This sample persuasive outline illustrates matters of form (I, A, 1, etc.; margins and indentations; use of complete sentences; the four parts of a speech).

INSTALL SEAT BELTS

Introduction

I. The experience of the French racing car driver is a dramatic example of the importance of equipping automobiles with safety belts.

II. The installation of belt anchorings as standard equipment on most automobiles leads to further discussion of the question of seat belts.

Central Idea

My purpose today is to urge you to have seat belts installed in the car you operate.

[18] Erwin P. Bettinghaus, "The Operation of Congruity in an Oral Communication Situation," *Speech Monographs,* XXVIII (August, 1961), 131-142. This finding should alert the student to listen critically to what the speaker *says.* Moreover it should be clear that if *content* and *delivery* are both good the effect of the speech will be more durable.

Body

I. Seat belts increase your chances of surviving an accident.

   A. In the event of an accident you are safer if you are not thrown from the car.

      1. Cornell studies of crash injury show that 12.8 percent of car occupants ejected through open doors, contrasted with 2.6 percent of those who remain in the car, are killed.

      2. The American Medical Association estimates that 5000 lives could be saved annually by controlling the hazard of ejection from the car.

   B. In the event of an accident your chances of injury are reduced if you are not thrown into the windshield.

      1. The American Medical Association estimates that you may be as much as 60% safer if you are held in place by a seat belt.

      2. Consumers' Union says that there is some evidence to suggest that in this respect even a poor belt is better than no belt at all.

   C. Cornell studies of crash injury estimate that seat belts in all cars would reduce fatal and major injuries by 35 per cent.

II. Commonly-heard objections to seat belts are not justified.

   A. The fear of being trapped in a wreck is ill-founded.

      1. Fires break out in only 2/10 of 1 per cent of injury-producing auto accidents.

      2. Submersion is involved in only 3/10 of 1 per cent.

      3. As your belt will more than likely keep you from being knocked unconscious, you have a better chance to escape than if you had no belt and were unconscious.

      4. Seat belts can be unfastened in an instant.

         a. The new metal-to-metal fasteners are easy to operate.

         b. Lt. Leslie Williams of the Connecticut state police can release his belt and draw his automatic with one quick move of his right hand.

   B. The problem of requiring children to hook their belts may be solved in various ways.

      1. Younger children may be told the family car is a space ship, requiring that belts be fastened before blast-off.

      2. Older children may be taught that fastening belts is a

safety procedure, like operating a direction-indicator signal.

    C. Isolated cases of belt failure may be traced to poor design or faulty installation.

III. Many firms and organizations use seat belts.

    A. Belts are required equipment on the 1700 cars owned by Allstate Insurance.

    B. Belts are installed on all cars operated by the U. S. Department of Health, Education, and Welfare.

    C. Belts are widely used by the highway patrols of at least 26 states.

    D. Belts are provided on the official cars of New York State.

IV. Informed individuals endorse seat belts.

    A. John Moore, director of the Cornell studies, who has seven children, has his 9-passenger station wagon equipped with 9 seat belts.

    B. Col. John Stopp, director of the Air Force Aero-Medical Field Laboratory, says: "I wouldn't be without them."

    C. Dr. R. Arnold Griswold, chairman of the American College of Surgeons' Committee on Trauma, has seat belts installed in his car.

Conclusion

Seat belts are not a substitute for careful driving, but they increase your chances of survival if you are involved in an accident.

Note on sources: Data in the above outline may be found in magazines usually available in any public or college library. Those principally consulted were: *Consumers' Bulletin*, March, 1957; *Consumers' Reports*, February, 1960, March, 1960; *Reader's Digest*, March, 1961; *Good Housekeeping*, August, 1961; *Saturday Evening Post*, July 16, 1955; *Today's Health*, October, 1958, July, 1960. Many facts presented in these articles come from basic research conducted by the Cornell University Automotive Crash Injury Research program. Objections to seat belts are reviewed in *Consumers' Bulletin*, March, 1957.

The outline does not include specific examples of lives saved, but a speaker could add interest to his speech by consulting the *Saturday Evening Post*, July 16, 1955, which refers to "eighteen instances of life-belt rescues" cited by Dr. Horace E. Campbell of the American College of Surgeons as reported in the *Bulletin of the American College of Surgeons*.

Questions for Classroom Discussion

1. When would you suggest the use of instances and when the use of illustrations?

2. What are common ways in which statistics are misused?

3. What are common ways in which quotations from authority are misused? From the point of view of delivery, how can the presentation of quoted material be improved?

4. How can visual aids be used in the persuasive speech?

5. What basic assumptions underlie the arguments that college authorities can regulate the use of automobiles by students? that the American system of education is preferable to the British? that the voting age be lowered to 18?

Speech-Related Projects

1. Examine reference works like *World Almanac, Britannica Book of the Year, Statesman's Yearbook, U. S. Census Reports,* and magazines like *U. S. News and World Report* as sources of factual material.

2. Examine the library collection of special periodical indexes (*Education Index, Art Index, Public Affairs Information Service, New York Times Index,* etc.) as sources of factual material for speakers.

3. Secure a recent issue of *Vital Speeches.* Study three speeches in this issue that best illustrate logical argument. Note uses of statistics, causal relationship, example and illustration.

Speaking Assignment 17

A Speech to Change a Belief

Make a speech of ...... minutes in which your purpose is to change or modify a belief of your listeners.

Choose a topic for which immediate action on the part of the listener is not required. This topic may deal with a campus, social, political, religious, or educational problem. Consult the list of topics on pages 47-48, 245, 347-348.

This speech should be well fortified with logical proofs. Instead of mere unsupported assertion or opinion, use facts, evidence. Recall what your chapter says about statistics, examples, instances, quotations from well-informed authorities. Consult reference sources such as *Readers' Guide to Periodical Literature* or *New York Times Index.* For some topics you may wish to interview local authorities on your campus or in your community.

For a sample outline, see pages 263-265.

REFERENCES ON THE PERSUASIVE SPEECH

A. Craig Baird and Franklin H. Knower, Chapter 17, "Persuasive Speaking," in *General Speech*, 2nd ed. (New York, McGraw-Hill Book Company, Inc., 1957).

John W. Black and Wilbur E. Moore, Chapter 9, "The Motivation of Speech," in *Speech: Code, Meaning, and Communication* (New York, McGraw-Hill Book Company, Inc., 1955).

Milton Dickens, Chapter 19, "Building Audience Attitudes" and Chapter 20, "Releasing Audience Attitudes," in *Speech: Dynamic Communication* (New York, Harcourt, Brace and Company, 1954).

John E. Dietrich and Keith Brooks, Chapter 9, "Learn to Persuade," in *Practical Speaking for the Technical Man* (Englewood Cliffs, N. J., Prentice-Hall, Inc., 1958).

Giles Wilkeson Gray and Claude M. Wise, Chapter 7, "The Psychological Basis of Speech," in *The Bases of Speech*, 3rd ed. (New York, Harper and Brothers, 1959).

James H. McBurney and Ernest J. Wrage, Chapter 17, "Advocacy," in *Guide to Good Speech* (Englewood Cliffs, N. J., Prentice-Hall, Inc., 1955).

Wayne C. Minnick, *The Art of Persuasion* (Boston, Houghton Mifflin Company, 1957).

Alan H. Monroe, Chapter 7, "How to Develop Talks to Convince and Persuade," in *Principles of Speech*, 4th ed. (Chicago, Scott, Foresman and Company, 1955).

Robert T. Oliver, Chapter 7, "Suggestion," in *Psychology of Persuasive Speech*, 2nd ed. (New York, Longmans, Green and Company, 1957).

Raymond G. Smith, Chapter 9, "Appeal Through Emotion" and Chapter 12, "Persuading," in *Principles of Speaking* (New York, The Ronald Press Company, 1958).

Paul L. Soper, Chapter 11, "Motivating the Audience in Persuasive Speech" and Chapter 12, "Planning the Persuasive Speech" in *Basic Public Speaking*, 2nd ed. (New York, Oxford University Press, 1956).

CHAPTER 18

Persuading Through Emotions, Attitudes

Especially when a logical basis also exists for urging others to believe or to act, emotional appeals are effective and ethically justifiable. These appeals include duty, fear, self-preservation, loyalty, anger, pride. ■ *The speaker's personal character is also a powerful persuasive force: his intelligence, integrity and sincerity, fairness, candor, good will, judgment, and reputation.* ■ *Repetition, verbal labels, arrangement, proportion are ways of emphasizing speech materials. The use of suggestion.*

ONE WOULD NEED UNUSUAL PERSISTENCE to believe something or do something that his wisest friends told him was contrary to reason and logic. Justice Oliver Wendell Holmes once said that a sensible man would recognize that if he were in a minority of one he was likely to get locked up.[1] At the same time one likes to *feel* that his belief or action is suitable to his own sentiments and emotions.

Those who study the art of speaking therefore, must first of all be able to present fact, example, statistic, testimony, as explained in the preceding chapter. They must also study the non-logical, non-factual aspects of persuading. One of these is emotional appeal; a second is the force of the speaker's character. A still different group of factors involves emphasis through repetition and arrangement.

I. Appeals to Emotion

No speaker can overlook the role of emotion in human behavior. The great speakers have learned this lesson well; the last stage of

[1] Dorothy I. Anderson, "The Public Speeches of Justice Oliver Wendell Holmes," in *American Public Address: Studies in Honor of Albert Craig Baird* (Columbia, University of Missouri Press, 1961), p. 9.

Lincoln's development as a speaker, as narrated on page 220, was to learn the vital significance of emotional appeal. Traveling on a train between Chicago and Washington, this author once met, in the diner, a Chicago lawyer. The conversation turned to speech making, and the lawyer confided that most of what he had learned about court room pleading he had picked up in the school of experience. One day, however, he decided to start reading legal addresses of famous lawyers, and found himself absorbed in the court room style of Daniel Webster. He reflected that although Webster used logical reasoning in the body of his jury pleas, in the conclusion he relied largely on emotional appeal. He may have been impressed by passages like that quoted on the next page, illustrating Webster's famous appeal to the jurymen to do their duty. He thereupon decided that he, too, would combine logical and emotional materials in his jury pleas, taking care to use his own language, not an imitation of Webster's. "From that time on," he concluded, "I became much more effective as a court-room speaker."[2]

The good salesman who points out that the suit is made of wool and dacron, that it has select tailored features, that it will not soil, that it is long-wearing, employs logical arguments; when he adds that it is a genuine Pinelli (*prestige, status*), that it is a popular model (*approval of the group*), and that it is becoming to *you* (*pride, physical attractiveness*), he is enlisting sentiment in support of logic. Thus the coach may say, "Win this one for me"; your teacher may urge, "Don't disappoint me"; the residence hall may decide, "Let's make it unanimous"; soldiers may be exhorted to remember the *Maine*, or the Alamo, or the traditions of the service. Some of the most unselfish, the most loyal, the most patriotic of our actions are motivated by our feelings.

The list of emotions and sentiments is long. We each crave *recognition, security,* and we will follow employers or leaders who speak of these. We value *honor, dignity, pride, self respect.* We want to live up to *our better selves,* and we capture renewed inspiration from those who show us how we can do this. We have *reverence* for things of the soul and the spirit. We want to *conform,* we

---

2 The author could draw a lengthy moral at this point, but will content himself with a short one, and bury it in this footnote. Part One of the moral is that a speaker must ever continue his study; much about speaking can be gleaned from the biographies of speakers and from collections of their speeches. Part Two is that the principles of effective speaking will actually work—but they must be studied anew and *understood* by each speaker. The Chicago attorney had found out for himself—late in his career, as Lincoln did—that listeners are reached through *understandings* and *feelings.* Moreover, the Chicago attorney hit upon the principle that the *conclusion* of a speech is the proper point to give the speech *climax, application, focus.*

seek to belong, we like *favorable attention.* We are capable of *anger,* or *indignation,* or *fear;* we can feel *pity* and *sympathy.* We have biological drives and needs like those growing out of *hunger, safety, sex.* We cherish *health, homes, family, children.* We can feel *shame;* and we can feel *confidence.* We want to do our *duty,* and we are *loyal.*

Each speaker has an ethical and a moral responsibility toward these non-logical materials. We should not stir up hatred nor provoke unwarranted anger. We should appeal to higher motives, not baser emotions. The cheap tricks of certain advertisers are not for us. Demagogues have had short-lived successes with lies and other verbal stunts. Although the truly eminent speakers, teachers, and spiritual leaders have been richly sentimental—think of Socrates, Lincoln, Churchill—because of their high personal integrity they command our admiration.

We can not in the discussion below illustrate all varieties of emotional appeal, but select a few to show how speakers have utilized these materials.

A. DUTY

A responsible individual will serve his country, canvass for charity, accept membership on an arduous committee, serve on a jury, hold an office, and do other irksome or time consuming things if he can be made to feel it is his *duty.*

One of the celebrated appeals to duty is that made by Daniel Webster urging a panel of jurors not to shrink from rendering a verdict in a murder trial:

> Gentlemen, your whole concern should be to do your duty, and leave consequences to take care of themselves. Your verdict, it is true, may endanger the prisoner's life, but then it is to save other lives. . . . You are the judges of the whole case. You owe a duty to the public, as well as to the prisoner at the bar. You can not presume to be wiser than the law. Your duty is a plain, straight-forward one. . . .

All of this would seem to be good reasoning—the logical, reasonable, and sensible support that men must have for their beliefs, and their actions. Webster continued—now in full, emotional vein:

> With consciences satisfied with the discharge of duty, no consequences can harm you. There is no evil that we cannot either face or fly from, but the consciousness of duty disregarded. A sense

of duty pursues us ever. It is omnipresent, like the Deity. If we take to ourselves the wings of the morning, and dwell in the uttermost parts of the sea . . .

(here Webster is quoting *Psalms*)

. . . duty performed, or duty violated, is still with us, for our happiness or our misery. . . . Our obligations are yet with us. We can not escape their power, nor fly from their presence. They are with us in this life, will be with us at its close; and in that scene of inconceivable solemnity, which lies yet farther onward, we shall still find ourselves surrounded, by the consciousness of duty, to pain us wherever it has been violated, and to console us so far as God may have given us grace to perform it.

Contrast Clarence Darrow's equally emotional plea to a jury not to hang his client: "You are trying the jury system. . . . No power on earth can relieve you of your obligation. This jury alone stands between this boy and the gallows. Bill Haywood can't die unless you kill him. You must tie the rope."[3]

B. FEAR

Listeners will behave wisely if they fear the outcome of not behaving wisely. If the speaker needs to scare his hearers into taking action, he needs to describe the consequences as vividly as possible.

A famous article, "—And Sudden Death," had great influence on those who read it originally in the *Reader's Digest*. Though an article, and not a speech, it illustrates effectively the appeal to fear, because the purpose of its author, J. C. Furnas, was to paint such a frightful picture of death on the highway that readers would be afterwards too terrified to drive at high speeds. Here is the ending:

And every time you pass on a blind curve, every time you hit it up on a slippery road, every time you step on it harder than your reflexes will safely take, every time you drive with your

---

[3] Horace G. Rahskopf, "The Speaking of Clarence Darrow," in *American Public Address: Studies in Honor of Albert Craig Baird* (Columbia, University of Missouri Press, 1961), pp. 41-42.

It is difficult to overvalue the importance of an *appeal*. An example from another field: Investigators mailed out 7000 mimeographed questionnaires on *half* of which had been written, by hand, "P.S. We need your help in this report. Could you please send it in promptly?" 24.7 per cent of those without the postscript, 31.4 per cent of those with it, came back. George Frazier and Kermit Bird, "Increasing the Response of a Mail Questionnaire." Reprinted from the *Journal of Marketing*, national quarterly publication of the American Marketing Association, XXIII (October, 1958), 186-187.

reactions slowed down by a drink or two, every time you follow the man ahead too closely, you're gambling a few seconds against blood and agony and sudden death.

Take a look at yourself as the man in the white jacket shakes his head over you, tells the boys with the stretcher not to bother and turns away to somebody else who isn't quite dead yet. And then take it easy.[4]

C. OTHER EMOTIONS

Much that is fine in speaking appeals to our better nature. Speakers say to us: Work hard, make sacrifices, do what is right and necessary. The emotions appealed to are those of affection, self-preservation, pride.

Charles Nutter, managing director of International House, concluded a thoughtful appraisal of the extent of Soviet penetration with these words:

I do not think that we can guarantee that our life will be easier or better for our children than it was for us. Frankly, I do not think that it will be. We must teach those children the meaning of responsibility and hard work, the necessity to sacrifice and help others, the real meaning, value and price of freedom.

During the dark days of World War II we readily accepted laws and regulations we would not otherwise have considered, we imposed rationing and shortages, we gave up rights and privileges, we made whatever sacrifices our leaders felt necessary for the war economy and victory.

We may yet have to go much farther along this road to hold our own. We may have to accept taxes far beyond anything we have yet dreamed, our national debt may soar to many times its present amount, our standard of living and economy may be greatly reduced. We can only guess what sacrifices we may have to endure.

Of course there always is the chance that the changing winds of Communism in China, where the commune is backfiring on the

---

[4] *Reader's Digest*, XLVII (December, 1945), 122. This article first appeared in the *Digest* in August, 1935. Within three months of publication, the *Digest* distributed 4,000,000 reprints to more than 8000 companies, clubs, civic associations, and other groups. James Playsted Wood in *Of Lasting Interest: The Story of the Reader's Digest* (Garden City, New York, Doubleday & Company, 1958), calls this "perhaps the most successful. widely circulated, read, and talked-about magazine article ever published." As this author describes it: "It was a grisly piece—blood, bones protruding through torn flesh, corpses strewn about the road, bodies smashed beyond recognition." One investigator "found a noticeable decrease in the number of highway accidents following its appearance" (no claim is made, of course, for an exact causal relationship here). (Pages 59-62.)

leaders there and causing concern in Moscow, may lead to disunity within the Communistic world and give us a breathing spell. But I do not think we can depend on this. We'll have to depend upon ourselves to save our civilization by our own efforts, and the way be rough and hard.[5]

Business men use appeals as well as reasoning. To conclude a talk filled with facts about American Motors and its product, George Romney used this thought:

Shakespeare wrote a great play about Henry V, an English king who had to take his troops to France to fight a crucial campaign. They had been on the march for three or four days, through hostile country; they were hungry and worn out when they were suddenly confronted in the evening by a French force five times their size, fresh and ready for battle.

That night Henry went among his troops encouraging them and building up their morale for the morning. They decided to attack before the French were set. As dawn approached the general of the English army said to the King, "Are we ready?" and the King gave this historic reply: "All things are ready if our minds be so."

Now we're ready to be the champions of basic excellence and to become the number 1 volume car sellers in America—if our minds be so. And there are many of you men here today that can put your dealerships into the number 1 position in the market during the coming year—and that's what I hope you'll do.[6]

Harold R. Medina, circuit judge of the United States Court of Appeals, gave a stirring address at the annual Congress of American Industry. His topic was "The Bill of Rights—Our Heritage." For his conclusion he used a personal experience:

[5] From a text supplied by Mr. Nutter. This speech appeared in *Vital Speeches*, XXV (March 1, 1959).

[6] Talk to dealers, introducing the 1960 Rambler, September 10, 1959, at Miami Beach. The incident is adapted from *King Henry V*, Act IV. From a tape recording supplied through the courtesy of Mr. Romney. The speaker wrote: "I have spoken in public ever since I was a small boy: As you may know, part of the training in my church involves self-expression. From a very early age, all youngsters are taught and encouraged to speak before large groups at church services and gatherings." (Letter of December 10, 1959.) He added that he makes about 35 talks a year. On one occasion he may be addressing dealers, as when he made the speech from which the foregoing excerpt was taken; on another he may be speaking to employees of American Motors in a mass meeting, urging them to keep up the quality of the company product; on still a third he may find himself talking to students at the University of Cincinnati on qualities of success needed in life. A Republican, he has long been interested in problems of citizenship; he was active in the constitutional convention of Michigan in 1961-1962, and takes a leading part in state and national politics.

In 1949 in the trial of the Communist leaders, charged with conspiracy to teach and advocate the overthrow of the United States Government by force and violence, we started off with a challenge to the entire panel of jurors. . . . I overruled the challenge. So we began to pick the jury with about 400 talesman in the courtroom. . . . Every single business man or executive begged off. I was positively ashamed. Even in a case where our whole future might be at stake, for all they knew, not a single one of these substantial business men was willing to make the sacrifice. The result was that we had a jury composed of the very persons who were claimed to have been excluded: three Negroes, including a Negro woman as the foreman, a number of housewives and working people.

My friends, this is not a healthy sign. We are a free and independent people; we have in our Bill of Rights a precious heritage which we must at all costs preserve; and we can preserve it only by fighting for it, fighting for it intelligently, persistently, and unselfishly.[7]

Webster ended a complex discussion of contracts with this emotional appeal in behalf of Dartmouth College and other colleges throughout the land:

Sir, you may destroy this little institution; it is weak; it is in your hands! I know it is one of the lesser lights on the literary horizon of our country. You may put it out. But if you do, you must carry through your work! You must extinguish, one after another, all those greater lights of science, which, for more than a century, have thrown their radiance over our land!

---

[7] *Vital Speeches,* XXV (December 15, 1958), 160. Read the complete speech in this issue, and also the analysis of Dr. Lionel Crocker, professor of speech at Denison University, that accompanies it.

Judge Medina's reflections on speech making contain practical advice to all students. He wrote (December 10, 1959):

"I think such capacity as I developed for public speaking is wholly the result of experience. I got a prize in prep school in a public speaking contest at commencement the year before I graduated but never had any formal training at all and did not participate in debating either in school or college. But practically from the time I got out of law school I was speaking constantly.

"I think the most valuable experience was in teaching large groups in the course I gave to prepare students for the bar examinations and also in the argument of appeals in the appellate courts. I would practice these arguments in appellate courts for hours on end in my office or in my apartment or in my library building down at Westhampton so that I could proceed without notes and with considerable flexibility.

"My own idea of the most valuable quality I possess in the line of public speaking is that of extreme sensitivity to the reactions of those to whom I am speaking, and an ability, the source of which I do not understand myself, to make the subject matter interesting so that people always listen to me. I also make a great effort always to stop at a time when the audience or the judges or the jurors would wish that I could only continue for a few minutes longer."

It is, sir, as I have said, a small college, and yet there are those who love it.[8]

Speakers sometimes challenge listeners by admitting that the speaker's view may be an unpopular one. A suggestion of this appears in Patrick Henry's defiant phrase, "I know not what course others may take." John Bright, one of the exceptionally eloquent orators in nineteenth century England, often used a thought like this: "*I am but one in this audience*," continuing: "and but one in the citizenship of this country; but if all other tongues are silent, mine shall speak." And speak he did, for the cause of those who were enslaved. Statements like these challenge others to follow the speaker's lead.

Sometimes a speaker can quite properly and effectively challenge listeners to become more concerned about their responsibility to defend their heritage through painting a word picture of the possible consequences of their failure to do so. In the excerpt which follows Florence Allen sketches briefly "a terrifying picture," followed with an appeal for "devotion, courage, and understanding":

We are fortunate in the present crisis to have an international organization actually functioning through which the moral opinion of the world may, and often does, speak. We are fortunate in having at its head a leader of judgment, courage and intelligence. And we Americans are supremely fortunate to have been born to a heritage of justice and freedom. But we see a terrifying picture. We behold the disintegration of that law which is based upon ethical standards, upon the dignity and equality of individuals before the law, and with that disintegration the destruction of human rights through great areas of the world. Make no mistake, if communism takes over America no great free university like this one, no church however large and powerful founded by men and women who wished to worship God according to their conscience, no private organization whatever its importance and value to the community will be permitted to survive. This poses a challenge not only to the government but also to the citizen. If the great mass of citizens responds with devotion, courage and understanding, the spread of this social and ethical disease which threatens to infect the whole world will be arrested, and free men and women will go forth to reestablish civilization.[9]

[8] From Webster's speech in the Dartmouth College case (1818). Tradition is that Chief Justice John Marshall wept upon hearing these words.

[9] Delivered August 26, 1960, at the commencement exercises at the University of Utah, Salt Lake City. In Lester Thonssen, ed. *Representative American Speeches: 1960-1961* (New York, The H. W. Wilson Co., 1961), 100-114. Used with the permission of the speaker.

Addressing an audience consisting mostly of women, Judge Allen concluded with this moving appeal:

> This is our supreme task, yours and mine; professional efficiency is not enough. We have to rebuild the spirit. We have not only to keep the home, not only to maintain the ethical standards, not only to cling to our faith; we have to teach the eager boys and girls the meaning of America so that they feel a tug upon their faculties and a sense of Partnership in the moral life about them. When we achieve this America will go on to a new birth of freedom; for when the coming race thrills to the meaning of the old American dream of justice and liberty it will become a reality.[10]

II. The Speaker's Character

All of us have to make so many decisions in fields where we can not make first-hand observations, and in situations where we can not understand the technical data involved, that we have to rely on each other continually for advice and counsel. Listeners feel that some speakers are more credible and believable than others. These characteristics are of prime importance:

A. COMPETENCE, SELF-ASSURANCE

Listeners like to be assured that the speaker is intelligent about his subject. A beginning speaker has the problem of letting his audience know that he is qualified to talk upon the topic he has selected. As modestly and as unassumingly as you can, let your

---

[10] The occasion was the dedication of Bevier Hall and the Child Development Laboratory on the campus of the University of Illinois, April 5, 1957. Title of the address: "Map for Living—50 Year Plan." The speaker was introduced as "the only woman in the world ever to sit on a federal court of general jurisdiction."
Text is supplied through the courtesy of Judge Allen. Answering an inquiry from the author, she wrote:
"You ask me about the amount and nature of my speech making. In my fairly long life I have addressed very many colleges and universities and conventions. Often I spoke on some subject connected with the administration of justice, using my personal experience as an Assistant Prosecutor in charge of framing hundreds of indictments, and actively trying hundreds of criminal cases, my experience as a trial judge and as a reviewing judge in the highest court of Ohio to add interest and point to my address. . . .
"My first training in public speaking I derived from my mother who was a fine speaker. She told me when I made any address to state my points briefly and with emphasis and then sit down. I have found this a good rule. I had a chance to try it out in speaking on behalf of woman suffrage in 1912. . . . The woman suffrage speeches I made in some 70 of the 88 counties of Ohio were not made to captive audiences. As a rule we would mount the steps of some court house and capture our audience in the first sentence we said. This helped me to be quicker and more effective than I otherwise would have been." (Letter of January 24, 1962.) Judge Allen is also quoted in this text on page 98.

hearers know about your special competence. If you spent a summer reading Jane Austen, tell us; that leads us to listen more carefully to your opinions of her novels. Similarly let us know if you have had special interviews or have been exposed to other sources of information that bear on your topic.

How do speakers reveal their competence to speak on a given subject? Listen to the senior senator from Illinois, reporting to his constituents on the crisis in Berlin: "The day Congress adjourned I left for Western Europe where I spent the bulk of my time in Germany and Berlin." Listen to the ambassador from Korea: "Just two weeks ago I returned from an intensive, consultative visit with my home government in Seoul." Listen to the United States Commissioner of Education: "We have just returned from a month-long study of the schools in the U.S.S.R." If well-known speakers with established reputations find these explanations necessary, a beginning speaker can spare the few words needed to show his listeners that he is better informed than they may suspect. A series of experiments conducted with student audiences at Northwestern University suggested that, for these college groups, "an especially high premium seemed to be placed upon the factor of competence."[11]

A speaker's self-assurance, his unshakable faith in himself, his firm belief in his policy, are of high importance. When in 1961 the mainland of France was threatened by invasion from Algeria led by four mutinous, retired generals, Charles de Gaulle made a brief but forceful appearance on television. "I forbid any Frenchman, and first of all any soldier, to execute any of their orders," he said, following with this appeal: "French men and women, look where France risks falling, and what she was about to become again. French men and women! help me!" The popular response to his plea was overwhelmingly favorable.

On this speech the *New York Times* commented: "De Gaulle and de Gaulle alone shattered the latest attempt on his authority." A maxim of this French general is said to be: "The man of character finds an especial attractiveness in difficulty, since it is only by coming to grips with difficulty that he can realize his potentialties."[12] De Gaulle's compelling, dramatic speech had immediate impact; and part of it is traceable to his massive self-assurance that he was spokesman for France itself. Of course self-assurance is not all; the self-confident person can be wrong; in the final analysis the listener must be assured

---

[11] Franklyn S. Haiman, "An Experimental Study of the Effects of Ethos in Public Speaking," in *Speech Monographs*, XVI (September, 1949), 202.
[12] C. L. Sulzberger in the *New York Times*, April 29, 1961, 22.

that there are also reason, logic, judgment, ethical standards. Nor are these paragraphs written to make an arrogant person happy in his arrogance but rather to persuade the quiet, sensible person to study a problem realistically instead of being conquered at the outset by fears and doubts.

B. INTEGRITY, SINCERITY

Through his language a speaker can show that he is accurate and honest. Consider statements like "fraternities are composed of irresponsible individuals" or "professors wait until they know we haven't studied then they spring a surprise quiz." If a listener senses that you are inaccurate in discussing the things *he* knows about, he may be less likely to accept your judgment in matters that he does not know about. Inconsistencies, contradictions, and exaggerations are sure to give an impression of insincerity.[13] Says Fosdick, who for more than two decades was "the most important popular figure in the Protestant pulpit": "There is no process by which wise and useful discourses can be distilled from unwise and useless personalities. . . . The ultimate necessity . . . is sound and intelligent character."[14]

Recall the line from the 1960 inaugural address, quoted in the Appendix: "To those peoples in the huts . . . we pledge our best efforts . . . not because the communists may be doing it . . . but because it is right."

Dr. Joseph Goebbels, considered an expert propagandist, was for a while able to lead and sway the German people. Yet long before World War II ended, they tuned their short-wave sets to BBC, London—because they sensed that BBC was telling the truth.

C. FAIRNESS

Any social, economic, or political issue about which we try to persuade others calls for shades of judgment and discernment. The more we study such a problem, the more of its complexities we appreciate. All the truth is not on one side. You will be more persuasive about the advantages of a large institution (or a small college) if you are equally ready to admit its faults. "The large university (or the small college) is not perfect, but here are two of its outstanding merits." Or: "At times I have been embarrassed by

[13] See Chapter 2 in Carl I. Hovland, Irving L. Janis, and Harold Kelley, *Communication and Persuasion* (New Haven, Yale University Press, 1953).
[14] Quoted by Roy C. McCall, "Harry Emerson Fosdick: A Study in Sources of Effectiveness," in *American Public Address: Studies in Honor of Albert Craig Baird*, p. 61.

the behavior of certain American overseas, but on these two matters we compare favorably with nationals of other countries." Again: "The stock market can go down as well as up, but a prudent investor should realize substantial gains from his purchases."

A speaker shows his fairness not only in his selection of materials for his speech, but also in his attitude toward his listeners.

When the Attorney General of the United States chose to talk about civil rights on the campus of the University of Georgia, the occasion being the Law Day exercises of its School of Law, he knew indeed that he was selecting a sensitive topic. Toward the close of his speech he said:

> You may ask, will we enforce the Civil Rights statutes.
> The answer is: "Yes, we will."
> We also will enforce the antitrust laws, the antiracketeering laws, the laws against kidnaping and robbing federal banks, and transporting stolen automobiles across state lines, the illicit traffic in narcotics and all the rest. . . .
> We will not make or interpret the laws. We shall enforce them—vigorously, without regional bias or political slant.
> All this we intend to do. But all the high rhetoric on Law Day about the noble mansions of the law; all the high-sounding speeches about liberty and justice, are meaningless unless people—you and I —breathe meaning and force into it. For our liberties depend upon our respect for the law.[15]

In these words the speaker attempted to reassure his listeners that he would perform his constitutional duty of enforcing the law "in every

---

[15] Robert F. Kennedy, May 6, 1961. The text of the speech was supplied this book by Jack Rosenthal, assistant director of public information in the Department of Justice and is used with permission. The speech also appeared in *Vital Speeches*, XXVII (June 1, 1961), 482-485, and in the *Journal* of the American Bar Association.

Mr. Kennedy, a Massachusetts man on this occasion visiting Georgia, ended his speech with a quotation from Henry W. Grady, a Georgian who in 1889 delivered a famous speech in Massachusetts: "This hour little needs the loyalty that is loyal to one section and yet holds the other in enduring suspicion and estrangement. Give us the broad and perfect loyalty that loves and trusts Georgia alike with Massachusetts." His activities as a speech maker during his February, 1962, world-wide tour attracted the attention of press and TV. An editorial by William Becker in the *Wall Street Journal* for February 27, 1962, commented:

Indonesia: "By Bobby's performance, . . . at least among some student leaders, years of Communist propaganda have been cancelled out in a few minutes."

Japan: "When a small knot of leftist students . . . in Tokyo . . . refused to let him speak, Mr. Kennedy invited their leader to the stage. . . . The youth went into a long harangue . . . Bobby patiently held the microphone for his adversary. . . . Eventually he managed to answer some questions and make a brief speech. That night nearly 200 students went to the American embassy to apologize" (p. 14).

field of law and every region . . . without regional bias or political slant."

D. CANDOR

Candor is a trait resembling fairness, but also carries the suggestion that the speaker wishes to state the issue frankly and honestly. It thus reveals that the speaker does not hesitate to utter a challenging responsibility nor to bring sober news. "I have nothing to offer but blood, toil, tears, and sweat" is more than being frank; it reflects great candor. The speaker may confess, "We have had our worst season in years." Or: "The remedy I propose is not an easy one." Or: "I wish I could report that our book pool showed a profit, but actually the figures show it has operated at a heavy loss." A good teacher can use candor to advantage: "The assignment for next week is one of the most difficult of the course." Statements like these will likely put listeners in a more receptive frame of mind than would soft-pedalling unpleasant news or overstating good features.

The address of Elmer Ellis, president of the University of Missouri, to the graduates of the Granite City, Illinois, high school, candidly presents the challenge of the future to citizens, to faculties, and especially to the students themselves:

> It is not only *more* education for *more* people that is being demanded, it is *better* education also. The years ahead will present to the colleges and universities both the opportunity and the challenge to improve their staffs, their practices, and the effectiveness of their educational programs. With a more vigorous interest than ever before on the part of the people generally, and surely with greater financial support than in the past, we must make higher education better in quality as well as broader in scope. There will be no place in next year's college for the idle student. Teachers and facilities are too scarce, and society's needs are too great, to waste time and effort on the indolent.[16]

[16] Text supplied this book through the courtesy of the speaker. The address was given at the midyear commencement of the high school, January 29, 1962.

As to the speech-making duties of a university president, Dr. Ellis makes the following observations:

"One who does much public speaking is likely to address many types of audiences. Among the many groups to which I speak each year, the three with which I meet most frequently are, in order: educational associations, university alumni, and business men's organizations. The most difficult speech I have to make is the biennial presentation of the university budget request to the appropriations committees of the General Assembly. The difficulty derives from the following sources: (1) the material must be exceptionally well organized and much of it committed to memory because the limited time of the committee requires that the presentation move rapidly; (2) all of the larger items of the request must be carefully justified, even though time does not permit the explanation of

Wide World (all photos)

CITIZENS OF THE REPUBLIC SPEAK ON VITAL ISSUES

Dwight D. Eisenhower answers emphatically a question by a reporter at a news conference. Adlai Stevenson comments on the possibility of a meeting of heads of state at a summit conference. Barry Goldwater addresses a forum meeting in New York City.

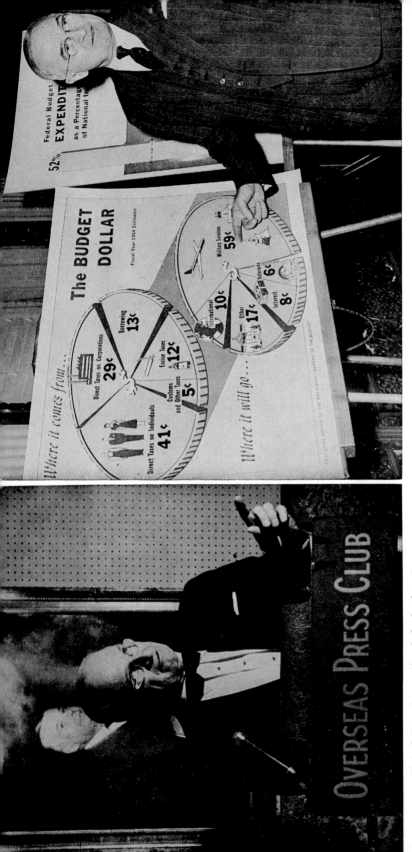

United Press International (both photos)

SPEECHES ARE MADE IN VARYING CIRCUMSTANCES

Left, private citizen Harry S. Truman addresses the Overseas Press Club in New York. He is there to help unveil a portrait of a former president of the club (shown in background). *Right*, President Harry S. Truman uses a pie graph to explain to newsmen at a press seminar the source and the expenditure of the budget dollar.

E. GOOD WILL

Irony and sarcasm have little place in persuasive speaking, though they flourished in an earlier century. Neither has bluntness nor rudeness. Generations ago a speaker might take pride in the fact that he could demolish an opponent with strong, salty, language; as now we are more sophisticated, we much prefer to see differences of opinion handled graciously and errors dealt with charitably. Speakers also show good will for listeners when they promise to be brief, and are brief; when they relate exactly what happened, the good along with the bad; when they are aware that the hour is late or that conditions do not favor comfortable listening; when they are considerate of the views of others.

A persuasive speech made in the United States Senate—one that is reputed to have changed votes—was made by Arthur H. Vandenberg endorsing the appointment of David E. Lilienthal as chairman of the Atomic Energy Commission. Note these short excerpts:

I wish briefly to make a matter of record my reasons for believing that under all existing circumstances Mr. David Lilienthal should be confirmed as Chairman of the Atomic Energy Commission without further delay.

I do so with no illusions that any Senator, at this late hour, after weeks and months of bitter controversy, is still open to persuasion. I do so with complete respect for the good conscience with which every Senator will take his position. I quarrel with none.

I have heard or read every word of the testimony. As a result, I have been driven away from the adverse prejudice with which I started. I have been driven to the belief that logic, equity, fair play, and a just regard to urgent public welfare combine to recommend Mr. Lilienthal's confirmation in the light of today's realities.

I say this with full appreciation of the earnest zeal with which others hold a contrary view, including many of my warmest friends. . . .

all needed background information; and (3) though the presentation may be well organized at the beginning, it may become disorganized at any moment by committee questions pertaining to matters already passed over, those not yet reached, or some not related to the budget request at all."

Dr. Ellis's counsel about organization, supporting evidence, and the importance of being able to meet question and inquiry may be applied not only to legislative committees but also to business or industrial situations in which budgets or other proposals must be presented to a board, committee, or other agency.

This opening part of the speech shows his resolution to take a firm position against many of his hearers, yet he was considerate of their views. To speak "with complete respect for the good conscience with which every Senator will take his position" invites a friendlier hearing than to say, in blunt language, "I flatly disagree . . . my friend is misinformed . . . he talked ten minutes and said nothing worth refuting . . . on my part I have absolutely proved . . ."[17]

F. JUDGMENT

A speaker is valued by the quality of the advice he offers. You can not expect to gain converts if your counsel is extreme, bizarre, radical, or reckless. Campus rules governing parking, rush week, social events, late hours, and the like, often complicated, are arrived at as the result of much experience. The student who argued that those who violate traffic regulations should be jailed touched a sensitive problem, but he had a poor solution. The issues confronting the nation and the world are complex. We need to feel that our speakers offer us wise counsel.

Lincoln deeply felt the responsibility of the speaker to offer good advice. "I always assume that my audiences are in many ways wiser than I am," he wrote, "and I say the most sensible thing I can."

G. REPUTATION

Haiman reported an experiment in which a recording of a persuasive speech on compulsory health insurance was played to three different student audiences. One audience was told that the speech was by the Secretary-General of the Communist Party; another was told it was by the Surgeon General of the United States; the third that it was by an anonymous Northwestern University sophomore. Opinion ballots taken before the speech showed that the three audiences were fairly comparable in their attitude toward the subject. The listeners, however, who thought they were listening to the Surgeon General, registered the greatest change towards the speaker's ideas.[18]

This discussion calls to mind the story told about the renowned classical scholar, Benjamin Jowett, who was invited to preach at a church then without a pastor. "But don't you recall," he said, "I happened to be in your church last Sunday, and, seeing you were

---

[17] From the *Congressional Record* for April 3, 1947. Quoted in A. Craig Baird, *Representative American Speeches*, 1946-1947, 122-123.

For another example of a highly persuasive speech, see, in the Appendix, Benjamin Franklin's "Plea to the Constitutional Convention."

[18] *Op. cit.*, 190-202. And see also the discussion of "trustworthy sources" in Part V, Chap. 6.

without a pastor, I preached the sermon." "Ah," said the parishioner extending the invitation, "at that time we did not know you were Benjamin Jowett."

A student in a public speaking class establishes a reputation with his classmates that may add to the effectiveness of his speaking. His reputation may be for competence in a special field, like sports, livestock judging, home economics education, or politics. It may be for fairness, a sense of humor, an appreciation of the good efforts of others. Even if his early speeches are poor, he will gain respect when he begins to solve his difficulties and demonstrate new abilities to stimulate interest and hold attention. When he graduates and enters civic, business, and professional worlds, his early efforts will help him build a reputation. Achievements in non-speaking fields may add to his prestige as an individual and, consequently, as a speaker. One can not make every speech better than the one preceding—no one can accomplish such an impossibility—but through the weeks, in school, and over the years, after school, one's reputation should be enhanced slowly even though irregularly.

H. COURAGE

How can any list of personal qualities be compiled without including one which—especially on critical occasions—looms most important of all—courage?

Deutsch rightly points out that the speaker is at times called upon by his conscience to display a special kind of courage. He says:

> To risk injury by rescuing a child from in front of a speeding train or single-handedly to charge a machine-gun nest are brave or courageous acts. This order of behavior, is essentially different from the courage displayed, for example, by the one representative in the Florida legislature who, in the face of unanimous opposition from his colleagues, spoke and voted against their school segregation bill.

This latter, he continues, may be defined as *social courage*.[19]

Times arise when a speaker *must* take a position. He *must* stand up and be counted. Simply to cast a silent vote, even a right one, may not be enough; the speaker's office or position, or his feelings of duty and responsibility, compel him to tell others why he believes as he does.

Especially we admire courage when at its side march courtesy

[19] Martin Deutsch, "Courage as a Concept in Social Psychology," *Journal of Social Psychology*, LV (October, 1961), 49-58.

and tact. Courage is also often properly seen in the company of moral and righteous indignation. Courage is less inspiring, however, when it uses a mask of ridicule, scorn, profanity, or other violent language.

Again we can listen to Lincoln's wisdom, which, as always, reflected his own quiet courage: "If the end brings me out all right, what is said against me won't amount to anything. If the end brings me out wrong, ten angels swearing I was right would make no difference."

I. ETHICAL RESPONSIBILITIES OF THE SPEAKER

This discussion of character affords opportunity to remind the speaker of his ethical responsibilities. One who addresses an audience should meet these standards:

1. *He should prepare thoroughly.* He has a positive responsibility to his audience to be well-informed. He should check the accuracy of his statements by research. To utter part-truths is moral flabbiness. To tell lies is even more reprehensible in public speaking than it is in private speaking.

2. *His personal interests and loyalties should be made clear.* One may speak as a citizen, as a member of a political party, as a spokesman for a religious faith, business, or organization. If, however, he appears to speak as a public official, whereas secretly he is working for a commercial firm, his ethical responsibilities are badly warped.

3. *When he offers advice, he should have the best interests of his listeners at heart.* Much that is significant in public speaking comes under the heading of advice and counsel. An audience deserves a speaker's best judgment, not his second-best or third-best judgment—just as a patient deserves the physician's best advice, not his next-best or third-best advice.

4. *A speaker should clearly label which ideas are his and which belong to some one else.* Don't use some one else's outline; don't repeat some one else's speech; don't use a striking phrase or a title that some one else has created—without giving credit to that other person. If it seems embarrassing to give credit, you probably should not use the material.

Though a good speaker compiles facts from many sources, he will identify his sources: that statistic comes from the Bureau of the Census, this quotation comes from the president of Bethlehem Steel. Yet his speech will reflect his own interpreting and thinking: sometimes by arrangement, sometimes by phrasing an idea, sometimes by showing new insights or relationships, sometimes by making application to the specific audience in front of him.

In business, professional, and public life, men and women often rely on others to gather speech materials for them. This situation brings up the term *ghost-written speech*. Often these are incredibly routine. When, however, the speaker refers to his own *personal* experiences, or when he draws the kinds of inferences that can be drawn only by a person in his position, the speech begins to grow in liveliness and impact. A business or public official must often use facts supplied by the lower echelons of his organization; the final wording, however, should be his own.

While you are a beginning speaker, set standards of ethical responsibility for yourself. Then when in later years you are confronted with ethical problems, you will, from life-long habit, put yourself on the side of those forces of morality and integrity that should enlist us all.

III. Other Factors

In order to be as persuasive as possible, speakers need to consider factors that affect the emphasis given an idea.

A. REPETITION

Some of the earliest studies in persuasion have shown that *repetition* has direct bearing on what is attended to and what is remembered. Making a statement and repeating it about twice, later in the speech, has been called one of the most effective ways of emphasizing an idea. A single utterance is not so effective.[20] Chapter 21, "Another Look at Speech Design," suggests that the use of a phrase or text which is stated and then is later reechoed and restated gives the speech high interest value. Often you will find it necessary to *state and restate* the title of the book you wish us to read, the time and place of the program you are recommending, the name of the Congressman we should be sure to write.

B. "NOW GET THIS"

The use of a phrase like "Now get this" has been shown to emphasize the idea that ensues.[21] This phrase seems to point a long

---

[20] Ray Ehrensberger, "An Experimental Study of the Relative Effectiveness of Certain Forms of Emphasis in Public Speaking," *Speech Monographs*, XII (1945), 94-111.
[21] Ehrensberger, *op. cit.*

finger at the words that follow, and makes them stick in the mind. We all learn that when the professor says, "Now, this is important," we should start underscoring our notes. This is an old lesson. Aristotle pointed out that these "calls for attention" may come at any part of the speech, although it was a little ridiculous to put them at the beginning when interest was strong anyway. "Choose therefore any point in the speech where such an appeal is needed," he counselled, "and then say, 'Now I beg you to note this point—it concerns you quite as much as myself.'" The "Now get this," or "Now this is important," or "Now I beg you to note this point" are all verbal colons that punctuate and thereby emphasize the longer statement to follow.

C. ARRANGEMENT

Speakers should give careful thought to the *order* in which they placed their arguments and appeals. Cicero argued that the strongest materials should be placed at the *opening* of the speech. Quintilian pointed out that this was not necessarily always the best arrangement; in certain instances the *closing* of the speech was the place for the strongest materials. All of this can be termed *emphasis by position.* Good historical precedent exists for *strongest, strong, stronger* or for *stronger, strong, strongest.* There is really no good place for *weak* materials; they can not very well be hidden or glossed over; better study further, say the experienced speakers, and leave the weak materials in the wastebasket. If you were making a speech about the advantages of sports cars, you could construct strong arguments about their *speed* and *maneuverability* but you could offer at best only a weak argument about their *roominess.*

At Yale University a group of 35 students in introductory psychology was divided into two groups, one containing 18 and the other 17. A speaker, introduced as a professor of psychology, appeared before one group and discussed the grading problem. He began by talking about the increasing number of high grades; he speculated on the probability of eventual lowering of grades, with the effect on parents and potential employers; he introduced a vague statement to the effect that the present situation had provoked confusion. He then talked about grading on the curve and presented it as an efficient system which would discriminate better among students and solve the present difficulties.

To complete the experiment, the same speaker appeared before the other group and used the same material, except that he described the system of curve grading first and the "need for the change" second. Later, questionnaires were administered to both **groups** and the results studied; they showed that the group which was aroused first and then presented with a solution was significantly more favorable to the idea of curve grading than the group which heard the *explanation* of curve grading first and the *need* for it second.[22]

Psychologists have given much attention to this matter of arrangement. The plan of using the *strongest argument first* is put under the heading of *primacy*. The plan of *closing with the strongest argument* is put under the heading of *recency*. The advantage of *primacy* lies in the persuasive effect of the first impression; the advantage of *recency* lies in the effectiveness of the last impression. The extensive research in this field is difficult to generalize, but perhaps it is partly true to say that not so much is claimed for the advantages of primacy as once was. Both primacy and recency are strategic positions that must be studied by the speaker as he reviews the subject, the occasion, and the audience;[23] such a review should help him make a wise decision.

Given three arguments labelled *strong, stronger, strongest,* should the order be

[22] See the complete study by Arthur R. Cohen in *The Order of Presentation in Persuasion,* in Vol. I of *Yale Studies in Attitude and Communication,* ed. Carl L. Hovland (New Haven: Yale University Press, 1957) 79-97. The student may be interested in reading Professor Hovland's summary of a series of experiments in the same volume, 129-157.

[23] In recent years *Speech Monographs* has published studies by Raymond G. Smith (1951), K. C. Beighley (1952, 1954), Harold Sponberg (1946), Harvey Cromwell (1950), Halbert E. Gulley and David K. Berlo (1956) and others discussing various problems of speech organization. As to whether organization is necessary so far as informing or persuading is concerned, certain of the studies suggest that, with some speeches, organization may not be critical. As speeches become longer, however, and materials more difficult, good organization is more imperative. In organizing a speech, these studies seem to agree, the speaker is advised to put his strongest argument towards the *end* of his speech rather than at the *beginning*; though circumstances alter cases.

Gulley and Berlo cite Gilkinson, Cromwell, and others, and their own research, to suggest a slight advantage in favor of arranging the arguments of a speech so that the strongest is last. See their study in *Speech Monographs,* XXIII (November, 1956), 288-297.

The Yale Institute of Human Relations studies, by Carl L. Hovland and others (see *The Order of Presentation in Persuasion,* New Haven, Yale University Press, 1957), also discuss these and related problems, such as whether arguments *for* a proposal should precede, or follow, arguments *against* a proposal. Selected conclusions: 1. When two sides of an issue are presented successively by different communicators, the side presented first does not necessarily have an advantage. 2. Order of presentation is a more significant factor in influencing opinion for listeners with relatively weak desire for understanding than for those with a strong desire; i.e., those who strongly desire to understand are less influenced by *order* of presentation. 3. Placing communications highly desirable to the listener first, followed by those less desirable, produces more opinion change than the reverse order. (Pages 130-136).

1. strongest argument
2. strong argument
3. stronger argument

or:

1. stronger argument
2. strong argument
3. strongest argument?

This book recommends the latter unless there are special circumstances. The worst order would probably be

1. strongest argument
2. stronger argument
3. strong argument

because this arrangement shows that the speaker is becoming weaker as he goes along—and puts his relatively weakest argument in the all-important *last* place.

An important purpose of this discussion is to remind the speaker not to arrange his arguments in haphazard fashion, but to arrange them after giving his best thought to the requirements of the subject, the audience, and the occasion.

After you have evolved what appears to be logically or psychologically the best order in which to present your arguments, give thought to the *conclusion* of your speech. This conclusion can take the form of a *summary, summary plus appeal, application, quotation, illustration* (see Chapter 12, "Beginning and Ending the Speech"). In this connection it is interesting to note that two experimenters, Hovland and Mandell, found that twice as many listeners changed opinions when the conclusion contained explicit recommendations than when it contained implicit (indirect) recommendations.[24]

The *length of time* given to a certain argument or appeal tends to emphasize it. If you spend twice as much time talking about *long-term advantages* of a proposal as you do to *short-term advantages,* the former will be emphasized in the listener's mind. This is termed *emphasis by proportion.*

D. SUGGESTION

Students should know about *suggestion* in part in order to be able to recognize it and to keep from being bamboozled by it.

[24] Carl I. Hovland and Wallace Mandell, "An Experimental Comparison of Conclusion-Drawing by the Communicator and by the Audience," *Journal of Abnormal and Social Psychology,* XLVII (1952), 588.
See also the section on "Importance of the Conclusion," pp. 171-172.

Suggestion is a form of communication presented in such a way as to make it unlikely that the listener will react critically or logically. In front of the hat-check girl is a saucer with quarters and half-dollars; this exhibit suggests that to offer small tips is not the thing to do. At the soft-drink counter the student says, "Coke"; the well-trained soda-dispenser says "Large one?" and the student, replies without reflecting, "Yes."

Suggestion may be *direct* as when speaker says, "Sign here," "Line up over here." It may be *indirect,* when the speaker wishes his real purpose to be concealed, like Iago's sly insinuations to Othello that his wife was unfaithful. Suggestion may be phrased in *positive* language when the speaker says "Vote for Hawkins" or in *negative* language when he says, "Don't buy common stocks." A speaker may use *counter suggestion* when he says one thing, hoping the listener will do the opposite. Thus he might say, "Miss Oliver is a demanding, exacting English teacher," hoping that his words, though discouraging, will challenge the listener to make a maximum effort. Counter suggestion, however, may boomerang; the listener may panic and drop the course altogether. In fact many kinds of suggestion may boomerang; not being founded on logical reasoning, they may not be substantial enough for the long pull.

Throughout this chapter principles are described which rely more on suggestion for their effect than upon reason. The speaker's personality, his use of emotional appeal, his telling a story rather than stating an argument, or asking a question rather than making a direct statement, may be received favorably by the listener without too much exercise of his critical faculties. Undoubtedly persuasion is more effective when it has a basis in logic and reason as well as in suggestion, emotional appeal, and other non-logical methods. Otherwise the listener may, after he has found time to reflect, decide not to do what was suggested, or to do it just this once, because he is committed, but to be more critical in the future.

Questions for Classroom Discussion

1. Considering that the art of persuasion gives great advantage to teacher, minister, salesman, statesman, and military leader, discuss: What are the ethical responsibilities of those who use the spoken word?

a. Does a speaker have an ethical responsibility in selecting examples, instances, other facts—in what he *chooses* and what he *omits?*

b. Does a speaker have an ethical responsibility in his *interpretation* of the facts—upon the emphasis, or importance, that he assigns to them?

2. Patrick Henry said, "I have but one lamp by which my feet are guided, and that is the lamp of experience." As Patrick Henry looked over that past experience with the British ministry, he thought the solution was *independence:* "Give me liberty, or give me death." Yet others, with that same experience, were recommending *conciliation.* How do you explain this type of conflict among speakers?

3. Is a speaker justified in declaring, "We will never surrender," when, actually, he can not know for sure? May he say, "This nation will endure forever" when, actually, he may not be around to verify it? May he say, "This is history's proudest hour" or "These are the most critical times in the history of the race" considering that history has had many proud hours, and the race has experienced many critical times? May he say "Prices will go up," or "shortages will not develop" or "the market will suffer a severe reversal during the six months just ahead" when every one's view of the future is inevitably uncertain?

Speech-Related Project

1. Study the advertisements in current magazines and newspaper, looking for examples of persuasion through emotional appeal.

2. Secure a copy of a recent volume of *Representative American Speeches*. Study typical speeches for examples of persuasion through emotional appeal. These appeals you will find, for example, not only in the sermons given in the volume, but also in presidential addresses and speeches by leaders in business and industry. Look also for sentences in which the speaker is attempting to convince listeners of his own honesty, integrity, and fairness.

Speaking Assignment 18
A Speech Urging Action

Make a speech of .... minutes in which your purpose is to get your listeners to take some specific action.

The action you seek may be to persuade them to sign a petition, attend a meeting, vote, write their Congressman, or buy something you are offering for sale.

Give us the strongest arguments you can muster in the time allowed. Feel free to appeal to our loyalty, pride, sense of duty and responsibility, or desire to improve our own health or financial position. If you want us to attend a political meeting, be specific about the time and place (repeat it, or write it on the board). If you want us to write a Congressman, give us the name and address. If you want us to take the pledge, have it there ready to sign.

For suggestions, consult the lists on pages 47-48, 245, 347-348. As usual, select a topic in which you have a deep, personal interest.

REFERENCES ON THE PERSUASIVE SPEECH

(NOTE. *See the list at the end of Chapter 17.*)

CHAPTER 19

Reading a Speech; Impromptu Speaking

Two entirely different but extremely useful forms of speech making: ■ *(1) the speech read from manuscript* ■ *(2) the impromptu talk.*

A STRIKING DEVELOPMENT in twentieth century speaking is the increasing use of the manuscript speech.

Although speakers in many ages have read speeches, our generation is exposed to more and more manuscript reading. The method is an easy one to use poorly. It is a difficult method to use well. Many speakers are opposed to it; former governor Arthur M. Hyde of Missouri expressed an objection colorfully when he declared, "Reading a speech is about the same as trying to make love to your best girl through a hedge fence. You can make her hear you all right, but the contact is bad."[1] Others, like Harry Emerson Fosdick, feel it necessary, in order to achieve both vigor of thought and expressiveness of language, to write and rewrite a speech manuscript. The speeches of Sir Winston Churchill, Harry S. Truman, Franklin D. Roosevelt, and countless business and professional men today, illustrate this latter sentiment.

Obviously, every student of public speaking should try to master more than one kind of presentation. Many public officials and business executives can use the extempore method impressively, but are dull and inept with a manuscript in their hands. Many can read a manuscript with skill, but fall apart in an impromptu situation. This chapter presents a few of the problems that accompany each of these two methods of delivering a speech.

[1] Robert P. Friedman, *The Public Speaking of Arthur M. Hyde* (unpublished Ph.D. dissertation, University of Missouri, 1954), p. 358.

I. Preparing the Manuscript Speech

In its early stages the planning of a manuscript speech is similar to that of other types of speeches. Important differences, however, show up in the later stages of the preparation of a speech that is to be read aloud.

A. GATHER, SELECT, ORGANIZE MATERIAL

These steps in the preparation of a manuscript speech are similar to those in the preparation of an extemporaneous speech. Recall what you have learned about gathering, selecting, organizing, and adapting materials. Recall also that examples, illustrations, instances, and striking or forceful details invariably have an important place in a manuscript speech.

B. PREPARE A WORKING DRAFT

In writing the first draft of your speech, keep in mind that you should set down on paper words that *sound like speaking* rather than words that *look like what some one has written.* The vocabulary of speaking differs from the vocabulary of writing: spoken words tend to be simpler, clearer, more vivid. The sentences of spoken style tend to be shorter. Connectives need to be more explicit; key words are freely repeated; extra pains are taken to make sure the listener understands immediately. Personal pronouns—*I, we, you*—make communication more direct between speaker and listener. Statistics may be used, but no more abundantly than a listener may be expected to hold in his memory. Abstract and generalized ideas may be presented, but the limitations of listening should not be forgotten; and if you have a few moments of abstract or complicated reasoning, follow with specific examples.

The following excerpts will recall the discussion on language in Chapter 16. The first one opens with a question and follows with an answer; the language is simple, and in places informal:

> You may well ask, is there any substitute for experience? My answer is, not entirely, but you can gain a great deal of it vicariously, through study. You can benefit from the experience of others. . . .
>
> One man can have only a limited number of personal experiences during his lifetime. If he could not learn from others, through the oral or written word, each man would have to start from scratch, like Adam, and find out everything for himself. No matter how bril-

liant he might be, he would still be a very primitive individual when he died, even though he reached the age of Methuselah.[2]

The second example contains statistics, but they are handled so that they are easily followed by a listener:

> You and I know that in the last few decades sizable gains have been made in the efficiency of fuel usage by American automobiles.
>
> We at Chrysler, for instance, have made detailed comparisons, under controlled conditions, of the fuel economy of a 1958 Plymouth weighing 3800 pounds, and a 1938 Chrysler weighing 3700 pounds. The same constant-speed test schedule was used for both cars. Gasoline was regular grade.
>
> In spite of the fact that the 1958 Plymouth was heavier, had more than twice the horsepower, and was equipped with automatic transmission, power steering, and power brakes, it showed an average gain of 22 per cent in miles per gallon over the 1938 Chrysler![3]

Part of the clarity is achieved through repetition: each car is mentioned twice by name. The listener thus finds it easy to keep in mind *1938 Chrysler* vs. *1958 Plymouth*. The following sentences from another speech are, by contrast, less inviting:

> Many newly-formed states flexing their young muscles and sovereignty and dealing with Communism may too late discover that they have become ensnared. In the present state of flux, bad planning and faculty implementation may lead to disaster.

The listener keeps waiting for something specific, concrete, vivid.

C. REHEARSAL

After you have prepared your draft, read it aloud to see how it sounds. *This test is important.* Even though you have attempted to write down words that sound like some one talking, you may now and then lapse into formalized, essay style.

You will need to read and reread your manuscript so often that you

[2] From "Foreign Service as an Art and as a Science," an address to the Georgetown University School of Foreign Service by George V. Allen, then director of the U. S. Information Agency. Copy of the speech supplied by Mr. Allen.
  George V. Allen took debating and public speaking courses in high school in North Carolina; he graduated from Duke and has an honorary LL.D. from Harvard. He spent many years as Ambassador, representing this country in Iran, India, and Greece. He delivers six to eight public speeches a month. Only rarely does he use a text, preferring to speak extemporaneously or from notes.
[3] *Vital Speeches*, XXIV (October 1, 1958), 764. This address, "Our Common Stake: The Future of Personal Transportation," is by Paul C. Ackerman, vice president in charge of engineering, Chrysler Corporation.

will practically have it memorized. You will need to know what each sentence says, and what it means; only thus will you be able to give each word the proper emphasis.

As you read, try especially to achieve these three goals:

1. *Make your reading sound like conversation.* Ordinary reading sounds mechanical. When you hear voices of people you can not see, you can invariably tell by the tones whether they are reading aloud or talking. Try to avoid the dull monotony of the average person reading a newspaper clipping.

2. *Avoid combinations of words that are difficult to say.* If you find yourself stumbling over a phrase, reword it.

3. *Look at your audience most of the time.* Develop the skill of glancing briefly at your manuscript, getting a sentence or two in mind, and then speaking that sentence *with your eyes on your listeners.* As you become increasingly familiar with your manuscript, you will find it less and less necessary to peer at it. Obviously you should be looking at your audience, not at your manuscript, when you are uttering emphatic words. And ordinarily you should be looking at your audience when you utter the closing words of your sentences.

Attention to these details will help you avoid the common fault of untrained speech readers who use a sing-song delivery, who frequently stumble over words, and who deliver the message to the manuscript instead of to the people out front.

Recall again the description of Sir Winston Churchill preparing a speech—mumbling words and phrases over and over to himself until they *sound* right; then dictating the preferred version to his secretary; then revising the secretarial transcript over and over.

D. PREPARE A READING DRAFT

You should type the draft of your manuscript that you are to use during actual speech delivery. Use a large type typewriter. Double or triple space the lines. Some speakers use lines of varying length, according to the meaning. Use short paragraphs; it is easy to get lost in a long paragraph. On the following pages are shown representations of manuscripts as prepared by two contemporary speakers.

Use heavy bond paper, standard letter size (8½ x 11) or half size (8½ x 5½). Number the pages; and use only one side of each sheet. If you number the pages with bold figures you can easily arrange them in proper order in the event of a spill or mix-up. If you use only one side of each sheet, you will not make false turns. And avoid excessive writing on the manuscript. You need to remember that a speaker is under tension, and should take precautions in advance to assure that he will not lose his place and will not get the sheets mixed. If you are to acknowledge others present by name, write the names down so your memory, under stress, will not play tricks on you.

Many speakers underscore words that they want to be sure to emphasize. They may also insert vertical marks to remind them to pause at strategic places. Both of these devices help the speaker to break up the monotonous vocal pattern that sometimes accompanies manuscript reading.[4]

REPRESENTATION OF PART OF A SPEECH MANUSCRIPT
OF PRIME MINISTER HAROLD MACMILLAN

(Used with permission)

Ours is really
  the only honest way
    to help the old people.

We have followed it in the past
  and pledge ourselves
    to follow it in the future.

Let me read
  what our manifesto says.

"We pledge ourselves to ensure
  that pensioners continue to share
    in the good things
      which a steadily
        expanding economy
          will bring."

---

4 A description of a speech manuscript prepared for reading by Sir Winston Churchill follows: "Churchill's . . . scripts . . . were typed to look like poems in free verse. The arrangement was actually to indicate the pauses for taking breath so as to be able to obtain the desired rhythm and emphasis. The lengths of the paragraphs and the intervals between them also varied according to the meaning of the sentences and the effect to be produced. It was also typed on a machine with exceptionally large letters." From *The Listener*, LXII (December 24, 1959).

II. Presenting the Manuscript Speech

As you sit on the platform with your manuscript awaiting your turn to speak, think of possible interpolations you can make in your manuscript that may help you adapt it to the chairman's introduction, the remarks of previous speakers, or other circumstances in the immediate occasion. You may need to acknowledge certain courtesies before you start reading.

You should not feel it necessary to explain why you choose to read a manuscript. The practice is well established by now. To say, "I wrote my speech out so I would not go overtime" inevitably sounds hollow.

Experienced manuscript readers often change the wording here and there as they go along. If you can do this, the practice will help make your delivery more conversational. You may insert comments one, two, or three sentences in length; this practice adds to variety of delivery. Don't overdo these interpolations, however, or you may appear to be stringing the material out beyond its proper length.

Try to read with all the sincerity, enthusiasm, directness, and force that is proper to the occasion. Emphasize important ideas vigorously.

```
Our greatest lack we share with all
we have too few young, alert and dev
leaders of the world today are old e
"sonny."   Eisenhower is 69, Syngma
is 83, Macmillan 65, Tito is 69, De
68.   Mao Tse-tung is 66.   Every ma
```

THE SPEECH MANUSCRIPT MAY BE TYPED IN LARGE TYPE

In order to make the reading of a speech easier, speakers may have the final draft typed on a large-type typewriter. The fragment above is reproduced from an address, "The Packaged People," delivered by Charles H. Brower, president, Batten, Barton, Durstine, and Osborn, Inc., to the Los Angeles Rotary Club. This part of the address is quoted on page 222). (Courtesy, Mr. Brower.)

Gesture is not out of place, especially when you are looking directly at the audience.

At times a speaker begins to read a manuscript, and finds it is less interesting to the audience than he imagined; or is taking more time than he planned; or his time has been cut to a length shorter than he was promised. In these situations do not try to read every paragraph; the plight of a speaker who can not shorten his speech is quickly communicated to an audience. Know your manuscript well enough so you can think ahead—even in the middle of the speech—and know where you can cut it. You can improvise something like "I have other evidence here that shows how competitive the market has become, but let me hurry over to my final question: How can we get a larger share of the export business?" and thus you can delete your speech the necessary amount. Don't be a slave to a manuscript if changing conditions require unanticipated adjustments.

Judge Harold R. Medina, previously quoted in this book, uses a manuscript on certain types of occasions, and has learned from experience that changes in wording, made at the moment of delivery, can be highly effective. He wrote the author as follows, for the guidance of students who use this text:

> One circumstance is important. I found over the years that when I had the speech all written out in advance, I inevitably did a certain amount of ad libbing here and there. Until I came across a couple of the speeches that had been recorded, I did not realize how much this ad libbing added to the effectiveness of the delivery. . . . The ad libbing comes along more or less instinctively to keep the audience alert, and some of it is the most effective part of the speech.

He goes on to write that these additions to or changes in the prepared speech depend "entirely upon a certain sensitivity to the reaction of the audience," which, he astutely observes, is *of the essence of effective public speaking.*[5]

Richard M. Nixon has made hundreds of formal and informal speeches during his political career. At one time a debater at Whittier College, he has long been interested in the problems of speech preparation and delivery:

---

[5] Judge Medina, quoted on pages 27 and 274, will be remembered as having presided in New York City over the long trial (January-October, 1949) of the 11 communists charged with conspiracy to advocate the overthrow of the U. S. government by force and violence. Judge Medina's speeches may be read in *The Anatomy of Freedom* (New York, Henry Holt & Company, 1959), and *Judge Medina Speaks* (New York, Matthew Bender & Company, 1954), the latter publication appearing under the auspices of the American Bar Association.

Although I participated in debating, I did not take any speech courses in school or college, and no doubt this is one reason why preparing a speech is about the hardest work I know.

Even when I speak off the cuff I have to devote a great amount of time to outlining in detail the thoughts I want to express.

As far as formal speeches which are to be read are concerned, I have not yet developed the ability to read effectively a speech somebody else has written. Consequently, I have to block out four or five days in which I do the extensive work necessary to get the speech in final form.

I usually begin by doing a great deal of reading in the particular field which I intend to cover. I then write down in longhand the various thoughts that I think might be worth developing. After that, I make a rough outline in which I try to develop one central theme. Incidentally, this is the longest and hardest part of the speech making process for me.

From there on I make usually three or four more outlines, the final one of which is almost a complete copy of the speech. From this final written draft I dictate into the dictaphone, primarily for the purpose of changing the written draft into what I sense is the spoken word. In the process of dictation, I make several changes when I come across words that do not sound as well as they read.[6]

Speech texts prepared by the office of the British Prime Minister for the use of newspaper reporters invariably carry a heading like "Please check carefully for any deviation in delivery," or "This text is made available to the press in advance only for the purpose of checking against delivery. There can be no guarantee that it will be adhered to and it should not be used without checking." These notations remind the reporters that the Prime Minister reserves the right to alter the wording of his speech. When reading your own manuscripts, remember that you can and should make changes that best express exactly what you want to say.

---

6 Letter of November 11, 1959.

The emphasis of the letter on the *hard work* involved in speech preparation can hardly be over-emphasized. "To deliver a speech is easy," once wrote a great teacher; "but to prepare it—ah, that is hard work." Not only must the speaker make careful preparation in advance, but he must also be ready to capitalize upon the inspiration of the moment. In other words, the preparation of a speech (manuscript or not) is not completed until the instant of delivery. The speaker is always alert to ways of improving the wording of his thought. (He has to depend upon his ever-watchful good judgment to make sure that, on the spur of the moment, he does not say something stupid.)

III. Impromptu Speaking

True *impromptu* speaking is speaking on the spur of the moment, *without previous notice*. *Extemporaneous* speaking, on the other hand, as the term is used in this and in most public speaking textbooks, is speaking from a *previously prepared* plan or outline. Scores of hours of preparation may enter into an extemporaneous speech, yet the speech is not memorized. The plan of the speech may be in the speaker's mind or on notes which he has in front of him as he speaks.

When the presiding officer says, "I see our former secretary, Dana Morrison, in the room; Dana, stand up and say a few words to us," the situation is set for a typical impromptu speech.

How does the trained speaker meet the requirements of the impromptu speaking situation?

A. ANTICIPATE THE IMPROMPTU SITUATION

Many so-called impromptu speeches are not impromptu at all; the speaker fully prepared himself in advance for this emergency. The story is told that William Ewart Gladstone was once overheard walking in the garden, saying in his resonant, baritone voice, "I had not expected to address the House tonight, but the remarks of the learned gentleman . . ." and on he went, anticipating his opponent's arguments and his own reply to them. Winston Churchill, in the earlier days of his career when he mistrusted his ability in impromptu debate, would prepare a series of short speeches, planning to use the one that best fitted the discussion to come. Richard Brinsley Sheridan at times was credited with uncanny skill in impromptu, crushing retort; later some of these crushers were discovered in his journals, thought out in advance but allowed to lie dormant in his mind until the proper occasion arose. The young William Pitt used to visit the House of Commons galleries, listening to the debates; when one speaker gave a telling argument, Pitt would think to himself how *he* would answer the argument if *he* were on the floor. The young Wendell Phillips made an unscheduled speech at an abolition meeting, and attracted favorable attention by his remarks.

You can easily appreciate the fact that these men, listening to the scheduled speeches, reacted to them *like speakers;* i.e., they asked themselves the question, "What would I say on this topic?" As the topics were familiar, they could rapidly organize ideas they had previously held, supporting them with examples and illustrations that applied to the immediate situation. While others were speaking, they listened, selected, arranged. The duration of the evening's program was time enough for them to plan their own remarks.

So there are ways of training yourself to speak impromptu, and ways of anticipating the impromptu situation. Suppose *you* are the former secretary of a high school club, and *you* find yourself returning to attend a meeting; you may say to yourself, "What will I say if I am suddenly called upon to say a few words?" Similarly, on occasions where you are to become an officer, or to receive an award, you may anticipate in advance what you will say if you are invited to talk.

B. THINK ON YOUR FEET

When you are called upon unexpectedly to say a few words, you need to prepare swiftly—in fact, instantly. Perhaps along these lines:

1. *Should I say something about the organization?* An answer to this question may supply your central idea: you may decide at once to talk on "What Rotary Has Meant to Me." One point is enough: "Rotary keeps reminding me to build my business on service to the customer." Or: "What Phi Delta Delta Has Meant to Me." Central idea: "Phi Delta Delta taught me the value of true friends."

2. *Should I bring greetings from the firm or institution I am now connected with?* Or should I report on what my district, or state, is doing? A short talk of this nature may be proper; and although you could speak at some length on this familiar topic, you quickly select a single example or illustration to develop.

3. *Is reminiscing in order?* Perhaps you would open by saying, "As I look over the new quarters of the club, I am reminded of an incident that happened in the old quarters." Such an impromptu talk, if kept brief, might be suitable.

4. *Should you commend or congratulate the organization, or its officers?* Something new or unusual may have come to your attention that you wish to comment on.

If the group is discussing a controversial issue, and the chairman unexpectedly turns to you and asks you what you think, you will have to state briefly what you *do* think: you favor the proposal, or you favor it with some change; or you are opposed to the proposal. Recall Chapter 8, "Organizing: the Short Speech"; as you rise, formulate your central idea: "Mr. Chairman, I favor the proposal, because . . ."; or "Mr. Chairman, I am planning to vote against the proposal, because . . ."; or "Mr. Chairman, I believe we can reconcile the disagreement here tonight by doing thus and so . . ."; or "Mr. Chairman, here is a situation that might arise if we adopt the proposal . . ."; and so on.

In short, the one-point-speech formula of "central idea followed by a supporting reason" is a useful one for meeting impromptu situations.

Questions for Classroom Discussion

1. Under what circumstances is one most likely to be called upon for a true *impromptu* speech? Under what circumstances will one most likely be able to *anticipate* being called upon to speak?

2. "Memory" has been called "the lost art." How does a good memory prove its value in speech making? in answering questions after the speech is given? in reporting the news on TV? in making a speech from notes or outline?

3. Since a large proportion of present-day speeches is read from a manuscript, is the development of a good, extemporaneous style worth the trouble it takes?

4. How can the *almost overwhelming disadvantages* of reading a manuscript speech be overcome? (Or do you agree that the disadvantages are almost overwhelming?)

5. Until an impromptu speaker has learned to concentrate on the wording and structure of his sentences as he utters them, he is likely to do violence to the English language. Fortunately, the listener is not so aware of strange and weird word arrangements as is the reader. When impromptu remarks are tape recorded and then transcribed, however, the poor sentence structure is exposed to the public glare. For example, a high-ranking public official was asked by news reporters whether Soviet leaders were to be invited to the United States. His impromptu answer was transcribed as follows:

No, I thought I was—certainly I meant, and it is possible that my wording was not as accurate as I had hoped, but it meant people not in official governmental positions, so it could be called a "summit" meeting between ourselves. I was talking about leaders of thought, and not, though, the people carrying official responsibility.

Comment on the foregoing, with respect to the following question: How can a speaker improve his ability not only to organize ideas when talking impromptu, but also to use good English grammar and syntax?

Speech-Related Projects

1. Report on speakers, lawyers, ministers, and professors you have heard, commenting upon whether they use the manuscript method ef-

fectively or ineffectively; if they use some other method, comment on it.

2. Report on the extemporaneous and other speaking contests conducted on your campus.

Speaking Assignment 19

A Manuscript Speech on a Research Topic

Make a speech of .... minutes on a research topic, using a manuscript.

Hand in (a) an outline, (b) note cards, (c) bibliography, as assigned. Review Chapter 5, "Gathering and Recording Material."

Your research topic may be an informative talk on a principle, theory, concept, procedure (social, economic, political, campus). Or it may be an inquiry into a problem in which presumably you present favorable and unfavorable aspects (use of automobiles by college students, cigarette smoking, required courses, suspending testing of nuclear weapons, parking, trend to early marriages, rising costs of education). Or it may be a persuasive talk, urging a change in belief or action. Review again the lists of suggested topics at the end of Chapter 4.

Prepare your manuscript with care: type it, double space it, underscore words to be emphasized (if this device is helpful to you) or places to pause.

Practice reading aloud, listening to sound as well as sense; revise awkward combinations of words or phrases. During your rehearsal, consider where you may interpolate a phrase or comment in order to add variety to the presentation. Try to make your *reading* sound like *talk;* this procedure will help you avoid chanting, or other sing-song or repeated vocal inflections.

REFERENCES ON MANUSCRIPT AND IMPROMPTU SPEAKING

Donald C. Bryant and Karl R. Wallace, Chapter 9, "Speaking Impromptu and Reading Aloud," in *Oral Communication,* 3d ed. (New York, Appleton-Century-Crofts, Inc., 1962).

Giles Wilkeson Gray and Waldo W. Braden, appropriate pages in Chapter 19, "Memory," in *Public Speaking: Principles and Practice* (New York, Harper and Brothers, 1951).

James H. McBurney and Ernest H. Wrage, appropriate pages in Chapter 23, "Delivery: Methods of Presentation," in *The Art of Good Speech* (New York, Prentice-Hall, Inc., 1953).

Eugene E. White and Clair R. Henderlider, Part I and Part II of Chapter 15, "Speeches of Special Types," in *Practical Public Speaking* (New York, The Macmillan Company, 1954).

CHAPTER 20

Five Types of
Short Speeches

Practice in making the speeches described in this chapter helps train the speaker in graciousness, cordiality, sincerity, appreciativeness. ■ *Purpose, content, plan, comment.*

THIS CHAPTER DISCUSSES SPEECHES of (1) introduction, (2) presentation, (3) acceptance, (4) welcome, (5) response to a welcome, (6) farewell.

I. Introducing a Speaker

By common custom a speaker is introduced to an audience before he makes his speech. The president of the organization that sponsors the speaker introduces him; or the chairman of the program committee; or some member who is not only a friend of the speaker but who is also prominent in the group. In public speaking classes, students frequently introduce one another.

A. PURPOSE

A good speech of introduction makes the audience interested in hearing the speaker. It assures the speaker that he is among people who appreciate his being with them. It serves as an ice-breaker. In all these ways it helps the speaker to make a better speech.

B. WHAT TO SAY

Your ideas may be drawn from the following sources:

1. *The speaker.* Tell about his important accomplishments. If he is a well-known personage, look him up in *Who's Who in America, Dictionary of American Scholars, Current Biography,* or other references. Do not, however, give an exhaustive list of his honors; select

items that bear on his subject, or that may be of special interest to the audience. Don't overlook items of human interest: perhaps his hobby is tennis; perhaps he has seven children, or has served in the armed forces. If you are introducing a classmate, interview him in advance about his achievements. Besides revealing his class, his major field of study, and his home town, you may refer to his principal activities. And, as in the instance of the celebrity, he may have a vocation or hobby that you will want to mention.

2. *The occasion.* If the occasion for the speech is special, like a tenth anniversary, call attention to that fact. Maybe this is the last meeting in an old building, or the opening convocation in a new; perhaps it is the first meeting of the year or the last. Perhaps your gathering has a special timeliness because of a current happening.

3. *The audience.* Mention anything unusual about the audience. Maybe this is the first ladies' night of the year; perhaps it is a combined meeting of all the churches or all the service clubs. On rare occasion a resourceful and imaginative introducer has, instead of introducing the speaker to the audience, introduced the audience to the speaker. ("Mr. Speaker, we know you well, but you may not know us; so tonight instead of introducing the speaker to the audience, let me introduce the audience to the speaker. Out in front we have a group of earnest, devoted, hard working students . . ." and so on, characterizing faculty, alumni, townspeople, in light vein.)

4. *The subject.* You will, of course, state the speaker's exact topic; but you may, in addition, say something about the importance of his topic. Here you must be brief, as you do not want to say anything that he might have planned to say. You do not want him to have to confess that you stole his thunder.

These are the four standard groups of ideas out of which speeches of introduction are composed. In addition, you may ask the speaker if there is something he would especially like to have you include. You may be able to make a casual comment that will serve as a springboard for an anecdote that he particularly wants to relate.

5. *The greeting.* Fully as important as the above is what may be termed the greeting: that part of your speech in which you reassure him that the group is looking forward to his address. Here you should be as cordial as possible.

C. PLAN OF DEVELOPMENT

Following is a typical plan of development:

After addressing the audience, open by expressing your pleasure in having the opportunity to introduce the speaker. Avoid trite expressions, "It gives me great pleasure," and that most trite expression of all, "without further ado," but put your thoughts in your own language: "I can not tell you how pleased I am to introduce to this group a man who is my classmate and a personal friend of more than two years. I have heard him speak on many occasions, and I always look forward to his talks with delight and at times even with amazement."

By custom the name of the speaker is not uttered until toward the end of the speech of introduction. So you continue, refraining from mentioning his name: "You know, of course, that he is a member of this class; you recall his speeches on the recognition of Red China and the revision of the immigration laws. And of course you know that he is co-captain of the football team. Maybe you did not know that he was valedictorian of his high school in Milan, that he is married and has a baby daughter, that he sings in the Presbyterian choir, and that he teaches a class of junior high boys every Sunday. Now, because of some of these experiences, and because this is our annual Religion and Life week, he has decided to talk upon a religious theme.

"I now want to present to you, speaking on the topic, 'Church Preference: None,' our classmate, Bob Dickinson." Slight nod to the speaker: "Bob."

Or the last sentences may end with the topic instead of the speaker: "I now want to introduce to you, our classmate, Bob Dickinson, whose topic for today is, 'Church Preference: None.'"

If you know a humorous story fitting to the occasion, include it. Do not, however, make your speech of introduction too long. From three to six minutes should certainly be sufficient to introduce a thirty to fifty minute lecture. Your instructor may want you to make speeches of introduction of ample length, however, for purpose of classroom instruction, even though the classmate you are introducing is to speak only a few minutes.

D. COMMENT

Don't forget to be gracious in your manner, or the impact of your speech will be lessened. If you are "highly pleased," let your voice, facial expression, and general bearing show this along with the words themselves.

Try to give this speech *without any notes whatever*. Reassure yourself as to the proper pronunciation of the speaker's name and the exact title of his speech. If the introducer says, ". . . who will speak on the very important subject" (long, penetrating glance at notes) **"Are *You* a Citizen?"** his poor preparation immediately betrays him.

With a little rehearsal you will be able to keep facts in mind like "graduated from Northwestern University in 1950 and went on to Chicago for a master's degree in 1953" along with "wrote a popular textbook in economics" and "is married and has three children, all girls."

An earnest endeavor on your part to give the foregoing kind of speech of introduction is far better than the often-heard, brief, perfunctory, soulless "Your next speaker is Rogers Meadows, who will speak on (quick rustle of notes) 'Breaking Through the Exam Barrier.' Mr. Meadows." Be careful, also, not to commit such other faults as building up the speaker too much, mispronouncing his name, or apologizing for the fact that he was a substitute secured at the last minute, thereby implying that he will not be nearly so good as the speaker originally booked. Professional speakers have many tales to tell about stupid and graceless comments uttered by half-prepared program chairmen. William Jennings Bryan was introduced by one, who, momentarily separated from all notions of courtesy, thought it would be amusing to tell the large, outdoor audience that this was probably the first time they had ever heard Colonel Bryan without paying for it. Designed as a witty jibe at Bryan's well-known ample lecture fees, it disturbed the speaker, who felt it necessary to open with a reminder that he had given thousands of political speeches all over the country without any admission price whatever attached.

II. Speech of Presentation

Those who do distinguished service are presented awards, citations, certificates, medals, letters, diplomas, gifts. An important ingredient of the honor is that it be *conferred in public,* with suitable words spoken. If an organization awards a ten-year membership pin, it is more gratifying to the recipient, and more inspiring to others, to make the presentation in public.

A. PURPOSE

The purpose of the speech of presentation is two-fold: (1) to honor the recipient and (2) to inspire others to emulate his record. The second purpose, often left unmentioned, is none the less operative.

B. WHAT TO SAY

Your ideas may be drawn from one or more of the following sources:

1. *The recipient.* You may review the good qualities of his character

and the nature of the achievements that have brought him recognition. Make your praise genuine, cordial, sincere. A little humor helps to offset any tendency to become overly-emotional, though a certain amount of sentiment needs to be felt and expressed. Remember that sometimes you should withhold the *name* of the recipient to the very end.

2. *The occasion.* You may mention the occasion at which the award is being presented, taking note of anything unusual in the situation.

3. *The giver.* You may want to say something about the organization in whose name you are making the presentation. If you are presenting an award to the winner of a speaking contest, you might note that the Athenian Club exists for the sole purpose of encouraging better speaking, and that former members have gone on to distinguished posts. If the organization is a fraternity or sorority, mention the ideals for which the group stands (and which presumably the recipient fully exemplifies).

4. *The award.* Make mention of the award itself. If you see special appropriateness in *this* recipient receiving *this* award, call attention to that fact. A copy of a dictionary or thesaurus presented to a winning speaker who had always shown an interest in the accurate and effective use of language illustrates the kind of comment that may be made.

5. *The presentation.* At the end of your talk, express your pleasure at having the opportunity of making the presentation, extend your congratulations to the recipient by a warm handshake, and *then* present the gift to him. Don't try to shake hands and present the gift at the same time. And don't hang on to the gift after you have offered it to him.

C. PLAN OF DEVELOPMENT

Following is a typical plan of development:

After addressing the audience, talk about the qualities of personality or character, or attainments and achievements, that justify the presentation. Avoid trite sentimentalities, but put your cordial feelings in your own words. "Now we come to a part of the program that we have looked forward to with expectation. Each year the club has conducted a secret ballot to locate the individual who has given the greatest service to the club during the school year. We have kept in mind such qualities as (here you can mention a few). We have voted to honor a young woman who is well-known to us for (here mention traits of character that led to her selection). I would like to ask Dora Hampton to come forward."

When Dora comes to the front of the room, indicate to her where she is to stand. She should stand so that those present will get a good view of her face, rather than just the back of her head. The rest of your talk may be given to Dora, the audience overhearing what you have to say: "This certificate I am about to present you, Dora, has on it a citation, which I should like to read." (Here you can read all or part of it.) "You are the seventeenth person to receive this award, and I know how proud we are that you can join the distinguished list of people who have stood here before you to receive a similar citation. We are grateful to you for what you have done for us; we feel that we are honoring ourselves in presenting this award. I want to congratulate you personally (shaking hands) and, in behalf of all your many friends and associates here tonight, want to present you this certificate (handing her the certificate)."

D. COMMENT

Nearly always the award or gift is a token of relatively slight monetary value. An organization could ordinarily not afford to repay, in cash, the dedicated and devoted service that members and officers give it. Yet through the ceremony of a public presentation it can honor these servants in a notable and memorable way. The individual who makes the presentation can make the ceremony outstanding if he is sensitive to the occasion and if he expresses his thoughts sincerely.

III. Speech of Acceptance

When you are presented with an award or gift in public you are expected to make reply. Although speeches of acceptance are usually brief, and may be impromptu, on formal occasions like the acceptance of a building or a recreation center by a college they may be ten or fifteen minutes or longer.

A. PURPOSE

The purpose of the speech of acceptance is primarily to express the individual's appreciation of the award or gift and of the sentiment underlying it. A secondary purpose may be to reaffirm his affection for the organization presenting the gift.

B. WHAT TO SAY

Your ideas may be drawn from one or more of the following sources:
1. *The gift*. The gift, or award, will attract your immediate at-

tention. If it is wrapped in a box, you may ask "May I open it?" This will give you a chance to show the group what the committee has purchased for you, and will enable you to express your appreciation more specifically. If it is a medal, certificate, plaque, or similar award, accept it and express your appreciation of it.

2. *The giver.* You may say that you have cherished your associations with the members of the group or organization, and perhaps briefly comment on what your participation has meant to you. Often you say, and with entire honesty, that you could not have won such an award without the help and cooperation of others in the group.

3. *The occasion.* You may make reference to the occasion, especially if there is something unusual about it: "I am especially pleased to have received this award on the silver anniversary of our Founders' Day."

4. *The acceptance.* Perhaps you should conclude with a final reference to the fact that you accept the gift with keen pleasure, and add a word about how you will use it or what it will mean to you.

C. PLAN OF DEVELOPMENT

You may begin by saying, "I certainly want to thank you, President Algord, and all the members of the Athenian Club, for the certificate and for this very handsome dictionary. I hope each of you will come up and look at it, because it is indeed attractively bound and indexed. I just took a peek at the inside cover and noticed your autographs. This feature I will especially cherish, as you know I could not have earned this prize or any prize at all without the fine cooperation and help every one has given me. I would like to say before I sit down that being a member of the Athenian Club has been one of the rich experiences of my college career. What we have done together in our monthly programs has added a new dimension to our education. This is my last year, but I know that the newer members of the club will not only carry on our present hopes and ambitions, but will add new lustre to them."

You may return to the gift as follows:

"Thank you again for the dictionary. I appreciate it because, as you said, President Algord, it comes with the good wishes of everybody here. I am especially pleased to have received this award on our Silver Anniversary. I guess I need a dictionary as badly as anyone, and I will keep this one on my study table, where it will remind me of the good times we have had together."

D. COMMENT

This speech of acceptance is longer than most. If many awards are being presented, each acceptance speech should be brief. Perhaps, however, in addition to the perfunctory "Thank you very much," you can add a few sentences, along the general lines suggested above, to enhance the importance of the ceremony. Remember that, in honoring you, the organization is trying to encourage younger members to follow in your footsteps; this thought gives you a reason for participating in the ceremony a little more fully than a barren, stripped-down "thanks."

One student of public speaking did take this lesson to heart; did receive an award; did take a few minutes to express to the group what the award signified, and what the responsibilities of individuals toward the group should be; and later reported to the class that this short talk invested the whole ceremony with a meaning and significance which up to that point it had not attained. You should therefore be able to improve on the studied, artificial, highly self-conscious impression given on TV by many Oscar and Emmy winners. You can be brief without being perfunctory, and you can express your appreciation for the gift and your regard for the giver in a way that will be forceful and impressive.

IV. Speech of Welcome

A speech of welcome may be made in behalf of a congregation to a new minister; in behalf of a faculty to a new president; in behalf of a firm to a new manager; in behalf of an organization to a former member who has been absent on military service; and on scores of similar circumstances. You may of course address a speech of welcome to a group as well as to an individual.

A. PURPOSE

The purpose of the speech of welcome is to greet the newcomer or the returnee. Extending the greeting in public enhances the honor and makes it more impressive. A secondary purpose may be to review the aims and goals of the group extending the welcome.

B. WHAT TO SAY

Your ideas may be drawn from one or more of the following sources:

1. *The recipient of the welcome.* After a sentence extending the

welcome, you may review the attainments of the individual, or of the group, being welcomed. If the welcome is being extended to an individual returning from military service, or from residence elsewhere, you may suggest that you have followed with interest his career while he was away.

2. *The group extending the welcome.* If you are the mayor of Chicago, welcoming the annual convention of chemists, you may mention Chicago's leading chemical industries and contributions. If you are the president of a local fraternity welcoming other chapters in your state or region, you may talk a little about your own chapter. You mention, of course, that you extend the welcome in behalf of your group. Most of your talk, however, will focus on the welcome rather than the welcomer.

3. *The occasion.* If you are president of the student government association welcoming a new president, you may make reference to the occasion at which the welcoming takes place. You may mention the different groups that have come together for the occasion. Perhaps the last such occasion was twenty years ago, and you have done research to compare or contrast the two occasions. If you are welcoming another group or groups, express your hope that the joint meeting will be of benefit to all.

4. *The welcome.* You should probably end with a sentence restating the welcome and your pleasure, speaking for your group, in extending it.

C. PLAN OF DEVELOPMENT

Your opening sentence may be, "Our purpose in meeting this evening is to extend a welcome in behalf of the Theatre Workshop of Center College to the other student theatrical groups in this tri-state area."

You may continue by saying, "Our Workshop Group has for some time now been making preparations for your coming. We have read with interest the correspondence that told us that first one of your groups and then another was planning to be here. We became familiar with many of your names long before you arrived. Some of you are personally known to some of us from other similar conferences of this sort."

You may refer to the occasion in words like these: "Center College is especially pleased to be your host at this fifth meeting. When a conference is five years old, it is beginning to acquire a certain dignity and majesty. And we are pleased to have you here this year because we are opening our new theatre in the Fine Arts building."

You may continue by describing special features of the conference, pointing out ways in which the meetings will be mutually helpful to all, and close by renewing your welcome: "Let me say again how pleased is the Theatre Workshop of Center College to welcome you to our campus. If there is anything we can do for you in the way of housing, transportation, food, medical attention, short-term loans, general hospitality and cultural uplift, and you think of it before we do, feel free to command our services. The place belongs to you; we are glad you are here, and we are looking forward to these days we are to spend together."

D. COMMENT

Again, the purpose of this speech is to enlarge upon a ceremonial occasion, and you can enhance the hospitality of your welcome by the friendly way in which you speak a few, sincere, carefully-selected words.

V. Speech Responding to a Welcome

After a formal speech of welcome, the individual should respond in his own behalf, or in behalf of the groups being welcomed.

A. PURPOSE

The purpose of the response is to express appreciation for the courtesy extended. A secondary purpose may be to review what the individual, or the group, hopes to accomplish through association with the welcoming group. For example, a new president, welcomed by the students and faculty, would be inclined to talk briefly about his hopes for the institution. A new member welcomed into an organization would find it proper to reaffirm his pleasure at being invited to join.

B. WHAT TO SAY

Your ideas may be drawn from one or more of the following sources:

1. *The welcome itself.* Express your pleasure at the friendly spirit shown.

2. *The group extending the welcome.* Comment upon your high regard for the group welcoming you. Mention any accomplishments that have come to your attention. You may recall the pleasure of former visits or associations with the group.

3. *The occasion.* Mention any unusual feature of the present

occasion. Comment upon what you hope to contribute to the occasion, or to the group or groups present.

Conclude with a sentence restating your pleasure at being welcomed by this group in this way.

C. PLAN OF DEVELOPMENT

You may open with a comment like, "In behalf of Mrs. Allerton and me, I want to thank the students, the faculty, the alumni, and the friends of Waterloo College for this cordial and delightful welcome."

You may refer to the welcomer: "George Jasper certainly managed to express a great deal of genuine friendliness and hospitality in that welcome, and the Allerton family is deeply touched by his words and by your generous response to them. As you know, this is not our first visit to the campus; Mrs. Allerton and I were students here together, years ago; we met here and were married shortly after her graduation. I have kept in close touch with your athletic, educational, and cultural progress all these intervening years."

You may briefly describe some of the things you hope to accomplish, warning in a friendly way that you will need the help and counsel of all present. You may conclude by referring again to the welcome: "Let me thank you again for your friendly greeting and welcome and assure you that this is one of the occasions we will cherish during the years to come."

D. COMMENT

Your response to the speech of welcome will help to emphasize the general feeling of good-will and friendship and thus contribute to the broader purpose of the occasion.

VI. Speech of Farewell

A speech of farewell may be made by a person going to another community or to another institution or company.

A. PURPOSE

The purpose of the public farewell speech is to express your regrets at severing a connection that you have enjoyed for some time.

B. WHAT TO SAY

Your ideas may be drawn from one or more of the following sources:

1. *Your mixed feelings.* One who says farewell usually regrets to leave, but is looking forward to his new field of endeavor.

2. *Your past association with the group.* You may recall the progress the group has made since you first joined it, highlighting the important events. You may mention individuals who have served the group prominently.

3. *Your new post.* Your listeners will be curious to know about your new work or your new location, so you may refer briefly to your own future.

4. *Your hope of seeing your friends later on.* You may invite your friends to visit you in your new location; or promise to return to renew acquaintances; or look forward to seeing your business or professional friends at state or national conventions.

5. *Your farewell itself.* A brief but important part of your speech will be saying good-bye and extending your continued good wishes.

C. PLAN OF DEVELOPMENT

You may begin by saying, "Professor Rush has told me I might make a short speech of farewell since I am leaving the class in the middle of the year to begin a three-year term of military service."

Continue by describing your mixed feelings: "I am looking forward to my tour of duty, since I have been offered an opportunity to do intensive work in electronics, which is my specialty, and have hope of being stationed overseas. At the same time I hate to leave my friends in this class and on this campus. I have mixed feelings, like the fellow who saw his mother-in-law drive off a cliff in his new Cadillac."

You may reminisce: "I have certainly enjoyed my work with you in this class. I am sorry I will no longer be able to hear those gems of humor by our friend, Bill Short." (You may make other brief, personal references.) "Moreover, I have learned a great deal from Professor Rush's instruction, so that when I am called upon to make any speeches in the Army, I will know how to proceed."

You may look forward to seeing your friends again: "By the time I have concluded my tour of duty I am sure all of you will have graduated long since, even Horace here, who told us the other day about his difficulties in keeping his grades up. But I expect I may see two or three of you also in uniform before long. And of course we will all get back for Homecoming whenever we can."

Conclude with the farewell: "Well, the time has come to say good-bye. I want to thank all of you for being such wonderful friends and I want to wish you good fortune and good luck."

D. COMMENT

A farewell speech, like the other ceremonial speeches, not only accomplishes its obvious purpose—in this instance to say good-bye— but at the same time an equally worthy purpose—in this instance to applaud the work of the group, remind every one of the military obligation that citizenship imposes, demonstrate a good attitude for one to have who is entering military service, and remind one and all of their mutual experiences and responsibilities.

VII. Special Comment

Although this chapter has been specific in explaining what a speaker may say on these ceremonial occasions, you should in planning your own speeches rely entirely on your own thoughts. A common fault is that these kinds of talks sound artificial and memorized and consequently less genuine and sincere. Strike a happy medium, also, between being too long and too brief. For examples of brief talks given on ceremonial occasions, see the Appendix of this text.

Questions for Classroom Discussion

1. Assume you are introducing a speaker, and have at hand facts about degrees, honors, and positions taken from *Who's Who in America.* How can you select, arrange, or augment this material in order to make an informal, friendly introduction?

2. In the situation in which the honoree receives a gift, a moment's awkwardness often arises at the time of receiving and handling the award. At times the recipient's speech of acceptance is too glib, as if memorized in advance; at other times it is stumbling, hesitant, or even inaudible. What advice can you offer him?

3. Welcome speeches and responses to welcome speeches are often too stiff, formal, memorized. How can they be made more gracious and cordial? What is the place for humor in this type of situation?

4. When a well-known person moves to another city, or retires, those who attend the farewell ceremonies like to feel that the proper amount of sentiment is expressed, but that sentimentality is not overdone. How can a friendly yet respectful tone be established for speeches on this kind of occasion?

Speaking Assignment 20

Speeches of Introduction and Acknowledgment

Assume that a classmate is to be the featured speaker at a future campus occasion. Make a speech of .... minutes in which you introduce him. After your introduction he will take the platform long enough to acknowledge your comments, but stop short of making the actual speech. The time limit for the acknowledgment is .... minutes.

This assignment assumes that the class will be divided in twos, each member of the pair taking turns in introducing, and responding to, the other.

Not infrequently on an occasion of this sort the chairman will prepare a helpful introduction which the speaker will dispose of with a perfunctory "Thank you, Mr. Chairman." More frequently the introduction will be an unimaginative reading of biographical data from a sheet. On occasion the introduction is too long; at other times it is too brief. The purpose of the introduction is to arouse the interest of the listeners in the speaker and his message; fix this purpose in mind as you prepare your talk.

Speaking Assignment 21

Speeches of Presentation and Acceptance

Each member of the class will write his name on a slip of paper and drop it in a hat; each member will then draw a name.

Purchase and gift-wrap a present, costing not more than .... cents, for the person whose name you draw. Prepare a speech of .... minutes in which you present it to him. He will follow with a suitable speech of acceptance of not more than .... minutes.

In making a speech of presentation, subtly remind the listeners of the occasion you have invented by alluding to "this Faculty-Alumni Banquet" or "this dedication of our new golf course." Make the occasion and the award realistic by adapting it to the known interests of the recipient.

Those who are to receive awards at ceremonial occasions usually know that the presentation is to be made; at times, however, the announcement of the award is planned as a surprise. If the class decides to follow this latter practice, then the responses will resemble a true impromptu situation.

Speaking Assignment 22

Speeches of Welcome and Response

Divide the class in twos for a speaking assignment of .... minutes in which each prepares a speech of welcome for the other.

Each pair will work out suitable occasions for which a speech of welcome would be appropriate. One day one member of each pair will give the welcome; the other will respond in a talk of .... minutes. On another day the situations will be reversed.

If a speech of welcome is to achieve its purpose, it should make the recipient feel that he is being cordially received. All listeners should, in fact, feel that the newcomer will be a fine addition to the institution, school, church, or community. Strike a note of friendliness and graciousness, with some sentiment, and perhaps a touch of humor.

Speaking Assignment 23

Speeches of Farewell and Response

Make a speech of .... minutes in which you bid farewell to the class. Tell your classmates of a new position you are accepting; or a decision to go to another campus, or to begin a period of military service. Although the occasion will be imaginary, make it as realistic as possible.

A member of the class should be chosen to respond, in a talk of .... minutes, to the speech of farewell.

NOTE: The instructor may elect one or more of the four speaking assignments just above; or he may assign part of the class to one project, another part to another. The speech of presentation and acceptance is appropriate at a meeting just before holidays.

REFERENCES ON TYPES OF SHORT SPEECHES

A. Craig Baird and Franklin H. Knower, Chapter 21, "Speeches for Special Occasions," in *General Speech*, 2nd ed. (New York, McGraw-Hill Book Company, Inc., 1957).

Donald C. Bryant and Karl R. Wallace, Chapter 24, "Speeches for Special Occasions," in *Fundamentals of Speaking*, 3d ed. (New York, Appleton-Century-Crofts, Inc., 1960).

Giles Wilkeson Gray and Waldo W. Braden, Chapter 10, "The Occasional Speech," in *Public Speaking: Principles and Practice* (New York, Harper and Brothers, 1951).

Alan H. Monroe, Chapters 24-29 in Part 5, "Special Types of Public Speech," in *Principles and Types of Speech*, 4th ed. (Chicago, Scott, Foresman and Company, 1955).

David C. Phillips, Chapter 12, "Occasional Speeches," in *Oral Communication in Business* (New York, McGraw-Hill Book Company, Inc., 1955).

Eugene E. White and Clair R. Henderlider, Chapter 15, "Speeches of Special Types," in *Practical Public Speaking* (New York, The Macmillan Company, 1954).

Yeager, Willard Hayes, Chapters 4, 5, 6, 8, 9, 10 in *Effective Speaking for Every Occasion* (New York, Prentice-Hall, Inc., 1940). Speeches of praise and blame, response and farewell, celebration, good-will, inspirational and entertaining occasions; principles and examples.

CHAPTER 21

Another Look at Speech Design

Designing a speech causes a speaker to consider its structure as a whole. An unusual or striking design may increase the interest of the audience. ■ Discussed and illustrated are (1) special list, (2) mnemonic device, (3) design based on a text, (4) design based on counter suggestion, (5) change-of-position design, (6) problem-solution design.

EARLIER CHAPTERS HAVE DISCUSSED basic principles of organizing a speech. Chapter 10 on "Development by Expository Methods" described time order, space order, comparison and contrast, definition, analysis. Each is a method of developing an idea to make it more clear. Chapter 17 on "Persuading Through Argument" described inductive, deductive, and causal arrangements. Each is a method of developing an idea to make it more persuasive.

Methods like these may also be referred to as designs for speeches. The word *design* leads us to think of the speech as an artistic and integrated *whole*. We know the importance of design in practical and fine arts. *Design* influences not only the manufacture of automobiles but also the building of college halls and churches. If a theatre is well designed, it can do better the things that theatres are supposed to do. If a speech is well designed, it can better accomplish the things a speech is supposed to accomplish: the ideas in the speech, for example, should be longer remembered.

The kinds of design described below are not necessarily more complex than the methods of development described in other chapters. But times will come in your own career when you want to make an especially striking speech. Your final speech in the public speaking course may be such an instance. A speech to be spoken in a contest may be another. Still a third may be a speech to be given under the auspices of your campus Speakers' Bureau. After graduation you will encounter other important situations. The examples below may suggest to you types of design that suit the specific purpose you have in mind better than more conventional arrangements.

I. The Special-List Design

Chapter 8 noted that a simple way of planning a speech was to build it around a list of topics. Senator Paul H. Douglas made a radio network address on "Five Great Americans." "In this age of denunciations and counterdenunciations," he opened, "I thought it might be well tonight to speak about five Americans, who are in danger of being forgotten but who by their work and lives have helped to make us all better men and women."[1] His choices were John Woolman, who fought slavery; John Peter Altgeld, a courageous governor of Illinois; Jane Addams, who gave her lifetime to the service of the poor and unfortunate; and two senators, Robert M. La Follette of Wisconsin and George W. Norris of Nebraska. Another simple list was used by Rabbi Charles E. Shulman, who, in discussing "Four Philosophies of Modern Life," listed cynicism, nihilism, materialism, idealism.[2]

A simple list plan may itself be highly effective; or the plan may be amplified and extended. Speaking at the 1959 commencement of Syracuse University, Dr. Finla G. Crawford, its retiring vice chancellor, chose "University Hallmarks."[3] He opened with a brief comment on the meaning of *hallmark;* generally applied, he said the term is "the *evidence* of *quality,* of *fine workmanship,* of *superior design,* of *honest weight,* and of *integrity.*"

The speaker continued: "My purpose . . . is to describe some of the hallmarks to be found in universities." He went on:

> The library is the number one hallmark of a university. A university library is not a building nor even a collection of books; it is more than brick and stone and marble or equipment and

[1] *Representative American Speeches, 1951-1952,* 85-90. This speech is quoted briefly on page 111.

[2] *Ibid.,* 1957-1958, 174-183. Address before the Ad-Sell League, Omaha, February 5, 1957.

[3] *Vital Speeches,* XXV (July 15, 1959), 606-608. Dr. Crawford, who gives 20 or 30 talks a year before educational, public affairs, and political groups, wrote: "Speech training for me was constant practice, the avoidance of difficult words until they were mastered, and careful organization of material before speaking. You can rarely speak well unless you have mastered your subject." (Letter of November 10, 1959.)

collections and staff. If it is to be the heart of a university, and I believe that it is—then it must play its proper role as the organ that keeps all else alive. . . .

Truly, the library becomes my number one hallmark for it is in the library we find the *evidence of quality,* of *fine workmanship,* of *superior design,* of *honest weight,* of *integrity.*

The second hallmark, the speaker declared, consists of "the books and articles that have made history." Another hallmark of a university is its active interest in diffusing knowledge. "When we seek the sign of superior design and integrity of a University," he continued, we must look for evidence of how its university press adds lustre to the academic program. After discussing other hallmarks— the faculty and students of the institution, and its freedom of inquiry —he concluded:

As one examines a cherished piece of silver, one must study closely a university and look beyond the bricks and mortar to find the hallmarks; and when one does, they signify the evidence of *quality,* of *fine workmanship,* of *superior design,* of *honest weight,* and of *integrity.* If a university has these hallmarks, it will be a great university. Its future will be secure.

The speaker might have planned his speech in this wise: "My purpose today is to describe the five characteristics of a great university. First of all is its library." You can judge for yourself what is added by substituting *hallmark* for *characteristic,* and by the repetition of phrases like *"quality . . . fine workmanship . . . superior design."*

Paul B. Wishart, president of the Minneapolis-Honeywell Regulator Company, concerned about a severe business slump, said to his audience of business men attending a marketing conference sponsored by the National Industrial Conference Board:

I have given a great deal of thought in recent months to an examination of some of the less obvious factors that underlie the surface of our economy. And it seems to me that I have found five in particular that hold the key to the mystery of what is wrong with selling today."[4]

---

[4] *Vital Speeches,* XXV (October 15, 1958), 20-21. Mr. Wishart's speaking experience had its roots in extracurricular activities in school. President of one of the large, growing corporations of the country, he replied to an inquiry: "I generally try to make not more than one major talk before outside organizations annually, plus one appearance before security analysts in one of the principal cities in the country. . . . From the stand-point of making informal talks, I probably average one a week throughout the year within my own organization before an audience that varies with the subject matter from twenty-five to several hundreds." (Letter of November 17, 1959.)

This speaker, too, could have developed his speech with a simple list of "five factors." But since they were "less obvious factors," and since he was speaking to highly-trained technical people in this highly-technical age, he continued:

I call these five factors "the invisible sound barriers in selling."

Here are his five:

First, there is a broad-based criticism of the profit motive. . . .

Second, there is a widely-held public resentment against the application of pressure. . . .

Third, there is a rapidly-growing sophistication of the buyer in our economy.

Fourth, there is a new emphasis on social and economic security that has brought . . . a lack of direct response to executive direction.

Fifth . . . there has developed in recent years a diffusion of the salesman's responsibility.

As these reasons are "less obvious," they are appropriately called "invisible sound barriers." Designating them by that phrase undoubtedly presented them in a more striking way to the listeners.

G. Keith Funston, president of the New York Stock Exchange, told the graduating classes of the University of Maryland:

I would like to describe briefly four yardsticks employers will use to measure your progress.

These were:

One: Your employer will look for people who can get along with others. . . .

Two: Your employer will look for creative ability—for the initiative and imagination required to range beyond the immediate job. . . .

Three: Your employer will look, at the same time, for people with measured judgment. . . .

Four: Your employer will look for men and women with firm beliefs and the ability to articulate them. . . .

Each of these four yardsticks was briefly but forcefully described. The formal listing of the yardsticks, "one—two—three—four" and the parallel wording, "Your employer will look for . . ." helped to emphasize the point to the listener.[5]

Henry Cabot Lodge, Jr., when United States delegate to the United Nations, wanted in an official speech to impress upon the General

---

[5] *Representative American Speeches, 1957-1958,* 141-142. Another excerpt from this speech is on pages 138-139.

Assembly the ways in which the Soviet regime in Hungary had betrayed the Hungarian people during the days of the Hungarian revolution.

He listed them as *promises:*

> Promise Number One: Withdrawal of Soviet troops. . . . Mr. President, that promise has been broken.

> Promise Number Two: No reprisals against Freedom Fighters. . . . The record shows that the authorities in Hungary have broken their solemn promise. . . .

And thus to:

> Promise Number Eight: Freedom of religion. . . . This promise too was broken. . . .

> Mr. President, there are eight broken promises of the regime in Hungary. The list could be extended. But I have chosen these eight because they all concern basic rights of every human being. Judged by the standards which it set for itself, the Soviet puppet regime has grievously wronged the Hungarian people."[6]

Do you agree with the speaker's choice of *promises* as opposed to other terms available to him: *pledges, agreements, understandings?* To use the word *promise* puts the issue in clear, human terms. And obviously *promises* is better than saying "eight *things* the Soviet regime failed to do" or "eight *ways* in which the Soviet regime failed to keep its word."

Another speech using a special list was delivered by United States Senator Kenneth B. Keating, Republican, New York, in a fund-raising dinner preceding the 1960 campaign. He described five leading Democratic candidates for the presidential nomination, each as a missile. Of a Minnesota senator he said:

> The Hurtling Hubert is a missile of extremely long range. In a test firing last year, the Hurtling Hubert actually reached Soviet Russia, where its communication system kept running at top speed

---

[6] *Ibid.*, 36-46. Wallace Irwin, Jr., then member of the staff of the United States Mission to the United Nations, wrote that Mr. Lodge's main experience in public speaking came after he entered public life. As to the number and kinds of speeches Lodge makes in a year, the letter (November 25, 1959) continued: "In official United Nations meetings, where he speaks as the United States representative, he has spoken at least 41 times in the past year; some of these statements have been only brief remarks but about a dozen have been major statements of the United States view. In addition he made 7 speeches as the President's personal representative accompanying Mr. Khrushchev in September. And in addition to that he made 27 prepared speeches to non-governmental audiences in various parts of the United States. This does not count off-the-cuff talks of which he also gave quite a number."

for eight consecutive hours. It is in constant television contact with the earth. Its fuel supply was developed largely in the mid-1930's, and some scientific circles feel a more modern source of thrust is needed.

He also discussed "the Missouri Fury, a short-range, anti-defense missile," "Texas Titan, a big missile, . . . known to have tremendous thrust," and "the Intercontinental Adlai, unsuccessful in its first two firings."[7]

II. The Mnemonic-Word Design

Mnemonic, from a Greek word meaning *remember,* is a way of aiding the memory. "Thirty days hath September" is a mnemonic device to help one remember the number of days in each month.

A speech on "The Three I's of Success" might have as its three supporting ideas, *industry, initiative, imagination.* The use of this device aids each listener in remembering the speaker's three main points. Other speakers have used *ships,* as *friendship, scholarship, clerkship,* to show that a good teacher must be a *friend,* a *scholar,* and a *clerk.* Others have selected a key word, the initial letters of which represent an idea: thus the four qualities of *youth, ambition, loyalty,* and *enterprise* spell *Yale.* The three R's of education are well known; one speaker proposed a new set of three R's: *right, reason,* and *response.* Still another discussed the triangle of life: *evolution, education,* and *resolution.*

If key words representing your supporting ideas fall naturally into a mnemonic arrangement, there is no reason why you should not capitalize upon the "Four H's" or the "Three J's." Do not, however, ordinarily use words in strained and distorted meanings to achieve a mnemonic effect (though every one appreciates the gentle humor of the original three R's—readin', 'ritin', 'rithmetic—for several reasons).

III. The Design Based on a Text

The development of a text is a favorite sermon design of preachers. Laymen, too, use this plan at times with good result.

[7] From a copy of the speech supplied by Senator Keating (Rep., N. Y.). Senator Keating, Harvard law school graduate, gained his public speaking experience through the practice of law, and in politics. Of other training he writes: "The only formal training in my earlier years was a course in elocution. Frankly, I have tried to forget what I was taught in that course. Since that time, I am aware, methods and techniques have greatly improved."

An interesting theme was employed by Tom E. Shearer, president of the College of Idaho, in a speech delivered to the students of Boise Junior College. He opened with:

This theme for my remarks today relates to some new, and yet very old, standards of excellence. The title comes from an incident which occurred down in the hills of southern Iowa. The driver of an automobile had lost his way, and inquired of one of the local residents how he could get to Ottumwa. The native scratched his head a moment and replied, "Mr., I don't reckon you can get there from here."

As the speaker developed his theme, "getting there from here" proved to be a striking way of describing the road one travels to his desired goal. One example was that of Kenneth Roberts, the author, who determined to be a novelist. By driving himself to write one chapter every four days, he in six months of writing turned out *Arundel,* which sold only 9,266 copies. But:

After continuing to pour out his energies on other novels, for *eight more years,* he finally hit the market with a critically acceptable and financially successful book—*Northwest Passage.*
. . . That's how he got there from here.

Madame Curie, born poor, had no money, always studied:

She was allowed to perform some elementary chemical experiments in a real laboratory. She found a way to get to Paris to study at the Sorbonne. Solitude and near starvation meant nothing to her as long as part of her day could be spent in a laboratory.
. . . In 1903 along with her husband she received the Nobel prize for physics. . . . In 1911 she received the Nobel prize for chemistry. . . . Twice winner of a Nobel prize, that is how she got there from here.[8]

---

[8] *Vital Speeches,* XXV (August 1, 1959), 633-634.
President Shearer replied to an inquiry by writing that he did a good deal of declamatory work in high school which "was certainly most helpful preparation for my subsequent work in public speaking." At his alma mater, the State University of Iowa, he took principles of speech during his freshman year and a course in argumentation and debate his sophomore year. "I make as many as 30 to 35 talks or speeches during a year," he continues. "About ten of these are more or less formally prepared, with about three or four during the year being what I would call major addresses. In addition, there are numerous occasions when, by reason of my position, I am called upon to make brief remarks of five to ten minutes. Some of these are extemporaneous, while others, of course, require real preparation."

IV. The Design Based on Counter Suggestion

Counter suggestion has long been known as a persuasive device. Basically it consists of telling some one to do or not to do something, hoping and expecting that he will do the opposite. To forbid boys to climb a water tower is almost to guarantee that they will attempt it. Read the following rules for rearing delinquent children:

Begin with infancy to give the child everything he wants. In this way he will grow up to believe the world owes him a living.

When he picks up bad words, laugh at him. This will make him think he's cute. It will also encourage him to pick up cuter phrases that will blow off the top of your head later.

Let him read any printed matter he can get his hands on. Be careful that the silverware and drinking glasses are sterilized, but let his mind feast on garbage.

Obviously in offering these rules on "How to Rear Delinquent Children," the compiler is in reality offering rules on "How to Rear Children Who Are Not Delinquent." Listener and speaker alike realize that no one is being fooled. The listener is intrigued by the novelty of the suggestions, yet he sees the wisdom behind them.

Another speaker gave the counter suggestion design an interesting variation when he wanted to talk on "Food Poisoning." He was eager to impress upon food-handlers the proper way of preparing and storing food. Instead he reversed the procedure; he began by asking the question, "Suppose you deliberately tried to cause food-poisoning. What would you do?" The way in which he described wrong practices led his audience to see that he was in reality advocating good practice.

Consider the design of the following sermon entitled, "Six Reasons for Drinking More Liquor":

Many people of our day have accepted the practice of drinking liquor, and in many areas of our society one is suspected of being queer if he does not drink. Sometimes it has seemed that the only dissenting group has been the Protestant clergy, and many times some church people are almost embarrassed by the unrelenting stand of their ministers.

But living in a college community, we are trained in the ways of free and honest thought. We can find facts and deal with them logically, and with our contemporary viewpoint, this we must do, regardless of how we may differ with voices around us.

Thus we can find factual and logical reasons for drinking more liquor.

The foregoing statement, coming from a Methodist pulpit, aroused tremendous interest in the large congregation. The minister continued:

The first of these reasons is that this is the best method we have for keeping the population explosion from making the earth too crowded.

By this time the audience was showing a high degree of alertness, as the minister went on:

We are able to eliminate more people by highway slaughter than by any other way. War is pretty good, but we kill more people month by month on our highways than any month of fatalities of American lives in either World War I or II.[9]

Read the complete speech in the Appendix. The special twist given to the wording of the reasons, combined with the factual evidence presented, made the sermon an impressive one.

V. The Change-of-Position Design

Consider a speech that opens with these words:

I am a registered member of the Democratic Party. Already I have voted in two national and two congressional elections, and each time I have voted for the complete Democratic slate. My parents have been life-long Democrats; in fact my father for six years held a political office in the Truman administration.

Such an opening naturally leads listeners to feel that the speaker is establishing his authority to speak as a Democrat. But let him continue:

When this year opened, I looked with favor upon the candidacies of the various Democratic aspirants to the presidential nomination. As the months have gone by, however, I have been forced to conclude that this November I should support the Republican candidate.

Now the speech has fallen into the change-of-position design; the speaker opened with a statement of his former position; his central idea is a strong statement of his changed position; the supporting ideas will present reasons for his change.

[9] Delivered by the Reverend Mr. Monk Bryan, minister of the Methodist Church, Columbia, Mo., January 11, 1958. Reprinted in *Missouri Methodist Messenger*, XIX, 10 (March 6, 1959), 2.

Here is another illustration:

When I was a high school senior and first began to think seriously about my future, I resolved that I would not get married until I had a good job and a thousand dollars in the bank.

Then I came to college, and took part in lots of bull sessions; but whenever the question of marriage was discussed, I insisted that no one should get married until he had a good job and a thousand dollars in the bank. My senior year I started going with a charming girl, and inevitably we found ourselves one evening talking about marriage; she agreed with me when I expressed my view that we should not get married until I had a good job and a thousand dollars in the bank.

This opening sets the stage for the change-of-position plan:

Well, I was finally graduated, worked a while, and went off to graduate school; but I got more and more lonesome, and one day I hunted up the little blonde and told her I wanted to get married. "Do you have a good job?" she asked, and I had to say "No, I don't have any job at all; and I've got two more years of graduate school." She reflected on that a second, and continued: "Do you have a thousand dollars in the bank?" I had to confess that all I had was two hundred dollars and forty cents. "That's close enough," she said, and soon we were married.

Then comes the central idea:

I've decided since then that it is just as foolish to be too cautious about marriage as it is to be too reckless about marriage. It is just as bad to underestimate what two people can do in order to establish a home as to overestimate what they can do. And here's why.

The speaker states his reasons, with examples, and so proceeds to his conclusion.

In general we expect people to be consistent. We feel that if they change their position on one issue, they might be equally wrong on other issues. On the other hand it takes some courage to admit having been wrong. History is filled with famous converts: Saul of Tarsus for one, St. Augustine for another. When a speaker has a genuine change of position, he may use it as an effective way of persuading others to change also.

VI. The Problem-Solution Design

An interesting design suggested previously in this text is one in which the speaker describes a puzzling problem, then states its solution. This procedure not only provokes the listener's curiosity and increases his suspense, but also makes him appreciate the solution when explained to him.

Suppose the problem is that of building a flying machine. An early solution was to construct machines with flapping wings; these failed. Another was to construct glider-like frames to be guided by the pilot's shifting his weight; these had only a partial success. Explaining these preliminary solutions helps the speaker set the stage for the successful solution evolved by the Wright brothers: the use of movable wing and tail surfaces.

The design of this type of speech may be summarized as follows: First, state the problem ("What accounts for the origin of new species?" "How can we account for the great phenomenon known as the Grand Canyon?" "What caused the irregularities in the orbit of Uranus?" "How can we get tanks across the river and still surprise the enemy?" "How was seed corn improved?"). Second, explain the preliminary solutions ("First we tried A, and that failed; next we tried B, and that failed"). Third, explain the successful solution.

Questions for Classroom Discussion

1. What speeches do you recall in which the design of the speech seemed impressive and effective?

2. How does the basic principle, "Real art conceals art," apply to the problem of speech design?

Speech-Related Project

Study recent issues of *Vital Speeches* and recent volumes of *Representative American Speeches* in search of speeches with noteworthy designs. Report your findings to the class.

Speaking Assignment 24
A Speech Illustrating a Special Design

Make a speech of .... minutes in which your persuasive material is organized according to one of the designs suggested in this chapter, or another design of your own invention.

Consider, for example:

a. A special list
b. A mnemonic device
c. A text
d. Counter suggestion
e. Change of position
f. Problem solution

The design should be prominent enough to capture the listener's interest, and lend support to the ideas of speech, and yet at the same time should not be strained, forced, or artificial.

Hand in an outline in the form requested by your instructor.

REFERENCES ON SPEECH DESIGN

W. Norwood Brigance, Chapter 6, "Organizing the Speech into Concise and Orderly Form," in *Speech Communication,* 2nd ed. (New York, Appleton-Century-Crofts, Inc., 1955). Study the five "thought patterns" presented.

Lionel Crocker, Chapter 17, "Techniques of Structuring the Speech," in *Public Speaking,* 3rd ed. (New York, American Book Company, 1956). Seven ways of developing the idea: definition, particulars and details, comparison and contrast, illustration, presenting reasons, applying a principle, stating cause and effect.

Milton Dickens, section on "Stock Speech Designs," pages 274-285, in *Speech: Dynamic Communication* (New York, Harcourt, Brace and Company, 1954). Describes types of design, illustrated with short outlines.

Alan H. Monroe, Chapter 16, "Organizing the Complete Speech: the Motivated Sequence," in *Principles and Types of Speech,* 4th ed. (Chicago, Scott, Foresman and Company, 1955). Read the five steps of the motivated sequence.

Eugene E. White and Clair R. Henderlider, section on "More Advanced Patterns of Organization," pages 90-105, in *Practical Public Speaking* (New York, The Macmillan Company, 1954). Describes and outlines (a) problem-solution, (b) cause-and-effect, (c) proposition of "fact."

CHAPTER 22

Group Discussion

The nature of discussion; suggested definitions; five steps in analyzing a discussion topic. ■ *Types of discussion: single leader, panel, symposium, forum, role-playing, brainstorming.* ■ *Steps in choosing a topic. Suggestions for presiding officer and participants.*

IN 1787 DELEGATES FROM THE COLONIES met in Philadelphia. Today it is difficult to imagine the host of turbulent issues on which delegates had conflicting interests. It helps to remember that those present represented sovereign states. No one thought of himself primarily as being an American; those present identified themselves as Virginians, New Yorkers, Pennsylvanians, and so on. They had different kinds of money and were properly suspicious of one another's currency. They had had boundary disputes and trade disputes: sensitive matters that touched pride and pocketbook. Large states arranged themselves against small states, Northern states were opposed to Southern, free states argued against slave states, New York was against almost everybody.

Coming from differing backgrounds, the delegates had differing opinions about what to do. Some wanted to amend the old Articles of Confederation; others wanted to compose a new instrument. As meetings dragged on still other disagreements came to light.

What is being described here is perhaps the most significant *discussion* group that ever foregathered on this planet. The outcome was, as every American knows, to create a new nation, "conceived in liberty, and dedicated to the proposition that all men are created equal."

Often the delegates became discouraged, but somehow they managed to adjust their differences. Fortunately there was a strong desire to give and take, to work out original formulas for difficult problems, to produce a document that all the colonies could accept. Moreover important matters like placing the common defense and the regulation of commerce in the hands of the central government met relatively less disagreement. And perhaps most significant of all, influential men were present who had had long association with the processes of discussion. George Washington was a fine presiding officer, partly because of his prestige, partly because of his vast experience with groups. Another persuasive individual was the old and distinguished Benjamin Franklin. Once when the going got rough he told an entertaining story; on another occasion he offered a prayer; at the conclusion of the deliberations he appealed to everybody to sign the document, whether or not he personally agreed with every line of it, simply because it was the best the group had been able to work out. You can read in the Appendix his words on that occasion.

The Constitutional Convention also had an *agenda;* part of it is known to history as the Virginia plan. At one stage of the agenda the convention deadlocked, because no one could formulate a method of resolving the bitter conflict of interests between large states and small. Now if a group begins its deliberations by adopting an agenda, it makes a tacit promise to itself to discuss all of it. When in the Convention a deadlock arose, the presiding officer decided to drop that item on the agenda temporarily, and proceed to the next item on the list. Later the group returned to the troublesome point, and then could reach an agreement.

The Convention could have broken up in disorder, and delegates could have returned to their state governments bearing the dark message of failure. What the effect of such a message would have been, no one can now say. That the Convention did not fail speaks much for the statesmanship and wisdom of those present, and for their abilities to *evolve a solution through discussion.*

I. Nature of Discussion

Discussion has been variously defined. Gulley states that discussion occurs "when a group with group orientation purposefully interacts orally for enlightment or policy-determination."[1] Barnlund and Haiman note that discussion groups "consist of a number of persons who perceive each other as participants in a common activity, who

---

[1] Halbert E. Gulley, *Discussion, Conference and Group Process* (New York, Henry Holt and Company, 1960), 4.

interact dynamically with one another, and who communicate their responses chiefly through words."[2]

These definitions suggest that discussion involves: (1) a **group**, which, though varying in size, has a kind of identity: a committee, a class, or other common interest; (2) oral communication: spoken words that carry with them meanings inherent in words plus the meanings of vocal inflection and gesture; and (3) a purpose, which usually, though not invariably, involves learning or the determining or implementing of policy. The Constitutional Convention disseminated information, worked out solutions of minor and major problems, and at the end arrived at a series of recommendations, drawn into a formal document, later to be presented to the state legislatures for ratification or rejection.

A. FIVE STEPS IN DISCUSSION

Thus far in your classroom speeches you have been aware that you as speaker were a lone individual at the focus of the communication situation. You were given a length of time in which to express your ideas, and were deferred to by your listeners as *the* speaker. To be sure your classmates have ways of expressing themselves also—somewhat subtly while you are speaking, somewhat more openly in any questioning period that followed—but you stood at the front of the room, the principal spokesman. In the discussion process, as our definitions suggest, you *and* the members of the group participate in a common activity. The center of communication shifts freely from one individual in the group to another.

Discussion is often described in language that originated with philosopher-educator John Dewey. Discussion begins with (1) a *question* or *problem*. Your group asks itself, "How can we lessen the number of traffic accidents in this community," or puts before itself some other topic. Next (2) comes a *definition* and *analysis* of the problem. This is an important step indeed. A participant should observe, read, interview, just as he would for an important speech. If the group wants to make constructive suggestions for reducing traffic fatalities, it should know that 43 per cent of deaths on the highway come from exceeding speed limits, that 18 per cent of fatal accidents occur between 1 a.m. and 6 a.m., that 36 per cent of pedestrians who are killed met their deaths while trying to cross a street between intersections. If a board of directors is trying to discover why the company lost money, it needs to know whether the

---

[2] Dean C. Barnlund and Franklyn S. Haiman, *The Dynamics of Discussion* (Boston, Houghton Mifflin Company, 1960), 20.

difficulty is low income or high expenses or both, and it will want to look at a breakdown of figures to determine the low-income projects and the high-cost areas.

The group next considers (3) *possible solutions.* Several solutions may be presented to the group, bearing on everything from new statutes or ordinances to changing requirements for drivers' licenses. Possible solutions are then combined or narrowed to (4) the *most feasible* solution. This solution is finally (5) *formally stated* and presented to the group as its consensus, or phrased as a recommendation for consideration by another group or agency.

What has been outlined above applies primarily to the kind of discussion in which *learning* or *policy making* takes place. You are familiar with other types of discussion groups, such as, for example, informal sessions around the coffee table or in your residence-hall lounge, or, on the other extreme, action-taking groups, such as a board of trustees or board of directors, which will not only evolve a solution but put it into effect. The purpose of your classroom discussion will be primarily to share information, to test reasoning, to develop ability to work with others in finding a solution; in some instances, and with some questions, you may, like the Constitutional Convention delegates, undertake to recommend a change in policy.

Not all discussion proceeds in this orderly arrangement of analysis through possible solutions to statement of best solution. Sometimes the creative process refuses to be channeled into this set groove, but instead expresses itself in irregular, unexpected, unsummoned, and unannounced hunches and flashes of insight. Ordinarily the leader of a discussion group will quite wisely suggest a plan or agenda for the approval of members and then somewhat firmly follow it step by step; situations may arise, however, when he will consent to items being discussed at greater length or in different order when he sees that the long-term interest of the group is being served.

B. TYPES OF DISCUSSION

Let us now discuss the conventional forms, and others not so conventional, that classroom discussion can follow. Your instructor may select one or more of these forms for use in this course; others are appended for your information, since you will encounter most of them in nearly any career you ever undertake.

1. *Group discussion with a leader*

Discussion with a leader consists of a group of individuals—for example your public speaking class—and a member of the group chosen as leader (chairman or moderator). The discussion opens with a statement by the leader explaining the question to be discussed: "How can the United States best meet the challenge of communism in this hemisphere?" "In what ways can the American high school be improved?" He may comment briefly on why the question is important and why it comes up for discussion at this time, giving information that may stimulate the thinking of members of the group. He may follow the steps in the Dewey problem-solution outline, (1) inviting the group to help him define and expand the statement of the problem; next (2) after the problem seems well explained, asking members to suggest solutions; and thus through the remaining steps in the outline. He makes the necessary transitions as he leads the group from one phase of the discussion to another, and closes with a summary of what has been agreed upon.

2. Panel discussion

A panel discussion may be described as a conversation in front of an audience. It is characterized by informal interchange of opinion, as contrasted with the series of short, previously-prepared speeches that describe the *symposium* (see below). It requires a leader and a panel of discussion participants; three is a good number, as this small size means that every one will have a chance to contribute.

A panel on the topic "Should the Schools Educate for Marriage" could proceed as follows:

The chairman may comment on the importance of the subject: couples marry at younger ages now than fifteen years ago; the situation is complicated because of the draft and military training.

The chairman and the panel speakers may first explore the topic, "What is the present situation?" Are families doing acceptably the job of educating their children for marriage? Is there evidence that young people are marrying without proper knowledge of their new responsibilities? What conclusions can be reached from the fact that the divorce rate is increasing? During this part of the discussion, the chairman will require his panel speakers to talk about the present situation. Some one may want to leap ahead and offer a solution, but the chairman will tactfully remind him that solutions come later; the present task is to understand the problem itself as fully as possible.

The second phase of the discussion should answer the question, "What can we do to meet the problem?" Should a special course be offered? A series of lectures? What are other institutions doing? What topics should be included in such a course? Should the course be coeducational? Various solutions may be suggested.

The third part of the discussion naturally follows: "What appears to be the best solution of the problem?" Here members of the panel will begin to take sides, in favor of one solution as against another. Perhaps a member of the panel can offer a resolution: "It is the opinion of this group that a series of lectures on the problem of education for marriage would be helpful, and we recommend that a faculty-student committee be appointed to study the matter further."

During the discussion the leader keeps an eye on the clock so he can keep the panel on the main thread of the argument. When the panel has finished its discussion, he invites questions from the audience. He should also summarize if the panel itself did not arrive at a formal resolution or specific proposal.

Before the panel meets, the chairman should collect his panel members and talk about matters to come up for discussion. Each member may be detailed to investigate certain aspects: one may look into the divorce question, another into the kinds of marriage courses taught at other institutions, another may interview students or young married couples. This kind of preparation will give substance to the discussion and keep it from becoming meaningless.

3. *Symposium*

The symposium is more formal in its operation than is the panel. It consists of a leader and a selected group of participants—three or four in number. The discussion begins with an opening statement from the leader. Participant 1 is then introduced and makes a short speech on some aspect of the question. Participant 2 follows with another short speech; and thus the symposium continues until all participants have spoken. The discussion then becomes more informal, as the leader invites members of the symposium to ask questions of one another. After this interlude, listeners may ask questions of participants.

Assume that the question is, "What Should Be Done to Promote Greater Safety on the Highway?" In an opening talk the chairman describes the gravity of the present situation: he may point out that 36,981 Americans lost their lives in motor vehicle accidents, including X deaths in the state of Y (the 1959 figures ranges from 7 in the Virgin Islands to 3,588 in California—consult the current issue of the *World Almanac* for later figures for your own state). Speaker A, who has consulted many magazines and has corresponded with various state highway commissions, talks about what is now being done: education, highway patrol, legislation. Speaker B, a student majoring in civil engineering, talks about highways: good and bad types oι highway design and construction, the importance of a highway engineer to a safety program, lessons learned from the construction of freeways and throughways. Speaker C talks about drivers: he has investigated men versus women drivers, young versus old drivers, accident-prone drivers. When Speaker C resumes his seat, the leader invites members of the symposium to interrogate one another; after a few minutes' exchange of ideas, the leader then invites members of the audience to ask questions or offer brief comment. At the end he summarizes the discussion.

4. *Forum: other conventional types*

The *forum period* is a term describing the time spent in questioning the leader, lecturer, panel, or symposium speakers. Groups appreciate the opportunity of having a say, and the popularity of the practice gives rise to self-explanatory terms like *panel-forum, symposium-forum, debate-forum, lecture-forum,* when a panel, symposium, debate, or lecture, respectively, is followed by a question period.

Round table, staff conference, committee meeting, meeting of governing board or board of directors, colloquy, bargaining session, public hearing are forms of discussion that do not call for special treatment here. With the exception of the last-named, the *public hearing,* discussions are carried on by a small group, usually with no audience present. These groups explore questions, the chairman following a discussion outline or formal agenda. Presentations may be made, as by a budget officer or supply officer at a staff conference, or by the representative of an organization, institution, or individual at a public hearing or bargaining session; but these formal interludes are likely to be followed by informal discussion. The *round table* is so called because the participants sit around a large table, in a fashion that suggests each is on an equal footing with every one else; the discussion that follows is likely to be exploratory or informative rather than policy-making. A *colloquy* resembles a panel except that the term *colloquy* suggests the presence of highly-qualified experts (although the distinction is not hard and fast; panel experts may be as authoritative as colloquy experts). Meetings of *committees, governing boards, boards of directors,* may or may not be open to the public, and may or may not hear expert opinion or testimony. They bring in reports, recommendations, fact-finding studies, and even resolutions or decisions.

5. *Other types of discussion*

Discussion is often stimulated by devices other than the problem-solution approach.

Role-playing (psychodrama, sociodrama) is a device that may be used to initiate a discussion. Instead of a formal statement by the leader, a small group may enact a little improvised (or rehearsed) play showing poor sportsmanship, customer complaints, good versus bad on-the-job instruction, good versus bad handling of a worker's grievance. For additional effect, one of the employees present may be asked to play the part of the foreman, and a foreman may be invited to assume the role of a new man just starting work. The play may consist of the new man (actually the foreman) asking questions of the sort that a beginner would likely ask, and the foreman (actually an employee) giving curt, gruff, and overly-technical replies. This play could be followed by another version in which the foreman demonstrated a more helpful attitude.[3] Afterwards members of the group are invited to comment and question; the role-playing has reminded them of other situations arising in employer-employee relationships that may not have been effectively handled.

Brainstorming is a method of stimulating the imagination to produce ideas. It is not specifically designed to solve a problem, but to accumulate a list of approaches, possibilities, or schemes. Its methods are different from those described elsewhere in this chapter, but the general procedure is described here for those who want to try it. It requires a leader, a recorder, and a group of ten or twelve.[4] The technique follows four rules: (1) *Adverse criticism* is taboo. Don't find fault with the suggestions of some one else. The thought is that creativity suffers in a critical atmosphere. (2) *Free wheeling* is invited. Wild, daring, even improbable ideas are welcomed and cheered. (3) *A quantity* of ideas is desired. (4) *Combination and improvement* of idea is sought. Modifying a previously-expressed idea is termed *hitch-hiking.*

After explaining the rules, the leader states the question. A recorder writes the ideas on the board as they are offered. The purpose of the session is to collect a large number of ideas. Appraisal of the ideas is usually made in another session. Some seemingly-improbable suggestions may prove to have merit if considered open-mindedly and imaginatively.

C. VALUES OF DISCUSSION

Values of discussion include:

1. *Discussion evolves a better solution.* The group will nearly always

---

[3] Role-playing may help convert the participant to the point of view represented by the role he plays. See the discussion in Joseph T. Klapper, *The Effects of Mass Communication* (Glencoe, Ill., The Free Press, 1961), 80-84.

[4] The method was suggested by Alex F. Osborn, of Batten, Barton, Durstine and Osborn, in his *Applied Imagination,* New York, Charles Scribner's Sons, 1954 (revised, 1957). See also Arthur M. Coon, "Brainstorming—A Creative Problem-Solving Technique," *Journal of Communication* (Autumn, 1957), 111-118.

foresee more difficulties, explore more facets, visualize more outcomes, than can a single individual.

2. *Discussion improves group spirit.* People like to be consulted. They like to be in on prospective developments. They cherish a feeling of being a member of the group. Points of friction between faculty and students, between labor and management, and between other groups—even between nations—can be resolved through discussion.

3. *The agreed-upon solution is more likely to work.* Some bugs will have been removed by process of discussion itself. The individuals participating, moreover, will exert extra effort to make the solution a success. Those involved in D-Day invasion plans, for example, from commanding generals to airmen, sailors, infantrymen, and paratroopers, felt confident that the invasion would be successful, and were better able to meet the many contingencies that later arose because of their foreknowledge of the objectives. Evidence is increasing that decisions are more effectively carried out when they have been made by the group concerned. Those present see that others also are willing to accept the decision of the group (pay the fee, change working hours, close the branch office, join the community committee) and understand the reasons for it.

4. *Discussion is vital to the survival of democracy.* When issues of massive concern sweep a country, the forums, panels, symposiums, debates, hearings, buzz sessions, and discussions of all kinds, formal and informal, organized and spontaneous, legislative and non-legislative, help a free people to analyze the problem, ascertain the facts, weigh the possible outcomes, and take the necessary steps.

II. Choosing a Question

The examples presented thus far suggest that preparation for discussion should begin with the selection of a question. Single words or phrases are not sufficient. If the leader announces, "Today we are going to discuss juvenile delinquency," he has not done enough home work. *Juvenile delinquency* is a phrase, not a question. If he announces, "How Can We Better Prevent Juvenile Delinquency in Middletown?" he has formulated a better statement of the problem to be discussed.

Problems for discussion may be loosely catalogued as *questions of fact, questions of value,* or *questions of policy.*

1. *Questions of fact* propose an inquiry. They may or may not be good subjects for discussion. A question like "What league has the

best hitters this season?" would not make a good subject, since the answers can be found simply by consulting printed batting averages. A question like "Is the Free World Winning the Cold War" could be profitable, as the facts must be sought in a variety of places, as needed facts will inevitably be missing, as facts that are located will require interpretation. A question like "Do Students Approve Proposal X For Modifying the Calendar of Vacations" could better be answered by a survey than by a discussion (though a discussion might be helpful to bring out pros and cons).

2. *Questions of value* ask for judgments: Was it wrong to drop the atomic bomb on Hiroshima? Is segregation harmful? Is euthanasia justified? Questions like these bring up questions of ethics, morals, personal standards.

3. *Questions of policy* discuss what people should do. Most discussion questions probably fall in this category. "What should be the policy of the United States on disarmament?" "What should be the agricultural policy of the United States?" "How can the United States best meet the challenge of communism?" "What should be our policy towards Cuba?" "Should we adopt a policy of free trade?" "Should Congress fix minimum wages and maximum hours for industry?" "Should diplomatic recognition be extended to the Communist government of China?" Local or campus questions of policy may be considered: "Should this institution adopt the trimester plan?"

In choosing a topic for discussion, follow the requirements for choosing a topic for a speech: consult your interests, the interests of the group, the availability of material, the timeliness or other aspect of the occasion.

III. Techniques of Presiding

The qualities of good presiding may be briefly stated: the leader should be able to get along with others; he should preside with tact and fairness; he should be able to keep in the background, not monopolizing the discussion, but drawing out the others; he should be able to express himself clearly as he opens the discussion, guides it, and summarizes it; he needs to keep a plan before him, leading the group through the various phases of analyzing the problem, gathering solutions, and working out the most feasible solution.

The suggestions below apply in the main to the more conventional discussion situations. Procedures like role-playing and brainstorming call for modifications.

A. ADVANCE ARRANGEMENTS

Whatever the nature of the discussion, certain plans need to be made in advance. These questions are suggested:

1. *How is the question to be worded?* It should not be too broad or too narrow. It should have focus. The question form is used: "Should students finish college before doing military service?" "How can we increase chapel attendance?"

2. *Who is to participate?* Unless the membership of the group is fixed, the presiding officer needs to invite the participants. Different points of view should be represented: in a discussion of "The Tensions of Big-City Living," the discussants included a corporation executive, the president of a labor union, a physician, a judge. Each saw the problem differently, and the group as a whole was able to cover a variety of aspects. Moreover the participants were well-informed and articulate. If you were planning a discussion of the forthcoming city election, you would certainly want students representing both "Reform" and "Liberal" tickets.

3. *What kind of discussion plan should be worked out?* For a policy making group, this may take the form of an agenda which may look like this:

AGENDA FOR A CONFERENCE

1. Minutes of last meeting.
2. Consideration of next year's calendar.
   a. Report of committee on examinations.
   b. Report of committee on review week.
   c. Report of committee on calendars of other institutions.
   d. Report of committee on student questionnaire.
3. Summary by chairman of recommendations.

The discussion plan may include such questions as, "What is the nature of the problem?" "What are possible solutions?" and "What is the best solution?"

4. *Is a rehearsal or preliminary discussion necessary?* In some instances a discussion is improved if participants meet in advance and agree upon a discussion outline and the points of view that each is to express. Even in formal committee sessions it is helpful to send an agenda to participants before the meeting, or to notify key people ahead of time to be prepared to discuss certain aspects. At the meeting itself the chairman may distribute copies of the agenda, and ask the group to approve or modify it.

5. *What publicity should be given the discussion?* If the public is to be invited, many possible news channels should be explored.

6. *What visual aids are to be employed?* Here the leader should ask himself what will be necessary in the way of graphs, charts, slides, films, exhibits.

7. *What other arrangements need to be made?* Here the check list consists of items concerned with reserving the room, notifying or reminding the participants, procuring and preparing ash trays, scratch pads, copies of the agenda or outline, name cards, and the like.

B. PROCEDURES DURING THE MEETING

The presiding officer should note the following suggestions:

1. *Make the preliminary remarks brief.* The presiding officer should introduce the participants; state the topic; open the discussion with a brief comment. After the comment, he may then introduce the first speaker, or ask a question. His opening remarks can become too lengthy. He should take care of essentials, but as quickly as possible should get the discussion under way.

2. *Insert brief summaries.* He should guide the progress of the discussion by occasional brief summaries that tie the discussion into the agenda or program outline.

3. *Ask questions.* Consider the forms that a question may take:

a. *Indirect* question (aimed at no one in particular). "How prevalent is dishonesty in examinations?" or "What are some of the procedures used by cheaters?"

b. *Direct* question (aimed at a specific individual). "Dean Thompson, how many cases of academic dishonesty have come before your office this year?"

c. *Relay* question. Some one asks a question of the chairman, but he relays it to the group: Member: "Mr. Chairman, how extensive is the problem of cheating?" Chairman: "You've heard the question, 'How extensive is the problem of cheating.' Dean Thompson, can you answer that?"

d. *Reverse* question. Some one asks a question of the chairman, but he reverses it to the questioner himself: Dean Thompson: "Mr. Chairman, how extensive is the problem of cheating?" Chairman: "Well, to start with, Dean Thompson, how many cases has your office turned up this year?"

Questions help meet situations that arise during discussion. This list of suggestions by Ewbank and Auer is indispensable:

To question the source of information or argument: "Who gathered these statistics that you spoke of?" "Who is Mr. Gish whose opinion has been quoted?" "Do you know that as a fact, or is it your opinion?"

To suggest that the discussion is wandering from the point: "Can someone tell me what bearing this has on our problem?" "Your point is an interesting one, but can't we get back to our subject?"

To register steps of agreement (or disagreement): "Am I correct in assuming that we all agree (or disagree) on this point?"

To handle the impatient, cure-all member: "But would your plan work in all cases? Who has an idea on that?" "Hadn't we better reserve judgment until we all know more about this problem?"

To suggest that personalities be avoided: "I wonder what bearing this has on the question before us?"

To suggest that some are talking too much: "Are there those who haven't spoken who have ideas they would like to present?"

To suggest the value of compromise: "Do you suppose the best course of action lies between these two points of view?"

To draw the timid but informed member into the discussion: "Spelvin here, lived for quite a while in China. Suppose we ask him whether he ever saw . . .?"[5]

Barnlund's studies show that the following represent the principal functions of the group leader.[6] The items are listed in the order showing the frequency with which they were used in the discussions under observation:

Summarizing or asking for summary 51
Directing group to new or former issues 44
Ascertaining group opinion 38
Resolving differences 33
Insuring recording of decisions 29
Stimulating further exploration of ideas 27
Checking time limits 23
Noting digressions from agenda 22
Clarifying agreements or disagreements 22
Restating problem or re-orienting 19

Experienced presiding officers raise this question: Can a discussion have *too much* guiding? On this point the chairman must ever exer-

[5] Read the complete list of questions in *Discussion and Debate,* 2nd ed. (New York, Appleton-Century-Crofts, Inc., 1951), pp. 287-288.
[6] Dean C. Barnlund, "Experiments in Leadership Training for Decision Making Discussion Groups," *Speech Monographs,* XXII (March, 1955), 6.

cise judgment. Out of what appears to be wandering, digressing, or reminiscing may develop the idea that best solves the problem. A discussion may be slowed down simply to give everyone his say; but what is lost in minutes may be gained in morale. Experienced chairmen combine careful guidance with flexible management so as to achieve the greatest amount of creativity. A good leader has enough command of the situation so that he can either follow the agenda rigidly or allow digressions that may develop a long-term value.

To contrast a group-centered discussion and a leader-centered discussion, consider these parallel columns:

Group-Centered	*Leader-Centered*
1. Leader asks a group member to summarize wherever possible.	1. Leader summarizes periodically, emphasizing ideas *he* considers important.
2. Leader clarifies and reflects member ideas without attempting to influence.	2. Leader interprets, rephrases, and modifies a member's contributions to conform with what *he* considers most important.

These and similar items show a distinct difference in the leader's views of his own responsibilities.[7]

IV. Techniques of Participation

A member of a discussing group can be helpful in various ways:

By keeping in mind the agenda or discussion outline. He will thus be able to make his contributions at the times when they are most pertinent and useful.

By understanding the nature and purpose of discussion. He will thus be able to enter into the problem-solving (or information-disseminating) spirit of the group.

By avoiding excessive talkativeness. Sometimes the most useful member of the discussion group is the one who has the most to say. Almost any experienced discussion leader, however, knows the type of dis-

---

[7] From Richard R. Wischmeier, "Group-Centered and Leader-Centered Leadership: An Experimental Study," *Speech Monographs,* XXII (March, 1955), 43-48. See the study itself for further contrasting items and for appraisals by subjects of the two methods.

See also William E. Utterback, "The Influence of Style of Moderation on the Outcomes of Discussion," *Quarterly Journal of Speech,* XLIV (April, 1958), 149-152. "Full moderation [keeping discussion focused, making suggestions regarding analysis of problem, clarifying discussion, etc.] was more favorable than partial [moderation] to progress toward consensus."

cusser who requires too many words to express his ideas, and who is too aggressive and dominating.

By avoiding excessive silence. A participant can not offer information that he does not have. In almost any discussion, moreover, are aspects about which some participants know nothing at all. On the other hand, just as it is easy to fall into the habit of saying too much, it is also easy to fall into the habit of saying too little. And then, "sometimes the quiet fellow has already said all he knows."

Good discussers avoid the extremes just described. They are active mentally throughout the discussion. They supply information; they ask questions; they challenge or stimulate differing points of view; they help keep the discussion on the main track, Avoiding personalities, they stick to the central problem. They praise a point well made and to help the chairman draw out one who may be hesitant. Their contributions sparkle with specific facts and pointed examples.

V. Concluding Note

One does not have to participate in very many discussions before he begins to realize that some individuals have more *power* (influence) than others. The power may come from the fact that one member is a colonel, whereas the others are captains; or from the fact that one member is well-informed, whereas the others are less well informed. Power also may flow from wealth, seniority, social standing, or other kinds of status. An individual may have high power in one group and low power in another; among the group of captains, the colonel had high power; among a group of generals, he might have low power. At college a freshman may have low power among a group of seniors (he is new, inexperienced, younger); but if he returned to his high school and sat with a committee of high school seniors to discuss "How can a high school senior best spend his senior year so as to prepare himself for college," our college freshman would have high power indeed (more information, greater experience, older). Again, suppose this college freshman was a life-long Gilbert and Sullivan fan; had seen all the operettas and could play most of the scores; then suppose he found himself in a discussion situation with a group of college seniors who wanted to produce *The Mikado* but had only average acquaintance with it; here the freshman would be in a position of high power (knowledge, background, talent).

Power is only one of the interpersonal relationships that operate in group discussion. To learn more about these phenomena, read the references at the end of this chapter.

Discussion and conference play an important part in business, industry, and the professions. Much thinking and planning is done by teams or committees. Your exposure to discussion—as leader, participant, listener—should help prepare you for the team or committee assignments that come to you in the pursuit of your own career.

Questions for Classroom Discussion

1. Make a list of suitable questions for a panel discussion.

2. Review the good and bad qualities of discussion participants; of the discussion leader.

3. Make a list of the various kinds of discussion situations encountered by members of the class.

4. Consider the advantages and disadvantages of a tightly-reined, closely-scheduled discussion; of a loosely-run, permissive, flexible discussion.

Speaking Assignment 25

A Panel Discussion of a Controversial Topic

Select a topic for a panel discussion. Sample topics are suggested below:[8]

1. How can we get out the vote for the X election?

2. What can be done to reduce automobile accidents?

3. Should "war criminals" be punished?

4. What can be done to reduce traffic in narcotics?

5. Should we adopt a program of compulsory health insurance?

6. Should we have Federal aid to education?

7. What can be done to improve mental hospitals?

8. How can college better prepare one for the business world?

9. What can we do to increase church attendance?

10. What can be done to improve the quality of TV programs?

11. How can we encourage intellectual activity on the campus?

12. Should a policy of gradual reduction of tariffs be encouraged?

13. What can be done to help students more effectively choose a vocation?

14. What can be done to make this a better institution of higher learning?

[8] Some of these topics are adapted from Marilyn Myers and Lionel Crocker, "One Hundred Questions for Public Discussion," in *Speech Teacher*, II (November, 1953), 266-272. Consult the complete article for further topics, and for suggestions for discussing each topic.

15. What should be the policy of the United States on disarmament?

16. How can the United States best meet the challenge of communism?

17. What should be our policy towards Cuba?

18. Should diplomatic recognition be extended to the Communist government of China?

19. Is the free world winning the cold war?

20. Should parents he held responsible by law for the misdeeds of their juvenile delinquents?

21. Is marriage undesirable for college undergraduates?

22. Should Berlin be made an international city under UN control?

23. Should school remain in regular session the year round?

24. Should gambling be legalized in all states?

25. Should subsidies be abolished for college athletes?

Select a leader and panel to discuss the chosen topic.

The leader and panel should arrange a meeting to consider the topic further and work out an agenda or outline for discussion.

On the date assigned, present the discussion to the class, allowing .... minutes for the panel contribution and .... minutes for class discussion and critique.

REFERENCES ON DISCUSSION

Auer, J. Jeffery and Henry Lee Ewbank, *Discussion and Debate,* 2nd ed. (New York, Appleton-Century-Crofts, Inc., 1951). The suggestions for presiding given on pages 343-344 come from this helpful text.

Barnlund, Dean C. and Franklyn S. Haiman, *The Dynamics of Discussion* (Boston, Houghton Mifflin Company, 1960). Especially good for its relating of principles of discussion to theory and experimental findings from psychology and sociology.

Braden, Waldo W. and Earnest Brandenburg, *Oral Decision-Making: Principles of Discussion and Debate* (New York, Harper and Brothers, 1955). Contains a helpful section on scoring and appraising discussion.

Cartwright, Dorwin and Alvin Zander, *Group Dynamics: Research and Theory,* 2nd ed. (Evanston, Row, Peterson and Company, 1960). Part 6, "The Structural Properties of Groups," discusses problems of communication in groups, and the varying amounts of influence exerted by different members.

Gulley, Halbert E., *Discussion, Conference, and Group Process* (New York, Henry Holt and Company, 1960). Well balanced between theory and practice. See for example Chapter 5, "Interaction," for a discussion of power relationships and interpersonal relations.

CHAPTER 23

Parliamentary Procedure

The basic principles of parliamentary procedure are rooted in British and American legislative institutions. ■ *Forming an organization calls for preliminary planning, from the calling of the first meeting through the adopting of the constitution.* ■ *Main, privileged, subsidiary, incidental, and unclassified motions are considered from the requirements of (1) precedence, (2) whether they need a second, (3) debatability, (4) amendability, (5) vote, (6) whether they will interrupt a speaker, (7) whether they can be reconsidered.*

AS MUCH SPEAKING IS DONE in situations in which parliamentary procedure is followed, this chapter will consider the important principles and rules governing the making of motions.

I. Basic Principles

American parliamentary procedure is of Anglo-Saxon origin; the British Parliament is accurately called *the mother of parliaments.* The procedures you will use are those based on the *Rules of Order* first published by General Henry M. Robert in 1876. Although this work differs from the other systems in details, it has become a standard for organizations throughout the country. Any social, honorary, or professional club to which you belong undoubtedly follows, after its own constitution, by-laws, and standing rules, this monumental guide compiled by General Robert for the vast amount of procedural detail not otherwise specifically mentioned.

Regardless of relatively minor differences, groups operating under this British-American tradition follow these basic principles.

1. *The majority rules.* This obvious principle evolved after a futile striving to maintain a rule that everything must be done by unanimous consent. Now we agree that the wish of the majority governs the whole group. Although the outcome may hinge on a single vote, we accept even this slender margin as establishing the will of the group.[1]

2. *Members have equal rights to speak and vote.* Only through carefully-defined procedures may discussion be limited or halted. During debate everyone may have his say. And it has been a century or more since anyone seriously introduced a bill that some people should have two votes each.

3. *Only one matter should be discussed at any one time.* This rule also evolved in the House of Commons, and then only after it had been repeatedly shown that a group could not profitably and efficiently consider two or three things at once. When a parliamentary situation seems hopelessly snarled, the cause may be that the group is trying to make several decisions at the same time.

4. *A courteous atmosphere must prevail.* This principle is of the highest importance. Parliament, the Congress, and the several state legislatures have established ingenious but positive prohibitions against name-calling, improper epithets, and disorderly conduct. The presiding officer has a special official, the sergeant-at-arms, to help maintain order when the chair's own request is insufficient. Each member of the House of Commons must stand behind a red line, woven into the carpet, when he speaks; this line, preventing him from getting too close to his opponents, reminds him that the House is for speaking, not fighting. In groups governed by parliamentary procedure improper language is strictly out of order; an offending person is subject to any discipline necessary to restore harmony to the discussion. The long-established tradition is to *speak to the motion; leave personalities out.* Experienced legislators have realized that they have to work with political friends and political opponents for years; they have learned that two people can disagree firmly on one issue, but can work together on another.

This is the attitude to carry into any society or club of which you are a member. These statements constitute *the basic philosophy of parliamentary law.*[2]

---

[1] Recall that Andrew Johnson missed impeachment by one vote; 35 to 19 for acquittal, one short of the necessary two-thirds. Rutherford B. Hayes was elected President by 185 electoral votes to 184; the committee vote preceding this decision favored him by 8 to 7. In 1941 the House of Representatives renewed the 1940 Selective Service Act by a shudderingly-close vote of 203 to 202. A hundred days later: Pearl Harbor. And recall various 5-4 Supreme Court decisions of 1959.

[2] See Giles Wilkeson Gray, "A Philosophy of Parliamentary Law," *Quarterly Journal of Speech*, XXVII (October, 1941), 437-441.

II. Forming a Parliamentary Organization

Your class may form a parliamentary organization to operate within the framework of the public speaking course, or you may some time need to know how to form a new society or club. Here is an outline of the necessary steps:

A. CALL A PRELIMINARY MEETING

Call together for an informal meeting others who may also be interested in establishing a group. If the proposal seems advisable, talk about a possible time for a first meeting. Select someone to call this meeting to order (say, Miss Allen), and to explain the purpose of the new organization. Select others to be named as temporary chairman (Mr. Bachelor) and temporary secretary. Others should be prepared to make other necessary motions. Set a date for a public meeting to discuss the proposed club, and make plans to publicize this meeting.

B. CALL A MEETING TO DISCUSS THE PROPOSED CLUB

When this meeting opens, Miss Allen, previously chosen for this purpose, steps forward and calls the meeting to order. She will point out that the group should have a duly-elected temporary chairman, and will say, "I move that Mr. Bachelor (also previously selected) serve as temporary chairman." Mr. Christian (previously selected) seconds the motion. As this is a motion, other nominations are not called for, and Miss Allen calls for the vote. If the motion carries, Mr. Bachelor takes the chair; if it is lost, another nomination for temporary chairman is in order, and may be made, seconded, and voted on.

Mr. Bachelor's first duty is to call for the election of a temporary secretary, following the procedure described above.

Mr. Bachelor calls upon Miss Devine (previously selected) to explain the purpose of the meeting. Others may take part in the discussion that follows by making comments or asking questions.

Mr. Bachelor then calls upon Mr. Ervin (previously selected) to introduce a motion calling for the establishing of a club: "I move that this group establish a Speakers' Club for the purpose of discussing current social, economic, and political issues." After this motion is seconded, the chairman calls for discussion. After it has been discussed, along with any amendments that may also have been offered, the chairman calls for a vote (voting first, of course, on the amendments, if any). If the proposal carries, the chairman declares that it is in order to select a committee to draw up the constitution and by-laws. Mr.

Gladdon says: "I move that the chair appoint a committee of three to prepare the constitution and by-laws, and present them at a meeting one week from today." If this is seconded, it may be discussed and amended. The chairman announces: "I appoint Miss Devine, Mr. Ervin, and Mr. How as members of the constitutional committee, and ask them to report to the group one week from today." The time is set for the second meeting, and the meeting is adjourned.

During the week, the committee of three prepares a draft of a constitution and by-laws. Their work may read as follows:

CONSTITUTION OF

THE YOUNG SPEAKERS' CLUB

Article I. Name and Purpose

Section 1. This organization shall be known as the Young Speakers' Club.

Section 2. The purpose of this organization shall be to provide opportunities for its members to discuss current social, political, and economic problems.

Article II. Membership

Section 1. Membership shall be limited to students regularly enrolled in Section B of Public Speaking 101.

Section 2. Faculty may be admitted as ex-officio members.

Article III. Officers

Section 1. Officers shall be: President, Vice-President, Secretary, Treasurer.

Section 2. Officers shall be elected at the last regular meeting of the year.

Article IV. Meetings

Section 1. Regular meetings shall be held each month during the school year.

Section 2. Special meetings may be called by the President, or by a majority vote of those present at any regular meeting.

Article V. Amendments

Section 1. The constitution may be amended by a two-thirds vote of the members present at any regular meeting, provided the amendment has been presented at a previous meeting; or at a special meeting, provided that the special meeting is held at least two weeks after the meeting at which the amendment was presented.

The committee should also prepare the proper by-laws. By-laws contain lesser details: (1) dues, (2) method of electing officers, (3) duties of officers, (4) standing committees and their duties, (5) order of business, (6) statement of a quorum, (7) statement of parliamentary authority, (8) method of amending by-laws. As by-laws are made more easily amended than is the constitution, it contains details more likely to need changing, as, for example, the amount of dues.

At the second meeting the temporary chairman calls for the reading of the minutes by the temporary secretary. The chairman of the constitutional committee then reads the constitution and by-laws and moves that they be adopted. Copies should be provided members. The chairman instructs the secretary to read the document section by section. Members are given an opportunity to offer amendments. Next the document is read as a whole, as amended, so that members may consider it in its entirety, especially being on the lookout for conflicting provisions, omissions, and the like. After this discussion, the constitution is read again in its final form; its adoption is then voted on. By-laws are then presented, discussed, and amended, following this procedure. Members may then sign the document. Steps are then taken to elect permanent officers for the group.

III. Qualifications of the Presiding Officer

The concept of having, as the executive agent of the organization, a single person, with well-defined authority, was developed over the centuries after other, less-efficient, plans were tried. It might seem eminently fair, for example, to have presiding officers rotate frequently; this procedure would give many people opportunity to preside. Although this plan was tried by the National Assembly during the French Revolution, it did not work. Presiding calls for traits and skills which individuals have in various degrees, so experience now dictates that the presiding officer should be carefully chosen, and elected for a term of office.

The presiding officer should be courteous, fair, and impartial, but also firm. He should be able to supply parliamentary information that members need in order to understand the status of the motion before the group or the effect of proposed motions. He is not expected to display his parliamentary knowledge; hence, he should not make procedures unnecessarily cumbersome. Often he is assisted by a member of the group elected as *parliamentarian,* who helps him keep in mind various parliamentary details.

When matters get complicated, a good chairman will not hesitate to explain to the group exactly what the situation is.

IV. Qualifications of the Secretary

The secretary is the record-keeper of the club. He should keep the minutes of each meeting. The degree of completeness of minutes largely depends on the nature of the club. He may or may not summarize discussions, but he at least needs to make sure that the minutes show (1) time and place of meeting, (2) name of presiding officer, (3) names of those present, (4) a record of all business transacted with names of movers and seconders (this would include all main motions except those withdrawn, and all other motions not withdrawn or lost), (5) other items that should go into the club's permanent record, (6) time of adjournment, (7) signature of secretary.

V. Order of Business

Following is the usual order of business, subject to the rules of the organization:
1. Call to order.
2. Reading minutes of previous meeting.
3. Correcting and approving minutes of previous meeting.
4. Report of officers.
5. Announcements.
6. Reports of standing committees.
7. Reports of special committees.
8. Unfinished business.
9. New business.
10. Program.
11. Adjournment.

VI. Quorum

No business can be transacted unless a legal minimum number of members, known as a *quorum*, is present. By-laws may state the number of members, or the percentage of the total membership, necessary to constitute a quorum. If the by-laws do not specify what constitutes a quorum, it may be presumed to be a majority of the membership.

VII. The Main Motion

The business of the group is transacted not through informal suggestions, but through *main* (or *principal*) *motions*.

To get a main motion before the group:

A. THE MEMBER ADDRESSES THE CHAIR

Since the group should discuss only one proposal at a time, the member needs to *get the floor,* i.e., *the right to speak.* This he does by addressing the chair: "Mr. Chairman" (or "Mr. President," or whatever the title is). If a woman is presiding, the form of address is "Madame (not "Miss" or "Mrs.") Chairman" (or "Madame President," etc.).

B. THE CHAIR RECOGNIZES THE MEMBER

This he does by nodding towards the member and calling his name. If he does not know the member's name, he may make inquiry. ("Will the member please state his name?") The secretary records the names of those who participate in parliamentary business.

C. THE MEMBER STATES HIS MOTION

The member states his motion by saying, "I move," followed by his proposal: "that the Club increase the fee for the dance to $5.00 per couple." He may, of course, offer remarks in support of his motion, before or after making it.

D. ANOTHER MEMBER SECONDS THE MOTION

No motion may be debated by a parliamentary group unless at least two members are willing; hence the second. The formula is, "I second the motion," or simply "Second." The seconder does not need to be recognized by the chair (unless the meeting is a large one, like a district or state convention). The seconder does not necessarily need to *favor* the motion; his second says simply that he is willing to have it discussed.

E. THE CHAIRMAN STATES THE MOTION

The chairman puts the motion officially before the group by saying, "It has been moved and seconded that the Club increase the fee for the dance to $5.00 per couple. Is there any discussion?" If there is no second he may inquire, "Is there a second?" If not, he says, "The motion is lost for lack of a second. Is there further business?" Once a motion is formally before a group, it may be referred to as *the question* or the *pending question.*

When the chairman calls for discussion, members may discuss, offer relevant amendments, or any privileged, subsidiary, incidental, or miscellaneous motion (see below) that applies. Those who wish to discuss will stand and say, "Mr. Chairman." If two or more claim the floor at the same time, the chairman will give the floor to the one who first caught his eye. Ordinarily he will not allow one member to speak twice (except to answer a question) until all who wish have spoken once. Robert's *Rules of Order* provides a time limit of ten minutes for each speaker. Your club does not have the filibustering rights of the United States Senate unless your constitution or by-laws specifically provides.

If, during the discussion of a motion, two or more members of a group begin to talk back and forth without going through the chair, order quickly breaks down and other members become confused about what is going on. Show your chairman and colleagues every courtesy.

When, as a member of a club, you see that there has been ample time for discussion, you may call out "Question!" This is considered an informal request to the chairman to call for the vote. The chairman may honor your request and proceed to call for the vote; or he may see others desiring to speak, and hear from them. This informal call for the question is not to be confused with *Previous Question* (see below, page 360), a high-ranking subsidiary motion requiring a second and a two-thirds vote.

A *second* main motion is out of order until the one before the group is disposed of.

F. THE CHAIRMAN PUTS THE QUESTION

When members call for the question, or when the chairman thinks discussion is finished, he says, "Are you ready for the question?" Members will then say, "Question," and he continues: "The question has been called for. Those in favor of the motion (restating it) indicate by saying *aye*." (Chorus of *ayes*.) "Those opposed, say *no*." (A few *noes*.) "The *ayes* have it and the question (motion) is carried." Or, if the *noes* predominate: "The *noes* have it and the question (motion) is lost." If the vote is close, his decision will have to be his best appraisal of the situation. If it is extremely close, he may say say, "The chair is in doubt," and take a new vote in some other manner. If members wish a new vote to be taken, they simply call out "Division," and the chairman takes a vote by *show of hands* or by *rising;* if someone so moves, by *ballot.*

Note that a good chairman *always makes clear* how the member will register his vote: "Those in favor, indicate by holding up the right hand; those opposed, same sign"; or "Those in favor, please stand."

When a main motion is carried, or defeated, the floor is clear for further business.

VIII. Other Motions

Motions may be grouped as follows: privileged, subsidiary, incidental, unclassified.

A presiding officer must know:

1. *What is the precedence of the motion?* (See page 369, below.)
2. *Does the motion require a second?*
3. *Is the motion debatable?* If so, he will call for discussion; if not, he will act on it at once or call for a vote.
4. *Is the motion amendable?*
5. *What vote is required?* Most motions require a simple majority vote. A few require a two-thirds vote; a few no vote at all.

Less frequently he needs to know:

6. *Is the motion in order when another has the floor?* A few motions are of such priority that they may be made any time.
7. *Can the motion be reconsidered?*

This information is indicated briefly in the discussions of the motions that follow.

A. PRIVILEGED MOTIONS

1. *Fix the time to which to adjourn*
2. *Adjourn*
3. *Take a recess*   Learn these
4. *Question of privilege*   motions
5. *Call for the order of the day*   in order

Precedence: These are the five highest ranking motions, and are accordingly numbered 1 through 5, 1 having precedence over all the others, 2 having precedence over all but 1, etc.[3]

1. *Fix the time to which to adjourn*

The purpose of this motion is to fix the time of the next meeting. The usual wording of the motion is: "Mr. Chairman, I move that when we adjourn, we adjourn to meet next Friday at 10:00." This motion has such high precedence that it is in order even after a vote on the adjournment of the present meeting has been taken, if the result of that vote has not been announced. Moreover, it is in order

---

[3] To repeat: *Privileged* motions are numbered from 1 to 5 to show their precedence, or ranking. No. 1 ranks over No. 2 and all others bearing a higher number; No. 4 ranks over No. 5 and all others bearing a still higher number, but No. 4 is outranked by Nos. 1, 2, and 3.

Subsidiary motions are numbered from 6 through 12. Thus, *all* of the *privileged* motions outrank any of the *subsidiary* motions.

when there is no quorum (i.e. less than a legal number to do business can set the time of the next meeting).

(SUMMARY: *Requires a second; not debatable if made when another motion is before the assembly; amendable; majority vote; not in order when another has the floor; can be reconsidered.*)

2. *Adjourn*

The purpose of this motion is to bring the meeting to an end. After it is seconded and voted upon, but before the chairman announces the result, he should call for announcements so the meeting will not break up too hastily. Note that this motion is considered *privileged* only in the form, "Mr. Chairman, I move that the meeting adjourn." If the maker of the motion adds a *time for adjournment,* as "Mr. Chairman, I move that we adjourn *at 10:30,*" his motion is no longer *privileged,* but has the rank of a main motion.

(SUMMARY: *Requires a second; not debatable; not amendable; majority vote; not in order when another has the floor; can not be reconsidered.*)

3. *Recess*

The purpose of this motion is to enable the assembly to take a rest. The motion may be worded as follows: "Mr. Chairman, I move that we recess for fifteen minutes [or until 10:00]." A recess may be taken for a coffee break, for luncheon, to inspect exhibits, etc. When the group reassembles, business continues from the point at which it had been interrupted.

(SUMMARY: *Requires a second; not debatable if made when another motion is before the assembly; amendable; majority vote; not in order when another has the floor; can not be reconsidered.*)

4. *Question of privilege*

Sometimes it is advisable to request immediate action by the assembly: the room may have become too cold, too stuffy; there may be a disturbance in a part of the room; members at the back may find themselves unable to hear. Or a special situation may arise. The motion may be worded as follows: "Mr. Chairman, I rise to a question of privilege." The chairman replies, "State your question of privilege." (No second is necessary.) The member continues, "Our first president, Mr. Burke, has just entered the room. I have learned that he will be here only a few minutes. I am sure the members would want him to say a word of greeting to us." Ordinarily the chairman will say, "If there is no objection," and then comply with the member's wish.[4] Or

---

[4] When a chairman says "If there is no objection" he is asking for what is called "general consent" (unanimous consent). See page 370.

the motion may be handled formally, in which event it requires a second, is debatable, amendable, and requires a majority vote.

(SUMMARY: *Does not require a second; not debatable; not amendable; majority vote. But—see just above—this motion is usually handled informally, without vote, by general consent, if there is no objection. In order when another has the floor; can not be reconsidered.*)

5. Call for the order of the day

When the assembly has agreed to take up certain business at a fixed hour, that business becomes the order of the day (i.e. must be taken up) at the hour set. Suppose the assembly had previously agreed that at 10:00 a.m. it will take up the long-delayed problem of increasing dues. Suppose, further, that when the hour of 10:00 comes around, the chairman has overlooked this scheduled event and is going ahead with other business. The proper way of reminding him is: "Mr. Chairman, I call for the order of the day." The chairman says: "The order of the day has been called for. If there is no objection, we shall proceed to the business previously scheduled." If there is an objection, he says, "What is the will of the assembly? Those in favor of the order of the day say *aye*," etc.

(SUMMARY: *Does not require a second; not debatable; not amendable; majority vote—but usually handled by general consent; in order when another has the floor; can not be reconsidered.*)

B. SUBSIDIARY MOTIONS

6. *Lay on the table*
7. *Previous question*
8. *Limit debate*
9. *Postpone to a definite time* } Learn these motions in order
10. *Refer to a committee*
11. *Amend*
12. *Postpone indefinitely*

As this group of seven motions has a lower rank than the five privileged motions described above, subsidiary motions are assigned the numbers 6 through 12. Thus the lowest ranking privileged motion (*call for the order of the day*: rank 5) takes precedence over the highest ranking subsidiary motion (*lay on the table*: rank 6).

6. Lay on the table

This highest-ranking subsidiary motion is designed to delay discussion of the main motion for the time being; the expectation is that discussion will be resumed later on. The member says, "Mr.

Chairman, I move that the question (or motion) be laid on the table." The "table" referred to here is the secretary's table; that officer has duly recorded the main motion and will also record this proposed action. This motion requires a second, but it is not debatable or amendable, so action on it can be taken rapidly. It requires a majority vote.

After intervening business, and when no other business is on the floor, a member may move to "take from the table" (see below, p. 367), and thus the proposal is before the assembly again. Of course if no one moves to "take from the table," the main motion is killed; and thus what started out to be a temporary deferment has become a permanent postponement.

(SUMMARY: *Requires a second; not debatable; not amendable; majority vote; not in order when another has the floor; can not be reconsidered.*)

7. *Previous question*

Parliamentary discussion is sometimes criticized as being too time-consuming. Although freedom of debate is a virtue rather than a defect, members should know that discussion can be stopped through the operation of the *previous question* motion. The member says, "I call for the previous question on the amendment," which says, in effect, "I move we stop discussion on the amendment and vote." Or he may say, "I move the previous question on all motions before the assembly," which would stop discussion, for example, on both a main motion and an amendment. If he says simply, "I move the previous question," the chairman should interpret this as proposing to stop debate on the *immediately* pending question (which may be a motion to refer, an amendment, etc., or the main motion itself if no subsidiary motions are pending). The motion requires a second.

The chairman's response is, "The previous question (or the previous question on the amendment, etc.) has been called for." As the motion is not debatable or amendable, he proceeds immediately to take the vote.[5] As this motion restricts the right of freedom of debate, it requires a two-thirds vote. If the motion carries, the chairman immediately calls for a vote on whatever motion or motions

---

[5] When a motion is not debatable, the chairman, instead of saying "Is there any discussion," uses the other parliamentary form: "Are you ready for the question." If, at this point, a member seeks the floor, the chairman may ask him for what purpose he rises, since he may have a legitimate purpose, such as making a parliamentary inquiry. Of course if he begins a discussion or debate, the chairman should courteously interrupt him and remind him that the motion is not debatable.

to which it has been agreed to apply the previous question (the amendment, etc., or the main motion and the amendment, etc., as specified by the wording of the previous question motion itself).

(SUMMARY: *Requires a second; not debatable; not amendable; two-thirds vote; not in order when another has the floor; can not be reconsidered after a vote has been taken on the motion to which it has been applied.*)

8. *Limit debate*

This motion may be used to regulate the amount of time given to discussion. The member may say, for example, "Mr. Chairman, I move that debate on the pending question end at 10:00 a.m." or "I move that debate on the pending question be limited to three minutes per member." The motion requires a second and is not debatable. It may, however, be amended: "Mr. Chairman, I move that '10:30' be substituted for '10:00,' " or "I move that 'two' be substituted for 'three.' " As this motion restricts the right of freedom of debate, it requires a two-thirds vote.

(SUMMARY: *Requires a second; not debatable; amendable; two-thirds vote; not in order when another has the floor; can be reconsidered.*)

9. *Postpone to a definite time*

The purpose of this motion is to defer action on a pending question until a specified time. The member may say, for example, "Mr. Chairman, I move to postpone discussion of the question until 10:00 (or until after we have heard the program, etc.)." The motion requires a second, and may be amended and debated. The proposed postponement may be to any time during the present meeting, or the next meeting, but not later. The motion requires a majority vote, and if carried, the secretary will make a note that the motion to which it applies is an order of business for the time specified.

(SUMMARY: *Requires a second; debatable; amendable; majority vote; not in order when another has the floor; can be reconsidered.*)

10. *Refer to a committee*

The purpose of this well known subsidiary motion is to turn over to a specific group the question before the house. Obviously a selected, representative committee can give the question more careful study than can the entire group. The motion may include phrases to (1) fix the size of the committee, (2) indicate how the committee is to be named, and (3) state whether it is to act in the name of the assembly, or is to report back to the assembly. Thus the motion to refer should be specific: "Mr. Chairman, I move that the question be referred to a committee of five, appointed by the chair, to report back to the assembly at the next meeting." Or: "Mr. Chairman, I move that the question be referred to a committee of five, appointed by the chair, with power to act." The motion requires a second, is debatable and amendable, and may be carried by a majority vote.

A member may move that the matter be referred to a specific committee, i.e. the Finance Committee, or he may specify the committee: "consisting of Mr. Alpha as chairman, Mr. Bravo, and Mr. Charley"; but a common procedure is to ask the chairman to appoint the committee. The first-named appointment is customarily the chairman of the committee, unless the presiding officer specifies differently. Ordinarily it is advisable for the chairman to appoint the committee at once, taking special care to make the appointments represent all the different interests or groups that may be involved (i.e. both men and women, enlisted men and officers, students of different classes or divisions, etc.). This practice is not only simple fairness, but shows good executive ability. Those appointed should be concerned and competent. If you are appointed to a committee you should willingly serve because of your loyalty to the group; if you can not serve, you should inform the presiding officer at once.

(SUMMARY: *Requires a second; debatable; amendable; majority vote; not in order when another has the floor; can not be reconsidered after a committee has begun its work, though the committee can be discharged at any time by a two-thirds vote.*)

11. *Amend*

The purpose of this motion is to change the wording of the question before the assembly. Next to the main motion, the subsidiary motion *to amend* is the most widely used of all motions.

Assume that the main motion is, "that the Club invite the Dean of the College and the Mayor of the City to address it at the May 15 meeting," that this motion has been duly seconded, and that the Chairman has placed it before the group by stating it and by adding the phrase, "Is there any discussion?"

Following the general principle that your amendment should be specifically worded, for the convenience of the secretary and the group, you may amend in these ways:

By *adding:* "I move to amend the motion by adding the words, 'and that the usual business of the meeting be dispensed with.' "

By *deleting:* "I move to amend the motion by deleting the words, 'and the Mayor of the City.' "

By *inserting:* "I move to amend the motion by inserting the words 'of Fine Arts' between 'Dean of the College' and 'and the Mayor of the City' so that the motion as amended will read, 'invite the Dean of the College of Fine Arts and the Mayor of the City to address it at the May 15 meeting.' "

By *striking out and inserting:* "I move to amend the motion by striking out 'Dean' and inserting 'President.' "

All of the foregoing are primary amendments: that is, they apply to the *main motion.* When a main motion and a primary amendment are before the house, no other primary amendment (and of course no other main motion) is in order. Thus, if the main motion were:

"I move that the Club invite the Dean of the College and the Mayor of the City to address it at the May 15 meeting."

and if the primary amendment were:

"I move that we strike out 'Dean' and insert 'President.' "

it would be out of order for someone to move *another* primary amendment:

"I move that we strike out 'May 15' and insert 'May 22.' "

When a main motion and a primary amendment are before the assembly, a member is in order to move a *secondary* amendment, which, by definition, is an amendment of a primary amendment. In the situation above, with the primary amendment

"I move that we strike out 'Dean' and insert 'President,' "

it would be in order to amend the primary amendment (which actually consists of the single word 'President') by saying:

"I move that we strike out 'President' and insert 'Provost.' "

Amendments of the third degree, however, are out of order. If someone thought the best speaker of all would be the Dean of Students, he would have to wait until the secondary amendment ("insert 'Provost' ") had either been carried or lost (leaving—if carried—an *amended primary amendment* or—if lost—the original *primary amendment*); then he could propose his new secondary amendment, "insert 'Dean of Students.' "

Often in parliamentary law one procedure is out of order if the same result can be achieved in a more direct way. Rather than complicate a situation by amendments of the third, fourth, etc., degree, parliamentary law rules them out of order. No member is thereby barred from *eventually* making his amendment; as can be seen, he is not even much delayed.

An amendment that negates is out of order: i.e., it is out of order to insert the word "not." The member who wishes to insert the "not" can achieve his purpose by the more direct method of voting against the motion.

An amendment must, moreover, be *germane* to (relevant to, or in harmony with) the main motion. The chairman should rule out of order irrelevant or frivolous amendments.

(SUMMARY: *Requires a second; debatable; amendable; majority vote; not in order when another has the floor; can be reconsidered.* But note: if a motion is non-debatable, an amendment to it is also non-debatable.)

12. *Postpone indefinitely*

The purpose of this motion is to kill the pending question without voting on the question itself. At times it is used to test the vote on the question without voting on the question itself. The member says, "Mr. Chairman, I move to postpone the question indefinitely." It is debatable and reopens debate on the motion to which it applies, it is not amendable, and requires a majority vote.

(SUMMARY: *Requires a second; debatable; not amendable; majority vote; not in order when another has the floor; negative vote on this question can not be reconsidered.*)

C. INCIDENTAL MOTIONS

> *Point of order*
> *Appeal*
> *Parliamentary inquiry*
> *Leave to withdraw a motion*
> *Division of the assembly*
> *Division of the question*
> *Suspension of the rules*
> *Object to the consideration of the question*

Incidental motions have no precedence among themselves, and are therefore listed above, unnumbered.

Point of order

If a member thinks a provision of parliamentary law is being violated, he may say, "Mr. Chairman, I rise to a point of order." The Chairman says, "Please state your point of order." The Chairman then makes his ruling and business proceeds. If he chooses, he may put the point of order to a vote, a majority deciding.

(SUMMARY: *Does not require a second; not debatable; not amendable; usually not necessary to put to a vote, but if put to a vote, a majority carries; in order when another has the floor; can not be reconsidered.*)

Appeal

If a member disputes a ruling of the Chairman, he says: "Mr. Chairman, I appeal from the decision of the chair." This motion requires a second. The member may state the reason for his appeal, and the Chairman may briefly explain his decision. He then says: "The decision of the chair has been appealed from. The question is: Shall the chair be sustained? Those in favor, say *aye* . . . those opposed, say *no*." A tie vote automatically sustains the chair, since it is assumed the chairman, if he did vote, would vote to sustain himself.

(SUMMARY: *Requires a second; usually debatable with certain exceptions: when it relates to a question which is in itself not debatable, or to indecorum, etc.; not amendable; majority vote; in order when another has the floor but can not interrupt a speaker; can be reconsidered.*)

Parliamentary inquiry

The purpose of this motion is to secure information. The member says: "Mr. Chairman, I rise to a parliamentary inquiry." The Chairman says: "State your parliamentary inquiry." The member then asks about a point of parliamentary procedure, and the Chairman supplies the information.

(SUMMARY: *Does not require a second; not debatable; not amendable; no vote; in order when another has the floor; can not be reconsidered.*)

Leave to withdraw a motion

Until a motion is formally stated by the chair, the member who made it may withdraw it or change it without asking consent of anyone. If he changes the wording, the seconder may withdraw his second. After it is stated by the chair, it may be withdrawn by general consent. If anyone objects, a vote on the motion to withdraw is taken. No second is required; the motion to withdraw is not debatable or amendable, and requires a majority vote.

(SUMMARY: *Does not require a second; not debatable; not amendable; usually handled by general consent, otherwise by majority vote; not in order when another has the floor; affirmative vote on this motion can not be reconsidered.*)

Division of the assembly

When a member thinks the chairman has erroneously announced the result of a vote, he may call out, "Division." The chairman proceeds immediately to take a new vote, by show of hands or by standing.

(SUMMARY: *Does not require a second; not debatable; not amendable; no vote required; in order when another has the floor, but can not interrupt a speaker; can not be reconsidered.*)

Division of the question

If a member wishes to consider the parts of a motion separately (that Mr. Howe and Miss Ingord be invited to join the club), he may say: "Mr. Chairman, I move to divide the question in two parts and consider the invitations to Mr. Howe and Miss Ingord separately." Ordinarily the chairman will say, "If there is no objection, the motion will be considered in two parts," and the assembly will act separately on each part. If there is objection, the motion to divide is formally presented. A second is not needed if the motion relates to different subjects independent of each other; it is not debatable nor amendable, and takes a majority vote.

(SUMMARY: *If the motion relates to different subjects independent of each other, no second is required, and the motion must be divided on the request of one member. If the parts of the motion relate to the same subject but can be divided, they may be divided on a regular motion and majority vote. Not debatable; can be amended; in order when another has the floor if motion relates to different, independent subjects; can not be reconsidered.*)

Suspension of the rules

If a member wishes to set aside certain standing rules—not provisions of the constitution, nor provisions of the by-laws unless the by-laws specifically provide for such suspension—he may move to suspend the rule which is interfering with his proposed action.

(SUMMARY: *Requires a second; not debatable; not amendable; requires a two-thirds vote although certain standing rules may be suspended by majority vote; not in order when another has the floor; can not be reconsidered.*)

Object to the consideration of the question

If a member wishes to object to the consideration of a main motion, he may achieve that purpose provided he objects before debate begins on the main motion. He says, "Mr. Chairman, I object to the consideration of the question." The chairman immediately puts the vote: "The consideration of the question has been objected to; shall the question be considered?" A two-thirds vote is required.

(SUMMARY: *Does not require a second; not debatable; not amendable; two-thirds vote; in order when another has the floor; an affirmative vote can not be reconsidered.*)

D. UNCLASSIFIED MOTIONS

Take from the table
Reconsider
Reconsider and enter on the minutes
Rescind

These motions have the same rank as a main motion, and generally can not be introduced when other business is pending.

Take from the table

This motion has already been mentioned (see page 360). The member moves, "Mr. Chairman, I move to take the motion . . . from the table."

(SUMMARY: *Requires a second; not debatable; not amendable; majority vote; not in order when another has the floor; can not be reconsidered.*)

Reconsider

The motion to reconsider has been called the American motion, because Americans frequently change their minds. If a question has already been voted upon, and a member who voted on the prevailing (winning) side changes his mind, he may move: "Mr. Chairman, I move to reconsider the vote on . . ." It requires a second, is debatable, unless the motion to be reconsidered is not debatable, is not amendable, and requires a majority vote.

This motion must be made at the same meeting at which the vote on the original motion took place, or at the following meeting; otherwise it is too late to move to reconsider.

In addition to the main motion, certain other motions may be reconsidered; below is a list of the most important:

Amendment
Appeal
Limit debate
Fix the time to which to adjourn
Postpone to a definite time
Main motion

An affirmative vote can not be reconsidered on motions to rescind, leave to withdraw a motion, and objection to the consideration of a question. A negative vote can not be reconsidered on the motion to postpone indefinitely. The motion to refer can not be reconsidered after the committee has begun its work. The motion for the previous question can not be reconsidered after a vote has been taken on the question to which it has been applied.

These motions may not be reconsidered:
Adjourn (when privileged)
Division of the assembly
Division of the question
Lay on the table
Making and closing nominations
Point of order and call for the order of the day
Parliamentary inquiry
Questions of privilege
Recess
Reconsider
Reconsider and have entered on the minutes
Suspension of the rules
Take from the table

(SUMMARY: *Requires a second; not debatable when the motion to be reconsidered is not debatable; not amendable; majority vote; in order when another has the floor; can not be reconsidered.*)

Reconsider and have entered on the minutes

This is an interesting motion to be used on occasions when attendance at a meeting is small, and a group that is usually in the minority finds that it has enough of its members present to pass a motion that would be voted down in a better-attended meeting. Suppose an editorial board of fifteen members normally consists of nine seniors and six juniors. At a meeting, there are present the six juniors and only four seniors; a junior moves that George Hovey, a junior, represent the board at the national convention. This honor is ordinarily reserved for senior members of the board. To forestall the temporary majority of juniors from overriding the wishes of the larger group, some of the seniors should vote with the juniors to pass the motion. Immediately afterwards one of the seniors (who voted with the winning side) moves to "reconsider the motion and have it entered on the minutes." The making of the motion suspends action on the vote on the main motion (to send George Hovey to the national convention). The matter is thus postponed to the next meeting, at which time the seniors can be sure to have a full turnout, and, presumably, elect a senior.

(SUMMARY: *Requires a second; not amendable; not debatable; no vote; in order when another has the floor; can not be reconsidered.*)

Rescind

Whereas the motion to reconsider must be made at the same meeting when the vote which it is proposed to reconsider was taken, or at the following meeting, the motion to rescind may be made at any time. The member says: "Mr. Chairman, I move to rescind the action taken . . ." The motion requires a second, is debatable, and is amendable. If previous notice has been given the membership, a majority vote carries; or a majority vote of the entire membership carries; otherwise a two-thirds vote of those present and voting is required.

(SUMMARY: *Requires a second; debatable; amendable; two-thirds vote, unless previous notice given membership (see paragraph above); not in order when another has the floor; an affirmative vote on this motion can not be reconsidered.*)

IX. Precedence

The main motion (and a few other motions like *take from the table, reconsider, rescind,* etc.) have the lowest precedence: i.e., they may be made only when *no other business* is pending.

Starting with this fact, precedence may be best understood by recalling the five privileged motions (assigned ranks 1 through 5) and the seven subsidiary motions (assigned ranks 6 through 12). All of these take precedence over the main motion; and they take precedence over one another in the order of their rank (number 1 being highest).

When a main motion is pending, an amendment (number 11) is in order. Thus:

Main motion: Mr. Albert: "I move that the class take a picnic on Lake LaSalle next Friday." (Seconded.)

The Chairman: "It has been moved and seconded that the class take a picnic on Lake LaSalle next Friday. Is there any discussion?"

Mr. Benjamin: "I move to amend the main motion by striking out 'Lake LaSalle' and inserting 'Lake Clair.'" (Seconded.)

The Chairman: "It has been moved and seconded to strike out 'Lake LaSalle' and insert 'Lake Clair.' Is there any discussion?"

Mr. Charles: "I move to refer the matter to a committee of three appointed by the chair, with power to make all arrangements." (Seconded.)

The Chairman: "It has been moved and seconded to refer the matter to a committee of three appointed by the chair, with power to make all arrangements. Is there any discussion?"

Note that these motions are all in order. No vote has as yet been taken on any of them. The amendment (number 11) yielded to the motion to refer (number 10). It would also now be in order *to postpone* discussion until the next meeting (number 9), or to move any subsidiary or privileged motion numbering 8 through 1.

If a vote is taken on the motion to refer, and it *carries,* the chairman appoints the committee of three, and the whole matter is disposed of until the committee reports. The committee can consider the amendment or not, as it likes.

If the vote on the motion to refer is *lost,* the chairman takes up the amendment. If the amendment fails to pass, he takes up the main motion. If the main motion carries, the class has formally agreed to the picnic on Lake LaSalle next Friday, and can then make further plans about the picnic, or turn to an other item of business.

The method of general consent can be freely used when the meeting is informal and when members are obviously in agreement. Division of the question, question of privilege, modifying or withdrawing a motion, are often handled by general consent. The chairman says: "If there is no objection, we will divide the question (or grant the request) (or change the wording of the motion) as the member wishes." A member who objects may say "I object," and the motion can be handled formally. General consent should be sought only when the matter is believed to be non-controversial.

X. Nominations

Most well-ordered clubs appoint a nominating committee to present names for official posts. Although the report of the committee is usually adopted, members may submit additional nominations from the floor. Nominations do not require a second (here procedure of organizations differs from that followed in national political conventions where nominations are seconded by long, prepared speeches). A member may move to close the nominations; this motion requires a two-thirds vote.

A special situation arises in elections when there are three or more candidates; the term *plurality* is used to describe the margin by which the leading candidate is ahead of the candidate with the next highest number of votes. Thus if Marshall has 21, Burks 15, and Morton 10, Marshall has a plurality of 6 votes; he does not have a majority (i.e. he does not have more than half of the total votes cast). If Marshall has 21, Burks 10, and Morton 5, Marshall has a plurality of 11 *and* a majority of 6. Unless a group has a rule to the contrary, a plurality should not elect; the successful candidate should have a majority.

(SUMMARY: *Nominations do not need a second (exception: unusually large gatherings); debatable; majority vote; not in order when another has the floor; can not be reconsidered.)*

(Reopening nominations: requires a second; not debatable; amendable; majority vote; not in order when another has the floor; affirmative vote can not be reconsidered.)

XI. Summary

Precedence	Name and type of motion	Requires a second	Debatable	Amendable	Vote
	Privileged motions				
1	Fix time to which to adjourn	Yes	No[3]	Yes	Maj.
2	Adjourn (when privileged)	Yes	No	No	Maj.
3	Take a recess (when privileged)	Yes	No[3]	Yes	Maj.
4	Questions of privilege	No	No	No	No
5	Call for orders of the day	No	No	No	No
	Subsidiary motions				
6	Lay on the table	Yes	No	No	Maj.
7	Previous question	Yes	No	No	⅔
8	Limit debate	Yes	No	Yes	⅔
9	Postpone to a definite date	Yes	Yes	Yes	Maj.
10	Refer to a committee	Yes	Yes	Yes	Maj.
11	Amend	Yes	Yes[2]	Yes	Maj.
12	Postpone indefinitely	Yes	Yes	No	Maj.
	Incidental motions				
	Appeal	Yes	Yes[6]	No	Maj.
	Division of assembly	No	No	No	No
	Division of question	No[1]	No	Yes[1]	Maj.
	Leave to withdraw a motion	No	No	No	Maj.
	Objection to consideration	No	No	No	⅔
	Parliamentary inquiry	No	No	No	No
	Points of order	No	No	No	Maj.
	Suspension of the rules	Yes	No	No	⅔
	Unclassified motions				
	Reconsider	Yes	Yes[4]	No	Maj.
	Reconsider and enter on minutes	Yes	No	No	No
	Rescind	Yes	Yes	Yes	⅔[5]
	Take from the table	Yes	No	No	Maj.
	MAIN MOTION	Yes	Yes	Yes	Maj.

[1] If the motion relates to different subjects that are independent of each other (see discussion in text). [2] An amendment is not debatable if the motion being amended is not debatable. [3] Not debatable when another motion is before the assembly. [4] Not debatable when the motion being reconsidered is not debatable. [5] But: a majority vote is sufficient if previous notice has been given to the membership (see discussion in text). [6] Usually debatable; see discussion in text.

For a quick summary of which motions can and can not be reconsidered, see pages 367-368.

Questions for Classroom Discussion

1. What general reasoning underlies the rule that each of the following motions is not debatable:
   a. Lay on the table
   b. Take a recess
   c. Previous question
   d. Limit debate

2. What general reasoning underlies the rule that each of the following motions requires a 2/3 vote for passage:
   a. Close nominations
   b. Suspend the rules
   c. Previous question
   d. Limit debate

3. What general reasoning underlies the rule that each of the following motions is amendable:
   a. Take a recess
   b. Limit debate
   c. Postpone to a definite date
   d. Refer to a committee

4. What general reasoning underlies the rule that each of the following motions is not amendable:
   a. Take from the table
   b. Lay on the table
   c. Postpone indefinitely

5. In your organization the following is pending:
   MAIN MOTION: That we invite the Mayor to address the club on Friday. Seconded.
   PRIMARY AMENDMENT: That we strike out "Friday" and insert "Saturday." Seconded.
   a. Would it be in order to refer the matter to a committee?
   b. If the motion to refer were made and seconded, would it then be in order to move to lay on the table?

6. Assume that the same motion and primary amendment as stated in Question 5 are pending.
   a. Would it then be in order to move to postpone indefinitely?
   b. Would it then be in order to move to strike out "the Mayor" and substitute "the City Attorney"?

7. Assume that the same main motion and primary amendment as stated in Question 5 are pending.
   a. Assume that the primary amendment is defeated. Would it

then be in order to move to strike out "the Mayor" and substitute "the City Attorney"?

8. You are the chairman, and a main motion is made and seconded. You call for discussion, and a member moves the previous question; this also is seconded. Since the previous question is not debatable, you say, "Are you ready to vote?" At this point another member rises. Should you recognize him?

9. You are presiding, and business has reached the point where the following are pending:

MAIN MOTION: That the Club have a dinner at the Hotel Baltimore on May 15, followed by a dance. Seconded.

PRIMARY AMENDMENT: That we strike out "May 15" and substitute "May 17." Seconded.

SECONDARY AMENDMENT: That we strike out "May 17" and substitute "May 19." Seconded.

a. At this point a member rises and says: "I move that we strike out "May 19" and substitute "May 22." Although it is seconded, you properly rule it out of order. Why?

b. You call for a vote on the secondary amendment, to strike out "May 17" and substitute "May 19." The amendment carries. It then would be in order to move to strike out "May 19" and substitute "May 22." Why?

c. Assume, however, you called for a vote on the secondary amendment, to strike out "May 17" and substitute "May 19," and the motion lost. It then would be in order to move to strike out "May 17" and substitute "May 22." Why?

10. Does a chairman have the right to rule out of order motions that are frivolous? Does he have the right to rule out of order motions made to kill time or delay the work of the group? Does a member of an organization have the right to filibuster?

Speech-Related Project

1. Organize the class.
   a. Select a steering committee to make plans for the organizing meeting, seeing that the proper information is presented, and appropriate motions introduced at the right time.
   b. Hold an organizing meeting. The temporary chairman selected will appoint committees to draw up a provisional constitution and by-laws.
   c. Hold a perfecting meeting. Hear reports from the constitution committee. Adopt constitution and by-laws, with amendments as seem desirable. Elect officers.

REFERENCES ON PARLIAMENTARY PROCEDURE

Auer, J. Jeffery, *Essentials of Parliamentary Procedure,* 2nd ed. (New York, Appleton-Century-Crofts, Inc., 1942).

Donald C. Bryant and Karl R. Wallace, Chapter 26, "Parliamentary Procedure," in *Fundamentals of Public Speaking,* 3d ed. (New York, Appleton-Century-Crofts, Inc., 1960).

Henry A. Davidson, *A Handbook of Parliamentary Procedure* (New York, The Ronald Press Company, 1955).

Wilbur E. Gilman, Bower Aly, and Loren Reid, Chapter 27, "Parliamentary Procedure," in *The Fundamentals of Speaking* (New York, The Macmillan Company, 1951).

Wayne E. Hoogestraat and Donald E. Sikkink, *Modern Parliamentary Practices* (Minneapolis, Burgess Publishing Company, 1962).

Alan H. Monroe, Chapter 33, "Parliamentary Law for Informal Groups," in *Principles and Types of Speech,* 4th ed. (Chicago, Scott, Foresman and Company, 1955).

H. M. Robert, *Rules of Order Revised* (Chicago, Scott, Foresman and Company, 1951).

Alice F. Sturgis, *Learning Parliamentary Procedure* (New York, McGraw-Hill Book Company, Inc., 1953).

APPENDIX

SPEECHES FOR STUDY

1.

PLEA TO THE CONSTITUTIONAL CONVENTION

BENJAMIN FRANKLIN

Words make a difference. The scene: final day of the Constitutional Convention. The document had been drawn up, filled with compromises. In its entirety it seemed to please no one. Before the aged Franklin moved that the Constitution be signed by the delegates, his speech, written for this purpose, was read by James Wilson of Pennsylvania:

I confess that there are several parts of this Constitution which I do not at present approve, but I am not sure I shall never approve them; for, having lived long, I have experienced many instances of being obliged by better information or fuller consideration to change opinions, even on important subjects, which I once thought right but found to be otherwise. It is therefore that the older I grow the more apt I am to doubt my own judgment and to pay attention to the judgment of others. Most men, indeed, as well as most sects in religion think themselves in possession of all truth. . . .

In these sentiments, Sir, I agree to this Constitution with all its faults, if they are such; because I think a general government necessary for us, and there is no form of government but what may be a blessing to the people if well administered; and believe farther that this is likely to be well administered for a course of years and can only end in despotism, as other forms have done before it, when the people shall become so corrupt as to need despotic government, being incapable of any other. I doubt too whether any other convention we can obtain may be able to make a better Constitution. For when you assemble a number of men to have the advantage of their joint wisdom, you inevitably assemble with those men all their prejudices, their passions, their errors of opinion, their local interests, and their selfish views. From such an assembly can a perfect production be expected? It therefore astonishes me, Sir, to find this system approaching so near to perfection as it does. . . .

Thus I consent, Sir, to this Constitution because I expect no better, and because I am not sure that it is not the best. The opinions I have had of its errors I sacrifice to the public good. I have never whispered a syllable of them abroad. Within these walls they were born, and here they shall die. . . .

On the whole, Sir, I cannot help expressing a wish that every member of the Convention who may still have objections to it would, with me, on this occasion doubt a little of his infallibility, and, to make manifest our unanimity, put his name to this instrument.[1]

Of 65 qualified delegates, only 39 signed to express the "unanimous consent of the states present"; on this slender margin, the document went to the several states. Of those who did sign, several had misgivings; perhaps Franklin supplied the reassurance they needed.

Some day you may find yourself a member of a group that has the responsibility of forging a constitution, a charter, or some legislation; you may similarly observe that no member present is entirely happy with the document drawn up by the group. On that occasion perhaps you can recall Franklin's wisdom . . . could any other group we might obtain "be able to make a better Constitution?" . . . and will every member "on this occasion doubt a little of his infallibility?"

2.

RESPONSE AT THE LORD MAYOR'S BANQUET

WILLIAM PITT

In the autumn of 1805, William Pitt, prime minister of Great Britain, was under heavy criticism because of the ill success of British arms in the Napoleonic conflict. Across the channel at Boulogne, Napoleon's troops and boats had been massing to mount an invasion. At Ulm, Napoleon had defeated Britain's ally, Austria, capturing 30,000 men. In the midst of these black days came word of a naval victory at Trafalgar; Admiral Nelson, though he had lost his life, had whipped the combined fleets of the enemy in "the last great battle of sailing ships," leaving England once more mistress of the seas.

The news of Trafalgar arrived in London on a Tuesday, November 5. On Saturday of that week had long been scheduled the annual banquet for installing the new Lord Mayor; now the banquet could also serve as a climax to the victory celebrations. Eleven hundred

[1] From Carl van Doren, *Benjamin Franklin* (New York, The Viking Press, 1938), III, 753-754.

*distinguished Englishmen and their ladies turned out at Guildhall
to dine and to hear the formerly-criticized Prime Minister now
toasted as "the Man to whom at present the World was looking up
as the Barrier that was to save Europe from Universal Slavery."
Applause was deafening, tumultuous, like repeated claps of thunder.
Pitt's reply was brief; according to four London newspapers he said,
"My Lord Mayor: I beg to return your Lordship my sincere thanks
for the great, but unmerited, honour you have done me. The security
of Europe will be owing to very different causes*—ENGLAND *has saved
itself by its firmness; I trust it will save* EUROPE *by its example."*

*Impressive as was the response, early biographers of Pitt omitted ref-
erence to it. In 1867, however, a more distinguished biographer, Stanhope, who in the course of his investigations had had a revealing conversation with a member of Pitt's audience, the Duke of Wellington,
recreated the event and supplied readers with a new text, based
largely upon Wellington's recollections. Biographers following Stanhope were equally intrigued by the event—after he had described it—
and without further investigation, accepted the Stanhope version.*[2] *So
here it is—now "a legend beyond recall":*

I return you many thanks for the honour you have done me; but
Europe is not to be saved by any single man. England has saved herself by her exertions, and will, as I trust, save Europe by her example.

*Lord Curzon says that this speech, Lincoln's Gettysburg Address and
his Second Inaugural, are the three outstanding examples of eloquence
in the English tongue.*[3] *Shortly after delivering the speech Pitt fell
ill, and died on January 23, 1806; it was, therefore, his last public
utterance.*

3.

THE GOVERNMENT STILL LIVES

JAMES A. GARFIELD

*Abraham Lincoln died April 15, 1865. His assassination deeply stirred
the people, especially in the North; no one could be sure of the full
extent of the plot against the government. In New York City, on April
17, a public meeting had been called at the Wall Street Exchange
Building. Masses of men, bewildered by the death of the President,*

---

[2] *Modern Parliamentary Eloquence* (London, The Macmillan Company, 1913), 73.

[3] Earl Stanhope, *Life of the Right Honourable William Pitt* (London, John Murray, 1867), IV, 346.

torn by rumors that Seward was dying, fearful that the government might fall, became excited. A dangerous riot seemed imminent.

The 34-year-old Major General James A. Garfield, in New York on business, stepped forward and made the following brief address:

Fellow citizens! Clouds and darkness are round about Him! His pavilion is dark waters and thick clouds of the skies! Justice and judgment are the habitation of His throne! Mercy and truth shall go before His face! Fellow-citizens! God reigns and the government at Washington still lives.

The majestic language of the speech, mostly from the Old Testament, and the dignity of the speaker, calmed the crowd, and the turbulence subsided.

Or so legend has it. The exact wording of the speech has caused some doubt. "The tradition of the speech was so well established during Garfield's own life time," writes Theodore Clarke Smith, "as to become a familiar commonplace, yet it is a curious fact that no clipping of it exists among Garfield's papers."[4] *Garfield was in New York—the* Times *for April 16 records a speech he made to the crowds mourning Lincoln's death—and he was an effective speaker: his address "elicited such continuous and tremendous shouts of applause as Wall-street hitherto knew nothing of." The rest of the story must for the time be sustained by tradition. Four presidential terms later Garfield became head of state, and was himself assassinated after four months in office.*

To the extent that the speech is correctly reported, it shows the persuasive impact of the speaker's character and of emotional appeal.

4.

WHICH KNEW NOT JOSEPH

BRUCE BARTON

This address by Bruce Barton, delivered before the Public Relations Section of the National Electric Light Association, in New York City, in 1923, has appeared in many textbooks of public speaking and in collections of speeches. Mr. Barton, for two terms a member of Congress, is chairman of the board of Batten, Barton, Durstine, & Osborn, Inc.

---

[4] *The Life and Letters of James Abram Garfield* (New Haven, Yale University Press, 1925), I, 383-384.

There are two stories—and neither of them is new—which I desire to tell you, because they have a direct application to everyone's business. The first concerns a member of my profession, an advertising man, who was in the employ of a circus. It was his function to precede the circus into various communities, distribute tickets to the editor, put up on the barns pictures of the bearded lady and the man-eating snakes, and finally to get in touch with the proprietor of some store and persuade him to purchase the space on either side of the elephant for his advertisement in the parade.

Coming one day to a crossroads town, our friend found that there was only one store. The proprietor did not receive him enthusiastically. "Why should I advertise?" he demanded. "I have been here for twenty years. There isn't a man, woman or child around these parts that doesn't know where I am and what I sell." The advertising man answered very promptly (because in our business if we hesitate we are lost), and he said to the proprietor, pointing across the street, "What is that building over there?" The proprietor answered, "That is the Methodist Episcopal Church." The advertising man said, "How long has that been there?" The proprietor said, "Oh, I don't know; seventy-five years probably." "And yet," exclaimed the advertising man, *"they ring the church bell every Sunday morning."*

My second story has also a religious flavor. It relates to a gentleman named Joseph, who is now deceased.

Those of you who were brought up on the Bible may have found there some account of his very remarkable business career. Those of you who have not read that book may have heard of Joseph through the works of Rudyard Kipling.

Said Mr. Kipling:

> Who shall doubt the secret hid
> Under Cheops' pyramid
> Was that the contractor did
> Cheops out of several millions.
> And that Joseph's sudden rise
> To comptroller of supplies
> Was a graft of monstrous size
> Worked on Pharaoh's swart civilians.

The account of Joseph in the Old Testament is much more complete and to his credit. It tells how he left his country under difficulties and, coming into a strange country, he rose, through his diligence, to become the principal person in the state, second only to the King.

Now, gentlemen, the Biblical narrative brings us to that point—the point where Joseph had public relations with all the other ancient nations, while his private relations held all the best-paying jobs—it brings us up to the climax of his career and then it hands us an awful jolt. Without any words of preparation or explanation, it says bluntly:

"And Joseph died, and there arose a new king in Egypt which knew not Joseph."

I submit, gentlemen, that this is one of the most staggering lines which has ever been written in a business biography. Here was a man so famous that everybody knew him and presto, a few people die, a few new ones are born, and *nobody* knows him. The tide of human life has moved on; the king who exalted the friends of Joseph is followed by a king who makes them slaves; all the advertising that the name "Joseph" had enjoyed in one generation is futile and of no avail, *because that generation has gone.*

Now, what has all that to do with you? Very much indeed. When we gathered in this room this afternoon, there were in this country, in bed, sick, several thousand old men. It perhaps is indelicate for me to refer to that fact, but it is a fact, and we are grown up and we have to face these things. On those old men you gentlemen collectively have spent a considerable amount of time and a considerable amount of money. It is to be supposed that you have made some impression upon them regarding your service and your purposes and your necessities. But in this interval, while we have been sitting here, those old men have died and all your time and all your money and whatever you have built up in the way of good-will in their minds—*all* your labor and investment have passed out with them.

In the same brief interval, there have been born in this country several thousand lusty boys and girls to whom you gentlemen mean no more than the Einstein theory. They do not know the difference between a Mazda lamp and a stick of Wrigley's chewing gum. Nobody has ever told them that Ivory Soap floats or that children cry for Castoria, or what sort of soap you ought to use if you want to have a skin that people would like to touch. The whole job of giving them the information they are going to need in order to form an intelligent public opinion and to exercise an intelligent influence in the community has to be started from the beginning and done over again.

So the first very simple thing that I would say to you (and it is so simple that it seems to me it ought to be said at every convention of this kind) is that this business of public relations is a very constant business, that the fact that you told your story yesterday should not lead you into the delusion of supposing that you have ever told it. There is probably no fact in the United States that is easier to impress upon people's minds than that Ivory Soap floats, and yet the manufacturers of Ivory Soap think it is not inconsistent or wasteful to spend more than a million dollars a year in repeating that truth over and over again.

Cultivating good-will is a day-by-day and hour-by-hour business, gentlemen. Every day and every hour the "king" dies and there arises a new "king" to whom you and all your works mean absolutely nothing.

Now, the second very simple thing which I might say to you is that in your dealings with the public, in what you write and say, you must be genuine.

When I came to New York a great many years ago I had a lot of trouble with banks. It was very hard to find any bank that would be willing to accept the very paltry weekly deposit that I wanted to make. Finally I discovered one which was not as closely guarded as the others, and I succeeded for a period of three years in being insulted by the teller every Saturday. At the end of three years when I came to draw out my money I had an audience with the vice-president who wanted personally to insult me. I said to myself, if I live and grow old in this town, some day I think I would like to take a crack at this situation.

And so as the years passed (as they have the habit of doing), and I lived and grew old, one day a bank official came in to us and said he would like to have us do some advertising for him. I said to this banker, "Now you go back to your office and shave off all the side-whiskers that there are in your bank and you take all the high hats and carry them out into the back yard of the bank and put them in a pile and light a match to the pile and burn them, because I am going to advertise to people that you're human, and it may be a shock to have them come in and find you as you are."

So he went back to his bank and I wrote an advertisement which said:

"There is a young man in this town who is looking for a friendly bank; a bank where the officers will remember his name and where some interest will be shown when he comes in," etc.

It was very successful. It was *too* successful. It was so successful that we could not control it, and all over the country there broke out a perfect epidemic, a kind of measles, of "friendly banks." Bankers who had not smiled since infancy and who never had had or needed an electric fan in their offices suddenly sat up and said, "Why, we are friendly."

Well, our bank dropped out. The competition was too keen. But it culminated, I think, in a letter which I saw and which was mailed by the president of a really very important bank in a large city. I won't attempt to quote it verbatim, but it was to this effect:

"Dear Customer: As I sit here all alone in my office on Christmas Eve thinking of you and how much we love you, I really wish that you and every customer could come in here personally so I could give you a good, sound kiss."

Well, that is a trifle exaggerated, but the fact is this—if you don't feel these things you can't make other people feel them. Emerson said, as you will remember, "What you are thunders so loud I cannot hear what you say." Unless there is back of this desire for better public relations a real conviction, a real genuine feeling that you are in business as a matter of service, not merely as a matter of advertising service—unless there is that, then it is very dangerous, indeed, to attempt to talk to the public. For as sure as you live the public will find you out.

The third very simple thing, and the last thing that I suggest, is this: In dealing with the public the great thing is to deal with them simply, briefly, and in language that they can understand.

Two men delivered speeches about sixty years ago at Gettysburg. One man was the greatest orator of his day, and he spoke for two hours and a half, and probably nobody in the room can remember a single word that he said. The other man spoke for considerably less than five minutes, and every school child has at some time learned Lincoln's Gettysburg Address, and remembers it more or less all his life. Many prayers have been uttered in the world—many long, fine-sounding prayers—but the only prayer that any large majority of people have ever learned is the Lord's Prayer, and it is less than two hundred words long. The same thing is true of the Twenty-third Psalm, and there is hardly a Latin word in it. They are short, simple, easily understood words.

You electric light people have one difficulty. I was in Europe this spring, and I rode a great deal in taxicabs. In England I sat in a taxicab and watched the little clock go around in terms of shillings. Then I flew over to Amsterdam and watched it go around in terms of guilders. Then I went down to Brussels and it went around in terms of francs. Then I went to France and it went around in terms of francs of a different value.

I would sit there trying to divide fifteen into one hundred and multiply it by seven, and wonder just where I was getting off, and I have no doubt that really I was transported in Europe at a very reasonable cost, but because those meters talked to me in terms that were unfamiliar I never stepped out of a taxicab without having a haunting suspicion that probably I had been "gyped."

In a degree you suffer like those taxicab men. You come to Mrs. Barton and you say, "Buy this washing machine and it will do your washing for just a few cents an hour." She says, "Isn't that wonderful!" She buys it, and at the end of the month she sits with your bill in her hands and she says, "We have run this five hours, and that will probably be so and so." Then she opens the bill and finds that she has not run it five hours; that she has run it 41 kw. and 11 amp. and 32 volts, and that the amount is not so-and-so but it is $2.67.

Well, that is a matter that I suppose you will eventually straighten out.

Asking an advertising man to talk about advertising at a convention like this is a good deal like asking a doctor to talk about health. I have listened to many such addresses and they are all about the same. The eminent physician says, "Drink plenty of water. Stay outdoors as much as you can. Eat good food. Don't worry. Get eight hours' sleep. And if you have anything the matter with you, call a doctor."

So I say to you that there is a certain technique about this matter of dealing with the public, and if you have anything seriously the matter with you—whether it be a big advertising problem or merely a bad letterhead (and some of you have wretched letterheads)—there probably is some advertising doctor in your town who has made a business of the thing, and it may be worth your while to call him in. But in the meantime, and in this very informal and necessarily general talk, I say to you, "Be genuine, be simple, be brief; talk to people in language that they understand; and finally, and most of all, be persistent." You can't expect to advertise in flush times and live on the memory of it when you are hard up. You can't expect to advertise when you are in trouble, or about to be in trouble, and expect to get anything in that direction. It is a day-by-day and hour-by-hour business. If the money that has been thrown away by people who advertised spasmodically was all gathered together it would found and endow the most wonderful home in the world for aged advertising men and their widows. Don't throw any more of that money away. If advertising is worth doing at all, it is worth doing all the time. For every day, gentlemen, the "king" dies, and there arises a new "king" who knows not Joseph.

Reprinted by permission of the speaker.

5.

SPEECH AT HIGH WYCOMBE

LT. GEN. IRA C. EAKER

Shortly after General Eaker moved into Wycombe Abbey at High Wycombe in April, 1942, with the first nucleus of the VIII Bomber Command, the Mayor of High Wycombe extended an invitation to have dinner with him and his councilmen. After dinner the Mayor asked the General to go across the street to the Town Meeting Hall where several hundred local citizens were gathered at a dance for the RAF and the WAAF, men and women stationed in that area. General Eaker assured the Mayor that he did not want to make any public appearances as he was entirely occupied with the war; the Mayor replied that no talk was expected, but was most urgent that the General put in a brief appearance.[5] At the Town Hall, after a very friendly introduction, General Eaker was asked to say a few words, and responded as follows:

I do not intend to do any talking until we have done some fighting; but this I can say now, I hope when we have gone you will be glad we came.

General Eaker was accompanied to the meeting by his aide, Major, later Colonel, Beirne Lay, who recorded the brief talk and sent it to the Reader's Digest, *where it was published. It also attracted wide attention among the English people. Eaker was described as a "natural diplomat" whose brief but moving speech in a room where Benjamin Disraeli had once spoken, out-Disraeli-ed Queen Victoria's prime minister. "His words landed with pin-point accuracy in the hearts of the British as news about what he had said reached all corners of the island."*

6.

SPEECH ACCEPTING AN HONORARY LL.D.

SIR WINSTON CHURCHILL

On March 5, 1946, Sir Winston Churchill delivered his famous "iron curtain" speech at Fulton, Missouri. Upon being presented the honorary degree of Doctor of Laws by Dr. Franc L. McCluer, then president of Westminster College, the former British prime minister re-

---

[5] Letter to the author, April 26, 1961. General Eaker is now associated with Douglas Aircraft Company, Inc. An excerpt from another speech appears on page 252 of this book.

sponded as follows. The text is a fine example of the impromptu speaking of one who at that time had probably delivered more than fifteen thousand speeches. Successive sentences touch various emotions as the speaker moved swiftly from his ever-present sense of fun to his deep personal sentiment and profound regard both for his own country and for that of his beloved mother.

Mr. President, President McCluer, Members of the Faculty—in fact I'm not sure I mayn't say "fellow members of the faculty" (*laughter and prolonged applause*):

I am most grateful to you, to the authorities of the State of Missouri, and to the college authorities, for their great kindness in conferring upon me another of these degrees, which I value so highly, and as I was saying only the other day at Miami, which have the double attraction for me that they do not require any preliminary examination. (Applause.)

I value very much this token of good will, which comes from a center of education in the very heart of the United States and in the state which is so dear to the heart of the president of this great country.

I shall endeavor to inculcate sound principles of education on persons of all ages, especially those of riper years (*laughter*), during such period of useful activity as may be left me.

I also thank you all here for the great patience, indulgence, kindness, attention, to which you listened to what I had to say, what I am quite sure on reflection will have been found right and wise to say, at this juncture. I am very glad to have this opportunity, and grateful to all who have come here and assisted me to discharge my task.

I am of course unswerving in my allegiance to my own King and country, and (*chuckling*) I can never feel entirely a foreigner in the United States, which is my motherland, and where my ancestors, forebears, on that side of the family for five generations are buried. (Applause.) I was, however, a little puzzled the other day when one branch of the Sons of the Revolution invited me to become a member (*laughter*) on the grounds that my forebears undoubtedly fought in Washington's army (*laughter*). I felt on the whole that I was on both sides then (*laughter*) and therefore I should adopt as far as possible an unbiased attitude towards history (*laughter*). But I need scarcely tell you how profound is my love for this great, mighty nation and empire of the United States, who have long been a refuge to the oppressed of every race and every clime and are now the foremost sun of civilization in upholding the forward march of man. (Applause.)[6]

7.

SIX REASONS FOR DRINKING MORE LIQUOR

MONK BRYAN

This sermon was delivered on Sunday, January 11, 1959, in the Missouri Methodist Church, Columbia, Missouri. Its unusual approach plus its concrete and specific evidence made a forceful impact upon the large congregation of students, faculty members, and townspeople that heard it.

Many people of our day have accepted the practice of drinking liquor, and in many areas of our society one is suspected of being queer if he does not drink. Sometimes it has seemed that the only dissenting group has been the Protestant clergy, and many times some church people are almost embarrassed by the unrelenting stand of their ministers.

But living in a college community, we are trained in the ways of free and honest thought. We can find facts and deal with them logically; and with our contemporary viewpoint, this we must do, regardless of how we may differ with voices around us.

Thus we can find factual and logical reasons for drinking more liquor.

The first of the reasons is that this is the best method we have for keeping the population explosion from making the earth too crowded.

We are able to eliminate more people by highway slaughter than by any other way. War is pretty good, but we kill more people month by month on our highways than in any month of fatalities of American lives in either World War I or II.

And we know that liquor is the largest single factor in highway deaths. The National Safety Council (the vice president of which is the president of a distillery) has conservatively discovered that liquor was the determining factor in 28 per cent of the accidents and involved in some 60 per cent. The last year for which we have full figures saw 38,300 highway deaths and three times that many injuries needing a physician or hospital care.

We must drink more so that we can kill off enough people.

---

6 From an electrical transcription of the speech, as broadcast.

Next, we can clearly realize that we must continue to drink, and drink more, in order that we can keep on having great health problems.

Physicians keep on moving in and eliminating certain diseases, like scarlet fever and typhoid. But we must keep work for doctors and must keep our hospitals filled. The year before the Salk vaccine took effect, the five chief health problems in the United States were, in this order: heart, alcohol, TB, cancer, polio. The only change has been to drop polio. Liquor is not first, but note this. Add the 1,200,000 cases of TB and the 711,000 cases of cancer and the 38,000 cases of polio that year, and then double that total, and you have just about the number of cases of alcohol sickness requiring medical attention. As long as we can keep increasing our drinking, we can be sure that we will have stupendous health problems.

Having just admitted that alcohol is only the second highest cause of physical health problems, we can now be stronger in advocating drink for it is No. 1 in the causes of emotional and mental failures.

Mental and emotional deterioration require just about as many hospital beds as do sickness which is primarily physical, and the largest single group of these people who need psychiatric care are the results of drink.

Our magazines and newspapers give us appealing articles on how over-crowded our mental hospitals are. And we can be assured that we can keep them that way if we will just keep up our drinking. Because in making liquor, we have $400,000,000 a year to spend in advertising, more than any other contract. We can be sure that the press will not do much to tell the public about our secret or how to keep up the number of mental deteriorations.

Again, we can clearly see that we must continue to drink and get more people to drink if we are to keep unchallenged our world supremacy in crime.

Again, in advocating more liquor the facts are on our side. . . . Over a period of 25 years, we find that those crimes directly related to liquor have increased 28.6 per cent while other crimes have increased only 9.4 per cent.

Here is another way we know that we are keeping America with the highest crime record in the world through drink. For a month or more keep a record of all crime recorded in any given city newspaper. On one sheet—it won't take a big one—record all crimes where there is no mention of liquor. Then on another—it will take several pages—record those that have to do with selling or distributing liquor, or where folks have just been drinking, or either they were in a tavern or the people have just left a tavern.

We must drink more or else there is no hope of keeping our crime rate on the increase.

For our fifth reason let us look at home life. We must keep the bottles handy if we are to keep way out front with the highest divorce rate in history.

As long as we can keep cracking up so many marriages, folks will know we don't really go for this stuff about Mother's Day and family love. All of us who deal with marital adjustments, even those who drink, know that this is the first cause of discord and maladjustment in the home.

A few years ago we knew that drinking had about reached the saturation point among certain groups. We still had three groups to go: women, Protestant church folks, and high school students. So we stepped up our promotion and captured the mass media of communication.

In 1915 we had to get 25 alcoholics in order to get one woman. But in 20 years, by 1935, we did better, so that out of each six alcoholics, one was a woman. We have continued to press onward until in 1955 one out of every four alcoholics in America is a woman—or girl.

And think how we can help children by getting them out of homes with normal parents and into orphanages; some orphanages find that three out of every five children committed to orphanages now are sent there by drink.

The last of many reasons for drinking more liquor is that we can keep civilization and history from going very far.

The final development of civilization are emotional maturity, intelligence, and an ethical conscience. It is precisely at these points that liquor hits first, and so we must get more people to drink or else schools and education and science and art and faith will make us emotionally mature, intelligent, ethical people.

But the wonderful thing about liquor is that if we will just drink a little, just start, we can count on it to do the rest. We know that there is no way to predict the alcoholic or the problem drinker. He may be young or old, healthy or sick, rich or poor, educated or ignorant, having been drinking for two months or twenty years—we just can't tell. But this we do know, that out of every eight people who take a drink, one will become a problem drinker. And out of each 16 who drink, one will become an alcoholic.

With the people who do the drinking and with the lives involved by others who drink, we are approaching the record of taking five per cent of the population out of productive, well rounded lives.

Here are facts, and we have dealt with them logically. Now, with these points I am sure that all of us agree:

First, out of the some seven million alcoholics in the United States there is not one who took his first drink with the intention of becoming an alcoholic. Do you agree?

Second, out of all those fathers and mothers who first reached down in some grocery store to take home a pack of beer to the kitchen, not one did it with the intention of breaking up the home or sending another youth into juvenile delinquency. Are we agreed?

Third, of all the folks who for the first time went to some cocktail party in a home or club or fraternity, not one went there because he wanted to have a wreck that night and kill some body. Do you agree?

Lastly, I don't ask you to agree to this. I ask you to take it home, cleave it, break it up, throw it out if you can. I don't know what we can do in the future. But I submit to you that as of January 11, 1959, we either will not drink at all, not once, not anywhere, not under any condition, not any amount—or else the facts and logic just developed will obtain. There is no third alternative, there is no middle ground. It is either: drink liquor for the reasons given here or don't drink at all.[7]

8.

ON ACCEPTING THE NATIONAL FOOTBALL FOUNDATION'S GOLD MEDAL AWARD

GENERAL OF THE ARMY DOUGLAS MacARTHUR

At the second annual Awards Dinner of the National Football Foundation and Hall of Fame, General Douglas MacArthur received the Gold Medal Award and made the principal speech of the evening. He had no prepared text; what follows is a transcript from a recording made by Armed Forces Radio.

Mr. Toastmaster, President LaRoche, members of the Football Hall of Fame, gentlemen of the gridiron:

No honor I have ever received moved me as deeply as this one.

Perhaps this is because no honor I have ever received is less deserved by me.

[7] Text from the *Missouri Methodist Messenger*, XIX (March 6, 1959), 2.

Many among you undoubtedly more fully merit this award, but none among you could possibly more fully appreciate it.

I can accept it only as symbolic of those unnamed thousands who through the years have loyally supported this great national sport.

Unhappily, President LaRoche, I possess neither that eloquence of diction, that poetry of imagination, nor that brilliance of metaphor, to say adequately what I feel. I can only express my gratitude, sir, in a very simple, but very heartfelt—Thank You.

I belong to the ancient football vintage of Walter Camp and Alonzo Stagg. I thrilled to the blaze of Hinkey and Heffelfinger, of Horton and Brickley, Poe and Trenchard and Tuxton Hare. I collaborated with Charley Daly and Pat Graves and Joe Beecham and that fine midshipman back, Bill Halsey, who was destined to become our great fighting admiral and my beloved comrade in arms in the Pacific War. . . .

In all my own long public service, both in war and peace, it is in football men that I have found my greatest reliance.

I recall so vividly a group from West Point who joined me in Korea and for what turned out to be my last campaign. Two names I shall never forget—the first was the captain of the unbeaten 1949 eleven, John Trent. He was one of the Army's finest defensive ends. He was assigned to the command of a platoon on the extreme end of our line. The enemy launched an enveloping movement to turn that flank, but failed largely because of the determined resistance of Trent's unit. He was mortally wounded and as he lay dying on the field his commanding officer knelt over him to catch his final words and through those bloody lips came that last gasping whisper, "Stupid, thinking they could turn my end!"

And, the other was from the same undefeated team, its quarterback, noted for his long-ball passing, Arnold Galiffa. He was given command of a key platoon in one of our attacks, but the enemy held in spite of all our fire power to dislodge him. Our whole line shivered to a halt some thirty yards short of its objective. But, suddenly, Galiffa rose up, seized a package of hand grenades and began rapidly lobbing them into the enemy's machine gun nest, barking in his staccato signal voice, "Colonel Blaik always told me when we were stopped in the line to go through the air."

The breach was blasted, his platoon went through the hole; the goal was reached and victory was won.

Thus, just as on the gridiron, the very essence of success in war requires the same combination of strength and speed and skill, the same close coordination of men and maneuver and the same indomitable courage which alone provides the will for victory.

I can repeat with the added conviction of time what I said many years ago on the plain in West Point—*On the fields of friendly strife are sown the seeds which on other fields and other days will bring forth victory.*

No greater accolade could be given this game than to recall its personal impact upon the contemporary Chief Magistrates of our great nation. . . .

I can still remember a remark of President Theodore Roosevelt, made to me more than fifty years ago, when I was his aide de camp, on the day of the Harvard-Yale game. "Douglas," he said, "I would rather be in the Harvard backfield today than be in the White House."

And, President William Taft, father of my old friend, the late Senator, when signing my commission as captain of engineers, saying smilingly, "As a Yale man I wish I could settle my political quarrels with your former Harvard commander in chief, Theodore Roosevelt, now the Bull Moose leader, with the same directness, the same decisiveness, and the same gallantry with which Yale and Harvard settled their football differences on the gridiron."

And, President Woodrow Wilson, when I called to thank him at the close of the first World War for giving me the command at West Point, remarking, "General, I would like the football game between West Point and Annapolis resumed. If we could only extend and expand this game throughout the world, perhaps we would not need a League of Nations." . . .

And, President Franklin Roosevelt, as I was about to terminate my tour as Chief of Staff and enter upon that long, lonesome, bitter sixteen years of unbroken service in the Far East, asking my recommendation of a successor and when I named the possibilities, his prompt query, "Which, Douglas, was a football man?" And, that was the one who was named, Malvin Craig, an Army back of the Flying 1897 team.

And, President Harry Truman surely tried to look like a fullback when he kicked me out of Korea. . . .

Since that never-to-be-forgotten first scrimmage on the field of Rutgers, the world has turned over many, many times.

The thrust into space of the satellites, spheres, and missiles marks the beginning of a new epoch in the long story of mankind, the chapter of the Space Age. . . .

We deal now not with things of this world only, but with the illimitable distances and as yet unfathomed mysteries of the Universe. We have found the lost horizon; we have discovered a new and boundless frontier. We speak now in strange new terms, of harnessing the cosmic energy, of making the winds and the tides work for us, of purifying sea water for our drinking, of creating new and unheard of synthetic materials to supplement or even replace our old standard basics, of mining ocean floors for new fields of wealth and food, of disease preventatives to expand life into the hundreds of years, of controlling the weather for a more equitable distribution of heat and cold, of rain and shine, of space ships to the moon, of the primary target in war—no longer the armed forces of an enemy, but instead his civil populations—of the ultimate struggle between a united human race and the sinister forces of some other planetary galaxy, of such dreams and fantasies as to make life the most exciting of all time.

And, to all this wealth of change and development it cannot fail to be a source of inspiration to football enthusiasts and supporters to realize how steadily and invincibly their great tradition has continued to command the absorbing interests of our people.

For youth, as it crosses the threshold of manhood, it has become a rallying point to build courage when courage seems to die, to restore faith where there seems to be little cause for faith, to create hope as hope becomes forlorn.

And, this mantle of good embraces not only our Foundation, but the schools which feed the college campus and the post-graduates who form the backbone of the professional ranks—all with their unsurpassed ability to provide mental and physical relaxation for the millions who watch from the sidelines.

Thank you for coming tonight.[8]

9.

INAUGURAL ADDRESS

JOHN F. KENNEDY

On January 20, 1961, John F. Kennedy delivered his Inaugural Address upon assuming the duties of President of the United States. Critics on both sides of the Atlantic ranked it among the outstanding examples of inaugural eloquence, calling to mind also Abraham Lincoln's Second and Franklin D. Roosevelt's First. The text was supplied this book by the White House with permission to reprint.

[8] From the *Footballetter*, II (January, 1960), 2-4.

Vice President Johnson, Mr. Speaker, Mr. Chief Justice, President Eisenhower, Vice President Nixon, President Truman, Reverend Clergy, Fellow Citizens:

We observe today not a victory of party but a celebration of freedom—symbolizing an end as well as a beginning—signifying renewal as well as change. For I have sworn before you and Almighty God the same solemn oath our forebears prescribed nearly a century and three quarters ago.

The world is very different now. For man holds in his mortal hands the power to abolish all forms of human poverty and all forms of human life. And yet the same revolutionary beliefs for which our forebears fought are still at issue around the globe—the belief that the rights of man come not from the generosity of the state but from the hand of God.

We dare not forget today that we are the heirs of that first revolution. Let the word go forth from this time and place, to friend and foe alike, that the torch has been passed to a new generation of Americans—born in this century, tempered by war, disciplined by a hard and bitter peace, proud of our ancient heritage—and unwilling to witness or permit the slow undoing of those human rights to which this nation has always been committed, and to which we are committed today at home and around the world.

Let every nation know, whether it wishes us well or ill, that we shall pay any price, bear any burden, meet any hardship, support any friend, oppose any foe to assure the survival and the success of liberty.

This much we pledge—and more.

To those old allies whose cultural and spiritual origins we share, we pledge the loyalty of faithful friends. United, there is little we cannot do in a host of cooperative ventures. Divided, there is little we can do—for we dare not meet a powerful challenge at odds and split asunder.

To those new states whom we welcome to the ranks of the free, we pledge our word that one form of colonial control shall not have passed away merely to be replaced by a far more iron tyranny. We shall not always expect to find them supporting our view. But we shall always hope to find them strongly supporting their own freedom —and to remember that, in the past, those who foolishly sought power by riding the back of the tiger ended up inside.

To those peoples in the huts and villages of half the globe struggling to break the bonds of mass misery, we pledge our best efforts to help them help themselves, for whatever period is required—not because the communists may be doing it, not because we seek their votes, but because it is right. If a free society cannot help the many who are poor, it cannot save the few who are rich.

To our sister republics south of our border, we offer a special pledge —to convert our good words into good deeds—in a new alliance for progress—to assist free men and free governments in casting off the chains of poverty. But this peaceful revolution of hope cannot become the prey of hostile powers. Let all our neighbors know that we shall join with them to oppose aggression or subversion anywhere in the Americas. And let every other power know that this Hemisphere intends to remain the master of its own house.

To that world assembly of sovereign states, the United Nations, our last best hope in an age where the instruments of war have far outpaced the instruments of peace, we renew our pledge of support—to prevent it from becoming merely a forum for invective—to strengthen its shield of the new and the weak—and to enlarge the area in which its writ may run.

Finally, to those nations who would make themselves our adversary, we offer not a pledge but a request: that both sides begin anew the quest for peace, before the dark powers of destruction unleashed by science engulf all humanity in planned or accidental self-destruction.

We dare not tempt them with weakness. For only when our arms are sufficient beyond doubt can we be certain beyond doubt that they will never be employed.

But neither can two great and powerful groups of nations take comfort from our present course—both sides overburdened by the cost of modern weapons, both rightly alarmed by the steady spread of the deadly atom, yet both racing to alter that uncertain balance of terror that stays the hand of mankind's final war.

So let us begin anew—remembering on both sides that civility is not a sign of weakness, and sincerity is always subject to proof. Let us never negotiate out of fear. But let us never fear to negotiate.

Let both sides explore what problems unite us instead of belaboring those problems which divide us.

Let both sides, for the first time, formulate serious and precise proposals for the inspection and control of arms—and bring the absolute power to destroy other nations under the absolute control of all nations.

Let both sides seek to invoke the wonders of science instead of its terrors. Together let us explore the stars, conquer the deserts, eradicate disease, tap the ocean depths and encourage the arts and commerce.

Let both sides unite to heed in all corners of the earth the command of Isaiah—to "undo the heavy burdens . . . (and) let the oppressed go free."

And if a beach-head of cooperation may push back the jungle of suspicion, let both sides join in creating a new endeavor, not a new balance of power, but a new world of law, where the strong are just and the weak secure and the peace preserved.

All this will not be finished in the first one hundred days. Nor will it be finished in the first one thousand days, nor in the life of this Administration, nor even perhaps in our lifetime on this planet. But let us begin.

In your hands, my fellow citizens, more than mine, will rest the final success or failure of our course. Since this country was founded, each generation of Americans has been summoned to give testimony to its national loyalty. The graves of young Americans who answered the call to service surround the globe.

Now the trumpet summons us again—not as a call to bear arms, though arms we need—not as a call to battle, though embattled we are—but a call to bear the burden of a long twilight struggle, year in and year out, "rejoicing in hope, patient in tribulation"—a struggle against the common enemies of man: tyranny, poverty, disease and war itself.

Can we forge against these enemies a grand and global alliance, North and South, East and West, that can assure a more fruitful life for all mankind? Will you join in that historic effort?

In the long history of the world, only a few generations have been granted the role of defending freedom in its hour of maximum danger. I do not shrink from this responsibility—I welcome it. I do not believe that any of us would exchange places with any other people or any other generation. The energy, the faith, the devotion which we bring to this endeavor will light our country and all who serve it—and the glow from that fire can truly light the world.

And so, my fellow Americans: ask not what your country can do for you—ask what you can do for your country.

My fellow citizens of the world: ask not what America will do for you, but what together we can do for the freedom of man.

Finally, whether you are citizens of America or citizens of the world, ask of us here the same high standards of strength and sacrifice which we ask of you. With a good conscience our only sure reward, with history the final judge of our deeds, let us go forth to lead the land we love, asking His blessing and His help, but knowing that here on earth God's work must truly be our own.

10.

PRESENTING THE DISTINGUISHED SERVICE MEDAL TO LT. COL. JOHN H. GLENN, JR.

JOHN F. KENNEDY

On February 20, 1962, Lt. Col. John H. Glenn, Jr., became the first American astronaut to perform orbital flight. Three days later, at Hangar "S," Cape Canaveral, Florida, the President of the United States presented him with the National Aeronautics and Space Administration's Distinguished Service Medal.

THE PRESIDENT: Colonel Glenn, will you step forward. Seventeen years ago today, a group of Marines put the American Flag on Mount Suribachi, so it is very appropriate that today we decorate Colonel Glenn of the United States Marine Corps, and also realize that in the not too distant future a Marine or a Naval man or an Air Force man will put the American Flag on the moon.

I present this Citation. The President of the United States takes pleasure in awarding the National Aeronautics and Space Administration's Distinguished Service Medal to Lieutenant Colonel John H. Glenn, Jr., United States Marine Corps, for services set forth in the following: For exceptionally meritorious service to the government of the United States in a duty of great responsibility as the first American astronaut to perform orbital flight. Lieutenant Colonel Glenn's orbital flight on February 20, 1962, made an outstanding contribution to the advancement of human knowledge of space technology and in demonstration of man's capabilities in space flight.

His performance was marked by his great professional knowledge, his skill as a test pilot, his unflinching courage, and his extraordinary ability to perform most difficult tasks under conditions of great physical stress and personal danger. His performance in fulfillment of this most dangerous assignment reflects the highest credit upon himself and the United States.

Colonel, we appreciate what you have done! (Great applause.)

We have Mr. and Mrs. Glenn, who launched Colonel Glenn originally—they are right here in the front row—and also Mrs. Glenn and David and Lynn.

And we would like to have you say a word to everybody.

RESPONSE

LT. COL. JOHN H. GLENN, JR.

COLONEL GLENN: All right—fine, thank you. Sit down, please—it's hot.

I can't express my appreciation adequately, to be here accepting this, when I know how many thousands of people all over the country were involved in helping accomplish what we did last Tuesday—and knowing how, particularly this group here at the Cape, and many of the group here on the platform, our own group of astronauts who were scattered all around the world who performed their functions here at the Cape also—we all acted literally and figuratively as a team. It was a real team effort all the way.

We have stressed the team effort in Project Mercury. It goes across the board—I think sort of a cross-cut of Americana, of industry, and military, and Civil Service—government work—contractors. It's almost a cross-cut of American effort in the technical field—I think it wasn't specialized by any one particular group. It was headed up by NASA, of course, but thousands and thousands of people have contributed, certainly as much or more than I have to the Project.

I would like to consider that I was sort of a figure-head for the whole big, tremendous effort. And I am very proud of the Medal I have on my lapel here, for all of us—you included—because I think it represents all of our efforts—not just mine.

Thank you very much. And thank you, Mr. President.

The text of the speeches given at this ceremony is furnished by and used with the permission of the White House Press Secretary.

Index

A Note on the Type in Which This Book Is Set

The type faces selected for this book are Baskerville for the body and Cochin for the larger headings.

John Baskerville, eighteenth century English typographer, was originally a cutter of epitaphs on tombstones. One day as he was carving away he no doubt said to himself, "There must be a better way of making a living"; so he decided to design a new type. Since at that time a sturdy letter named Caslon was in almost universal use, to undertake to compete with it was venturesome indeed. Baskerville's correspondence describes how he labored away at his new type; on one day he might redesign the tail of the R, on another he might take the splay out of the Y.

Although the result was more graceful and readable than Caslon, many did not like it because it was different. A staunch defender of the new face was an American printer often seen in England, Benjamin Franklin. When one reader claimed that Baskerville hurt his eyes, Franklin secured a sheet printed in Caslon, blandly said it was Baskerville, showed it to this loud-screaming critic, and asked him how he liked it. The critic looked at the sheet of Caslon and, thinking it Baskerville, announced that his eyes began to ache at once; thus he was exposed as an opinionated phony. (So that the reader may test *his* eyes, this paragraph is set in a modern version of Caslon.)

Teachers of public speaking will recognize Baskerville, long used in publications of the Speech Association of America and the American Educational Theatre Association. It was selected for the *Quarterly Journal of Speech* in 1942 by the editor, the late W. Norwood Brigance. *Harper's,* the *Atlantic,* and *American Heritage* are among many that happily dress themselves in Baskerville.

Chapter headings and subheadings for this book could have been set in any one of a hundred different fonts (i.e. type faces), but the choice fell on a striking face introduced in 1912 by a French foundry and named after the great French engraver, Nicholas Cochin.

All of us should be grateful to those who over the centuries have patiently and dedicatedly developed, letter by letter, new type fonts. Otherwise, we would have to peer at page after page of an old-manuscript face that inaugurated the invention of movable types five hundred years ago.

CREDITS: COCHIN HEADINGS BY WARWICK TYPOGRAPHERS, ST. LOUIS
BASKERVILLE COMPOSITION AND PRESSWORK BY ARTCRAFT PRESS, COLUMBIA
BINDING BY THE BECKTOLD COMPANY, ST. LOUIS